Metropolitan
HILARION ALFEYEV

JESUS CHRIST

His Life and Teaching

In Six Volumes

VOLUME THREE

THE MIRACLES
OF JESUS

Translated by Nicholas Kotar

ST VLADIMIR'S SEMINARY PRESS
YONKERS, NEW YORK
2020

Library of Congress Cataloging-in-Publication Data

Names: Ilarion, Metropolitan of Volokolamsk, 1966– author.
Title: The miracles of Jesus / Metropolitan Hilarion Alfeyev.
Other titles: 880-01 Chudesa Iisusa. English
Description: Yonkers, New York : St Vladimir's Seminary Press, 2020. | Series: Jesus
    Christ : his life and teaching ; volume 3 | Translation of: Chudesa Iisusa. | Includes
    bibliographical references. | Summary: "The third volume of Met. Hilarion Alfeyev's
    series Jesus Christ: His Life and Teaching examines the miracles of Jesus. He
    places them in the context of recent scholarship, as well as in the original historical
    and cultural context of Jesus' time, and, what is lacking in much contemporary
    scholarship, in the context of the tradition of reception in the Orthodox Church,
    from the period of the early Church Fathers down to the present day"-- Provided by
    publisher.
Identifiers: LCCN 2020038214 (print) | LCCN 2020038215 (ebook) | ISBN
    9780881416695 (paperback) | ISBN 9780881416701 (Kindle edition)
Subjects: LCSH: Jesus Christ--Miracles.
Classification: LCC BT366.3 .I4313 2020 (print) | LCC BT366.3 (ebook) |
    DDC 226.7/06--dc23
LC record available at https://lccn.loc.gov/2020038214
LC ebook record available at https://lccn.loc.gov/2020038215

COPYRIGHT © 2020

ST VLADIMIR'S SEMINARY PRESS
575 Scarsdale Road, Yonkers, NY 10707
1-800-204-2665
www.svspress.com

Unless noted otherwise, scriptural quotations are taken from the King James Version,
with some modifications for accuracy or ease of comprehension. Psalm texts are
taken from a draft translation of the Psalter, edited by Hieromonk Herman (Majkrzak)
and Priest Ignatius Green, and used by permission; Psalms are cited according to the
Septuagint (LXX) numbering, which differs from the Hebrew numbering (used by most
English translations) in Pss 9–147: LXX Ps 9 = Heb. Pss 9–10; LXX Pss 10–112 = Heb.
11–113; LXX 113 = Heb. 114–115; LXX 114 = Heb. 16.1–9; LXX 115 = Heb. 116.10–19;
LXX 116–145 = Heb. 117–146; LXX 146 = Heb. 147.1–11; LXX 147 = Heb. 147.12–20.

ISBN 978–088141–669–5 (paper)
ISBN 978–088141–670–1 (electronic)

PRINTED IN THE UNITED STATES OF AMERICA

TABLE OF CONTENTS

Chapter 4
CASTING OUT DEMONS   193

Chapter 5
MIRACLES CONNECTED WITH THE NATURAL WORLD   253

INTRODUCTION

This book continues a series of investigations into the life and teaching of Jesus Christ.

The foundational principle of most such investigations is often chronology; that is, the events in the life of Jesus are examined in a chronological order that is determined by the harmonization of the accounts of the four Gospels. Another equally widespread approach is a systematic analysis of the material found in each of the four Gospels, or one of them. There is a third approach, which divides all the material in the Gospels thematically. Consequently, all the parables of Jesus are treated separately, then all his miracles, then the history of the Passion. This is the foundational approach of this series of books, titled Jesus Christ: His Life and Teaching. Each theme is treated in a separate volume.

In the first volume of this series, we summarized the general principles that lie at the foundation of this investigation; we informed the reader of the most important directions in contemporary New Testament scholarship; and we treated the Gospels as the primary source of our knowledge

The Passions,
Anonymous
artist, 15th
century

Dome of an Orthodox
church in Cana of Galilee

about Jesus. Finally, we examined the introductory chapters of all four Gospels and underlined the essential themes to be fully treated in the subsequent volumes.

The second volume was dedicated to the Sermon on the Mount—the longest public address of Jesus included in the Synoptic Gospels. In it, he formulated the fundamental principles of his moral teaching, his view concerning certain prescriptions of the Law of Moses, the qualities that his followers must acquire, as well as his teaching concerning fasting, prayer, and almsgiving.

This third volume is dedicated to the miracles of Jesus, as described in the four Gospels.

The miracles are the aspect of Jesus Christ's activity that inspired the greatest interest of his contemporaries. Crowds of people, attracted by his fame as a healer, surrounded him, no matter where he went. Even in the first stages of his public ministry in Galilee, "And his fame went throughout all Syria: and they brought unto him all sick people that were taken with divers diseases and torments, and those which were possessed with demons, and those which were epileptic, and those that had the palsy; and he healed them. And there followed him great multitudes of people from Galilee, and from Decapolis, and from Jerusalem, and from Judaea, and from beyond Jordan." (Mt 4.24–25) With time, his fame only grew, and some of the people he healed, among them women, joined the number of his disciples (see Lk 8.2–3).

If we were to follow the generally accepted chronology that is based on the Gospel of John, then all the miracles of Jesus, except for the very first one (transforming water into wine at the wedding in Cana of Galilee) were accomplished in the space of three years—between the first and fourth Passovers of his public ministry.

By what principle did the evangelists choose—from the vast multitude of miracles performed by Jesus—the ones that they include in their accounts? We can only guess that they chose first of all those miracles

The Transfiguration, Giovanni Bellini, 1480–85.

that were memorable for their vibrancy and unexpectedness, for example the calming of the storm, walking on water, and casting out the legion of demons from the possessed man. One or another of the events could have been chosen if the healed person was not simply one of the many sick in the crowds who came to Jesus in tens and hundreds, but a memorable figure. For example, he may have begun a dialogue with Jesus (such as the centurion from Mt 8.5–13 and Lk 7.1–10), or the apostles may have paid special attention to him (for example, the man born blind from birth in Jn 9.1–7), or he may have returned to give thanks to Jesus (for example, one of the ten healed lepers in Lk 17.12–19). Some miracles were mentioned because they occurred on the Sabbath, when Jesus attended the synagogue, which often incited the anger of the Jews (in such miracle accounts, the evangelist often describes the miracle, then recounts Jesus' dialogue with the Jews). Finally, the evangelists pay special attention to the miracles that were performed for individuals of a different ethnicity or religious confession, such as the Canaanite (or Syrophoenician) woman, the Samaritan woman, and the centurion.

In this book, the story of Jesus Christ's miracles will be preceded by an introductory section, in which we will examine the phenomenon of miracles from a scientific and historical point of view, analyzing the arguments of those who reject the possibility of miracles on the basis of reason. Then, we will speak of the miracles of the Old Testament prophets, after which we will attempt to systematically analyze the miracles contained in the four Gospels.

Chapter 1

THE MIRACLE AS A RELIGIOUS PHENOMENON

The generally accepted definition of "miracle" is that it is a phenomenon that transcends the laws of nature and is, therefore, supernatural. When analyzing and interpreting a miracle, the worldview of the person approaching this phenomenon is key.

There is a widely held opinion that in the ancient world, faith in miracles was universal, and only in modern times, under the influence of scientific progress, did this faith waver. Some also assert that faith in miracles is a defining characteristic of all religious traditions, while only the irreligious deny the possibility of miracles. But in ancient times, faith in miracles was by no means universal. And by far not all religious traditions consider miracles to be a necessary attribute of faith and holiness. The founders of three world religions—Confucius, Buddha, and Muhammad— were skeptical or even disparaging of miracles, even if, after their deaths, stories of their own lives were elaborated with miraculous details.

Moreover, a rejection of the possibility of miracles is not a necessary attribute of atheism or agnosticism. In our enlightened age, often regarded as the age of scientific and technological progress, faith in miracles has spread widely, even among people with no religion. Many psychics and so-called

Confucius

Buddha

Mohammed, represented with a covered face, Illustration of Siera Nebi, 16th century

healers, witch doctors and conjurors, specialists in predicting the future and removing the "evil eye," make good business on such faith. Some of these even use supernatural powers, the nature of which neither they, nor their clients, know much about. This faith—against which the Church is engaged in a fierce battle to this day—is the reason for the popularity of horoscopes, fortune telling, and various superstitions that comfortably co-exist with an atheist mindset.

There is also another popular opinion that miracles could have occurred in past times, but do not occur today. This opinion can also be refuted based on the many documented cases of healings that have occurred in our time.[1] Naturally, every miracle can be interpreted as a coincidental series of events, a fortunate accident; alternately, one can always argue for the historicity of any miracle.

One cannot ignore the fact that for some Christian traditions (including Catholicism), the presence of documentary evidence of a miracle is an absolute necessity for the canonization on a future saint. In this case, the miracle becomes a part of a formal process, dressed up in scientific language, requiring proofs, witnesses, documents, and even something like a juridical process, when one of the members of the canonization committee acts as a "devil's advocate," summarizing arguments against the miracle. This example alone shows that for the Christian tradition, the miracle remains an experience that is not limited only to the past.

---

[1]C. S. Keener's recent, two-volume work on miracles contains descriptions of many phenomena that are interpreted as miracles in many parts of the world, as well as documented cases of possession and exorcism. See Craig S. Keener, *Miracles: The Credibility of the New Testament Accounts* (Grand Rapids, MI: Baker Academic, 2001), 1:264–358; 2:788–856.

1. "There are no miracles"

Reason-based argumentation against miracles has many centuries of history behind it. Even in the Classical world, faith in miracles was subjected to the criticism of philosophical rationalism. The Roman orator Cicero, for example, completely denied the possibility of miracles, coming to this position through several logical deductions:

> Nothing can happen without a cause; nothing actually happens that cannot happen; if that has happened which could have happened, then it should not be considered a miracle; therefore there are no such things as miracles. . . . That which could not have happened never did happen; and that which could have happened is no miracle; therefore, in any view, there is no such thing as a miracle.[2]

In the modern age, the development of criticism concerning miracles is directly connected with scientific and technological progress. During the Enlightenment, many thinkers sincerely believed that any natural phenomenon could be explained with science; if a phenomenon did not fit within any scientific explanation, then either it was false, or it would be explained by future scientific discoveries. This period also witnessed many efforts to create a "religion of reason," that is, a religious worldview that would fit within a rationalistic mindset, and, consequently, would exclude everything that appeared unusual or supernatural.

The writings of the philosopher Benedict Spinoza (1632–77) are imbued with naïve positivism and a blind faith that everything can be explained with science. He dedicated an entire chapter to

Cicero

---

[2]Cicero, *On Divination* 2.28 (Falconer, LCL; translation slightly altered: "miracle" translates *portentum*). [Here Cicero gives the arguments of the Stoic philosopher Chrysippus (*c.* 279–*c.* 206 BC).—*Ed.*]

Benedict Spinoza,
Portrait (1666)

miracles in his *Theologico-Political Treatise*, in which he intended to debunk the Church's interpretation of the Old Testament. According to the philosopher, who echoed the aforementioned opinion of Cicero, "Nothing comes about in nature, therefore, which conflicts with its universal laws. Nor yet is there anything that does not agree with them or follow from them."[3] The power and strength of nature is nothing other than the power and strength of God:

For, since the virtue and power of nature are the very virtue and power of God, and the laws and rules of nature are the very decrees of God, it is altogether to be believed that the power of nature is infinite and that its laws are so wide as to extend to all things that are conceieved by the divine understanding itself. For otherwise what else is being stated thant that God created a nature so impotent and established such sterile laws and rules for it that he is often compelled to reinforce it anew if he wants ti to be preserved and that things succeed one another on the basis of prayer: this, I figure, is very alient to sound reason.[4]

This is what he has to say concerning "miracles" (*miraculum*): "Form these things, accordingly . . . it very clearly follows that the noun 'miracle' cannot be understood except with respect to the opinions of human beings, and signifies nothing else but a whork whose natural cause we cannot explain on the model of some other, usual thing; or, at least, that the one who writes or narrates the miracle cannot so explain."[5]

Any phenomenon that claims to be a miracle, according to the philosopher, can be explained. But since in ancient times, "But since miracles were made to suit the grasp of the vulgar, who were plainly ignaorant of

[3]Benedict Spinoza, *Theologico-Political Treatise* 6.1.16. Translation in Benedict Spinoza, *Theologico-Political Treatise*, trans. Martin D. Yaffe (Newburyport, MA: Focus Publishing, 2004), 69.

[4]Ibid.

[5]Spinoza, *Theologico-Political Treatise* 6.1.17. (Yaffe, p. 69).

the principles of natural things, it is certain that the ancients considered as a miracle what they could not explain in the mode in which the vulgar are used to explaining things."[6] Therefore, they accepted as miraculous anything that they could not explain. In the meantime, much that the Holy Scripture things "are narrated as miracles whose causes can easily be explained on the basis of the recognized principles of natural things."[7]

Another philosopher-positivist, who lived a hundred years later, David Hume (1711–76), dedicates a chapter of his treatise *An Enquiry Concerning Human Understanding* to the subject of miracles:

A miracle is a violation of the laws of nature; and as a firm and unalterable experience has established these laws, the proof against a miracle, from the very nature of the fact, is as entire as any argument from experience can possibly be imagined. Why is it more than probable, that all men must die; that lead cannot, of itself, remain suspended in the air; that fire consumes wood, and is extinguished by water; unless it be, that these events are found agreeable to the laws of nature, and there is required a violation of these laws, or in other words, a miracle to prevent them? Nothing is esteemed a miracle, if it ever happen in the common course of nature. It is no miracle that a man, seemingly in good health, should die on a sudden: because such a kind of death, though more unusual than any other, has yet been frequently observed to happen. But it is a miracle, that a dead man should come to life; because that has never been observed in any age or country. There must, therefore, be a uniform experience against every miraculous event, otherwise the event would not merit that appellation. And as a uniform experience amounts to a proof, there is here a direct and full proof, from the nature of the fact, against the existence of any miracle.[8]

Hume's logic corresponds exactly to the general mentality of those rationalist philosophers who rejected the possibility of miracles based

---

[6]Spinoza, *Theologico-Political Treatise* 6.1.18. (Yaffe, p. 69).

[7]Spinoza, *Theologico-Political Treatise* 6.1.19 (Yaffe, p. 70).

[8]David Hume, *An Enquiry Concerning Human Understanding* 10.1. David Hume, *An Enquiry Concerning Human Understanding* (Chicago: The Open Court Publishing Co., 1900), 120.

Immanuel Kant

on the fact that they contradicted both the laws of nature and "common sense." Being deists, these philosophers did not reject the existence of God, but their ideas concerning God could easily fit within their naturalistic and scientific worldview. In their understanding, God was the one who originated the mechanism of the laws of nature and, after this, no longer interfered in the world. More than that, according to Spinoza, God's interference in the natural phenomena of the created world would have contradicted the perfection of God's mind, which was the foundation of all these laws, since then one would have to assume that God created them imperfectly, not capable of acting always and everywhere the same, but rather requiring constant correction.

One of the sections of Immanuel Kant's (1724–1804) *Religion within the Boundaries of Pure Reason* is dedicated to the subject of miracles. According to him, "moral religion" sees its goal "not in rites, observances, or traditions, but in the cordial intent to fulfill all our duties, as if divinely commanded."[9] Therefore, faith in miracles is extraneous. Kant even cites Christ's own words: "Except ye see signs and wonders, ye will not believe" (Jn 4.48), as well as his teaching that God must be worshiped in "spirit and in truth" (Jn 4.23). If a religion that was founded on ritualism and cultic observances could have no authority without miracles, then a new religion—which Kant calls his readers to establish—founded on a moral way of thinking, must exist on the foundation of reason, "although once upon a time it may have required such supports to aid it."[10]

Thus, according to Kant, faith in miracles is a sign of primitive religiosity, while progressive religion, founded on reason, needs no miracles. According to Kant, in theory wise people may believe that miracles occur, but in

---

[9]Immanuel Kant, *Religion Within the Boundaries of Pure Reason*, Book 2, Apotome 2, General Scholion. Translation in Immanuel Kant, *Religion Within the Boundaries of Pure Reason*, trans. J. W. Semple (Edinburgh: Thomas Allen & Co., 1838), 103 (slightly modified).

[10]Ibid, 104 (slightly altered).

practice, they do not accept any miracles as true. This is why "enlightened governments have upon this ground at once conceded, or even decided and enacted . . . that miracles happened in days of yore; but that nowadays no new miracle may be permitted."[11]

Kant believed that the presence of "theistic miracles," that is, those connected with God's interference in human history, contradict the idea of a creator and ruler of the word, who is "the causal-agency of an almighty and moral being."[12] He continues: "On the hypothesis that, in some particular cases, it should seem fit to the divine wisdom to control and modify the course of the physical system in that sensible effect called a miracle, then we have not the smallest notion, neither can we ever hope to attain any, of the law agreeably to which God conducts the operation of such sign. . . . Here the understanding is brought at once to a stand."[13] In these thoughts, Kant echoes Spinoza.

In 1795, a mere two years after the publication of *Religion within the Boundaries of Pure Reason*, Georg Wilhelm Friedrich Hegel (1770–1831) published *The Life of Jesus*, in which a rationalistic approach to the phenomenon of religion is consistently applied to the earthly history of Jesus of Nazareth. The book is a free retelling of the Gospel with significant redactions. It opens with a very characteristic introduction, which is intended to remind the reader of the prologue to the Gospel of John: "Pure reason, transcending all limits, is divinity itself—whereby and in accordance with which the very plan of the world is ordered. Through reason man learns of his destiny, the unconditional purpose of his life. And although at times reason is obscured, it continues to glimmer faintly even in the darkest age, for it never totally extinguished."[14]

The book presents Jesus as a moralizer who teaches rational behavior to people. Hegel's work completely omits all of Christ's miracles with no explanation. The same events that in the Gospels are presented as having a supernatural character are reinterpreted in a rationalistic spirit. Thus, for

[11]Ibid, 105.
[12]Ibid, 107.
[13]Ibid.
[14]G. W. F. Hegel, *Three Essays, 1793–1795: The Tübingen Essay, Berne Fragments, the Life of Jesus* (Notre Dame: University of Notre Dame Press, 1984), 104.

Hegel, portrait by
Schlessinger, 1831

example, the temptation by the devil is interpreted in the sense that a thought occurred to Jesus:

Once, during an hour of solitary reflection (Lk 4; Mt 4), it occurred to him that perhaps by studying nature he might, in league with higher spirits, actually seek to transform base matter into a more precious substance, into something more immediately useful to man, e.g., converting stones into bread. Or perhaps that he might establish his own independence of nature altogether while hurtling down from a high place.[15]

However, "as he reflected on the limits nature has placed on man's power over her, he rejected such notions."[16]

The mystical supper is presented as a friendly dinner, during which, "in the manner of the Orientals (or the Arabs, who to this day promote lasting friendship by sharing the same piece of bread and drinking from the same chalice), Jesus served bread to each of them; and after the meal he had the chalice passed round, taking the occasion to say: 'When you dine like this in friendship, remember your old friend and teacher.'"[17] The book ends with the burial of Jesus. Naturally, the resurrection is missing, since it does not fit within "the boundaries of reason" as Hegel understood them.

These excerpts provide more than enough context to understand the intellectual atmosphere in which European biblical criticism of the eighteenth and nineteenth century developed. It was heavily influenced by philosophical rationalism, which left no place for the miracle as a historical phenomenon. It was exactly those biblical narratives that concerned miracles that became the main subject of criticism from Protestant theologians who tried to apply to their research the foundational methodological principles of rationalists such as Kant and Hegel. These narratives were either declared to be completely invented and, consequently, subject to

[15]Ibid, 106.
[16]Ibid.
[17]Ibid, 155.

redaction from the life of the "historical Jesus," or their historical seed was studied, so that it could be "freed" from mythological accretion.

David Friedrich Strauss (1808–74), a consistent follower of Hegel, wrote his own *Life of Jesus*, in which he applies the following method to the miracle narratives: "separate the natural fact—the nucleus of the historical reality—from its unhistorical and miraculous embellishments."[18] If there is nothing other than the miracle, then it is an invention. Thus, for example, the phenomena that accompany the casting out of demons can be explained thanks to physiology; consequently, there may be a historical element to the narratives concerning healing demoniacs. As for the healing of the man blind from birth, the narrative must be rejected as completely invented.

Ernest Renan (1823–92) goes even further, and in his version of *The Life of Jesus*, first published in 1863, he includes nothing that goes beyond the limits of the natural and quotidian:

> The idea of the impossibilities of the supernatural is coincident with the beginnings of the experimental science of nature. The man who is destitute of any notion of physical laws, who believes that by praying he can change the clouds in their courses, stay disease and even death, finds nothing extraordinary in miracle, since to him the whole course of things is the result of the free will of the Deity. This intellectual state was that of Jesus during all his life. . . . As to miracles, they were considered at this epoch the indispensable mark of the divine, and the sign of prophetic vocation. . . . It must be remembered that the whole ancient world, with the exception of the great scientific schools of Greece and their Roman disciples, accepted miracles; and that Jesus not only believed in them, but had not the least idea of an order of nature under the reign of law.[19]

---

[18]David Friedrich Strauss, *The Life of Jesus, Critically Examined*, Vol. 1, trans. Marian Evans (New York: C. Blanchard, 1860), 35. [The English translator is the novelist better known by her pen name: George Elliot.—*Ed.*]

[19]Ernest Renan, *Renan's Life of Jesus*, trans. William G. Hutchison (London: Walter Scott, Ltd., 1897), 27, 162.

Leo Tolstoy (1828–10), of all the authors here mentioned, has perhaps gone the farthest in this direction. His criticism of miracles is also based on rationalism. Following Hegel, he also rewrote the prologue to the Gospel of John in his own style: "The comprehension of life became the beginning of all. And the comprehension of life stood for God. And that same comprehension of life became God. It grew to be the beginning of everything for God."[20] His work *The Four Gospels Harmonized and Translated* was intended as a severe anti-ecclesiastical pamphlet, filled not only with perversions (the text is very different from what might be considered a translation; it is more like a free and highly biased retelling), but also with abject blasphemies.

Tolstoy rejected all the Gospel miracles based on the same worldview that was typical of the German and French rationalists like Strauss and Renan. He described the healing of the paralytic at the pool of Bethesda thus:

> A sick man had been waiting for twenty years for a miracle to happen, and Jesus says to him, Do not wait for anything; what is in thee, that will be. Wake up. If thou hast the power to get up and walk, walk. He tried, got up, and walked.
>
> All this passage, which is taken as a miracle, is an indication of the fact that there can be no miracles, and that the man who is waiting for a miracle to happen is sick. That life is the greatest miracle, while the event itself is very simple, can frequently be seen in our midst. I know a lady who lay in bed for twenty years and got up only when morphine injections were administered to her; after twenty years the doctor who administered the injections confessed to her that he injected water only, and when the lady heard that she took up her bed, and walked.[21]

Here we encounter not so much a rejection of the miracle as a historical event, but rather a crude, naturalistic reinterpretation of it.

---

[20]Leo Tolstoy, *The Four Gospels Harmonized and Translated*, Vol. 1, trans. Leo Wiener, *The Complete Works of Count Tolstoy*, Volume 14 (Boston: Dana Estes & Co., 1904), 24, 26, 30.

[21]Ibid, 327.

Rationalism, which reached its apex during the Enlightenment, worked out two approaches to miracles: the first is a rejection of their possibility, while the second is an explanation using natural phenomena. According to this second approach, a miracle can only be miraculous in appearance—one can always find a natural explanation for it.

According to such an approach, the casting out of a demon from a demoniac is interpreted as the sudden cessation of psychological illness, as healing from a disease, as a restoration to health thanks to natural processes or because of suggestion. The res-

The remnants of the pool of Siloam, Current view, Aben

urrection from the dead is nothing more than sudden cessation of lethargic torpor or coming out of a coma. More than that, the sickness itself could have been imagined, as in the case of the paralytic and the woman that Tolstoy wrote about.

The views of the rationalists concerning miracles are based on nothing more than a banality passed on from one author to another, from Cicero all the way to Renan and Tolstoy: there are no miracles. Even in our time, many people accept this "maxim" as axiomatic. If anyone, anywhere speaks about a miracle, this means that the story is unreliable or that there was no real miracle at all, but rather there was some phenomenon or event that for whatever reason we cannot yet explain. However, a rational explanation will be found eventually. Faith in the progress of science continues to shut many people's eyes to obvious miracles occurring all around them, so that "they seeing see not; and hearing they hear not" (Mt 13.13). Jesus spoke of such people thus: "neither will they be persuaded, though one rose from the dead" (Lk 16.31).

2. Miracles in the
Old Testament

The God of the Old Testament has little in common with the abstract and distant divinity of the deists. In fact, he is almost the complete opposite.

According to most deists, God is an exalted, intelligent principle with the capacity for self-knowledge who created the world and established the natural laws that govern it. But he then left the world behind and allowed it to develop on its own. The God of the deists is like a clockmaker who wound up the clockwork mechanism, then left to do other things. Some philosopher-deists allowed for the possibility of God's limited interference in the world, but more commonly they insisted that God cannot defy the laws that he himself created. This, by definition, excludes the possibility of miracles. The god of the deists has no relationship with human history. He is a priori outside of history, completely transcendent with reference to the world and man. No personal relationship is possible with him, since he is not a person.

The God of the Old Testament, on the contrary, interferes in the affairs of men in the most active manner. He directly speaks to Adam, showing him from which trees he may eat fruit, and from which he must not (Gen 2.16–17). After Adam and Even transgressed the commandment, God seeks Adam in the garden, asking him "Where art thou?" (Gen 3.9). He addresses a similar question to Cain after he killed Abel: "Where is Abel thy brother?" (Gen 4.9). God speaks to Noah, commanding him to build an ark, even giving him specific dimensions for its construction (Gen 6.13–16). After the end of the flood, God bestows the blessing of Adam on Noah, saying, "Be fruitful, and multiply, and replenish the earth." (Gen 9.1). God speaks to Abraham with these words: "Now the LORD had said unto Abram, 'Get thee out of thy country, and from thy kindred, and from thy father's house, unto a land that I will shew thee. And I will make of thee a great nation, and I will bless thee, and make thy name great; and thou shalt be a blessing'" (Gen 12.1–2). God speaks to Abraham many more times, as well as to his descendants and to other people in the book of Genesis.

The Creation of Adam, Michaelangelo, 1508–12

In Exodus, Moses is the man who speaks to God most often and intimately. He hears the voice of God coming from the burning bush, calling him to bring the Israelites out of the bondage of Egypt (Ex 3.3–10). From that moment the history of God's intense participation in the life of his people begins. Most of the book of Exodus is dedicated to conversations between God and Moses, with whom God spoke "face to face, as a man speaketh unto his friend" (Ex 33.11). These conversations alternate with narratives in which the majority of space is dedicated to the actions of God that have an inexplicable, supernatural, and miraculous character.

The miracle as the direct interference of God in human history is one of the foundational elements of the narrative of the Bible. The authors of the books of the Bible did not see any kind of defiance of God's established laws in this interference. On the contrary, for them the miracle is a supernatural event that surpasses human abilities and has a divine provenance.[22]

The book of Exodus contains descriptions of a great number of events of a supernatural character. They are denoted in the Hebrew Bible by the terms *ôt* and *môpet*. In the Septuagint, they are translated with the help of the words *sēmeion* ("sign") and *teras* ("miracle"). These terms are used both for the signs and miracles of God (Ex 7.3), as well as for miracles that Moses and Aaron perform by the command of God (Ex 7.9).

Moses' first miracle before Pharaoh was the transformation of his staff into a serpent. But when Pharaoh calls his magicians and wise men, they are able to perform the same miracle with their magic (Ex 7.14–22). Then

[22]See Graham H. Twelftree, *Paul and the Miraculous* (Grand Rapids, MI: Baker Academic, 2013), 21.

Moses before the Burning Bush, Icon, 12th century

Aaron stretches his rod over the waters of Egypt and calls forth frogs that cover the earth, and the Egyptian magicians are able to do the same (Ex 8.1–7). When Aaron turns the dust of Egypt in to lice, however, the magicians are unable to replicate the miracle. Here, for the first time, we encounter the notion that miracles are a manifestation of the power of God, while magic (or witchcraft) is manifestation of a different kind of power, having a demonic character. This is a major theme of the Bible.

In the rest of the narrative of the plagues of Egypt—God's punishments upon the Egyptians because of Pharaoh's refusal to release the Hebrew nation from bondage—only Moses performs miracles. There is no mention of the magicians repeating any of them. The last, tenth plague brings about the death of all the firstborn in the land of Egypt. This miracle God himself accomplishes (Ex 12.29). In remembrance of this plague, and of Israel's exodus from Egypt, God establishes the feast of the Passover (Ex 12.43–51).

The history of the exodus itself is also filled with miracles. God goes before the camp of Israelites "by day in a pillar of a cloud, to lead them the way; and by night in a pillar of fire, to give them light; to go by day and night" (Ex 13.21). When the Israelites approach the sea, the chariots of Pharaoh reach them, but Moses stretches out his rod over the sea, the waters part, and the Hebrews "went into the midst of the sea upon the dry ground" (Ex 14.22), while Pharaoh's chariots perish in the waters that came together again after the Israelites had passed. In Marah, the Israelites could not drink the bitter water; Moses then threw a tree into the water, and it became sweet (Ex 15.23–25). In the desert, the people had no food, and God sent manna from heaven that the Israelites ate for forty years (Ex 16.13–35). In Horeb, where the people had no water to drink, Moses creates a source of water from the side of a cliff (Ex 17.2–6). The book of Numbers records that many people died from snakebites during the Israelites' wandering in the desert; Moses, by God's command, fashioned a bronze

Joshua stops the sun, Gustave Doré, 1860's

serpent and placed it on a staff; anyone who looked upon the serpent was healed (Num 21.6–9; cf. Jn 3.14–15).

The series of miracles begun by Moses continued in the life of his disciple Joshua. Like Moses, who led the Hebrew nation across the Red Sea, Joshua led the people, together with the Ark of the Covenant, across the parted Jordan River (Josh 3.7–17). After the priests carried the Ark of the Covenant around the walls of Jericho for seven days at Joshua's command, the walls of the city fell, and the Israelites entered the city "And they utterly destroyed all that was in the city, both man and woman, young and old, and ox, and sheep, and ass, with the edge of the sword" (Josh 6.21). During the battle with the inhabitants of Gibeon, Joshua commanded the sun to stop moving, "And the sun stood still, and the moon stayed, until the people had avenged themselves upon their enemies. . . . And there was no day like that before it or after it, that the Lord hearkened unto the voice of a man: for the Lord fought for Israel" (Josh 10.13–14).

The story of Joshua's army destroying an entire city together with all its inhabitants is only one of many horrifying episodes that fill the Old Testament. The first such story is the description of the flood that covered all the earth, when God, having repented of creating man (Gen 6.6–7), destroyed all mankind, except for a single family. The next disturbing event is the destruction of two cities, when "the LORD rained upon Sodom and upon Gomorrah brimstone and fire from the LORD out of heaven; and he overthrew those cities, and all the plain, and all the inhabitants of the cities, and that which grew upon the ground" (Gen 19.24–25). Another similar account is the plagues of Egypt, which God unleashed on an entire nation, and then destroyed all their firstborn (Ex 7–12).

All these narratives contain miraculous elements, but the miracle is connected with such bloodshed that it is simply inexplicable from the perspective of human reason. Moreover, the one who initiates this massive carnage in these biblical narratives—if one reads them literally—is God himself! Only in the light of the revelation of the New Testament can these narratives of the Old Testament gain meaning that allows us to accept them from a different point of view, first and foremost as foreshadowing events connected to the promised Messiah coming into the world.

The miracles described in the historical books of the Old Testament have a direct reference to the New Testament not only as types, but as material used by Jesus in his sermons. The stories of Moses' miracles were the part of the holy history of the Israelites that every Jew knew. These were the stories used in schools and in the family to teach children. It was completely natural for Jesus to mention them many times. When conversing with Nicodemus, he said, "as Moses lifted up the serpent in the wilderness, even so must the Son of man be lifted up" (Jn 3.14). When answering the Jews who referred to their ancestors who ate manna in the wilderness, Jesus said, "Moses gave you not that bread from heaven, but my Father giveth you the true bread from heaven" (Jn 6.32).

When teaching the people, Jesus referred to the miracles of the prophets Elijah and Elisha in First and Second Kings. In these books, miracles play a secondary role.[23] The primary focus is on the acts of the kings from Solomon onward. Nevertheless, a significant amount of attention is given to the actions of the prophets Elijah, Elisha, Isaiah, and others.

In several vivid episodes of the first book of Kings, the Prophet Elijah is the main character. The narrative (1 Kg 17.8–24) tells how Elijah came to

---

[23]Barnabas Lindars, "Elijah, Elisha, and the Gospel Miracles," in *Miracles*, ed. C. F. D. Moule (London: Bowbray, 1965), 65.

Chirst and Nicodemus, A. A. Ivanov, 1850's

the home of a widow with one son in the days of famine and asked for water and bread. The woman answered that he had only a handful of flour. The prophet then promised her that if she listened to his request, "The barrel of meal shall not waste, neither shall the cruse of oil fail, until the day that the LORD sendeth rain upon the earth" (v. 14). And truly, for a long time "the barrel of meal wasted not, neither did the cruse of oil fail, according to the word of the LORD, which he spake by Elijah" (v. 16)

After this, the son of the woman fell ill, "his sickness was so sore, that there was no breath left in him" (v. 17) The woman rebuked Elijah, "What have I to do with thee, O thou man of God? Art thou come unto me to call my sin to remembrance, and to slay my son?" (v. 18) But Elijah took the boy, carried him into an upper room, put him in bed, and then, lying on top of him, called out to the Lord three times, after which the soul of the boy returned to his body and he came back to life. "And Elijah took the child, and brought him down out of the chamber into the house, and delivered him unto his mother. And Elijah said, 'See, thy son liveth.' And the woman said to Elijah, 'Now by this I know that thou art a man of God, and that the word of the LORD in thy mouth is truth.'" (vv. 23–24). When speaking with the people in the synagogue of Nazareth, Jesus mentions these events (Lk 4.26).

A similar situation is described in the second Book of Kings. Here, the Prophet Elisha resurrected the only son of a wealthy woman whom he

And icon of Elijah with episodes of his life, 16th century

had visited when hungry and in need of rest (2 Kg 4.8–37). In this book we also read about Naaman, the commander of the army of the king of Syria, was healed of his leprosy by the word of the prophet Elisha (2 Kg 5.1–14). Jesus also references this healing in his sermon in the synagogue of Nazareth (Lk 4.27).

Some of the prophets' actions are remarkable for their severity and are difficult to explain from the perspective of contemporary standards. Thus, for example, Samuel hacked King Agag to pieces with a sword (1 Sam 15.33). After Elijah was victorious over the 450 prophets of Baal, he ordered that they be seized, and he then personally killed every single one of them (1 Kg 18.40). Elisha punished his servant Gehazi for his dishonesty by transferring Naaman's leprosy to him, "And he went out from his presence a leper as white as snow" (2 Kg 5.27). Once, when Elisha was walking on the road, "There came forth little children out of the city, and mocked him, and said unto him, 'Go up, thou bald head; go up, thou bald head.' And he turned back, and looked on them, and cursed them in the name of the LORD. And there came forth two she bears out of the wood, and tore forty and two children of them." (2 Kg 2.23–24).

One of the images that Jesus constantly referred to during his ministry was the prophet Jonah. The book named after this prophet tells how Jonah, when he did not want to fulfill God's mission to preach to Nineveh, fled from God to Joppa, where he embarked on a ship bound for Tarshish. At sea, the ship was mired in a storm, and Jonah was thrown overboard. He was then swallowed by a "great fish," in which he remained for three days and three nights. Jonah then called to God from within the belly of the fish; God released him and sent him back to Nineveh. As a result of Jonah's prophecy, the Ninevites repented. "And God saw their works, that they turned from their evil way; and God repented of the evil, that he had said that he would do unto them; and he did it not" (Jon 3.10). Jesus reinterpreted the three days within the belly of the great fish as a foreshadowing of his own three-day sojourn in the "belly" of the earth (see Mt 12.39–41; 16.34; Lk 11.29–32).

The miracles that God performed in the Old Testament play several important roles. First of all, they indicate the real, active involvement of God in the fate of the Israelites. He himself traveled before the people as a pillar of fire (Ex 13.21). He himself came down to Mount Sinai in fire and calls Moses, in order to give the commandments and the Law to the people through Moses (Ex 19.18). When the Tabernacle was built, a cloud descended upon it, and the glory of the Lord filled it. When the cloud ascended, the sons of Israel would travel. If it did not ascend, they remained in place (Ex 40.35–58). When the Temple in Jerusalem was built instead of the Tabernacle, "the cloud filled the house of the LORD, so that the priests could not stand to minister because of the cloud: for the glory of the LORD had filled the house of the LORD" (1 Kg 8.10–11). The signs and miracles that God worked witness to his abiding presence among the Israelite nation, to his unwavering dedication to the fate of his nation, to his love for them.

God did not simply give commands to his people, then wait to see whether or not they would fulfill them. He himself helped those who were faithful to his commandments; however, those who turned away from his commands he punished severely. When the nation stopped worshiping God, God punished them; when the nation returned to him, he forgave them. God's actions toward the nation were as a jealous husband with his wife—this is the major significance of the images that open the book of the prophet Hosea. It is in this same sense that God is called "jealous" in the Old Testament (Ex 20:5; 34.14; Deut 4.24; 5.9), that is, he is the one who is jealous of his wife—the nation of Israel—and how she relates to other gods.

The miracles performed by God illustrate the majesty and power of the God of Israel compared to other, false gods that other nations worship. This theme, which appears as a leitmotif again and again throughout all of the Old Testament, is vividly expressed in the following passage from Deuteronomy:

> For the LORD thy God is a merciful God; he will not forsake thee, nei-
> ther destroy thee, nor forget the covenant of thy fathers which he swore
> unto them. For ask now of the days that are past, which were before
> thee, since the day that God created man upon the earth, and ask from
> the one side of heaven unto the other, whether there hath been any
> such thing as this great thing is, or hath been heard like it? Did ever
> people hear the voice of God speaking out of the midst of the fire, as
> thou hast heard, and live? Or hath God attempted to go and take him
> a nation from the midst of another nation, by temptations, by signs,
> and by wonders, and by war, and by a mighty hand, and by a stretched
> out arm, and by great terrors, according to all that the LORD your God
> did for you in Egypt before your eyes? (Deut 4.31–34)

The same theme emerges in the Psalms. Here the true God is contrasted with false gods, and the miracles that he accomplished for his people throughout history are one of the proofs that he is the true God:

Blessed is the Lord, the God of Israel, who alone does wondrous things. (Ps 71.18)

Among the gods, there is none like unto thee, O Lord; and there are no works like unto thy works. All the nations thou hast made shall come and worship before thee, O Lord, and shall glorify thy Name. For thou art great, and doest wonders; thou alone art God. (Ps 85.8–10)

O sing unto the Lord a new song; sing unto the Lord, all the earth. Sing unto the Lord, bless his Name, proclaim the glad tidings of his salvation from day to day. Declare his glory among the nations, his wonders among all peoples. For the Lord is great, and greatly to be praised; he is to be feared above all gods. For all the gods of the nations are demons; but the Lord made the heavens. (Ps 95.1–5)

O give thanks unto the God of gods, for his mercy endures forever. O give thanks unto the Lord of lords, for his mercy endures forever. To him who alone has done great wonders, for his mercy endures forever. (Ps 135.2–4)

The miracles and signs of God are meant to awaken and strengthen the faith of the chosen nation. Abraham, to whom God—against reason and contrary to all natural laws—promised to give an heir when he and Sarah were already very old, "believed in the LORD; and he counted it to him for righteousness" (Gen 15.6, cf. Gal 3.6). On the contrary, the nation often did not believe in God, in spite of all the signs that he accomplished for them (Ex 14.11). The Psalmist laments that though God showed the people many miracles, they "sinned yet more, and believed not in his wonders" (Ps 77.32). "They kept not the covenant of God, and would not walk in his law. And they forgot his benefits, and his wonders that he had showed to them" (Ps 77.10–11).

Figures like Moses and Joshua perform miracles for a variety of reasons. Sometimes a miracle is necessary for a prophet or a military leader to prove to the people that they are sent by God (Ex 4.1–9). In some episodes, a miracle accompanies battle, and the victory is ascribed to God, who acted through the leader or general (Ex 14.21–28; Josh 6.5–20; 10.12–14). In other cases, the miracle is necessary to strengthen faith in God (Ex 15.23–25; 17.2–6; Num 21.6–9).

The miracles of the prophets (e.g., Elijah, Elisha, and others) are often performed to demonstrate God's might and the falseness of the idols (1 Kg 18.38). The prophets also performed some miracles from pity or compassion toward specific people (1 Kg 17.8–24; 4 Kg 4.8–37; 4 Kg 5.1–14).

Further, angels are constantly active in the Old Testament. Their presence often sets a specific tone for a particular biblical episode, appropriate to miraculous narratives. The angel of the Lord appears to Old Testament saints and speaks with them on behalf of God (Gen 16.7; 21.17; 22.11; 32.1; 1 Kg 19.5–7). Angels appear before prophets, enter into dialogue with them, and often instruct them (Dan 9.21; Zech 1.9–14). Often righteous men and prophets saw angels in visions. Jacob saw a ladder that stood on the earth, but reached to heaven. Angels of God ascended and descended on it (Gen 28.12). Isaiah saw the Lord, sitting on a throne; around him stood six-winged seraphim, exclaiming, "Holy, holy, holy, is the LORD of Sabaoth, the whole earth is full of his glory" (Is 6.3). One of these seraphim flew up to the prophet and touched his lips with a fiery coal (Is 6.6–7).

In the Old Testament, angels appeared as hosts of warriors standing at the right and left hand of the Lord (1 Kg 22.19). The angels' task is to serve God their king, to be his courtiers, his retinue. The Lord sits on the cherubim (Ps 17.10; 79.1), and they also drive the chariot of the glory of God (Ez 10.9–19). At the same time, angels are the messengers of God who perform his will and his decrees for mankind. In this sense, angels are the intermediaries between God and the human race. Sometimes angels are agents of destruction (2 Sam 24.16; 2 Kg 19.35; 1 Chron 21.15–16, 2 Chron 32.21; Is 37.36); much more often, however, they are people's protectors (Ex 23.20; Tob 3.17; Ps 90.11), and they even act as saviors (Is 63.9). Every person has an angel-instructor who shows him the right path (Job 33.23).

Angels directly take part in many kinds of miraculous events in biblical narratives. Three angels come to Abraham, and one of them announces to him that he will have an heir (Gen 18.2–10). An angel stops the upraised hand of Abraham as he was ready to sacrifice Isaac (Gen 22.11). An angel

Abraham bows before the three angels under the Oak of Mamre, Mosaic, 12th century

appeared to Moses from the midst of the burning bush (Ex 3.2). An angel with his sword drawn stood in the way of Balaam (Num 22.22–35). The supreme commander of the Lord's hosts, also with his sword bared, appeared to Joshua before the battle of Jericho (Josh 5.13–15). An angel appeared to Manoah and his wife, the parents of Samson (Judg 13.3–21).

In many cases, the angel does not simply appear as a messenger speaking on behalf of God—he is directly identified with God himself. The three wanderers who appeared to Abraham at first are called men (Gen 18.2), but later one of them is addressed as "My LORD" (Gen 18.3),[24] with the other two as angels (Gen 19.1). He who appeared to Moses in the burning bush at first was called an angel (Ex 3.2), but then God (Ex 3.4–6). Manoah, after the conversation with the angel, said to his wife: "We shall surely die, because we have seen God" (Judg 13.22).

The Old Testament is filled with miracles; however, these events refer only to certain period of the history of the chosen nation:

[24]I.e., YHWH, the name of God (cf. Ex 3.14).—*Ed.*

The destruction of Sodom, G. I. Semiradskii, 1860's

If we set aside the history of the primordial age (Gen 1–11) . . . then the historical period described in the books of the Old Testament covers about 1,700 years. Considering that vast amount of time, there are not many miracles recounted, nor are they distributed equally throughout those years. They are almost completely absent from the history of the Patriarchs, except for the destruction of Sodom and Gomorrah (Gen 19.24–28) and the birth of a firstborn son to Sarah in her old age (Gen 21.1–7). However, the books of Exodus and the beginning of Joshua are filled with them; they are very rare in the histories of Elijah and Elisha (1 and 2 Kings), then they seem to disappear almost completely.[25]

In the memory of the Israelites, the events associated with the exodus stand out the most. These events formed the foundation for their major religious holidays, and these events were recalled often during sermons heard in synagogues. During various ages of its history, the Israelite nation continued to remember the glorious past described in the pages of the historical books of the Old Testament—to the signs and miracles performed by God.

[25] D. Galbiati and Alessandro Piazza, *Pagine difficili dell'Antico Testamento* [Difficult Pages of the Old Testament] (Genova : Bevilacqua & Solari, 1951). [Translated into English from the Russian translation—NK]

A synagogue in
Capernaum

A nostalgia for these miracles fills a majority of the Old Testament, beginning with the Psalter, where they are described as having occurred in ancient times (Ps 43.1, 142.5). The Psalmist says, "I will open my mouth in parables, I will utter dark sayings which have been from the beginning, even those things that we have heard and have known and which our fathers have told us. They were not hid from their children in another generation. They declared the praises of the Lord and his mighty acts and his wonders which he wrought" (Psalms 77.2–5). The prophet Isaiah exclaimed to God: "Awake, awake, put on strength, O arm of the LORD; awake, as in the ancient days, in the generations of old" (Is 51.9).

The sense that miracles belonged to a time long past, but were no longer a part of the present, that God had revealed his power at some past time, but now has ceased—this sense widely pervaded Israel for a very long time. By the time of John the Baptist and Jesus, this idea was already centuries old.

3. Miracles in the Gospels

The atmosphere of the miraculous found in the books of Genesis, Exodus, Joshua, and some of the prophetic books is reborn in the Gospel accounts and events that accompanied the birth of Jesus in Bethlehem. This atmosphere is created first of all thanks to the presence of angels in the events recounted.[26] In Matthew's account, an angel appears to Joseph in a dream three times (Mt 1.20, 2.13, 19). In Luke's account, the angel of the Lord appears to Zachariah (Lk 1.11–20), then the angel Gabriel is sent to the Virgin Mary (Lk 1.26–38). An angel announces the birth of the Christ child to the shepherds, then together with him, "There was with the angel a multitude of the heavenly host praising God, and saying, 'Glory to God in the highest, and on earth peace, good will toward men'" (Lk 2.13–14). After Jesus overcame all the temptations of the devil in the desert, "Then the devil leaveth him, and, behold, angels came and ministered unto him" (Mt 4.11).

Accounts of Jesus' miracles after the beginning of his ministry make up the major part of the Gospel accounts. In the Gospel according to Mark, miracles make up no less than a third of the entire text, and in the first ten chapters that precede the account of the Passion, they account for nearly half of the text.[27] In the other two Synoptic Gospels, the ratio of miracles to other accounts and the teachings of Jesus is somewhat different, but the miracles still occupy a significant place. Overall, Matthew recounts nineteen miracles, Mark records eighteen, and Luke includes twenty.[28] In the Gospel according to John, there are only seven miracles,[29] but the majority of them are described in vivid detail not found in the other accounts.

---

[26]E. M. Humphrey, "God and Angels" in *Jesus among Friends and Enemies*, ed. Chris Keith and Larry W. Hurtado (Grand Rapids: Baker Academic, 2011), 46–49.

[27]J. Meier, A *Marginal Jew: Rethinking the Historical Jesus, Volume 2: Mentor, Message, and Miracles* (New York: Doubleday, 1994), 619.

[28]P. J. Achtenmeier, *Jesus and the Miracle Tradition* (Eugene: Cascade Books, 2008), 12. Other researchers count twenty-one miracles in Mark.

[29]Stephen S. Kim, *The Miracles of Jesus according to John: Their Christological and Eschatological Significance* (Eugene, OR: Wipf and Stock, 2010), 109–87.

Differences between the evangelists are not limited to the number of miracles retold and the manner of the retelling alone. The evangelists' perspectives on the miracles also differ.

In the Gospel according to Matthew, the connection between Jesus' teaching ministry and his miracles is stressed. The accounts of ten miracles in chapters 8–9 follow immediately after the Sermon on the Mount, completing, as it were, the second half of a diptych. The miracles in Matthew confirm that Jesus is the Son of David and a new Moses. Matthew's descriptions of the miracles are generally shorter than Mark's, leaving out certain details.

The Mother of God and Archangel Gabriel, Russian icon, 19th century

For example, Matthew calls less attention to the theme of casting out demons than Mark does.[30]

For Mark, the miracles of Jesus are an eloquent and vivid proof of the fact that he is the Son of God. This cannot be hidden, even from the demons. Jesus as wonderworker cannot be separated from Jesus the teacher, and the miracles, like the parables, serve a pedagogic purpose. As one modern commentator puts it, the miracles attract attention to the sermon, while the sermon gives meaning to the miracle.[31] The miracle narratives are set within the larger context of the increasing conflict between Jesus and the religious leaders of the Hebrew nation. The theme of miracles is closely connected to the theme of faith—miracles increase the people's faith in Jesus as the Son of God. Without faith, there cannot be a miracle; lack of faith is a clear obstacle to the performance of a miracle.[32]

Luke, the author of two books—his account of the Gospel and the Acts of the Apostles—focuses on the theme of miracles in both. Jesus' miracles, which have their preceding types in the Old Testament, in turn foreshadow the miracles that will be performed by the apostle in his name. For Luke,

[30]For more on the miracles in the Gospel according to Matthew, see Graham. H. Twelftree, *Jesus the Miracle Worker* (Downer's Grove, IL: InterVarsity Press, 1999), 140–43.

[31]J. Knight, *Jesus: an Historical and Theological Introduction* (London: T&T Clarke International, 2004), 158.

[32]For more on the miracles in Mark, see Twelftree, *Jesus the Miracle Worker*, 93–100.

the miracles of Jesus are proof of the fact that he is truly the Messiah and Lord. The activity of the Holy Spirit is underlined both in the miracles of Jesus and the apostles. Even during his life, Jesus gave his disciples the power to perform miracles, while after his death and resurrection, this gift remains and increases in the community of the apostles.[33]

In the Gospel according to John, miracles fit in the general picture of the signs (σημεῖον, *sēmeia*) by which the Son of God reveals his glory to people, "the glory as of the only begotten of the Father" (Jn 1.14). The person of the pre-eternal Logos of God, who accepted human flesh, is revealed through each of these signs in different ways, and the majority of the miracle narratives are prologues to discussions in which different aspects of Jesus' ministry receive theological interpretations.[34] John's purpose in recounting Jesus' miracles is expressed by the author himself in the following words: "And many other signs truly did Jesus in the presence of his disciples, which are not written in this book; but these are written, that ye might believe that Jesus is the Christ, the Son of God; and that believing ye might have life through his name" (Jn 20.30–31). There were actually many more miracles, and if he were to write down all of them, then the entire world would not be able to contain the books written about them (Jn 21.25). He stresses that recounting Jesus' miracles is an integral part of the Gospel, since they are proofs that are intended to increase the faith of the reader. This faith is best expressed in Thomas' exclamation: "My Lord and my God!" (Jn 20.28)

Overall, we find in the Gospels around thirty-five complete accounts of miracles, not counting short recollections of various supernatural occurrences that accompanied the life and ministry of Jesus. These include sixteen healings, six exorcisms of the possessed, three resurrections, three examples of Jesus' power over nature (walking on water, calming the storm, and cursing the fig tree), and five other supernatural events (turning the water into wine, feeding the five thousand with five loaves of bread and seven thousand with four loaves of bread, as well as two miraculous

[33]For more on the miracles in Luke, see Twelftree, *Jesus the Miracle Worker*, 167–88.
[34]For more on the miracles in John, see Kim, *The Miracles of Jesus according to John*, 109–87.

*The Faith
of Thomas,*
Carravagio,
1601–1602

catches of fish). Two miracles are included only in Matthew, two only in Mark, five only in Luke, six only in John,[35] while the rest are mentioned by two or three evangelists (twelve are common to all Synoptics). Only one miracle (the feeding of the five thousand) is found in all four Gospel accounts.

Some researchers reduce the total number of miracles to twenty-seven;[36] however, this number is only possible if two events described by the evangelists themselves as distinct are assumed to be the same event (e.g., Mt 9.32–34 and 12.22–24; Lk 5.1–11 and Jn 21.1–19; Mt 14.13–21 and Mt 15.32–39). Other commentators, on the contrary, count thirty-eight total miracles, including short mentions of events that had an unusual or miraculous character (e.g., Mt 17.24; Lk 4.30, 22.51). But in both cases, these numbers only include those miracles that were more or less completely described by the evangelists.

As for the actual number of miracles that Jesus performed, there can be no way of counting. The number could be in the hundreds, if not in the thousands of healings and exorcisms. Many places in the Gospels witness to this fact:

[35]If we consider Luke 5.1–11 and John 21.1–19 to be two different events.
[36]Armaud Puig i Tarrech, *Jesus: a Biography* (Waco: Baylor University Press, 2011), 363–65.

And Jesus went about all Galilee, teaching in their synagogues, and preaching the Gospel of the kingdom, and healing all manner of sickness and all manner of disease among the people. And his fame went throughout all Syria: and they brought unto him all sick people that were taken with divers diseases and torments, and those which were possessed with demons, and those which were epileptic, and those that had the palsy; and he healed them. (Mt 4.23–24)

When the even was come, they brought unto him many that were possessed with demons, and he cast out the spirits with his word, and healed all that were sick, that it might be fulfilled which was spoken by Isaiah the prophet, saying, "He himself took our infirmities, and bore our sicknesses." (Mt 8.16–17)

But when Jesus knew it, he withdrew himself from thence, and great multitudes followed him, and he healed them all. (Mt 12.15)

And when the men of that place had knowledge of him, they sent out into all that country round about, and brought unto him all that were diseased, and besought him that they might only touch the hem of his garment; and as many as touched were made perfectly whole. (Mt 14.35–36)

And great multitudes came unto him, having with them those that were lame, blind, dumb, maimed, and many others, and cast them down at Jesus' feet, and he healed them, insomuch that the multitude wondered, when they saw the dumb to speak, the maimed to be whole, the lame to walk, and the blind to see; and they glorified the God of Israel. Mt 15.30–31)

And great multitudes followed him; and he healed them there. (Mt 19.2)

And the blind and the lame came to him in the temple; and he healed them. (Mt 21.14)

At evening, when the sun did set, they brought unto him all that were diseased, and them that were possessed with demons. And all the city was gathered together at the door. And he healed many that were sick of divers diseases, and cast out many demons; and suffered not the demons to speak, because they knew him. . . . And he preached in their synagogues throughout all Galilee, and cast out demons. (Mk 1.32–34, 39, cf. Lk 4.40–41)

For he had healed many; insomuch that they pressed upon him for to touch him, as many as had plagues. And unclean spirits, when they saw him, fell down before him, and cried, saying, "Thou art the Son of God." (Mk 3.10–11)

And when they were come out of the ship, straightway they knew him, and ran through that whole region round about, and began to carry about in beds those that were sick, where they heard he was. Wherever he entered, into villages, or cities, or country, they laid the sick in the streets, and besought him that they might touch if it were but the border of his garment; and as many as touched him were made whole. (Mk 6.54–56)

And he came down with them, and stood in the plain, and the company of his disciples, and a great multitude of people out of all Judaea and Jerusalem, and from the sea coast of Tyre and Sidon, which came to hear him, and to be healed of their diseases, and they that were vexed with unclean spirits, and they were healed. And the whole multitude sought to touch him, for there went power out of him, and healed them all. (Lk 6.17–19)

And in that same hour he cured many of their infirmities and plagues, and of evil spirits; and unto many that were blind he gave sight. (Lk 7.21)

And many other signs truly did Jesus in the presence of his disciples, which are not written in this book. (Jn 20.30)

The Gospels also mention certain personages, healed by Jesus, including "certain women, which had been healed of evil spirits and infirmities, Mary called Magdalene, out of whom went seven demons, and Joanna the wife of Chuza Herod's steward, and Susanna, and many others, which ministered unto him from their means." (Lk 8.2–3) Among those who constantly followed Jesus, there were probably more than a few who were also healed by him.

Commentators often avoid all these mentions of various miracles as not containing any indications of concrete events. However, they do paint a picture that is absolutely unique in history, both for the Hebrew nation and the world at large. Nowhere and never have so many mass healings been recorded as were in the Gospels. Crowds of people followed Jesus, sometimes as many as four-five thousand. If we consider the current scientific opinion that there were around a million and a half inhabitants of Palestine at that time,[37] while the population of towns such as Nazareth usually included no more than thirty-five families,[38] we can imagine that Jesus' arrival in a town would become an event known to all inhabitants. Sometimes, apparently, entire cities emptied, labor ceased entirely, if people followed Jesus by the thousands into the desert or to the hill where he led them to distract them from their daily toil and to force them to hear the word of God. But it was exactly the miracles and healings that he performed en masse that attracted the people to him, more so than his preaching.

The Gospels do not contain a single instance when Jesus ever refused to heal anyone. But he did refuse to perform miracles in cases when people demanded a sign from him as proof of his messianic dignity. He also chose not to perform a single miracle suggested to him by the demon. He refused the Pharisees and Sadducees, who asked to see a "sign from heaven" (Mt 16.1–4, Mk 8.11–12). He was not interested in miracles for the sake of miracles. Neither did he need to perform any miracles to prove his authority as

[37]Bruce Metzger, *The New Testament: Its Background, Growth, and Content* (Nashville, TN: Abingdon Press, 2003), 39.

[38]See George Ernest Wright, "Palestine in the Time of Christ," Chapter 9 in his *Biblical Arachaology* (Philadelphia: Westminster Press, 1960), 147–63.

Moses did (Ex 4.1–9). He had already accomplished so many miracles that there was absolutely no need of any additional demonstration or proof.

After all, the Pharisees required a sign allegedly so that they could believe in him, when in fact, faith is a prerequisite for a miracle: miracles are a consequence, not a source, of faith.[39] Those who did not want to believe in his miracles simply refused to see what was already obvious—like Cicero or the rationalists of the modern age who consider miracles to be impossible. There were many such rationalists in Palestine in Jesus' time—the Sadducees, for example, were among them.

To any impartial reader of the Gospel, this should be obvious: they speak of a personality that had never appeared in history, neither before, nor after. The miracles and healings are only one aspect of Jesus' activity. Healings and even resurrections, as we have seen, had been performed by Old Testament prophets, but these were rare cases. In the Old Testament, the majority of miracles were char-

Mary Magdalene,
N. K. Bodarevskii,
Mosaic, 1895–1907

acteristic only of certain ages (first of all, the time before the exodus from Egypt, when God decided to interfere in an unusual way in the fate of his people). The New Testament paints a picture of divine intervention unparalleled in human history. Even if we were to sum up all the miracles described in Exodus, there would be no more than twenty, including the plagues, and they all occurred during a space of time lasting at least forty years. The Gospels, on the contrary, shows us the ministry of Jesus, which lasted slightly more than three years (if we follow the chronology that is based mostly on the Gospel according to John); moreover, the number of miracles is in the hundreds, if not thousands.

[39]Mary Anne Tolbert, *Sowing the Gospel: Mark's Work in Literary-Historical Perspective* (Minneapolis: Fortress Press, 1996), 182.

Jesus' miracles differ from Old Testament miracles and signs not only in quantity, but in quality as well. In the Old Testament, there were few "gentle" miracles—the kind that inspire in the readers feelings of joy or love for God. Old Testament miracles are first and foremost "τέρατα" (*terata*), signs that are intended to incite fear or horror, forcing the reader not so much to bow before the mercy of God as to tremble before his majesty. In the New Testament, we see "God with a human face," both literally and figuratively. The miracles performed by the incarnate God fundamentally differ in their tone from the miracles of Moses and the Old Testament prophets, just as the teaching of Jesus, in its tone and content, differs from the commandments of Moses and the books of the prophets.

In the Synoptic Gospels, the term τέρατα (*terata*), is used mostly with reference to the miracles of false prophets (Mt 24.24, Mk 13.22). They use the term δυνάμεις (*dynameis*) when speaking of Jesus' miracles, meaning a manifestation of power and might (from δύναμις [*dynamis*], "power").[40] In the fourth Gospel, Jesus' miracles are described by the term "σημεῖα" (*sēmeia*), or "signs" (from σημεῖον [*sēmeion*], "sign"). For the Synoptics, a miracle is first of all a manifestation of the power of God through Jesus, while a sign is that which Jesus' opponents ask for, but do not receive from him (Mt 12.38–39; 16.1, 4; Mk 8.11–12). In John, on the contrary, every miracle is a σημεῖον (*sēmeion*)—a sign that indicates Jesus' divine nature, a cypher hiding the reality that is inaccessible to human eyes, but is revealed through the power of faith.

In general, there is no need to put too much stress on the specific meaning of these terms as used in the Synoptics as opposed to John. In the Gospel of Mark, the word σημεῖα (*sēmeia*) is used to refer not only to the miracles of false prophets (13.22), but also to the miracles that the disciples of Jesus will perform in his name (16.17). "The sign of the prophet Jonah"—this is the only miracle of Jesus that is termed by the Synoptics as "σημεῖον" (*sēmeion*). The other miracles in some sense are a foreshadowing of this most important miracle in the Gospel accounts.

---

[40]On the meaning of this term in Mark, see K. Kertelge, *Die Wunder Jesu im Markusevangelium: Eine redaktionsgeschichtliche Untersuchung* (Munich: Kösel, 1970), 120–25.

To perform a healing was just as natural for Jesus as for a doctor to prescribe medicine to a sick person. Healing power even flowed from him unbidden, even when he was not intentionally performing a miracle. People were healed simply by touching him (Lk 8.46).

The story of Jonah,
miniature, 10th century

Jesus' miracles were motivated first of all by his desire to help people, to lessen their suffering. We find no such motivation among the figures of the Old Testament, except for isolated incidents. In the synagogue in Nazareth, Jesus applied Isaiah's words to himself: "The Spirit of the Lord is upon me, because he hath anointed me to preach the Gospel to the poor; he hath sent me to heal the brokenhearted, to preach deliverance to the captives, and recovering of sight to the blind, to set at liberty them that are bruised, to preach the acceptable year of the Lord" (Lk 4.18–19, cf. Is 6.1–2). In these words, the prophet described one in whom all messianic yearnings were contained, to whom all looked with hoped, in whom all saw salvation. The history of the people of Israel had not known such a person before the coming of Jesus. He came to fulfill these expectations, and not merely to fulfill them, but to exceed them. This becomes evident in the words spoken by him to the disciples of John the Baptist: "Go and show John again those things which ye do hear and see: blind receive their sight, and the lame walk, the lepers are cleansed, and the deaf hear, the dead are raised up, and the poor have the Gospel preached to them" (Mt 11.4–5).

"The acceptable year of the Lord" had come with the coming of Jesus Christ to the world, and this is what best explains the great number of healings and miracles that accompanied his ministry. It pleased God in this exact moment of human history to send his Son into the world, so that he would transform the world forever. Yes, his miracles did not convince everyone, just as his teachings and parables did not lead to universal repentance. But we can assume that all who wanted to receive healing from him received it, just as all who wanted to follow his teaching followed him.

The New Year,
Fresco, 14th
century

Jesus, judging by everything we know, never rejected anyone, even if, for whatever reason, he did not immediately respond to a request for healing (Mt 15.23; Mk 7.27; Jn 11.6). Only those who did not want to be healed or to believe remained without healing or faith. Similarly, in our own time, in spite of the "cloud of witnesses" (Heb 12.1), some do not want to believe in the divinity of Jesus; others—in his miracles; and still others—that he even existed.

Were there ever any events in the life of Jesus when he could not heal someone? It turns out that there were. In the Gospel of Matthew, we hear of how the inhabitants of his own city did not want to accept Jesus as the Messiah because he was the son of a carpenter and because his brothers and sisters continued to live among them. That particular episode ends with the following words: "And he did not many mighty works there because of their unbelief" (Mt 13.58). In the parallel account in Mark, this is expressed even more starkly: "And he could there do no mighty work, save that he laid his hands upon a few sick folk, and healed them. And he marvelled because of their unbelief. And he went round about the villages, teaching" (Mk 6.5–6). Jesus could not perform a miracle if those to be healed did not have faith.[41]

[41][This is not a power lacking in Christ, who, as God, is all-powerful; rather, the lack of faith of those who needed to be healed precludes the reciprocal relationship of faith and power that is needed for miraculous healing. As St Gregory the Theologian explains: "Take, for example,

For Jesus' followers, every miracle he performed is an act of communion with God, because in his person, they encountered God incarnate. Therefore, many physical healings are also accompanied by spiritual illumination. Jesus asked the man blind from birth, whom he had healed, "Do you believe in the Son of God?" He, in turn, asked Jesus, "Who is he, Lord, that I may believe in him?" Jesus answered, "You have both seen him and it is he who is talking with you." The word "seen" here has a special meaning for a man who only a few hours or days before had no conception of what it meant to see, for whom the entire world was opened thanks to the healing power of Jesus. The formerly blind man answered, "Lord, I believe!" and he worshiped him (Jn 9.35–38). The physical healing of blindness progressed to spiritual illumination, which took place thanks to man's encounter with God.

In the Old Testament, only a few of God's chosen ones were found worthy of such communion with God, which one might call a face-to-face encounter. Concerning Moses, it is told with wonder that God spoke with him "face to face, as a man speaketh unto his friend" (Ex 33.11). In the Gospels, doens of people walk before our eyes, and with each of them the incarnate God speaks as with a friend. People hear his teachings, they are present at the miracles he performed, and every encounter with him becomes a meeting with God, with him who is no longer hidden from the people by the cloud on top of a mountain (Ex 19.16), but who comes into the very thick of everyday human life in order to make this everyday life into a miracle.

Christ's inability to do any signs in that area because of unbelief on the part of the recipients. Something essential for cures was required on both sides—faith on the part of the patients, power on that of the healer. So one side without its counterpart could not perform them. I am not sure whether this does not count as a case involing moral unsuitability as well—medical cure is out of place with people who are going to be damaged as a result by unbelief." St Gregory of Nazianzus, *Oration* 30.10 (PPS 23:100–101).—*Ed.*]

4. The Miracles of Jesus in Contemporary New Testament Scholarship

The miracles of Jesus do not lend themselves to rational explanation; however, to cast doubt on their possibility or to consider them merely pious legends invented by the followers of Jesus many decades after his death would mean to redact entirely huge and numerous swaths testimonies from the Gospel. Without miracles, the Gospel stops being the "good news," since the most important part of that good news has been taken out.[42]

"Jesus minus the miracles"[43] is a false academic construct that in no way corresponds to the Gospel depiction of Christ. Such works as Hegel or Renan's *Life of Jesus* lose all connection with the real, historical Jesus simply by virtue of ignoring the miracle narratives, not even trying to reflect on them or give them at least some kind of concrete interpretation. From such writers, it is only a small step to a complete denial of the historicity of Jesus of Nazareth.

We have already offered many telling citations from the books of rationalist philosophers concerning miracles. Some of these citations are so dated they are amusing, such as Kant's words concerning "enlightened governments" that might have "at once conceded, or even decided and enacted . . . that miracles happened in days of yore; but that nowadays no new miracle may be permitted." But this skepticism concerning the phenomenon of the miraculous, as well as everything supernatural that cannot be explained by human reason, is just as widespread in our times as during the Enlightenment. Today's arguments may sound different, but the verdicts of skeptics concerning miracles are just as dogmatic.[44] John Tyson, for example, insists:

---

[42]Thomas E. Crane, *The Synoptics: Mark, Matthew, and Luke Interpret the Gospel* (London: Sheed and Ward, Ltd., 1999) 34–35. Gerald O'Collins, *Jesus: a Portrait* (London: Darton, Longman and Todd, Ltd., 2008), 76.

[43]Meier, *A Marginal Jew*, 2:618.

[44]See Anthony Flew, "Neo-Humean Arguments About The Miraculous," in *In Defense of*

The problem from the modern historian is that he or she does not have the option of explaining events in terms of demon possession or miracle . . . We cannot simply adopt a worldview; it is part of the inheritance we have as citizens of the world at a particular time, and the ancient view of the world, as Bultmann described it, is obsolete.[45]

Rudolf Bultmann (1884–1976) was an influential German theologian of the twentieth century, the most famous proponent of the school of the "demythologizing" of the Gospels. He assumed that everything written in the Gospel accounts concerning healing and expulsion of demons was simply part of that mythological world in which the ancients lived and which has completely become a thing of the past. According to Bultmann, faith in miracles is incompatible with scientific and technological progress. He explores this idea categorically and thoroughly:

Also finished by knowledge of the forces and laws of nature is faith in spirits and demons. For us the stars are physical bodies whose motion is regulated by cosmic law; they are not demonic beings who can enslave men and women to serve them. If they have any influence on human life, it takes place in accordance with an intelligible order and is not due to their malevolence. Likewise, illnesses and their cures have natural causes and do not depend on the work of demons and on exorcising them. Thus, the wonders of the New Testament are also finished as wonders; anyone who seeks to salvage their historicity by recourse to nervous disorders, hypnotic influences, suggestion, and the like only confirms this. Even occultism pretends to be a science. We cannot use electric lights and radios and, in the event of illness, avail ourselves of modern medical and clinical means and at the time believe in the spirit and wonder world of the New Testament. And if we suppose that we can do so ourselves, we must be clear that we can represent this as the

Miracles: A Comprehensive Case for God's Action in History (Downers Grove: InterVarsity Press, 1997), 49–51.

[45]J. B. Tyson, *The New Testament and Early Christianity* (New York: Macmillan, 1984), 138.

attitude of Christian faith only by making the Christian proclamation unintelligible and impossible for our contemporaries.[46]

It is unclear why exactly Bultmann includes the stars in his line of argumentation. Nowhere in the Gospels are they ascribed any sort of demonic influence.[47] Attempts to explain away the Gospel's miracles with hypnosis, suggestion, or occultism are, in fact, unsound—that is easy to agree with. But as for any discussion of miracles being impossible in the light of electricity, such arguments can only be convincing to those who deny the possibility of miracles in principle. These argument smack of the same naïve positivism as the words of Kant concerning wise governments who do not allow miracles.

Few modern commentators follow Bultmann's logic in the same expressions that he used. Nevertheless, his influence continues to be pervasive. For many decades, Bultmann has poisoned Western New Testament scholarship with his speculations and fantasies, and many scholars continue to dedicate hundreds of pages of analysis to deepening his hypotheses instead of referring to the text of the Gospels themselves to find answers to questions about Jesus' life and teachings.

As for the miracles of Jesus, many authors offer approaches that differ from Bultmann's in language but are similar in content.[48] One is not required to accept the historicity of miracles, these authors insist, neither is one required to deny them outright. The important thing about the miracle narratives is the content, the message that they bear.

At the end of the nineteenth century, a new approach to the miracles arose that tried to interpret them the same way as the parables. Not

[46]Rudolf Bultmann, *The New Testament and Mythology & Other Basic Writings* (Philadelphia: Fortress Press, 1984), 4–5.

[47]Some of those healed by Jesus are described in Matthew 4.24 as *selēniazomenous* (σεληνιαζομένους; cf. Mt 17.15); modern translations render this as "epileptic," but the origin of the word is "moon," because some in the ancient world thought this condition was caused by the moon, and thus people suffering from epilepsy or similar diseases that caused seizures were thougt to be "moonstruck," or "lunatics" (the original meaning of the English word, which comes from the Latin word for "moon," and is used in the KJV). But this is merely the etymology of the Greek term, and nowhere in Scripture is this origin of the disease discussed or accepted.—*Ed.*

[48]See Gerd Theissen, *The Miracle Stories of the Early Christian Tradition* (Edinburgh: First Fortress Press, 2007), 1–40.

because they were fictions, and not because a tale that existed initially as a parable was then transformed by the early Church into a historical account, but because miracle narratives in the Gospel fulfill the same function as parables—they are indications of redemption.[49] This idea continues to have many adherents among scholars of the New Testament. One of them writes,

> The narratives of the nature miracles when examined in their earliest forms recoverable from the gospel texts depict in symbol the identical in-breaking kingdom, often with striking parallels in both imagery and significance to specific parables of Jesus. In short, the nature miracles and the parables closely cohere with each other. From these three propositions it therefore follows that the earliest forms of these miracle stories should be recognized as most probably historical (that is to say factual accounts of deeds from the life of Christ). . . . [There are] often overlooked parallels between the miracles and the parables and . . . the former make very good sense when viewed as genuine, symbolic enactments of the dawning new age by its harbinger, Jesus.[50]

Form criticism, which Bultmann himself promoted, is based on the strict separation between different literary forms and genres, to which this or that excerpt from the Gospels might belong. The parable and the miracle are two such forms, each of which requires its own hermeneutic approach. A group of modern scholars believes that functional criteria are more important than the formal—if the miracle narrative plays the same role as a parable in the Gospels, then one must interpret it using the same tools as one would use to interpret parables. Such a view allows for the assertion that the historicity of miracles is secondary to their function in the text.[51]

[49] Alexander Bruce, *The Miraculous Element in the Gospels* (New York: A. C. Armstrong & Son, 1886), 309.

[50] Craig L. Blomberg, "The Miracles as Parables," in *Gospel Perspectives*, Vol. 6: *The Miralces of Jesus*, ed. David Wenham and Craig Blomberg (Eugene, OR: Wif and Stock Publishers, 1986), 327–59, at 347–48.

[51] Craig L. Blomberg, *The Miracles as Parables* (Sheffield: JSOT Press, 1986), 327–28.

This opinion, however, is fraught with the dangers of allegorizing the miracles of Jesus, or turning them into mere symbols. If these miracles were not actual events, that means that we are dealing with falsified texts, even if that falsification is well-intended. Therefore, the opinion that in some cases "the entire narrative concerning the miracle could grow from a dramatization of a word or parable of Jesus"[52] must be rejected.

The most convincing approach seemingly belongs to those scholars who do not doubt the historicity of Jesus' miracles, though they may still underline the fact that in the Gospels, miracle narratives serve the same pedagogic function as parables. H. van der Loos, the author of a detailed examination of this topic, insists that the miracles in the Gospels are "historically reliable." He further notes:

> Now Jesus manifested himself not only in what he said, but also in what he did. . . . Word and miracle are both functions of the Kingdom which are *sui generis*, however "intertwined" they may sometimes appear to be. In both God "behaves" in a certain way, in both he enters into contact with man in his mental and physical need. . . . In both cases God makes "history" with man. . . . After all, a miracle, as part of God's actions, can never be placed in some pigeonhole of ordinary human history. It happens over and above ordinary events, and against the known order of things (*supra et contra naturam*).[53]

This scholar concludes that faith is the only possible prism through which we may correctly interpret the miracle. The miracles of Jesus

> may therefore not be "taken into consideration," even if this is done in the most sympathetic fashion. They are among the vital parts of the Gospels, which may not be cut away. . . . In his miracles as direct deeds Jesus revealed to mankind, with an intention, a new observable reality, which can only be fully understood by faith. In this new reality, outside and against the known laws of order and regularity in nature,

---

[52]Meier, *A Marginal Jew*, 2:647.
[53]H. van der Loos, *The Miracles of Jesus* (Leiden: E. J. Brill, 1965), 701–2.

he proclaimed his freedom, power and love as the Son and Lord sent by the Father.[54]

That which Bultmann called the "mythological vision of the world" in fact is nothing less than a religious worldview founded on biblical revelation. It assumes the existence not only of God, but angels and demons also; not only natural phenomena that fit within the known laws of nature, but supernatural events that supersede such laws as well. This is the worldview reflected in the pages of the Old and New Testaments, and it is within the frame of this worldview that the miracles of Jesus acquire that reliability that can only be established thanks to religious experience.

The criteria of reliability that are applied to the miracles by contemporary scholarship can be convincing only as additions to religious experience. Such criteria include the following: 1) many proofs in various sources (Matthew, Mark, Luke, John); 2) various literary genres in which the miracle narratives have come down to us (healings, casting out demons, miracles associated with natural phenomena, and resurrections); 3) agreement among the various witnesses (i.e., lack of contradictions among the available sources). The presence of these criteria argues against the possibility that all these stories were simply fabrications of the early Church.[55]

5. Son of God or "Divine Man"?

In the scholarly literature about Jesus' miracles, it is considered appropriate to compare Jesus with other miracle-workers of ancient times, such as Apollonius of Tyana (AD 1–98), a Neopythagorean philosopher who lived almost at the same time as Jesus, but who outlived him by many years.[56] The

---

[54]Ibid, 706.

[55]Meier, *A Marginal Jew*, 2:619–25, 630.

[56]Cf. Puig, *Jesus: a Biography*, 365, 371; Meier, *A Marginal Jew*, 2:576–81; T. Klutz, *The Exorcism Stories in Luke-Acts: a Socio-Stylistic Reading* (Cambridge: Cambridge University Press, 2004), 121–25; Achtenmeier, *Jesus and the Miracle Tradition*, 207.

Life of Apollonius of Tyana, written by Flavius Philostratus in the third century, contains descriptions of nine miracles, some of which have a certain external similarity to the miracles performed by Jesus. Thus, for example, the work describes the casting out of a demon from possessed young man at his mother's request. This episode is reminiscent of the healing of the daughter of the Canaanite woman (Mt 15.22–28; Mk 7.25–30).

The similarity between the miracles in the Gospel and the miracles described in the *Life of Apollonius* have forced some scholars to suggest that the evangelists may have been influenced by the oral traditions that gave rise to the *Life of Apollonius*.[57] Such an assertion, however, is not confirmed by any sources. The opposite influence is much more likely— Philostratus, living in the third century, could easily have been aware of Christian literature and could have appropriated the structure that undergirds his own miracle narratives. More than that, when one reads the life of Apollonius, especially the "miracles," one cannot fail to notice that these are simply parodies of the Gospel accounts of the miracles of Jesus.[58]

This is exactly how early Christians themselves perceived the work of Philostratus, a fact noted by Eusebius of Caesarea in the fourth century. According to Eusebius, during the persecutions of Diocletian, a certain Roman courtier named Hierocles, the prefect of Egypt from 307–308, used Philostratus' work to compare Apollonius with Christ in his work *To the Christians*. This work is not extant, but its rebuttal, written by Eusebius, has survived. The latter, throughout the entire rebuttal, demonstrates that Apollonius was a magician propped up by demonic power: "Even if we are to admit that the writer spoke the truth about the miracles, even from his own words it is clear that everything was done with the cooperation of demons."[59]

[57]G. Petzke, *Die Traditionen über Apollonius von Tyana und das Neue Testament* (Boston: Brill Academic Publishers, Inc., 1970), 68–72.

[58]In Apollonius' "miracles," scholars note an element of sleight of hand and delusion, while his interactions with other people are characterized by arrogance and pride. Cf. Craig Evans, *Jesus and his Contemporaries: Comparative Studies* (Boston: Brill Academic Publishers, Inc., 2001), 249–50.

[59]Eusebius, *The Treatise of Eusebius, the Son of Pamphilus, Against the Life of Apollonius of Tyana by Philostratus, Occasioned by the Parallel Drawn by Hierocles between Him and Christ.* Translation in *Philostratus: Life of Appolonius of Tyana, Vol. 2*, trans. F. C. Conybeare, Loeb Classical Library 17 (Cambridge: Harvard University Press, 2005), 484–605.

Appolonius of Tyana, Marble, 2nd century

This interest in Apollonius of Tyana among modern New Testament scholars is connected in large part with a desire to find a "scientific" explanation for the phenomenon of miracles, since they take up such a significant portion of the Gospel narrative of Jesus. Some scholars, considering the fact that several decades passed between the time of the "historical Jesus" and the actual writing of the Gospels (during which time his life gradually gathered "mythological details"), have developed a theory that the image of Christ in the Gospels was modeled on the "divine men" that appear in ancient Greek and Roman literature. The phrase "divine man" (*theios anēr or theios anthrōpos* [θεῖος ἀνήρ, θεῖος ἄνθρωπος]) does not appear in the New Testament at all. It was invented by scholars and continues to appear in scholarly literature concerning Jesus as miracle-worker.

The fact that the idea of a "divine man" is a completely far-fetched fabrication has already been mentioned in a previous volume of this series.[60] Jesus was not simply a man with the power to perform miracles. He was the Son of God, and only in the light of this understanding can his miracles be explained and appreciated in all their complexity. There are no actual analogues to his activity in Greek, Roman, or even later Jewish literature. Even if we were to accept the miracles in these later literary traditions as historically reliable, none of these literary characters comes even close to Jesus—not in the sheer number of miracles, not in the quality of his signs, miracles, and healings.

As we explore the miracles of Jesus in this book, we will make several fundamental assumptions: 1) all the miracle narratives are historically reliable; 2) in each case, Jesus is acting as both God and man at the same time; 3) each exploration of a miracle is not simply an account of what happened, but it also contains a certain spiritual and moral content; 4) every miracle is the fruit of synergy—a cooperative action between God and the specific person for whom the miracle is performed.

This last point requires further clarification. In the Old Testament, miracles were seen as proof of God's power and omnipotence—in most cases, people were not active participants, but passive recipients, or even unwilling victims, of these miracles. The healings of Jesus present a different reality. He often asks people whether or not they want to be healed, whether they believe that it will occur, and sometimes he requires specific actions as proof of that faith. For example, he said, "Go, show yourselves unto the priests" to the healed lepers (Lk 17.14), and "Go, wash in the pool of Siloam" to the blind man (Jn 9.7). Even when the healing occurs seemingly without his will, as a consequence of his power flowing out from him (Lk 8.43–48), it becomes possible only thanks to the faith of the one who hopes to be healed. We will return again and again to this point when speaking of specific miracle narratives in the Gospels.

---

[60]Met. Hilarion Alfeyev, *The Beginning of the Gospel*, Jesus Christ: His Life and Teaching, Vol. 1 (Yonkers, NY: St Vladimir's Seminary Press, 2018), 71–73.

Chapter 2

JESUS' FIRST MIRACLE

The Gospel according to John was written later than the first three Gospels. Both ancient writers and some modern commentators agree on this fact. They assume that the author of the fourth Gospel was largely motivated by a desire to tell about those things that the first three evangelists left out. Therefore, though his account in some ways comes into contact with the accounts of the Synoptics, the majority of events he describes are not mentioned by the Synoptics at all. John was probably a witness of many episodes he recounted, which gives his witness a special value. It is possible that he saw Jesus' first miracle as well, an event that begins the second chapter of the fourth Gospel.

The fact that John may have been present is suggested by the previous chapter, which includes an account of two disciples of John the Baptist who followed after Christ. One of them was Andrew, while the other, evidently, was John himself (Jn 1.35–40), though nameless in the account. John appears several times in the pages of his account without being named, and only toward the end is he revealed. That same day, the group of Jesus' disciples was enlarged by the addition of Simon Peter, and the day after that of Philip and Nathaniel. Three days later, Jesus and his disciples were already in Cana of Galilee (Jn 2.2). Thus, John found himself among a still small group of disciples. It was these five disciples that became the most reliable witnesses of Jesus' first miracle.

John's presence at the scene is further suggested by the fact that the account is given with many specific details. To hear the dialogue between Jesus and his mother would only be possible if John were in the immediate vicinity.

Apostles Andrew the First-called and John the Theologian, Icon, end of 17th to earthly 18th century

1. "There Was a Wedding in Cana of Galilee"

Cana of Galilee is mentioned only in the Gospel according to John. Nathaniel was born there (Jn 21.2). The fact that Jesus ended up in Cana three days after meeting Nathaniel could suggest that the family of the wedding party was in some way connected to Nathaniel. In a small Galilean town, it is likely that everyone knew each other, and intermarriage was common. If the family was not connected immediately with Nathaniel, at least the invitation to Jesus and his disciples could have come from him (otherwise how could Jesus, who was in Bethabara, have found out about a wedding in Cana of Galilee and about his being invited there as well?).

The beginning of the account tells that the Mother of Jesus (nowhere in the Gospel of John is she named) was already at the wedding when he arrived with his disciples. The word "both" in verse two shows that Jesus was not the most important guest invited:

> And the third day there was a marriage in Cana of Galilee; and the mother of Jesus was there, and both Jesus was called, and his disciples, to the marriage. And when they wanted wine, the mother of Jesus saith unto him, "They have no wine." Jesus saith unto her, "Woman, what have I to do with thee? Mine hour is not yet come." His mother saith unto the servants, "Whatsoever he saith unto you, do it." And there were set there six waterpots of stone, after the manner of the purifying of the Jews, containing two or three measures apiece [twenty or thirty gallons]. Jesus saith unto them, "Fill the waterpots with water." And they filled them up to the brim. And he saith unto them, "Draw out now, and bear unto the governor of the feast." And they bore it. When

the ruler of the feast had tasted the water that was made wine, and knew not whence it was (but the servants which drew the water knew), the governor of the feast called the bridegroom, and saith unto him, "Every man at the beginning doth set forth good wine, and when men have well drunk, then that which is worse; but thou hast kept the good wine until now." This beginning of miracles did Jesus in Cana of Galilee, and manifested forth his glory; and his disciples believed on him. (Jn 2.1–11)

The Martyrdom of the Apostle Bartholomew (Nathaniel), Mosaic, 12th century

In accordance with the practices of the time, the family of both bride and groom, as well as friends of both families, were invited to the wedding feast, which occurred in the house of the groom or his father. Wedding feasts usually continued for seven days (Judg 14.12; Tob 11.17); in special cases, one could last as long as two weeks (Tob 10.7).

Commentators offer various hypotheses concerning why the wine ran out during the feast. One of them is the unexpected arrival of Jesus and his disciples, who, contrary to tradition, did not bring any wine with them.[1] Another guess is that the feast lasted a long time. A third is that the family was poor, and this hypothesis is the most likely. The words of the Mother of Jesus ("They have no wine") suggest a certain distance between her and the events—she is clearly not a member of the family.

---

[1]The amount of wine at a wedding feast to some degree depended on how much the guests brought. Jesus and his disciples probably came empty-handed. See Raymond Brown, *The Gospel according to John (I-XII)* (New Haven: Yale University Press, 2007), 102.

The Marriage in Cana of Galilee, Veronese, 1562–63

2. "What Have I to Do With Thee?"

Jesus' answer to his mother's request is sometimes interpreted to mean that Jesus was in some way unhappy about his mother's question. According to Irenaeus of Lyons, "When Mary was urging [him] on to [perform] the wonderful miracle of the wine, and was desirous before the time to partake of the cup of emblematic significance, the Lord, checking her untimely haste, said, 'Woman, what have I to do with you? My hour is not yet come'—waiting for that hour which was foreknown by the Father."[2] The "cup of emblematic significance" can be understood as the cup of suffering that Jesus had to drink (Mt 26.39, 42), or as the cup of the Eucharist (concerning the eucharistic subtext, we will speak more later).

According to St John Chrysostom, "For she desired both to do them a favor, and through her Son to render herself more conspicuous; perhaps too she had some human feelings, like his brethren, when they said, 'Show yourself to the world' (Jn 17.4), desiring to gain credit from his miracles. Therefore he answered somewhat vehemently." He continues by saying

---

[2]Irenaeus of Lyons, *Against Heresies* 3.16.7 (ANF 1:443).

that "she, because she had borne him, claimed, according to the custom of other mothers, to direct him in all things, when she ought to have reverenced and worshipped him." Since she did not want to submit to him, "but would in all cases have claimed the superiority as being his mother, therefore he replied as he did to them who spoke to him; otherwise he could not have led up her thoughts from his present lowliness to his future exaltation, had she expected that she should always be honored by him as by a son, and not that he should come as her master."[3]

Some contemporary commentators go even farther, and insist that in his answer to his mother, Jesus expressed a categorical protest that would underline his independence from the start. Her words are nothing less than a desire for explicit action, a request, however implicit, for a miracle. And this is what inspires Jesus' seemingly strict response.[4]

Both Chrysostom and many contemporary commentators on the text take as their starting point the idea that Jesus' answer to his mother was not altogether respectful. The phrase "What does your concern have to do with me" is a particularly Semitic phrase. We find similar phrases in the Old Testament, for example addressed to the prophet Elijah by the widow: "What have I to do with thee, O thou man of God?" (1 Kg 17.18) The question of the widow contains a rebuke that the prophet came too late, for her son had already died. Chrysostom thinks that the intonation of rebuke can also be heard in the words of Jesus toward his mother "instructing her for the future not to do the like; because, though he was careful to honor his mother, yet he cared much more for the salvation of her soul, and for the doing good to the many, for which he took upon him the flesh. These then were the words, not of one speaking rudely to his mother, but belonging to a wise dispensation, which brought her into a right frame of mind, and provided that the miracles should be attended with that honor which was meet."[5]

But a rebuke is not the same as lack of respect. Some people, however, see a lack of respect in the fact that Jesus calls his mother "woman."

---

[3]John Chrysostom, *Homilies on the Gospel of John*, Homily 21 (NPNF¹ 14:74).

[4]John Ashton, *Understanding the Fourth Gospel* (Oxford: Oxford University Press, 2007), 172.

[5]John Chrysostom, *Homilies on the Gospel of John*, Homily 21 (NPNF¹ 14:75).

The Marriage in Cana,
detail from the *Maestà*
of Duccio, 1308–11

However, the word "woman" (*gynai*, γύναι) is one that Jesus used when referring to her at the moment when she stood by him at the cross. In fact, this was a typical form of address for women that Jesus used (see Jn 4.21 8.10, 20.13).

But was Jesus' response to his mother really a mere result of her failure to recognize his divine dignity? The words of Jesus— "My time has not yet come"—force us to seek another interpretation. The author of the fourth Gospel understands this expression exclusively in the context of the imminent suffering and death of Jesus—we find similar expressions in the fourth Gospel several times. When his brothers invited him to come to the feast in Jerusalem, Jesus said, "My time is not yet full come" (Jn 7.8). When the Jews wanted to seize him, no one could, "Because his hour was not yet come" (Jn 7.30). On the contrary, before the Passover, "Jesus knew that his hour was come that he should depart out of this world unto the Father" (Jn 13.1), and for this reason he washed the feet of his disciples. Mark records that in the garden of Gethsemane, Jesus prayed for the hour to pass him by, if possible (Mk 14.35).

Thus, even during the wedding in Cana of Galilee, at the very beginning of his ministry, Jesus spoke to his mother about the sufferings that awaited him. Did she know about them already, or did she only guess? Did he tell her before about all that awaited him? We do not know this, just as the disciple who witnessed this conversation did not know either. But the fact that at this moment Jesus found it necessary to remind or tell her about it force us to look at the entire conversation in a different light. From the moment of the wedding in Galilee, Jesus' path toward death began, a path followed by John through the entire fourth Gospel.

The words of Jesus' mother, directed at the listeners, also force us to doubt the aptness of an interpretation founded on the idea that she did not recognize the divine dignity of her Son. If that were so, why would she say to her listeners: "Whatsoever he saith unto you, do it" (Jn 2.5)? Up to this point, he had not accomplished any miracles yet, nor had he revealed his supernatural abilities in any way. He "lived as one among many."[6] So why the conviction in his mother concerning his ability to solve the problem? The Gospel does not provide a direct answer. We can only guess that her experience of daily life with Jesus for the last thirty years, beginning with the miraculous events of his birth and childhood, gave her a conviction of his divine dignity, as well as his supernatural abilities.

---

3. Transforming the Water into Wine: Interpretations

How are we to understand the miracle of the transformation of the water into wine? There are very many different rationalistic interpretations of this event, mostly belonging to the German theologians of the last few generations. In the beginning of the nineteenth century, H. Paulus suggested that Jesus came to the wedding with reserve wine that he kept back until the moment when all the wine in the house ran out. Mary knew that he had the wine with him, and she wondered why he waited to pass on the wine to the family; finally, Jesus got the wine and it was a pleasant surprise for everyone.[7] In the beginning of the twentieth century, H. Schäfer tried to prove that Jesus, having mastered the power of hypnotism, managed, by the power of suggestion, to change the mood of all the people present radically—this is what was taken as the miracle.[8] A little later, M. Dibelius suggested that the story of the transformation of water into wine came about as a result of the cult of Dionysius,[9] while the Christian feast of Theophany (January 6) was an updated version of the feast of Dionysius (January 5). The story of the miracle, therefore, became a linking point

---

[6]St John Chrysostom, *Homilies on the Gospel of John*, Homily 21 (NPNF[1] 14:74).

[7]H. E. Paulus, *Philologisch-kritischer und historischer Kommentar über das neue Testament*, 4.1:151.

[8]H. Schäfer, *Jesus in psychiatrischer Beleuchtung* (Berlin, 1910).

[9]M. Dibelius, *Die Formgeschichte des Evangeliums* (Tübingen: Mohr [Paul Siebeck], 1933), 98.

between the two religions.[10] All these theories are no longer accepted as serious additions to scholarship concerning this Gospel episode, except for Bultmann's opinion, which continues to exert a certain influence in New Testament scholarship.

To understand the meaning of the miracle in Cana, we must remember that in the Gospel according to John miracles are only mentioned when the evangelist sees a special theological meaning in them or an illustration of some theological truth. In contrast with the Synoptic writers, who record miracles one after the other and leave the interpretation of them to the reader, John interprets everything he sees and hears. In the episode of the healing of the paralytic, the multiplication of the loaves, and the healing of the man blind from birth (Jn 5.1–47; 6.4–54; 9.1–41), the interpretation is offered as part of the narrative itself or immediately afterward. As for the wedding in Cana of Galilee, a clear interpretation seems to be lacking, but it is necessary to understand why the evangelist mentions this miracle. What theological reality is he revealing in this account? What is the symbolism of the miracle?

The language of symbols is an extremely important and unique aspect of all the Johannine writings. John's ability to reveal theological truths with the help of symbols reaches its apogee in Revelation. But even in the Gospel there are many symbols that can be read and interpreted in light of the larger theological context. In this case, we have two symbols—water and wine. John wrote his Gospel in a time when the liturgical practice of the Christian Church had already been formulated as distinct from the Jewish. At its foundation were two sacraments—baptism and the Eucharist. Around these two sacraments, a symbolic language had developed, which was reflected, among other things, in the art of the Early Church.

Water was a symbol of baptism, while bread and wine were symbols of the Eucharist. The transformation of water into wine at the wedding feast doubtless has eucharistic connotations. This is how the event was understood in the early Church. It is no coincidence that in the frescoes and bas-reliefs of the Christian Roman catacombs, we often find two themes—

[10]R. Bultmann, *Das Evangelium des Johannes: Kritisch-exegetischer Kommentar über das Neue Testament*, 2nd ed. (Göttingen, 1952), 83.

the wedding at Cana and the multiplication of the loaves.[11] These two miracles are purposefully placed close to each other in the Gospel according to John, and the miracle of the multiplication of the loaves is explicitly interpreted in a eucharistic context (immediately after it follows the discussion of the bread that came down from heaven).

The Marriage in Cana, detail of a stained glass window in Chartres Cathedral, 13th century.

The image of the wedding feast also has deep symbolism for John. In Revelation, John paints a picture of the wedding of the Lamb, during which the angel says, "Blessed are they which are called unto the marriage supper of the Lamb" (Rev 19.9). This image is used by Jesus himself, including in the parable of those called to the wedding feast (Mt 22.1–14, Lk 14.16–24), which from earliest times was understood to be a symbol of the Eucharist.

Finally, the eucharistic context is indicated by what happened to the water—it is transformed into wine. Of all thirty miracles of Jesus that we find in the Gospels this is the only one where he transforms something into something else. A central point of the Eucharistic liturgy is the transformation of the bread and wine into the Body and Blood of Christ. It occurs immediately after the moment when the priest remembers the life of Christ and his Passions, underlining especially the Mystical Supper. It is impossible to deny the eucharistic interpretation of the marriage in Cana of Galilee, during which Christ foretold his suffering and death for the first time, then transformed the water into wine. At the very least, it would be difficult to explain why John included it in his Gospel otherwise.

We should also note that Jesus uses the symbol of wine to indicate the newness of his teaching compared to the Old Testament regulations, for example when he says that new wine should not be poured into old wineskins (Mt 9.17; Mk 2.22; Lk 5.37–38). In the wedding scene, we see "six waterpots of stone, after the manner of the purifying of the Jews" (Jn 2.6). These waterpots symbolize the old Jewish rituals and rites, which

---

[11]Lee Jefferson, *Christ the Miracle Worker in Early Christian Art* (Minneapolis: Fortress Press, 2014), 134–37.

are going to be transformed by a new teaching and new liturgical culture, centered on the Eucharist.[12] We also note that Jesus soundly criticized the rites associated with washing as an expression of hypocrisy typical of the Pharisees (Mk 7.1–8).

What other meanings, other than the eucharistic one, are concealed in the narrative concerning the marriage in Cana of Galilee? Here it would be appropriate to mention certain other biblical texts about wine and marriage. In the Old Testament, wine was taken to be a symbol of joy and happiness (Ps 103.15, Eccl 10.19). In the prophetic books, the coming of the era of the Messiah was symbolized by the image of wine:

> And in this mountain shall the LORD of hosts make unto all people a feast of fat things, a feast of wines on the lees, of fat things full of marrow, of wines on the lees well refined. (Is 25.6)

> Therefore they shall come and sing in the height of Zion, and shall flow together to the goodness of the LORD, for wheat, and for wine, and for oil, and for the young of the flock and of the herd: and their soul shall be as a watered garden; and they shall not sorrow any more at all. (Jer 31.12)

> "Behold, the days come," saith the LORD, "that the plowman shall overtake the reaper, and the treader of grapes him that soweth seed; and the mountains shall drop sweet wine, and all the hills shall melt. And I will bring again the captivity of my people of Israel, and they shall build the waste cities, and inhabit them; and they shall plant vineyards, and drink the wine thereof; they shall also make gardens, and eat the fruit of them." (Am 9.13–14)

Sometimes the symbols of marriage and wine are used together:

---

[12]See C. H. Dodd, *The Interpretation of the Fourth Gospel* (Cambridge: Cambridge University Press, 1998), 299–300; C. H. Dodd, *Historical Tradition in the Fourth Gospel* (Cambridge: Cambridge University Press, 1999), 223; R. Alan Culpepper, *Anatomy of the Fourth Gospel* (Minneapolis: Fortress Press, 1987), 193; G. R. Beasley-Murray, *Word Biblical Commentary, Volume 36: John* (Nashville: Thomas Nelson, Inc., 1999), 36.

As the bridegroom rejoiceth over the bride, so shall thy God rejoice over thee. . . . The LORD hath sworn by his right hand, and by the arm of his strength, "Surely I will no more give thy grain as food for thine enemies; and the sons of the stranger shall not drink thy wine, for which thou hast labored; they that have gathered it shall eat it, and praise the LORD; and they that have brought it together shall drink it in the courts of my holiness." (Is 62.5, 8–9)

All these texts were well known to John, who, when he wrote of the wedding in Cana of Galilee, could have been implicitly evoking them. The wedding feast, as described, can be understood as the beginning of a new era—the same that was foretold by the prophets. The end of the narrative attests to this: "This beginning of miracles did Jesus in Cana of Galilee, and manifested forth his glory; and his disciples believed on him" (Jn 2.11). John here uses the word *sēmeion* (σημεῖον, "sign"). In Cana, Jesus laid the foundation for the signs that were to fill the rest of his earthly ministry.

The term "glory" (δόξα, *doxa*) also deserves some added attention. This term, in John, means not simply human glory or fame.[13] It has a very specific meaning that points to the coming suffering and death of Jesus—it was precisely in these events that John saw the greatest manifestation of the glory of God. Just before his arrest, when Judas had already left to go to the high priest to arrange his betrayal, Jesus said to his disciples: "Now is the Son of man glorified, and God is glorified in him. If God be glorified in him, God shall also glorify him in himself, and shall straightway glorify him" (Jn 13.31–32). Then he uttered a prayer to his Father that begins with the words "Father, the hour is come; glorify thy Son, that thy Son also may glorify thee" (Jn 17.1).

In Cana of Galilee that hour—toward which the entire Gospel narrative moves—had not yet come. Jesus' ministry had only just begun. But having transformed the water into wine, he already revealed his glory—the glory that he had with his Father "before the world was" (Jn 17.5). Here, in a simple Jewish home, where there was not enough wine, this glory was

---

[13]"How can ye believe, which receive glory one of another, and seek not the glory that cometh from God only?" (Jn 5.44).

The Marriage in Cana, Bosch. 1560–80

revealed for the first time. Subsequently, it would be revealed in other miracles and signs performed by Jesus. It would reach its climax in that moment when Jesus, nailed to the cross, in the complete humiliation of his human nature, would reveal the full glory of his divine majesty.

In this moment—the culmination of the Gospel drama—he will once again turn to his mother, and point to that same disciple who wrote down the story of the wedding in Cana of Galilee: "Woman, behold thy son!" Then to the disciple, he will say, "Behold thy mother!" And from that moment, the disciple will take her to his own home (Jn 19.25–27). This will be the continuation of the relationship between John and the mother of Jesus—a story that begins at the wedding at Cana of Galilee.

The words of the steward of the feast, directed to the groom—"Every man at the beginning doth set forth good wine; and when men have well drunk, then that which is worse: but thou hast kept the good wine until now" (Jn 2.10)—are not included by accident. As in many other cases, the characters in the Gospel's narratives think exclusively in earthly terms; their consciousness has not surpassed the limits of the material world. In Jesus' conversations with Nicodemus (John 3) and the Samaritan woman (John 4), this is especially evident. Jesus speaks of one reality, but those he speaks with hear something entirely different. He speaks of the heavenly; they hear the earthly (Jn 3.12). In this case, Jesus does not speak to the steward of the feast, and the latter does not know that a miracle has occurred. The Evangelist John fixes the reader's attention not so much on Jesus' words, as on his actions, but the meaning of this action remains hidden to those not immediately touched by it. Its meaning is revealed to the disciples, who, having seen what happened, believed in Jesus.

4. The Blessing of Marriage

Christian tradition interprets Jesus' presence at the wedding in Cana as Christ's blessing of the marriage union and the bearing of children. According to St Cyril of Alexandria, Jesus was present in order "to sanctify the very beginning of the birth of man. . . . For it was fitting that he, who was renewing the very nature of man, and refashioning it all for the better, should not only impart his blessing to those already called into being, but also prepare before grace for those soon to be born, and make holy their entrance into being." St Cyril reminds the reader of the Old Testament curse: "In sorrow thou shalt bring forth children" (Gen 3.16). Woman needed to be freed from this curse, which is what Christ did: "For he, the delight and joy of all, honored marriage with his presence, that he might expel the old shame of child-bearing."[14]

This explanation is also included in the Orthodox marriage service. In the beginning of the rite, the deacon intones a litany that contains the

[14]Cyril of Alexandria, *Commentary on John*, trans. E. B. Pusey, *A Library of the Fathers of the Holy Catholic Church: Commentary on the Gospel according to S. John, by S. Cyril, Patriarch of Alexandria, Volume I: Saint John I–VIII* (Oxford: James Parker and Co., 1874), 155.

petition: "May this marriage be blessed as was the marriage in Cana of Galilee." In the prayer of the priest, we read the following:

> O Lord our God, who in thy saving providence didst vouchsafe by thy presence in Cana of Galilee to declare marriage honorable: Do thou the same Lord, now, also maintain in peace and concord thy servants, (*name*), and (*name*), whom thou hast been pleased to join together. Cause their marriage to be honorable. Preserve their bed undefiled. Mercifully grant that they may live together in purity; and enable them to reach a ripe old age, walking in thy commandments with a pure heart.

The transformation of water into wine, as we have already said, is a symbol of the transformation of the bread and wine into the Body and Blood of Christ. But it is also a symbol of the change that a husband and wife undergo in marriage, when two become one flesh (Gen 2.24). As St John Chrysostom said, "For he is not one who is not yet [united,] but the half of one. . . . Do you see the mystery of marriage? he made of one, one; and again, having made these two, one, he so makes one, so that now also man is produced of one. For man and wife are not two men, but one Man."[15] This union occurs thanks to the mutual love of the partners: "Since this is friendship, that the lover and the beloved should no longer be two persons divided, but in a manner one single person; a thing which no how takes place except from love."[16]

The transformation of water into wine is also a symbol of the transformation of the daily life of the family into a feast: "I wish you all the best," St Gregory the Theologian wrote to a newly married couple, "And one of these good things—for Christ to be present at your wedding, for wherever Christ is, there is prosperity, and there the water transforms to wine, that is, a transformation of everything for the best."[17]

The marriage union, in which God is invisibly present, must become a never-ending feast of the revelation of the face of Christ in each of the

---

[15]St John Chrysostom, *Homilies on Colossians*, Homily 12 (NPNF[1] 13:318).
[16]St John Chrysostom, *Homilies on 1 Corinthians*, Homily 33 (NPNF[1] 12:197).
[17]St Gregory the Theologian, Letter 232.

The Marriage in Cana, Mosaic, Ravenna, 4th century

partners for each other. It must be a transformation of all aspects of their life together.

Nevertheless, we we must be careful of the too-widely-held idea that Christ established the sacrament of marriage in Cana of Galilee. This understanding, which firmly entered textbooks of dogmatic theology in the nineteenth century, comes from the idea that all seven sacraments were established by Christ. But since there is no direct evidence concerning this establishment of the sacrament of marriage in the Holy Scriptures, some have suggested various times and places when Christ might have done this. Often Cana of Galilee is cited in such cases.[18]

Such an interpretation stretches credulity. The marriage union was established by God in Eden when he created Adam and Eve and said to them, "Be fruitful, and multiply" (Gen 1.28). As for marriage as a sacrament of the Church, it only entered the typicon of the Church gradually, over the course of several centuries.[19] Jesus came to Cana of Galilee not to

[18]Cf. Metropolitan Makary's textbook of dogmatic theology, where the metropolitan suggests that Christ either established the sacrament of marriage during the wedding in Cana or when he said to the Pharisees: "What God hath joined together, let no man put asunder" (Mt 19.6). Or it could have occurred during another event we do not know about.

[19]Cf., John Meyendorff, *Marriage: An Orthodox Perspective* (Crestwood, NY: St Vladimir's Seminary Press, 1975).

establish the sacrament of marriage, but he came to bless and sanctify the marriage union by his presence.

---

5. The Presence
of His Mother

We must also say something about the role of the miracle at Cana of Galilee in Christian teaching about the Virgin Mary. In the Gospels, there is so little written about her that many interpreters who have no connection to the interpretive tradition of the Church have concluded that she played no role whatsoever in his life or in the Christian community after his death. These commentators claim that only many centuries later, during the era of Christological controversies (5th century), the Church began to ascribe a special significance to her. Such an opinion can be strengthened by reading early sources (up to the 4th century), such as the aforementioned quote by St John Chrysostom, where the Mother of Jesus is spoken of without special piety.

Based on such a reading of the event and such an interpretation of the early Church's history, many Protestant scholars of the Gospel see in the events of the wedding at Cana a confirmation that the cult of the Mother of God is a rather late phenomenon, uncharacteristic of the faith of the Early Church. Catholic commentators, on the contrary, see in this story an indication of the Virgin Mary's special role in the history of salvation. Her words "Whatever he says to you, do it" are interpreted as a commandment to obey the Son of God, left behind as a testament for all times and for all mankind.

The story of the wedding in Cana of Galilee is the only miracle narrative in the Gospels where the presence of the mother of Jesus is mentioned. Moreover, this miracle is accomplished as a result of her request, and the servants who fill the waterpots with water are fulfilling her command. Though Jesus performs the miracle, she plays a significant role in the narrative. In the Gospel of John, the next time she appears in the text is at the

The Marriage in Cana, G. David, 16th century

cross of her Son. One cannot avoid seeing the connection between these two appearances of the Mother of Jesus—at the beginning of his public ministry, at his first miracle, and at the very end, at the climactic moment, at the Cross. It is as though John is indicating her continued, though invisible, presence during the entire Gospel narrative.

In addition, one cannot fail to remember the image of the woman "clothed with the sun" (Rev 12.1). In the Church's tradition, beginning with the writing of Hippolytus of Rome, this image is usually interpreted as a symbol of the Church,[20] not the mother of God. However, we must not reject the connection between this image and the mother of God (St Andrew of Caesarea mentions such an interpretation),[21] especially considering that the woman clothed with the sun gives birth to "a man child, who was to rule all nations with a rod of iron: and her child was caught up unto God, and to his throne" (Rev 12.5). Here there is a clear allusion to Psalm 2, which was interpreted as messianic by the Early Church: "The Lord said to me: thou art my Son, this day have I begotten thee. Ask of me,

[20]Hippolytus of Rome, *On Christ and the Antichrist*; Methodius of Patara, *The Banquet of the Ten Virgins* 8.5–8 (ANF 6:336–37).

[21]Andrew of Caesarea. *Commentary on the Apocaplypse* 33. Translation in *Greek Commentaries on Revelation: Oecumenius and Andrew of Caesarea*, trans. William C. Weinrich (Downers Grove, IL: InterVarsity Press, 2011), 154.

and I shall give thee the nations for thine inheritance, and the uttermost parts of the earth for thy possession. Thou shalt rule them with a rod of iron; thou shalt shatter them like a potter's vessel" (Ps 2.7–9). Even Jesus saw this Psalm as a reference to himself.

Even if we are to accept the woman clothed in the sun as a symbol of the Church, not the mother of God, we must remember that the Bible often conflates symbols with real historical figures.[22] In the Early Church, the Virgin Mary herself was used as a symbol for the Church. The words of the Psalmist, "Hearken, O daughter, and see, and incline thine ear; forget also thy people and thy father's house. And the King shall desire thy beauty" (Ps 44.10–11) are usually understood to be a prophecy of the Virgin Mary. However, Justin the Philosopher interprets this passage as a symbol of the Church: "Moreover, that the word of God speaks to those who believe in him as being one soul, and one synagogue, and one Church, as to a daughter; that it thus addresses the Church which has sprung from his name and partakes of his name."[23]

The apostle Paul spoke of Christ as the second Adam (1 Cor 15.45–49). Continuing this theological train of thought, by the second century, the Church began to speak of the Virgin Mary as the second Eve. According to St Irenaeus of Lyons, Eve "having become disobedient, was made the cause of death, both to herself and to the entire human race; so also did Mary . . . by yielding obedience, become the cause of salvation, both to herself and the whole human race." Through the obedience of Mary, the knot of Eve's disobedience was untied, "For what the virgin Eve had bound fast through unbelief, this did the virgin Mary set free through faith."[24]

The earthly path of Jesus was a path of humiliation and kenosis. On this path, from the beginning to the end, Jesus' mother accompanied him. For her, this path was also a way of kenosis and lessening—from the moment when Simeon told her that her soul would be pierced by a sword, until the moment when this prophecy was fulfilled at the cross of her Son. Her human humiliation was expressed, among other things, in that humble

[22]Brown, *The Gospel according to John (I–XII)*, 108.
[23]Justin Martyr, *Dialogue with Trypho* 63 (ANF 1:229).
[24]Irenaeus of Lyons, *Against the Heresies* 3.22.4 (ANF 1:455).

The Marriage in Cana, mosaic, 12th century

place that she occupied in the Gospel's narrative, where the central place—this is no great wonder—is given to Jesus. But when his hour came, his glory was also revealed. Her hour came after the resurrection of Jesus, when the Church recognized her as the new Eve and saw her as its own Mother.

From that time, the life of Mary began, not as a simple Jewish woman, whom Jesus simply addressed as "woman," but as the one whom the Church places at the head of the host of saints, calling her "more honorable than the cherubim and more glorious beyond compare than the Seraphim." From that time, her glory is inextricable from his glory.

Chapter 3

HEALINGS

The majority of Jesus' miracles, as recorded by the Gospels, are healings of various illnesses. The Gospels contain around twenty more or less detailed accounts of such healings. All together, Jesus' miracles can be counted in the thirties or forties.

1. Jesus As Healer

Were Jesus' healings exclusively a consequence of some special power that belonged to him, or did he use some kind of technique to achieve his desired ends, similar to other doctors and healers of his time? This question is often posed in scholarly literature. Before answering it, it is necessary to make a few general comments.

Many people know from personal experience that getting better from illness does not always occur, even when a doctor correctly diagnoses it and prescribes the correct medicines for the diagnosis. It often happens that, in spite of all the efforts of the doctors, the sickness gets worse. But it also sometimes happens that a person gets better in spite of his past history and even without any drugs or even contrary to medical logic. Such an unexpected rehabilitation is sometimes called a miracle, meaning that it happened contrary to the expectations created by all the attendant circumstances.

In spite of the colossal progress in medicine from the time of Jesus, medicine continues to be a discipline full of guess work. Many diseases are barely able to be cured or are simply incurable. There are many theories about how the human body reacts to disease and rehabilitation, how the inner physical state of a person can affect the battle against disease, and how the psychological state of a person can also influence physical health. Many kinds of medical techniques and approaches exist—from the so-called conservative approaches (that is, pharmaceutical-based and surgical) to various non-traditional medicines including homeopathy, hypnosis, or healing as a result of psychological suggestion.

As much as we can tell from the Gospels themselves, Jesus received no specialized medical training. He never used specifically technical terminology, and his ministry in no way resembles the practice of medicine of his time. He never used any medicines, nor did he perform any surgery. All this forces some modern scholars to see him as something like a folk healer, whose success is achieved with a combination of various healing practices and technologies or through the process of hypnotic suggestion.

The author of one such study, himself a medical doctor, considers all mentions of Jesus' ability to overcome natural laws as legendary (such as walking on water). At the same time, he does not deny that the narratives concerning healing have a verifiable historical basis. Nevertheless, he still interprets raising the dead as awakening from a comatose state, while leprosy, according to him, is nothing more than psoriasis.[1] As for being mute, blind, deaf, or paralyzed—these phenomena he explains as only partial losses due to dissociative psychological states such as conversion disorder.[2]

Since the illnesses have, in his opinion, psycho-neurological aspects, their healing would involve techniques of psychological suggestion. For him, two factors prove his hypothesis definitively. First of all, Jesus required faith in his ability to perform the healing from all his patients. Secondly, he announced aloud the forgiveness of their sins. "If we assume the psychological theory that sin is guilt or trauma projected out onto a god figure, then the elimination of sin is, psychologically speaking, formal permission to forgive oneself." Jesus "could present himself as the manifestation of God

---

[1]Stevan L. Davies, *Jesus the Healer: Possession, Trance and the Origins of Christianity* (New York: Continuum International Publishing Group, 1995), 67–68.

[2]Ibid., 71–72.

on earth, announce forgiveness and set in motion a comprehensible set of psychological factors that would lead to the elimination of the presenting symptoms."[3]

Except for the use of modern medical terminology, this explanation differs very little from the one given by Leo Tolstoy, when he compared the paralytic who lay at the pool for thirty-eight years with the lady who received a placebo injection of water instead of morphine. Davies assumes the same reality as Spinoza: it is impossible to break the laws of nature. However, he ignores something that most other scholars of Jesus' miracles pay attention to: "Modern scientific endeavor is continually compelling us to modify our understanding of the processes of the natural world. Hence the so-called laws of nature, by which we describe the limits of our experience, are under constant revision."[4]

One more question arises among scholars who research the healing miracles in the Gospels: do these healings have anything to do with magic? The accusation that Jesus cast out demons by the power of the prince of demons (Mt 12.24, Mk 3.22, Lk 11.15) was not accidental. For centuries, magic has operated through the influence of dark otherworldly powers, and in first-century Palestine magical practices were reasonably widespread.[5] We will examine this theme in greater detail when we turn to this specific expulsion of demons in the Gospels.

Here we will limit ourselves to noting that the Gospels contain no indications that Jesus used any element of magic in his healing of diseases. In part, this is evident in the fact that Jesus never invokes any spells, magical formulas, or gestures.

The power that Jesus used to perform his miracles is fundamentally opposed to the power used by magicians and sorcerers. The latter use various demonic energies, adding to them their own extrasensory abilities, if they have any. The power of Jesus came out of him directly (Lk 8.46), from his divine essence, which was indelibly united to his human nature. It

---

[3]Ibid, 75.

[4]Twelftree, *Jesus the Miracle Worker*, 51.

[5]See J. M. I. Hull, *Hellenistic Magic and the Synoptic Tradition* (London: SCM Press, 1974), 42–72.

St Nikolai (Velimirovich)
of Zhicha, Serbia, Icon,
20th century

was part of his nature and it healed all who touched him (Lk 6.19) or turned to him with faith in the possibility of healing. (Mk 9.23). The Serbian Orthodox theologian and hierarch St Nikolai (Velimirovich) wrote the following:

> Christ as Man is no less a miracle than Christ as God. One and the other is a miracle, and they together are a miracle of miracles. However, this miracle is not a miracle of magic, or necromancy, or simple sleight of hand. This is a miracle of God's wisdom, God's power, and God's love for man. The Lord performed miracles not for human glory. Does any of us go to the hospital, to the insane, the deaf and dumb, and the leprous to receive glory from them? Does the shepherd treat his sheep so that the sheep glorify him with their bleating? The Lord preformed miracles only to mercifully help the helpless sufferers; at the same time, he showed through them that God came to them because of mercy and love.[6]

The methods that Jesus used to heal were the simplest imaginable, having nothing to do either with magic or medicine. These methods were either his word or, in a series of cases, physically touching the body of the sick. In three separate cases, the evangelists mention Jesus using his own saliva (Lk 7.33, 8.23; Jn 9.6). No other special means, methods, or techniques are mentioned.

Physical touch was one of Jesus' most frequently used "methods" to heal the sick. In many cases, he touched the body of a sick person or even a specific organ that required healing. In the telling of the healing of the leper, Jesus, having stretched out his arm, healed him (Mt 8.3; Mk 1.41; Lk 5.13). The blind he healed by touching their eyes (Mt 9.29, 20:34), the deaf and dumb man by touching his tongue (Mk 7.33). In Bethsaida,

---

[6]Nikolai Velimirovich, *Tvoreniya* [Collected works] 1:423 (translated by DNK).

"They brought a blind man to him, and besought him to touch him" (Mk 8.22). Jesus took the blind man by his hand, leading him out of the village, then he spit in his eyes and put his hands on him, and his vision partially returned. Then Jesus placed his hands on his eyes, and his sight was fully restored (Mk 8.22–26). Many times when people touch Jesus of their own initiative (Mk 3.10; Lk 6.19), or touch his garments (Mt 9.20. 14.36; Mk 6.56), they receive healing.

Touching a sick person's body is a widely used practical gesture in medicine, most often used to diagnose an illness (for example, when a doctor palpates a painful spot) or for the purposes of healing (massage, rubbing in oils into the skin of an afflicted person). But whenever Jesus touched the body of a sick person, there were no indications that this touch constituted a medical method. One can hardly agree with the opinion of scholars who believe Jesus used various healing methods of the physicians of his own time (including physical touch).[7] It is more likely that the touch, as his word also, was necessary to pass on that spiritual energy that flowed from him, that had a supernatural character, and that contained healing power.

If we are to speak of parallels or associations inspired by this gesture of touching the body of the sick person, then it seems more similar to a blessing that is imparted by laying the right hand on a person, or sometimes both hands. "The hand of the Lord" is a typical image used by the Old Testament—usually it is used to indicate the majesty and power of God that is manifested both through blessing and punishment. The laying on of hands in the Old Testament is used as a gesture through which a blessing is passed from an older man to a younger, for example from a father to a son (Gen 48.14–19). The laying on of hands gave the Levites the right to serve God in the Tabernacle (Num 8.10).

Jesus sees in his actions a continuation of the activity of the Father: "My Father worketh hitherto, and I work" (Jn 5.17). This is fully applicable to the healings that he accomplished.

---

[7]See Frederick Gaiser, *Healing in the Bible* (Grand Rapids, MI: Baker Academic, 2010), 153–154.

What is said symbolically in the Old Testament about the hand of God manifests itself concretely in the New Testament in the hand of Jesus Christ, the Son of God. When Jesus touches a sick person, his immediate, creative, preserving power manifests itself in that action. The function of his word and his hand are identical! By that touch the sick person is "linked" to Jesus, he becomes the property of Jesus, and therefore he is mentally and physically healed.[8]

Physical touch, moreover, indicates the intimate union between Jesus as God, who had come down to earth, and the people for whom he had come. According to St Paul, "For in him dwelleth all the fullness of the Godhead bodily" (Col 2.9). Having a human body that was entirely filled with the presence of his divinity, Jesus conveyed this presence to other people by touching their bodies, and he healed with a touch to the afflicted areas of the body to impart health to them.

That being said, Jesus did not always touch the body of the sick person. In the account of the resurrection of the son of the widow of Nain, he touches the bed on which the dead youth was carried (Lk 7.14). In many other cases, there is no mention of any physical touch. Thus, for Jesus, touching the body of a sick person was in no way a requirement to heal. As St John Chrysostom said, "And sometimes he heals by words only, sometimes he even stretches forth his hand, sometimes he does both these things, to bring into sight his way of healing."[9]

In certain cases, healings happen in absentia, as it were: by his word alone, Jesus healed people who were in different places entirely. Consequently, even simple actions like touching a sick person or even speaking to him were not absolutely necessary for healing.

What words did Jesus use during his healings? Often, as he turned to the person being healed, he used short, imperative forms of a verb, for example: "I will; be thou clean" (Mt 8.3); "Arise, take up thy bed, and go unto thine house" (Mt 9.6); "Stretch forth thine hand" (Mt 12.13); "Damsel,

---

[8]H. van der Loos, *The Miracles of Jesus,* 321.
[9]St John Chrysostom, *Homilies on Matthew,* Homily 27 (NPNF[1] 10:185).

I say unto thee, arise" (Mk 5.41); "Go, shew yourselves unto the priests" (Lk 17.14); "Go, wash in the
pool of Siloam" (Jn 9.7).

In many miracle narratives, the central theme
is faith.[10] Jesus often required faith from those he
healed, or even tested their faith. When the two
blind men asked to be cured, he asked them, "Believe
ye that I am able to do this?" (Mt 9.28). He told the
father of the demoniac youth, "If thou canst believe,
all things are possible to him that believeth." The
answer of the father is significant: "Lord, I believe;
help thou mine unbelief" (Mk 9.23–24).

*The Raising of the Son of
the Widow of Nain*, mosaic,
12th century

No less often does Jesus constitute the fact of the
salvific faith of the one being healed: "Thy faith hath made thee whole" (Mt
9.22, Mk 10.52); "O woman, great is thy faith! Let it be unto thee as thou
wilt" (Mt 15.28, Mk 10.52); "Daughter, thy faith hath made thee whole; go
in peace, and be healed of thy plague" (Mk 5.34); "Arise, go thy way; thy
faith hath made thee whole" (Lk 17.19); "Receive thy sight; thy faith hath
saved thee" (Lk 18.42).

Faith is that state of the soul and mind of a person that is necessary for
healings to occur in the first place. Especially of note is the fact that Jesus
does not ascribe the healing power to himself, he does not say, "My word
has healed you." He puts the emphasis on the faith of the one asking to be
healed, and to this same faith he ascribes the salvific power. Faith is necessary as a reciprocal action of a person desiring the help of God. The miracle
then becomes the fruit of the synergy between God and man.

[10]Concerning the connection between faith and miracles narratives in general, see Günther
Bornkamm, G. Barth, and H. J. Held, *Tradition and Interpretation in Matthew* (Louisville, KY:
Westminster Press, 1963), 275–96.

2. Healing the Nobleman's Son and the Servant of the Centurion

It is not always possible to determine the exact chronological order of Jesus' miracles. Nonetheless, the Gospel according to John records two miracles that clearly happen one after the other. The first is the transformation of water into wine at the wedding in Cana of Galilee. The second is the healing of the son of the nobleman of Capernaum. It is possible that the author of the fourth Gospel witnessed to both of these miracles. The second miracle also occurred in Cana of Galilee (Jn 4.46), where Jesus returned after a short sojourn in Jerusalem:

> So Jesus came again into Cana of Galilee, where he made the water wine. And there was a certain nobleman, whose son was sick at Capernaum. When he heard that Jesus was come out of Judaea into Galilee, he went unto him, and besought him that he would come down, and heal his son, for he was at the point of death. Then said Jesus unto him, "Except ye see signs and wonders, ye will not believe." The nobleman saith unto him, "Sir, come down ere my child die." Jesus saith unto him, "Go thy way; thy son liveth." And the man believed the word that Jesus had spoken unto him, and he went his way. And as he was now going down, his servants met him, and told him, saying, "Thy son liveth." Then enquired he of them the hour when he began to amend. And they said unto him, "Yesterday at the seventh hour the fever left him." So the father knew that it was at the same hour, in the which Jesus said unto him, "Thy son liveth"; and he himself believed, and his whole house. This is again the second miracle that Jesus did, when he was come out of Judaea into Galilee. (Jn 4.46–54)

There are some similarities between this miracle and the one preceding it in the Gospel according to John. In both cases, Jesus initially seems

The Healing of the Son of the Nobleman, Veronese, 16th century

not to hurry to answer the request addressed to him. The suppliant then insists, and only after that does Jesus acquiesce. Both cases lead to a group of people (in the first, his disciples; in the second, the members of the nobleman's house) coming to believe in im. After both, Jesus left for Jerusalem.[11] There are valid reasons to believe that the evangelist consciously offers both miracles performed in Cana as a pair of connected events, with common characteristics and a similar meaning.

There is an even greater similarity between the healing of the nobleman's son and the healing of the servant of the centurion described in two Synoptic Gospels (Mt 8.5–13; Lk 7.1–10). Even such an early father as St Irenaeus of Lyons, citing the second miracle in Cana of Galilee, goes so far as to call the healed man the son of a centurion.[12] This could be an indirect confirmation of the fact that he considered the healing of the servant in the two Synoptics and the healing of the son of the nobleman in John to be three versions of the same event. In contemporary scholarship, this is a commonly-held view as well. There is indeed much in common among the three accounts.

Let us examine the account concerning the healing of the servant of the centurion in the Gospel according to Matthew:

[11]See Brown, *The Gospel according to John (I–XII)*, 194.
[12]Irenaeus of Lyons, *Against the Heresies* 2.22.3 (ANF 1:391).

And when Jesus was entered into Capernaum, there came unto him a centurion, beseeching him, and saying, "Lord, my servant lieth at home sick of the palsy, grievously tormented." And Jesus saith unto him, "I will come and heal him." The centurion answered and said, "Lord, I am not worthy that thou shouldest come under my roof, but speak the word only, and my servant shall be healed. For I am a man under authority, having soldiers under me, and I say to this man, 'Go,' and he goeth; and to another, 'Come,' and he cometh; and to my servant, 'Do this,' and he doeth it. When Jesus heard it, he marvelled, and said to them that followed, "Verily I say unto you, I have not found so great faith, no, not in Israel." And I say unto you that many shall come from the east and west, and shall sit down with Abraham, and Isaac, and Jacob, in the kingdom of heaven. But the children of the kingdom shall be cast out into outer darkness; there shall be weeping and gnashing of teeth." And Jesus said unto the centurion, "Go thy way, and as thou hast believed, so be it done unto thee." And his servant was healed in the selfsame hour. (Mt 8.5–13)

The narrative in Luke is closer to Matthew's version than John's, but there are a few interesting differences. Here is the account in Luke:

Now when he had ended all his sayings in the audience of the people, he entered into Capernaum. And a certain centurion's servant, who was dear unto him, was sick, and ready to die. And when he heard of Jesus, he sent unto him the elders of the Jews, beseeching him that he would come and heal his servant. And when they came to Jesus, they besought him instantly, saying, "He is worthy for whom he should do this, for he loveth our nation, and he hath built us a synagogue."

Then Jesus went with them. And when he was now not far from the house, the centurion sent friends to him, saying unto him, "Lord, trouble not thyself, for I am not worthy that thou shouldest enter under my roof; wherefore neither thought I myself worthy to come unto thee. But say in a word, and my servant shall be healed. For I also am a man set under authority, having under me soldiers, and I say unto one, 'Go,'

and he goeth; and to another, 'Come,' and he cometh; and to my servant, 'Do this,' and he doeth it."

When Jesus heard these things, he marvelled at him, and turned
him about, and said unto the people that followed him, "I say unto you,
I have not found so great faith, no, not in Israel." And they that were
sent, returning to the house, found the servant whole that had been
sick. (Lk 7.1–10)

The narratives in Matthew and Luke obviously show two different versions of the same story. In both, the event occurs in Capernaum and the
main character is called a "centurion," (ἑκατόνταρχος [*hekatontarchos*] in
Matthew and ἑκατοντάρχης [*hekatontarchēs*] in Luke), which indicates that
the man was a Roman in military service, a commander of one hundred
soldiers.[13] The rank of centurion was not high—he was a middling commander in the Roman army (similar to a major in our days). It is generally
accepted that the centurion served the Roman emperor; however, there
were no garrisoned Roman troops in Galilee at that time. Most likely, he
served in the army of Herod Antipas.[14] This actually adds to the similarity
between him and the nobleman in the Gospel according to John.

The sick person on whose behalf he requests Jesus' help is called in
Matthew "παῖς" (*pais*) which literally means "boy," "child," but this word can
be used both to indicate a servant and a son. In Luke, two terms are used
to identify him: παῖς (*pais*, "boy") and δοῦλος (*doulos*, "servant," "slave").
In Matthew, the centurion comes to Jesus in person, in Luke, he sends
the Jewish leaders on his behalf. In Matthew, Jesus immediately expresses
his readiness to come and heal the boy, but the centurion demurs—Jesus'
word alone suffices, and the boy will be healed. In Luke, the elders try to
persuade Jesus to come to the home of the centurion, and he begins to
walk there, when a servant meets him along the way and passes on the
same information that in Matthew is spoken directly by the centurion: "I

[13]In actual practice, a centurion could command a group of thirty to sixty as well. Meier, *A
Marginal Jew*, 2:721.

[14]Mark A. Chancey, *The Myth of a Gentile Galilee* (Cambridge: Cambridge University Press,
2002) 175, 176; *Greco-Roman Culture and the Galilee of Jesus* (Cambridge: Cambridge University
Press, 2007), 51–56.

am not worthy that thou shouldest come under my roof." Jesus' reaction is the same in both cases: he praises the faith of the pagan, using him as an example for the edification of the Jews who were following him. In both cases, the healing occurs from a distance—in Matthew, Jesus tells the centurion directly that his servant is healed, while in Luke, the servants find the boy healed in person.

In what ways are these two accounts similar and different from John's version? In all three, Capernaum is mentioned, but in John the action occurs in Cana, which is an entire day's journey from Capernaum. The fact that Jesus performed the healing at a distance without visiting the home of the petitioner is better explained by John's version than the version of the Synoptics (i.e., the boy was near death, and if Jesus had traveled there in person, then the boy could have died while Jesus was still on his way).

All three evangelists have the petitioner refer to Jesus as "Lord." Though this form of address could simply mean "sir," or "mister," in the Gospels it is often used to emphasize the divine dignity of Jesus.

In John the petitioner is called a "βασιλικός" (*basilikos*, a nobleman or member of a king's court); what this means most likely (in the Synoptics as well) is that this man served at Herod Antipas' court. We know nothing about the ethnicity of the nobleman, nor do we know what his religious affiliation was. He could have been either a pagan Roman or a Jew.

John uses two terms for the son: "υἱός" (*huios*, "son") mostly, and "παιδίον" (*paidion*, "child," a diminutive form of παῖς [*pais*]) as a secondary term. Matthew, when using the term "boy" without indicating the nature of the sick man's social status, in this case uses an intermediate term between John and Mark, who directly calls the sick boy a servant.

The physical state of the boy in John is expressed in two different ways: "he was sick" (ἠσθένει, *esthenei*) and "he was near death" (ἤμελλεν ἀποθνήσκειν, *ēmellen apothnēskein*; literally "he was about to die"). We see expressions similar in meaning in Luke: "he was sick" (κακῶς ἔχων, *kakōs exōn*; literally "he felt bad") and "near death" (ἤμελλεν τελευτᾶν, *ēmellen teleutan*). Matthew describes the sickness in a slightly different way: literally "he lay at home paralyzed, suffering terribly." John describes the symptoms of the sickness as πυρετός (*pyretos*, "fever") indicating a high temperature.

Jesus' words—"Except ye see signs and wonders, ye will not believe"— could have served as an indirect confirmation of the fact that the nobleman is a Jew. If these words were directed at the nobleman, then this could be a case of "Christ often humbling by his strictness those whom he desired to grace with his mercy."[15]

But it is also quite likely that these words were not directed at the nobleman, but at the Jews who were present at the scene (Jesus used the second person plural, not singular). The theme of signs and miracles appears constantly in Jesus' polemics with the Jews. In answer to their request that he show them a sign from heaven, Jesus "sighed deeply in his spirit, and saith, 'Why doth this generation seek after a sign? Verily I say unto you, there shall no sign be given unto this generation'" (Mk 8.12). Since the request was constantly repeated, the answer also was repeated more than once, sometimes in a more incisive form: "An evil and adulterous generation seeketh after a sign; and there shall no sign be given to it, but the sign of the prophet Jonah" (Mt 12.39). This phrase resonates with Jesus' words to the nobleman in John's version.

In John, the nobleman asks Jesus to come before his son dies. In this point, he differs from the centurion who, according to Matthew, asked Jesus not to come, but only to say the word (in Luke's version, he sends a servant to request the same).

All three evangelists place the faith of the petitioner at the center of the narrative. In John, this faith is emphasized by the narrator ("he believed him"), while in Mark and Luke it is expressed in the dialogue between the centurion and Jesus. Moreover, in John's version (in contrast to the Synoptics) the faith of the petitioner is not offered as an example to those in attendance. But only John ends the account with the words: "And he himself believed, and his whole house." For John, this is the most important result of the miracle—not the healing of the young man, but the way the nobleman's entire family reacts to the miracle. Here we can also remember

[15] Alexander Shargunov, *Evangelie dnya* [The Gospel of the day], 2 vols. (Moscow: Sretensky Monastery, 2010), 1:64.

Jesus' answer to the question about who sinned to deserve being born blind—the parents of the man or the blind man himself? "Jesus answered, 'Neither hath this man sinned, nor his parents, but that the works of God should be made manifest in him'" (Jn 9.3). The disease of the nobleman's son was necessary for the works of God to be manifested in him, and thanks to his healing, his entire family believed in Christ.

The healing itself occurs "in absentia" in all three versions. Jesus does not come into the house of the petitioner, does not see the boy, does not touch his body. The healing occurs by the word of Jesus, which the petitioner believed. Moreover, in John, he finds his son healthy, asks about the time of the healing and confirms that it coincided with the moment that Jesus said the words "Go thy way; thy son liveth." Matthew mentions that the boy was healed at that hour, that is, at the same moment that Jesus said, "Go thy way; and as thou hast believed, so be it done unto thee." Luke says nothing about the time of healing; those who were sent simply find the servant already healed when they return to the centurion's home.

We will add to what has already been said that in Matthew, as in John, the healing of the boy is the second miracle to be mentioned in their Gospel accounts. It occurs immediately after the Sermon on the Mount and the healing of the paralytic (Mt 8.2–4), which is the first in his list of miracles. Therefore, both evangelists ascribe this miracle to the early period of Jesus' earthly ministry. Luke's narrative is preceded by several other miracles, as well as the Sermon on the Plain (Lk 7.21–49), which has thematic resonance with the Sermon on the Mount. After it ends, Jesus finds himself in Capernaum, where the miracle occurs.

Thus, there are several differences among the accounts,[16] but the essential details are the same. In John's version, there seems to be more logical consistency—it is more likely that a Jewish nobleman would have come to Jesus than a Roman; the request to heal his son is more likely than the request to heal a slave; the fact that Jesus did not go to the house where the sick man lay is more easily explained by a matter of distance between Cana and Capernaum than if the events had occurred in the same city.

---

[16]Concerning the differences between John and the two Synoptics, see A. J. Köstenberger, *John* (Grand Rapids, MI: Baker Academic, 2004), 168–69.

The Healing of the Servant of the Centurion, fresco, 16th century

One can suppose that when the story was first retold, the use of the word παῖς (*pais*; found in both Luke and John) was interpreted differently by the Synoptics and John—the former assumed it to mean "servant," the latter "son." And the nobleman, for whatever reason, turned into a centurion. Neither should one exclude the possibility that John, who left out most of the miracles that the Synoptics included, placed this miracle in his Gospel account in order to clarify that the centurion was actually a nobleman, the servant was a son, and in general, the event was different from the way it was described in Matthew and Luke.

All these possibilities, frequently expressed by scholars,[17] are based on the similarities of the three accounts. Comparing both similarities and differences does not allow these scholars to make a single conclusion about the question of whether these accounts describe one event or two. No matter how this question is resolved, all three accounts can be examined together, since they show a single type of miracle—healing at a distance without any physical contact.

The evangelists do not disclose the "mechanism" or "technique" of healing. They only say that the healing occurred instantaneously, at the moment that Jesus uttered a "word," which, in Matthew's version, was the centurion's request in the first place.

[17]See van der Loos, *The Miracles of Jesus*, 530–33.

The term "word" in this context has an important connotation: it indicates Jesus' primary method of healing. What sort of a "word" did the
centurion expect from Jesus? Most likely not some kind of magical formula typical of healers and exorcists of Jesus' time. It is more likely that
he expected some sort of "command"—a formula that would ensure the
healing of the servant. According to Matthew, Jesus' formula was: "Go
thy way; and as thou hast believed, so be it done unto thee." In John, the
formula was shorter "Go thy way; thy son liveth."

In Luke, the centurion said, "For I also am a man set under authority,
having under me soldiers, and I say unto one, 'Go,' and he goeth; and to
another, 'Come,' and he cometh; and to my servant, 'Do this,' and he doeth
it." These words impress Jesus by their unexpectedness. In these words,
the centurion described the principle underlying military service in all
times—the principle of the soldier's absolute obedience to the orders of his
superior officer. The army is built along strictly hierarchical principles—
each soldier has his own immediate superior, and every superior has his
own commander, going all the way to the commander in chief. The orders
of a superior officer are not discussed or criticized, and not fulfilling an
order is strictly punished. An order is given in oral form, often in a short
phrase that is pithy and mandatory.

Why did the centurion speak this way concerning himself? He was
making a parallel between himself as a military commander and Jesus as
the ambassador of God, whose word must be just as mandatory as the
order of a military commander. In the same way that a centurion ordered
his soldiers and servants, Jesus should command the disease to retreat
from the boy. The commander received this "word," which he was expect-
ing, and the boy was healed.

Here it is appropriate to remember Old Testament passages concerning
the healing power of the word of God: "He sent forth his word, and healed
them" (Ps 106.20); "For thine oracle has given me life" (Ps 118.50); "For it
was neither herb, nor medicinal plaister, that restored them to health, but
thy word, O Lord, which healeth all things" (Wis 16.12). This last quote
references an event connected with the history of the Exodus from Egypt,
when poisonous snakes attacked the people in the desert (Num 21.6–9).

According to the Wisdom of Solomon, it was not the image of the snake that saved the people, but the word of God. In the mouth of Jesus, the word was a bearer of the same healing power that he has as God. He heals not with herbs or plasters, but with power that comes from him at the same moment that he utters the word.

It is not coincidental that so much attention is given to the centurion in the accounts of Matthew and Luke. According to Luke, though he was a Roman, he had such respect for the rites of the Jews that he built a synagogue for the inhabitants of the city. Now, when calamity struck him personally, the Jewish elders felt sorry for him. But they had no resources of theirs with which to help him, and so they interceded on his behalf before Jesus. Jesus then speaks in wonder to the people concerning him: "I say unto you, I have not found so great faith, no, not in Israel." Matthew also has these words of Jesus. Matthew adds a short monologue concerning the kingdom of heaven, about how many will come from the East and the West, "But the children of the kingdom shall be cast out into outer darkness."

Here Jesus touches on a theme that appears as a repeated motif in his preaching. The children of the kingdom—this is the Israelite nation, to whom he was sent. But it is exactly this nation, as it turns out, that responded to his preaching with the most resistance. Their lack of faith—which Jesus required of those who wished to be healed—becomes a reason for God to reject them as the chosen nation, and to choose a New Israel, the Church that unites people not by a nationalistic or ethnic principle, but only on the foundation of faith in Jesus as God and Savior.

Jesus develops this thesis in its most succinct form when speaking with the Jews in the Temple in Jerusalem: "Therefore say I unto you, the kingdom of God shall be taken from you, and given to a nation bringing forth the fruits thereof" (Mt 21.43). In this conversation, Jesus speaks of himself as the stone that the builders rejected, that has become the head of the corner (Mt 21.42). Subsequently, Jesus' teaching concerning the New Israel would be developed further by the Apostle Paul. For him, as for Jesus, faith is central:

What shall we say then? That the Gentiles, which followed not after righteousness, have attained to righteousness, even the righteousness

*Jesus among the
Teachers,* fresco
from Giotto's
workshop,
14th century

which is of faith. But Israel, which followed after the law of righteousness, hath not attained to the law of righteousness. Wherefore? Because
they sought it not by faith, but as it were by the works of the law. For
they stumbled at that stumblingstone. (Rom 9.30–32)

Paul lays out a series of questions, then answers them: "I say then, hath
God cast away his people? God forbid. . . . I say then, have they stumbled
that they should fall? God forbid; but rather through their fall salvation is
come unto the Gentiles, for to provoke them to jealousy" (Rom 11.1, 11).
In other words, thanks to the fact that the Israelites did not believe, the
chance for salvation opened up for the Gentiles. In terms of a historical
perspective, that is exactly what happened: after the apostles' first attempts
to preach among the Jews failed, the Church—first of all thanks to the
influence of Paul—decided to turn its chief attention to ministry among
the Gentiles. From that moment, the Church began to grow exponentially.
Moreover, the Apostle Paul continued to consider that the faithlessness of
Israel was only temporary: "Blindness in part is happened to Israel, until
the fulness of the Gentiles be come in. And so all Israel shall be saved"
(Rom 11.25–26).

The centurion of Capernaum was one of a pagans who received righteousness through faith. The history of the salvation of the Gentiles began

not with Paul, but with Jesus. He was the one who—contrary to long-established Jewish traditions—turned his attention to the pagans. In general, the Jews despised the pagans exceedingly; they did not even consider them to be people. Jesus' words in Matthew 18.17 ("let him be unto thee as an heathen man and a publican") fully reflect this mindset. However, for Jesus himself, this was not a characteristic attitude. Naturally, his preaching was directed primarily at the Jews; he himself said that he was sent only to the lost sheep of the house of Israel (Mt 15.24), and we do not find in the Gospels a single case when he preached before a group of pagans. However, he did not deny pagans the chance at healing, if they turned to him with faith, and in his conversations with the Jews, he sometimes offered the example of the faith of pagans, such as this centurion of Capernaum.

In Jesus' interactions with his own chosen nation, we see the same Old Testament story of God's relationship with the nation of Israel. Time and time again, God sent this nation various blessings and good things, revealing signs and miracles, but the people remained deaf to his call, blind to his miracles. Having in mind both the history of the Israelite nation and his own history, as well as the reaction of the Jews to the preaching of his disciples, Jesus speaks these frightening words to the Jews: "Wherefore, behold, I send unto you prophets, and wise men, and scribes: and some of them ye shall kill and crucify; and some of them shall ye scourge in your synagogues, and persecute them from city to city" (Mt 23.34). Citing the prophet Isaiah (Is 6.9–10) Jesus said of his own countrymen: "For this people's heart is waxed gross, and their ears are dull of hearing, and their eyes they have closed; lest at any time they should see with their eyes and hear with their ears, and should understand with their heart, and should be converted, and I should heal them" (Mt 13.15).

If Isaiah spoke of healing in a metaphorical sense, as the freeing from spiritual blindness and deafness, Jesus actually performed these miracles in a literal sense, and so the words of the ancient prophet acquired a new meaning coming from his lips. He underlined that faith is necessary for healing, and for faith, you must be ready to see and hear, not to close your eyes and stop up your ears to what would otherwise be obvious. The miracle occurs with a person who is capable of accepting it; if this person closes his eyes to the miracle, it will not occur with him, nor will he see how it occurs with others.

In his commentary on the healing of the servant, John Chrysostom notes the differences between the version of Matthew and Luke. He believes the differences to be merely apparent. If in Matthew the centurion himself came to Jesus, while in Luke he sent a servant, that only means that one evangelist filled out the account of the other—at first the centurion sent a servant to Jesus, then he came himself and said what he had intended to say through his servants. According to Chrysostom, the centurion's words about the subjection of those under his authority reflect the following thought: "If you command death not to approach the servant, it will not come." Thus, the centurion confessed that Jesus had power of life and death—the power to send a soul to hell and to raise it up again (1 Sam 2.6). In answer to this great faith, Jesus gave him much more than he could have expected—the centurion had asked for the healing of a servant, but he returned, having received the kingdom.[18]

As for the nobleman spoken of in the Gospel according to John, St John Chrysostom said, "Some indeed think that this is the man mentioned by Matthew, but he is shown to be a different person, not only from his dignity, but also from his faith. That other, even when Christ was willing to go to him, entreats him to tarry; this one, when he had made no such offer, draws him to his house." If the centurion, Chrysostom says, shows an example of faith, this nobleman, on the contrary, shows his weakness when he asked Christ to come: "As though he could not raise him after death, as though he knew not what state the child was in. It is for this that Christ rebukes him and touches his conscience, to show that his miracles were wrought principally for the sake of the soul. For here he heals the father, sick in mind, no less than the son, in order to persuade us to give heed to him, not by reason of his miracles, but of his teaching."[19]

Blessed Jerome, in his commentary on the healing of the servant of the centurion, mentions three virtues of the Roman military commander: faith, humility, and wisdom. These three qualities are what Jesus saw in the

[18]John Chrysostom, *Homilies on Matthew*, Homily 26 (NPNF[1] 10:180).
[19]John Chrysostom, *Homilies on the Gospel of John*, Homily 35 (NPNF[1] 14:124).

petitioner: "faith in that he as a Gentile believed that [his servant] could be healed by the Savior; humility because he judged himself unworthy to have the Lord come under his roof; wisdom because beneath the covering of the body he saw the concealed divinity."[20]

Returning to the theme of the "method" or "technique" that Jesus used to perform his healings, we must insist that based on both accounts there can be only one conclusion: Jesus had no specific technique at all. The miracle occurred thanks to two primary factors—the healing or miracle-working power that he contained as God, and the faith of the petitioner (stronger in the case of the centurion, weaker in the case of the nobleman).

In Matthew, the term "faith" (πίστις, *pistis*) is first found in the story of the healing of the servant of the centurion. It is possible that Matthew wants to emphasize the faith of the centurion as creating a precedent for the faith of all future petitioners in the miracle accounts in the Gospel.[21] Thus, the theme of faith, which has the most important significance for understanding the entire earthly ministry of Jesus, begins in the New Testament in the Gospel of Matthew with this account of the healing of the servant of the centurion.

The experience of people's interaction with Jesus in the Gospels is similar to the experience of prayer. When man turns to God in prayer, by this very action he shows his faith in him and his trust in him. God already knows in advance everything that the person can possibly say to him and everything that that person needs (Mt 6.7–8). At the same time, prayer has the character of actual communication with God—God is capable of reacting to the person's request, he does not predetermine the request, and his answer is not something that is established in advance. When a person says, "Thy will be done," that person still reveals his own will in the prayer. God's answer takes human will into account. If it is necessary to break the laws of nature to answer the person's will, God will accomplish such a miracle. In the mutual relationship between God and man the miracle

---

[20]Jerome, *Commentary on Matthew* 1.8.5–7 (FOTC 117:100).

[21]Walter Wilson, *Healing in the Gospel of Matthew: Reflections on Method and Ministry* (Minneapolis: Fortress Press, 2014), 62.

The Image not Made by Hands, icon, 14th century

is only one of many means by which God answers human petitions and reveals his mercy to mankind.

In this we find the greatest distinction between the God of the Bible and the deity of the deistic philosophers such as Spinoza and Kant. The deists' god created the world, established natural laws, then parted to its eternal mansions. The God of the Bible, having created man and the world, reveals an active participation in their fate, and, if necessary, he is ready to break the natural laws that he himself established.

The miracles that God performed while incarnate were doubtless violations of natural laws. Jesus performed these violations systematically and purposefully, and he did it on a massive scale. For God, no limits exist that he cannot overstep, no laws that he cannot break. Though a miracle has clearly delineated qualities within space and time, it still occurs in a different dimension in which earthly laws cease to work. This dimension is what Jesus called the kingdom of heaven or the kingdom of God. The announcement of the kingdom of God is the main theme of Jesus' preaching, and this kingdom of God comes into existence through his action, including his miracles.

The healings and exorcisms that Jesus performs are signs that the kingdom is not merely awaited, but already present.[22] Every one of his healings described in the pages of the Gospel become revelations of God's omnipotence, expressed in the acts of the incarnate Son of God and having as its object concrete people—noblemen and centurions, petitioners and those on whose behalf they ask, blind and deaf people, the mute and the paralyzed, the leprous and the possessed, women and men, people of various ages, social classes, ethnicity, and religion.

Anyone can become a participant in a miracle, but one condition must be met. He must have faith. Jesus said to his own disciples, "If ye have faith as a grain of mustard seed, ye shall say unto this mountain, 'Remove hence to yonder place,' and it shall remove; and nothing shall be impossible unto

[22]R. A. Horsley, *Jesus and the Spiral of Violence* (Minneapolis: Fortress Press, 1993), 181.

you" (Mt 17.20). For a believer, nothing is impossible. Miracles are a reality in his life, one that is just as evident and indisputable as the entire world surrounding him.

---

3. Healing Peter's Mother-in-Law

The healing of Peter's mother-in-law is one of Jesus' first miracles in all three Synoptic Gospels. In Matthew, this is the third healing, following immediately after the story of the healing of the centurion's servant. In Mark and Luke, this is the first healing, following immediately after the account of the first exorcism. Here is Mark's version:

> And forthwith, when they were come out of the synagogue, they entered into the house of Simon and Andrew, with James and John. But Simon's wife's mother lay sick of a fever, and anon they tell him of her. And he came and took her by the hand, and lifted her up; and immediately the fever left her, and she ministered unto them. (Mk 1.29–31)

The account is remarkable for its brevity in all three evangelists. In Luke's version, James and John are not mentioned; the house in which the event occurred was called the house of Simon, and Simon's mother-in-law "was taken with a great fever; and they besought him for her. And he stood over her, and rebuked the fever; and it left her" (Lk 4.38–39). During Jesus' time, high fevers were considered a serious illness in and of themselves, not symptoms of other diseases.[23] In addition, a difference was made between "fevers" and "strong fevers." The fact that Luke calls it a high fever, possibly, is an indication of his knowledge of medical terminology. It is known that he was a physician by profession (Col 4.14).

In Matthew, the presence of James and John is not mentioned, and no one asks Jesus about her—he sees her himself, then touches her hand, and her fever leaves her (Mt 8.14–15). Not one of the three versions mention

[23]Van der Loos, *The Miracles of Jesus*, 553.

*The Healing of
Peter's Mother-
in-Law*, fresco,
14th century

the presence of Peter; however, it is evident that Jesus came to his house
by Peter's invitation. Consequently, Peter was an eyewitness to the miracle.

Judging by the context, the healing of Peter's mother-in-law was not
Christ's main purpose in coming to Peter's house. More likely, he came to
Peter's house to eat—this is suggested by the conclusion of the account,
when the healed woman immediately got up to serve them food (the verb
"to serve" as in Jn 12.2, is used in the sense of "to prepare food," "to set a
table," "to offer food"; this is how Chrysostom understands this passage as
well).[24]

It is also possible that her sickness was unexpected for Peter as well.
From all three accounts, it is made clear that the sickness of his mother-
in-law was discovered only after Jesus entered the house with his disciples.
But Chrysostom thinks otherwise:

> For though he had his wife's mother at home lying ill, and very sick
> of a fever, he drew him not into his house, but waited first for the
> teaching to be finished, then for all the others to be healed; and then
> when he had come in, besought him. Thus from the beginning was
> he instructed to prefer the things of all others to his own. Therefore
> neither does he himself bring him in, but he entered of his own accord

[24]John Chrysostom, *Homilies on Matthew*, Homily 27 (NPNF[1] 10:184).

after the centurion had said, "I am not worthy that you should come under my roof" [Mt 8.8] to show how much favor he bestowed on his disciple.[25]

Matthew and Mark do not mention Jesus saying anything to Peter's mother-in-law. Luke's expression "rebuked her fever" could refer to the words used by Jesus, similar to those he used in other such situations. In Luke's Gospel, this word appears three times in three consecutive accounts. In the account of the casting out of the demon from the possessed man, Jesus also rebuked him, saying, "Hold thy peace, and come out of him" (Lk 4.35). In the account of the healing of Peter's mother-in-law, Jesus also rebukes the fever, and the fever leaves her.

The Apostle Peter,
icon, 1387–95

After this event comes another account of Jesus healing the sick, laying his hands on them, and casting out demons. As the demons came out of the possessed, they said, "Thou art Christ the Son of God. And he rebuking them suffered them not to speak: for they knew that he was Christ" (Lk 4.40–41). The verb "to rebuke" (ἐπιτιμάω, *epitimaō*) has a different meaning in each of these scenes, and the two first uses, in particular, point to Jesus' power, his ability to achieve an immediate and effective result. It is in this same meaning that "rebuke" is used in the account of Jesus calming the storm: "And he arose, and rebuked the wind, and said unto the sea, 'Peace, be still'" (Mk 4.39).

In Matthew, the healing occurs through Jesus touching the hand of the woman; Mark mentions that Jesus raised her up by the hand; Luke does not say anything about physical contact. In this episode, we are dealing with an instantaneous healing (Mark's characteristic description "immediately" [εὐθύς, *euthys*] here has a literal meaning). The healing occurs because Jesus saw the sick woman (or he was told of her), approached her, touched her hand, and, possibly, uttered some words.

[25]Ibid. (NPNF[1] 10:184).

4. "Lepers Are Cleansed"

Healing the Leper in Capernaum

Let us turn to the healing of the leper, which is the first healing mentioned in the Gospel according to Matthew (before the healing of the servant of the centurion and Peter's mother-in-law). In Luke, this is also one of the first miracles mentioned (it occurs after the healing of Peter's mother-in-law and the miraculous catch of fish).

In Matthew, this event occurs immediately after the Sermon on the Mount, the first in a series of accounts of healings and miracles.

> When he was come down from the mountain, great multitudes followed him, and behold, there came a leper and worshipped him, saying, "Lord, if thou wilt, thou canst make me clean." And Jesus put forth his hand, and touched him, saying, "I will; be thou clean." And immediately his leprosy was cleansed. And Jesus saith unto him, "See thou tell no man; but go thy way, shew thyself to the priest, and offer the gift that Moses commanded, for a testimony unto them." (Mt 8.1–4)

Mark's version gives more detail:

> And there came a leper to him, beseeching him, and kneeling down to him, and saying unto him, "If thou wilt, thou canst make me clean." And Jesus, moved with compassion, put forth his hand, and touched him, and saith unto him, "I will; be thou clean." And as soon as he had spoken, immediately the leprosy departed from him, and he was cleansed. And he straitly charged him, and forthwith sent him away; and saith unto him, "See thou say nothing to any man: but go thy way, shew thyself to the priest, and offer for thy cleansing those things which Moses commanded, for a testimony unto them." But he went out, and began to publish it much, and to blaze abroad the matter, insomuch that Jesus could no more openly enter into the city, but was without in desert places; and they came to him from every quarter. (Mk 1.40–45)

The Healing of the Leper in Capernaum, mosaic, 12th century

Luke's version is close to Matthew's, but the ending is different. If in Mark the healed man disobeys Jesus' command not to tell anyone of the healing, in Luke, Jesus' fame grows as an objective consequence of the miracles he performed: "But so much the more went there a fame abroad of him; and great multitudes came together to hear, and to be healed by him of their infirmities. And he withdrew himself into the wilderness, and prayed" (Lk 5.15–16).

In our opionion, reading these accounts together provides a good argument against the widely accepted (in scholarly circles) hypothesis that the Gospel according to Mark was the source material for both Matthew and Luke, who edited it to better serve the needs of their pastoral communities. In this case, Matthew's account is the shortest and most laconic, and it is difficult to accept that Mark is its source. If in Matthew the leper merely bows to Jesus, in Mark he begs Jesus and falls before him onto

The Evangelist Luke,
icon, 1350–60

his knees. Matthew leaves the emotional content offstage; Mark mentions that Jesus felt compassion for the leper. After the leprosy comes off the healed man, Mark mentions that Jesus strictly speaks to the man and tells him not to spread any word about the miracle. Matthew leaves out this detail, as he does the rest of the behavior of the former leper and its consequences.

If we are to assume that any of these three was a source for the other two, then it seems to us that Matthew's account fits, not only because of its brevity, but because of the mention of the gift that needed to be brought to the Temple in gratitude for healing, as prescribed by the Mosaic Law. The theme of the relationship between Jesus' teaching and the Law of Moses occupies a central place in the Sermon on the Mount. The story of the healing of the leper follows the Sermon on the Mount immediately. It is in this sermon only that Jesus said, "Think not that I am come to destroy the law, or the prophets: I am not come to destroy, but to fulfill" (Mt 5.17). There is no parallel to this phrase in any other Gospel. Matthew was much more interested in the theme of the Old Testament Law than either of the other two Synoptics. It is entirely possible that he was the first to record the words of Jesus spoken to the healed man, while the other two took the account from him and added the missing details.

However, all these considerations about the possible literary dependence of one evangelist on another is nothing more than speculation. It is entirely possible that there was no such dependence at all, and that every evangelist just wrote down his own version of the account that existed in oral tradition. In this case, we may consider the possibility of the existence of two oral traditions: a shorter one (reflected in Matthew) and a longer one, with more details, recorded in Mark and Luke.

Luke strengthens the emotional content of the narrative, mentioning that the paralytic "fell on his face, and besought him" (Lk 5.12). The phrase peson πεσὼν ἐπὶ πρόσωπον (*pesōn epi prosopōn*, "fell on his face") is a typical Semitic expression that we also find in Syriac patristic texts. Isaac the Syrian often uses it when he speaks of prayer:

> During periods of temptations, when someone is darkened, he ought to fall on his face in prayer, and not rise up until power come to him from heaven and a light which will support his hear in a faith that has no doubts.[26]

> Someone who shows a reverential posture during prayer, by stretching out his hands to heaven as he stands in modesty, or by falling on his face to the ground, will be accounted worthy of great grace from on high.[27]

Here the saint is speaking of the pose of a person at prayer when he falls to his feet and bows his face to the ground. Sometimes, this is called the pose of the prophet Elijah (1 Kg 18.42). One finds this pose frequently on icons. This is the pose that is implied in the account of Abraham, when he saw the three visitors, ran to greet them, and bowed to the ground (Gen 18.2). In the ancient world, it was customary to fall down to the ground as a sign of respect for powerful people of higher status, and also in cases when someone had a very important request to make. This last example explains the pose of the leper before Jesus.

To fully appreciate the significance of this healing of the paralytic for Jesus' contemporaries, we must stop to examine what exactly "leprosy" (λέπρα, *lepra*) meant in Jesus' time, as well as the social status of lepers. In the Septuagint, the term λέπρα (*lepra*) is used to translate the Hebrew term צָרַעַת (*tsaraath*). Its symptoms are described in detail in Leviticus: it includes swelling, inflammation of the skin, spots or open wounds on the skin, boils, rashes, indentations in the skin, scabs, and pus (Lev 13.2–53). No other disease in the Bible is given such a detailed description.

Leprosy was considered unclean, and those who contracted it had to live separately from everyone else, lest the leprosy be passed on to

---

[26]St Isaac the Syrian, *Ascetical Homilies* II/9.5, quoted in Hilarion Alfeyev, *The Spiritual World of Isaac the Syrian*, Cistercian Studies Series 175 (Kalamazoo, MI: Cistercian Publications, 2000), 104.

[27]Ibid., II/14.8–12, quoted in ibid., 153.

The Healing of the Leper in Capernaum, G. Tucco, 19th century

others: "And the leper in whom the plague is, his clothes shall be rent, and his head bare, and he shall put a covering upon his upper lip, and shall cry, "Unclean, unclean." All the days wherein the plague shall be in him he shall be defiled; he is unclean: he shall dwell alone; without the camp shall his habitation be" (Lev 13.45–46). The responsibility of declaring someone a leper belonged to the priests. They also declared a restoration of purity if the "leprosy be healed in the leper" (Lev 14.3). For this situation, certain rituals were prescribed, including the washing of the body of the healed person, shaving all the hair off the body, washing all his clothes, as well as a prescribed sacrifice for his sin (Lev 14.3–32).

Based on the symptoms, what is meant by leprosy is a series of skin diseases of varying severity—from eczema and psoriasis to a serious form of leprosy proper. The cause of leprosy (mycobacterium leprae) was only discovered in 1873; before that, no one knew the cause of the illness. In early stages of leprosy, which usually afflicted a person in his youth, the bacteria spread across the skin; however, when the illness advanced, the bacteria could afflict the lungs, the eyes, the nervous system, as well as the hands and feet. As a result of leprosy, the face of a person might change so much that he would no longer be recognizable.

The book of Job describes the symptoms of leprosy in detail: "So went Satan forth from the presence of the LORD, and smote Job with sore boils from the sole of his foot unto his crown. And he took him a potsherd to scrape himself withal; and he sat down among the ashes" (Job 2.7–8). As for how the disease affected him, Job himself said, "When I lie down, I say,

'When shall I arise, and the night be gone?' And I am full of tossings to and
fro unto the dawning of the day. My flesh is clothed with worms and clods
of dust; my skin is broken, and become loathsome" (Job 7.4–5). No less
painful are his psychological sufferings, because he becomes the recipient
of the scorn of his relatives, friends, and servants:

> Behold, I cry out of wrong, but I am not heard; I cry aloud, but there
> is no judgment. . . . He hath put my brethren far from me, and mine
> acquaintance are verily estranged from me. My kinsfolk have failed,
> and my familiar friends have forgotten me. . . . I called my servant,
> and he gave me no answer; I intreated him with my mouth. My
> breath is strange to my wife, though I intreated for the children's sake
> of mine own body. Yea, young children despised me; I arose, and they
> spake against me. My inward friends abhorred me, and they whom I
> loved are turned against me. My bone cleaveth to my skin and to my
> flesh, and I am escaped with the skin of my teeth. (Job 19.7, 13–14,
> 16–20)

Lepers were scorned not only for fear of contagion. Leprosy was considered a serious punishment for sins; it was understood to be a curse
sent by God. This is how Job's friends, who came to console him, understood his disease. Seeing him changed and whitened from the leprosy,
they "knew him not, they lifted up their voice, and wept; and they rent
every one his mantle, and sprinkled dust upon their heads toward heaven.
So they sat down with him upon the ground seven days and seven nights,
and none spoke a word unto him, for they saw that his grief was very
great" (Job 2.12–13). But later, they begin speaking with Job and expressing their understanding of God's justice. In summary, they believe that if
such misfortune attacks a person, that means that he is guilty before God;
more than that, God actually punishes a guilty person half as much as he
deserves (Job 11.5–6). Job does not consider himself to be guilty of the sins
that his friends imply he is guilty of. He sees his illness as an undeserved
punishment from God. Because of this, he cried out, "What is man, that
thou shouldest magnify him? And that thou shouldest set thine heart upon
him? And that thou shouldest visit him every morning, and try him every

Job on the Dungheap, Gračanica, Serbia, 14th century

moment? How long wilt thou not depart from me, nor let me alone till I swallow down my spittle? I have sinned; what shall I do unto thee, O thou preserver of men? Why hast thou set me as a mark against thee, so that I am a burden to myself?" (Job 7.17–20).

In ancient Israel, lepers were pariahs. They lived in small communities outside cities; they were forbidden from approaching healthy people, their relatives cast them off, their acquaintances and friends feared them. It seems, given the evidence, that the disease was fairly widespread and in its most serious form was practically incurable.

The leper mentioned in the three Synoptic Gospels approached Jesus with a request: "If thou wilt, thou canst make me clean." What do the words "if thou wilt" mean in this context? Do they mean that the leper doubts in Jesus' desire or ability to perform the healing? St John Chrysostom answers this question thus. In the words of the leper he sees a confirmation of the leper's sincere and fiery faith in Jesus—the leper does not insist on the fulfillment of his request, but he leaves everything to Jesus, trusting the decision to heal to his will alone.[28]

What is the point of his request? Some commentators of the nineteenth century insisted that the leper, seeing in Jesus an authority figure like the priests or Levites, asked to be declared clean, that is, to be given a "certificate of purity" that is required by Leviticus.[29] Certain modern commentators have repeated this opinion, conflating leprosy with psoriasis, making the healing nothing more than a ritual declaration of the end of the period of impurity:

> Jesus had a considerable reputation as a healer. People who were said to be lepers came to him and asked his opinion whether or not their condition remained leprous or not. He said sometimes that they were clean of leprosy; they rejoiced to hear his opinion and subsequently they journeyed to Jerusalem to have his opinion formally verified.[30]

But the fact that Jesus tells the healed leper to go to the priests and receive from them the confirmation of his purity proves the exact opposite—if Jesus himself gave out such "certificates," there would be no need to get priestly approval. Healing from leprosy was only the first step for a leper to be allowed back into society. Until the priests declared him clean, neither his relatives nor his acquaintances would receive him.

Jesus' words, "I will; be thou clean," indicate his immediate readiness to answer the leper's request. The healing itself occurred in a moment, when Jesus touched the sick man's body. This touch has a special significance. No one would touch a leper for fear of contagion, but also because of ritual impurity laws. Jesus ignored these laws.

If we compare this event with the healing of Naaman (whom Jesus mentioned in his sermon in Luke 4.27), as does St John Chrysostom, we see that the prophet Elisha did not want to touch the body of the sick

---

[28]John Chrysostom, *Homilies on Matthew*, Homily 25 (NPNF[1] 10:172).

[29]H. E. B. Paulus, *Exegetisches Handuch über die drei ersten Evangelien* (New York: Wentworth Press, 2018), 703.

[30]Davies, *Jesus the Healer*, 69.

man, but instead sent a servant out to him, an act that angered Naaman. Naaman's reaction to the prophet's desire not to touch him is expressed in strong language in the Bible: "But Naaman was wroth, and went away, and said, 'Behold, I thought, "He will surely come out to me, and stand, and call on the name of the LORD his God, and strike his hand over the place, and recover the leper." Are not Abana and Pharpar, rivers of Damascus, better than all the waters of Israel? May I not wash in them, and be clean? So he turned and went away in a rage'" (2 Kg 5.11–12). Chrysostom emphasizes that Jesus, unlike Elisha, "to signify that he heals not as a servant, but as absolute master, does also touch. For his hand became not unclean from the leprosy, but the leprous body was rendered clean by his holy hand."[31]

By his behavior, Jesus overturns an assumption concerning uncleanness that had persisted since the time of Moses, and he does this purposely and consistently. In the Old Testament, the source of impurity was considered to be anything external to a person, and he was assumed to be impure if he touched anything considered unclean. Some kinds of foods were unclean; if a person ate such food, he was considered defiled. Jesus, on the contrary, insisted, "There is nothing from outside a man, that entering into him can defile him, but the things which come out of him, those are they that defile the man" (Mk 7.15). These words, uttered in the presence of a crowd, he later explained to his disciples:

> And he said, "That which cometh out of the man, that defileth the man. For from within, out of the heart of men, proceed evil thoughts, adulteries, fornications, murders, thefts, covetousness, wickedness, deceit, lasciviousness, an evil eye, blasphemy, pride, foolishness: all these evil things come from within, and defile the man." (Mk 7.20–23)

As we have already mentioned, Mark's account of this healing differs from Matthew's in its greater detail. Especially worthy of attention are the following words: "And he straitly charged him, and forthwith sent him away, and saith unto him, 'See thou say nothing to any man, but go thy way, show thyself to the priest, and offer for thy cleansing those things

---

[31]John Chrysostom, *Homilies on Matthew*, Homily 25 (NPNF[1] 10:173).

which Moses commanded, for a testimony unto them'" (Mk 1.43–44). Many questions arise from this passage. Why did Jesus warn him "strictly" ("straitly")? Was he unhappy about the way he asked, or did he foresee that the man would not listen to his command not to tell about the miracle? What was the reason for this command—Jesus' desire to hide his healing or were there other reasons connected with the future fate of the healed man? Finally, what do the words "as a testimony to them" mean?

We cannot answer the first question definitively. We do not know why Jesus spoke strictly. Perhaps he recognized that this person was not fully trustworthy, not fully capable of fulfilling his command. We can compare this case with another healing described by John—there, Jesus healed the paralytic who lay at the pool for thirty-eight years; after this occurred, Jesus hid himself in the crowd. The Jews began to complain that Jesus broke the Sabbath, and said to the healed man that he should not be carrying his bed, which broke the injunction not to work on the Sabbath. The man then cited Jesus' words to him. When Jesus later found him in the temple he said, "Behold, thou art made whole; sin no more, lest a worse thing come unto thee" (Jn 5.14). But the former paralytic immediately went and informed the Jews that the man who healed him was Jesus. As a result, "the Jews persecuted Jesus, and sought to slay him, because he had done these things on the sabbath day" (5.16).

In spite of the fact that his healings were done en masse, Jesus—at least in the beginning of his ministry—did not want rumors about them to spread widely. In the Gospels, we find him forbidding the healed to speak about the miracle of their healing.[32] It seems there were two reasons for this. First, he did not want the climax of his conflict with the Pharisees to happen before its time. In the early stage of his ministry, he said, "Mine hour is not yet come" (Jn 2.4). He understood that he had a limited time on the earth, and he wanted to have time to do and say all the things he came

[32]Some scholars see in these cases Jesus' desire to conceal that he was the Messiah. The idea of the "Messianic secret" (Messiasgeheimnis) that became very popular in scholarly literature began with German New Testament scholar W. Wrede, who (mostly based on Mark's Gospel) insisted that Jesus did not reveal his messianic dignity until the very last part of his earthly ministry; see W. Wrede, *The Messianic Secret*, tr. J. C. G. Greig (Cambridge and London: James Clarke and Co., 1971).

The Healing of the Man Born Blind, Duccio, 14th century

to do and say. Second, excessive popularity, a constant crowd of people around him, and the rapidly increasing fame of the miracle-worker—all this hindered his ability to enter into cities, so that he had to hide in desert places (Mk 1.45). He did not seek human fame. He avoided it and did not want it to hinder his preaching.

It is also unclear why Jesus immediately sent the healed man away. His haste might be motivated by a desire to avoid a gathering crowd, which could give rise to the kinds of arguments that flared up after he healed the man blind from birth (Jn 9.8–34). After the healing was accomplished and the leprosy was gone, there was nothing left to do but for the man to show himself to the priests.

St Jerome indicates three reasons for sending the man away to the priests:

> First, for humility's sake, that he might be seen to defer to the priests. For there was a precept in the Law that those who had been cleansed of leprosy were to offer gifts to the priests. Second, so that those who saw that the leper had been cleansed might either believe in the Savior, or not believe. If they believed, they would be saved; if they refused to

believe, they would be without excuse. A concurrent reason is so that he would not seem to be breaking the Law. This was a charge with which they were very frequently accusing him.[33]

The words "as a testimony to them" could refer to the "certificate" that lepers were to receive from the priests after the official declaration that they were ritually clean. But these words can also be understood in the context of Christ's polemic against the Pharisees that accompanied his ministry from the very beginning. "They" could be the priests and Pharisees who did not believe in Jesus. The term "testimony" might be used here in the same sense as it would be used in court.

In another place, Jesus said to the Jews: "I told you, and ye believed not: the works that I do in my Father's name, they bear witness of me" (Jn 10.25). Here, the word "witness" refers the testimony of his deeds. The truth of Jesus' words is confirmed by his deeds, first of all by the healings he performed. These deeds should have become strong proofs against the accusers, who shut their eyes to obvious facts. This is how St John Chrysostom understands this passage:

> But what is, "for a testimony unto them?" For reproof, for demonstration, for accusation, if they be unthankful. For since they said, as a deceiver and impostor we persecute him, as an adversary of God, and a transgressor of the law; "You shall bear me witness," says he, "at that time, that I am not a transgressor of the law." Nay, for having healed you, I remit you to the law, and to the approval of the priests; which was the act of one honoring the law, and admiring Moses, and not setting himself in opposition to the ancient doctrines. . . . For this very thing he did indeed foreknow, and foretold it: not saying, for their correction, neither, for their instruction, but, for a testimony unto them, that is, for accusation, and for reproof, and for a witness that all has been done on my part; and though I foreknew they would continue incorrigible, not even so did I omit what ought to be done; only they continued keeping up to the end their own wickedness.[34]

[33]Jerome, *Commentary on Matthew* 1.8.4 (FOTC 117:99–100).
[34]John Chrysostom, *Homilies on Matthew*, Homily 25 (NPNF¹ 10:174).

The Healing of the Ten Lepers

Having examined the account described by the three Synoptics, we can pass to another case of healing of leprosy, which only Luke records. This event occurred during the final stages of Jesus' public ministry, when he was on his final journey from Galilee to Jerusalem. The exact place where this event occurred is not indicated.

> And it came to pass, as he went to Jerusalem, that he passed through the midst of Samaria and Galilee. And as he entered into a certain village, there met him ten men that were lepers, which stood afar off, and they lifted up their voices, and said, "Jesus, Master, have mercy on us." And when he saw them, he said unto them, "Go show yourselves unto the priests." And it came to pass, that, as they went, they were cleansed. And one of them, when he saw that he was healed, turned back, and with a loud voice glorified God, and fell down on his face at his feet, giving him thanks; and he was a Samaritan. And Jesus answering said, "Were there not ten cleansed? But where are the nine? There are not found that returned to give glory to God, save this stranger." And he said unto him, "Arise, go thy way; thy faith hath made thee whole." (Lk 17.11–19)

First of all, let us note that before us is a whole group of lepers. Lepers who lived in groups outside of cities often walked around together, either asking for alms or other forms of support. In the Old Testament, we find an account of four lepers who sat at the gates of a city (2 Kg 7.3). The lepers were not allowed inside the gates. Therefore, any chance of actually meeting Jesus was only when he entered into a certain village, that is we may assume he had not yet entered it. The lepers stopped at a distance, since it was forbidden for them to approach.

Calling Jesus by name and adding a title rarely found in the Gospels, ἐπιστάτα (*epistata*, "master" in the vocative case, found only in Lk 5.5; 8.24, 25; 9.33, 49; 17.13), the lepers witnessed to the fact that by this time, he had gathered wide acclaim. They recognized his face, considered him a person with authority, and hoped to receive healing.

Christ Heals the Ten Lepers, fresco, 14th century

In contrast with the previous healing, Jesus does not touch the lepers, and the healing does not occur instantaneously, but after they had departed from him. There is a similar event described in John. There Jesus anointed the eyes of a blind man with mud and sent him to the pool of Siloam, from which he returned with his sight (Jn 9.6–7). Consequently, the healing occurred either during the moment of immersion into the water or immediately afterwards, or on the way back. In the case of the ten lepers, it occurred on the return journey. Jesus went along the same route, then one of the healed men returned to him. The scene is vividly described—the healed man glorified God with a loud voice, fell to Jesus' feet, and thanked him. He was clearly affected by everything that happened and took the opportunity to come close to Jesus. After all, he had been denied this possibility as a leper. We can assume that the other nine continued on their journey toward Jerusalem.

The one who returned was a Samaritan; the others evidently were Jews. Some commentators believe that the return of the only Samaritan in the group is connected with the fact that he did not go to Jerusalem, but to the temple on Mount Gerizim, the center of the Samaritan religious cult (Jn 4.20), where he would have shown himself to the local priest. This explanation, however, is unlikely. The emotional state of the healed man,

*Christ Heals the
Ten Lepers*, Jean-
Marie Melchior,
1864

as described by the evangelist, witnesses to the fact that he returned with
a concrete purpose—to passionately thank his benefactor.

As in similar cases, when a foreigner shows more faith than Jesus' fellow countrymen, he uses him as an example for those surrounding him.
To the healed man, he says "rise up and go," indicating that during the
entire time that Jesus spoke with the people surrounding him, the healed
man remained prostrate at Jesus' feet. Jesus often accompanies his healing with the words "thy faith hath saved thee." The term "faith," as in other
such cases, refers exclusively to faith in Jesus. Nothing is said about the
difference between the belief systems of the Jews and Samaritans. This
completely corresponds to what Jesus said to the Samaritan woman when
she asked him where one must worship God—in Jerusalem or on Mount
Gerizim?

> Jesus saith unto her, "Woman, believe me, the hour cometh, when ye
> shall neither in this mountain, nor yet at Jerusalem, worship the Father.
> Ye worship ye know not what; we know what we worship, for salvation
> is of the Jews. But the hour cometh, and now is, when the true wor-
> shippers shall worship the Father in spirit and in truth; for the Father
> seeketh such to worship him." (Jn 4.21–23)

Having fallen down at the feet of Jesus, the healed Samaritan performed just such an act of worship, even if he did not fully understand that Jesus is God incarnate. His intuition suggested to him that he needed to thank God not by going to Jerusalem or Mount Gerizim, but to Jesus. The glorification of God and his gratitude to Jesus combine into a single expression, and bowing down before Jesus becomes an act of worship before God.

* * *

We have already mentioned the opinion of certain scholars who insist that the leprosy mentioned in the Gospels is nothing more than a minor skin disease such as psoriasis. We cannot agree with such a position, which lessens the significance of Jesus' miracles. In first-century Palestine, leprosy of a particularly virulent form was widely spread. The term λέπρα (*lepra*), which is how the disease is labeled in the Gospels, had the same meaning then that it does today, even if its meaning had broader application. Leprosy afflicted the entire body of a person. When he healed lepers, Jesus performed a miracle that was impossible to explain with any medical techniques. In a supernatural manner, he performed what was impossible to do using natural means.

Even in our time, leprosy is considered a disease that is very difficult to treat. Even one hundred years ago, it was widely spread in certain regions of Africa. In the first half of the twentieth century, Albert Schweitzer began to work with lepers in the Gabonian town of Lambarene:

> Leprosy in our consciousness is still associated with the ill-defined disease of the Bible and with the bell-riging outcasts of the Middle Ages, when all kinds of skin diseases were lumped together under this name. Leprosy, or as it is now often called, Hansen's disease, is about the least catching of all contagious diseases. No one knows exactly how contagion with Hansen's microbacillus takes place. Sometimes white workers have become infected, but these cases are rare and a special predispostion seems to be required. Since 1941, and thanks to an American scientist, Dr Guy Faget, effective drugs, the sulfones, have come into use which make it probable that this horrible social scourge

can be converted into a purely medical problem and eradicated within our lifetime [date of writing, 1959—*Ed.*].

In Africa, the sulfones have been in use only since the early 1950's, and hence one still finds innumberable persons who show the leonine features, the missing fingers and toes, and the unspeakable wounds of the classical leper. With the new drugs, new attitudes were introduced and leper villages became less and less something like garbage cans for leprous mankind.[35]

Schweitzer was one of the most impressive Christian humanists of the twentieth century. He began his career as a theologian and he wrote several important papers dedicated to the search of the "historical Jesus" between the end of the nineteenth and the beginning of the twentieth centuries. He left his mark in contemporary New Testament studies (Schweitzer rejected the divine nature of Jesus, instead emphasizing the eschatological character of Christianity and its moral content). Moreover, he was an excellent organist and musicologist—he wrote a brilliant study of Bach. When he turned forty, he decided to radically change his life. He received medical training and traveled to Africa, where he opened a hospital. One of his most important labors was the war against leprosy, and he achieved some notable successes in this area. In 1953, he received the Nobel Peace Prize. He used all the prize money to build a leper colony.

Having begun to study the life of Jesus in his youth, Schweitzer was inspired by Jesus' example of service, and dedicated his whole life to what Jesus did by his divine power—healing the sick. Following after other rationalist thinkers, Schweitzer was skeptical of the biblical narratives. All the same, he was a sincere man who saw in Jesus a great example for emulation. In 1931, he wrote:

> The study of the Life of Jesus has had a curious history. It set out in quest of the historical Jesus, believing that when it had found him it could bring him straight into our time as a Teacher and Saviour. It loosed the bands by which he had been riveted for centuries to the

[35]Frederick Franck, *Days with Albert Schweitzer: A Lambaréné Landscape* (New York: Henry Holt and Company, 1959), 45–46.

stony rocks of ecclesiastical doctrine, and rejoiced to see life and movement coming into the figure once more, and the historical Jesus advancing, as it seemed, to meet it. But he does not stay; he passes by our time and returns to his own. . . . Jesus means something to our world because a mighty spiritual force streams forth from him and flows through our time also. This fact can neither be shaken nor confirmed by any historical discovery. It is the solid foundation of Christianity.[36]

Albert Schweitzer
in Africa

By performing his miracles and healings, Jesus acted on the will of man through his own will. The power that came from him healed people who were ready to believe in him, to trust in him, to put their fate into his hands, to submit their wills to his will. This readiness was expressed in different ways. Some people called the master with a loud voice, begging him to save them. Others were more restrained, saying "If thou wilt, thou canst make me clean." But the element of faith and trust was present to a greater or lesser degree in all those who turned to Jesus for healing. In answer to their faith, to the submission of their will to his, they received healing.

5. "Arise, Take up Your Bed, and Walk"

Healing the Paralytic in Capernaum

The account of this healing follows the healing of the leper in the Gospels according to Mark and Luke; in Matthew, however, several other events occur between these two healings. We will include the account as recorded by Mark:

---

[36] Albert Schweitzer, *The Quest of the Historical Jesus: A Critical Study of its Progress from Reimarus to Wrede*, trans. W. Montgomery (London: A. & C. Black, Ltd, 1911), 399.

And again he entered into Capernaum after some days; and it was noised that he was in the house. And straightway many were gathered together, insomuch that there was no room to receive them, no, not so much as about the door; and he preached the word unto them. And they come unto him, bringing one sick of the palsy, which was borne of four. And when they could not come nigh unto him for the press, they uncovered the roof where he was; and when they had broken it up, they let down the bed wherein the sick of the palsy lay. When Jesus saw their faith, he said unto the sick of the palsy, "Son, thy sins be forgiven thee." But there were certain of the scribes sitting there, and reasoning in their hearts, "Why doth this man thus speak blasphemies? Who can forgive sins but God only?" And immediately when Jesus perceived in his spirit that they so reasoned within themselves, he said unto them, "Why reason ye these things in your hearts? Is it easier to say to the sick of the palsy, 'Thy sins be forgiven thee,' or to say, 'Arise, and take up thy bed, and walk'? But that ye may know that the Son of man hath power on earth to forgive sins," (he saith to the sick of the palsy), "I say unto thee, arise, and take up thy bed, and go thy way into thine house." And immediately he arose, took up the bed, and went forth before them all, insomuch that they were all amazed, and glorified God, saying, "We never saw it on this fashion." (Mk 2.1–12)

Here, as with the healings of Peter's mother-in-law and the leper, we see that Mark's version is significantly more detailed that Matthew's. In Matthew's account, Jesus was first on one shore of the lake, in the land of the Gergesenes, then returned into his boat and came back to his city (that is, Capernaum). Matthew's account does not include the fact that people took the roof apart—from his version, we have no idea how the paralytic's bed ended up before Jesus in the room. Matthew also does not include a description of the setting or context, other than mentioning a few scribes (see Mt 9.1–7). In all other details, his version matches up with the other two Synoptic Gospels.

Luke does not specify where the event occurred, opening the narrative with the following words: "And it came to pass on a certain day, as he was teaching, that there were Pharisees and teachers of the law sitting by, which were come out of every town of Galilee, and Judaea, and Jerusalem; and the power of the Lord was present to heal them. And, behold, men brought in a bed a man which was taken with a palsy . . ." (Lk 5.17–25). The rest of the account is almost the same as in Mark.

Thus we see Jesus sitting and teaching inside a house. Around him, there was a crowd of people, among whom were some scribes (Mt 9.3, Luke mentions both Pharisees and scribes). The house cannot fit all those who wish to enter. What house

The Evangelist Mark,
miniature, 13th century

is this? Evidently, this is Peter's house, since Jesus had no house of his own. If he did, he could have gone to his own house to sleep instead of traveling across the Sea of Galilee in the evening after healing Peter's mother-in-law, then coming back to Capernaum afterward (Mt 8.18–9.1).

The word paralytic is παραλυτικός (*paralytikos*) in the Greek (in Matthew and Mark, while Luke uses a medical term similar with a similar meaning, παραλελυμένος [*paralelymenos*]). Here, we must assume, the text is talking about a completely paralyzed man, who is supine without the ability to move at all.

Many commentators find the episode with the breaking up of the roof to be fantastical.[37] How could four people break through a roof without the conversation inside the house stopping, without the listeners being distracted, or without people complaining or even laughing? Any answer, of course, can only be hypothetical, but it seems that the roof was made of some light material, typical of the houses of people of limited means. It is possible that the house was being remodeled and part of the roof was exposed. Possibly, the house was built in such a way that one could enter through the roof as well as through a door. It is also entirely possible that when they started to break through the roof, the conversation in the room ended as everyone watched with interest to see how it would all end.

[37]Wendy Cotter, *The Christ of the Miracle Stories: Portrait through Encounter* (Grand Rapids, MI: Baker Academic, 2010), 92–101.

Healing the Paralytic,
icon, 15th century

In any case, the inventiveness of these four men inspired neither amazement nor anger in Jesus. In contrast to the episode with the leper, where Jesus was surprised at his words (see Mt 8.10), here he is not amazed at all, but rather seeing their faith (a comment included in all three accounts), he turns to the paralyzed man with words about the forgiveness of his sins. The word "they" could have indicated the entire group, including the paralytic (Chrysostom makes the point that if the sick man himself did not have faith, he would never have allowed himself to be lowered thus into Jesus' presence[38]). On the other hand, in many cases total paralysis includes partial or complete loss of speech—we do not know whether the man was even able to express his desire to be healed. Alternately, it is possible that his friends, in desperation at being unable to push through into the interior of the house, decided to risk breaking all forms of convention for the sake of their friend.

In any case, the paralytic is the only one to receive forgiveness of his sins, not the four men who carried him in. What does this suggest? It suggests that Jesus connected physical illness with the internal state of the man—sickness associated with sin. The words of Jesus, which angered the scribes, should not be understood in the sense that the paralytic had some secret sins that his friends did not know about, and that Jesus was pointing at specific sins that only he knew about. Such an interpretation, which can be found in scholarly literature, comes not from the context of the narrative itself, nor from comparison of this episode with other cases when Jesus told a healed person that his sins were forgiven, such as, for example, when he told the formerly paralyzed man, "Behold, thou art made whole; sin no more, lest a worse thing come unto thee" (Jn 5.14).

The connection between sin and illness is a separate, important theme, impossible to discuss here in the proper detail. Evidently, in some cases, certain diseases are a direct result of concrete sins (venereal diseases, for

[38]Chrysostom, *Homilies on Matthew*, Homily 29 (NPNF[1] 10:196).

example, are a consequence of the sin of sexual immorality). In the Old Testament, there are cases when God sent specific people disease as punishment for concrete sins (see 2 Chr 21.15). But the book of Job clearly shows that disease is not always connected with specific sins. It is a consequence of man's general sinfulness, which comes from the nature of Adam, twisted by sin, which all mortal people inherit. As the Apostle Paul said, "Wherefore, as by one man sin entered into the world, and death by sin . . . so death passed upon all men, for all have sinned" (Rom 5.12).

Diseases entered human history together with death after the fall of Adam and Eve. In the Old Testament, deliverance from diseases is directly connected with faithfulness to God, who said to Mosses, "If thou wilt diligently hearken to the voice of the LORD thy God, and wilt do that which is right in his sight, and wilt give ear to his commandments, and keep all his statutes, I will put none of these diseases upon thee, which I have brought upon the Egyptians, for I am the LORD that healeth thee" (Ex 15.26). In the Law of Moses, God commands his people thus: "And ye shall serve the LORD your God, and he shall bless thy bread, and thy water; and I will take sickness away from the midst of thee" (Ex 23.25). And the opposite is true as well: "If thou wilt not observe to do all the words of this law that are written in this book, that thou mayest fear this glorious and fearful name, THE LORD THY GOD; the LORD will make thy plagues wonderful, and the plagues of thy seed, even great plagues, and of long continuance, and sore sicknesses, and of long continuance. Moreover he will bring upon thee all the diseases of Egypt, which thou wast afraid of; and they shall cleave unto thee. Also every sickness, and every plague, which is not written in the book of this law, them will the LORD bring upon thee, until thou be destroyed" (Deut 28.58–61).

The connection between sickness and sin, and between confession of sin and freedom from disease, is clearly delineated in the thirty-first Psalm:

> Blessed are they whose iniquities are forgiven, and whose sins are
> covered.

Blessed is the man unto whom the Lord imputes no sin, and in
>   whose mouth there is no guile.
Because I kept silence, my bones waxed old through roaring all the
>   day long.
For day and night thy hand was heavy upon me, I was turned into
>   misery whilst the thorn stuck fast in me.
I acknowledged my sin, and mine iniquity have I not hid. I said: 'I will
>   confess mine iniquity before the Lord against myself,' and thou
>   forgavest the ungodliness of my heart. (Ps 31.1–5)

In the Old Testament, God dealt with an entire nation, and the main
function of the Law of Moses was to ensure the spiritual and physical
health of Israel as a nation. Faithfulness to the one God was the main
guarantee of this health. Therefore, we often encounter Old Testament
texts about diseases that become epidemics afflicting the entire nation or
a majority of its representatives. In the New Testament, the incarnate God
deals with individuals, each of whom he approaches individually. Each
healed person hears a word directed to him personally.

The three Synoptics offer three versions of Jesus' words to the paralytic:
"Son, thy sins be forgiven thee," "Son, be of good cheer; thy sins be forgiven
thee," and "Man, thy sins are forgiven thee." Nowhere else in the Synoptic
Gospels do we see a similar expression to these. In the Gospel according
to John, Jesus uses the phrase "thy sins be forgiven" when speaking to the
sinful woman who washed his feet with myrrh, adding that which he often
said to those he healed: "Thy faith hath saved thee; go in peace." Moreover,
in this case, the reaction of those with him were the same as the reaction
of the scribes to Jesus' words to the paralytic: "Who is this which speaketh
blasphemies? Who can forgive sins, but God alone?" (Lk 5.21).

The scribes' anger is expressed in different ways in these three accounts.
In Matthew, they "said within themselves, 'This man blasphemeth'" (9.3).
In Mark, he describes the "scribes sitting there, and reasoning in their
hearts, 'Why doth this man thus speak blasphemies? Who can forgive sins
but God only?'" (2.6–7) In Luke, they "began to reason, saying, 'Who is
this which speaketh blasphemies? Who can forgive sins, but God alone?'"

(5.21) Luke's words can be understood to mean that there was a discussion among the scribes as a result of what they heard. But in all three accounts, Jesus does not answer their words, but their thoughts; consequently, "began to reason" means "reasoning in their minds."

Sometimes the thoughts of a person can be read in his eyes or his facial expression. Jesus knew the thoughts of the scribes and Pharisees very well. When he uttered the words about forgiveness of sins, he could have immediately felt their reaction—it was written on their faces, even if they said nothing or even did not whisper to one another. However, this is not the only case when the evangelists emphasize that Jesus could read people's thoughts (see Mt 16.7; Lk 6.8, 9.47, 11.17). He was not simply perceptive. His ability to see people's inner world went beyond normal human capabilities.

The accusation of blasphemy is the worst that a Jew could utter against a countryman. And this is exactly the crime for which Jesus will be convicted by the high priest: "He hath spoken blasphemy; what further need have we of witnesses? Behold, now ye have heard his blasphemy" (Mt 26.65). But during this initial phase of his earthly ministry, the accusation of blasphemy is still only thought silently, though it would ultimately become the reason that the Jews would demand the death sentence for him.

Jesus asked the scribes: "Whether is it easier to say to the sick of the palsy, 'Thy sins be forgiven thee,' or to say, 'Arise, and take up thy bed, and walk'?" (Mk 2.9) The answer seems obvious—it is easier to say aloud that a person's sins are forgiven, because no one can prove whether they were or were not. It is harder to order a paralyzed man to stand up, because then everyone would expect the natural consequence of such words— that the man get up and walk. Why did this not occur immediately? Why, after Jesus announced that the man's sins were forgiven, did the paralytic remain supine, even if for a short time? From what the text says of him up to this moment, he exhibited no reaction to anything that occurred. It is very likely that he was simply unable to react, being completely paralyzed.

The forgiveness of sins was intended to heal his paralyzed, atrophied soul. His return to life, therefore, occurred in two stages—first, Jesus healed his soul, then his body. This is not the only case when healings occurred in two stages. Jesus did not return sight to the blind man immediately, but only after touching him a second time (see Mk 8.23–25). The ten lepers were not immediately healed, but only after they walked away from Jesus (Lk 17.14); another blind man was healed only after he bathed in a pool (Jn 9.7)

The reasons for this have nothing to do with an inability to achieve an immediate result. The reasons are more likely found in the person about to be healed—his body, evidently, is not always able to react instantaneously to the healing power of God. Moreover, the causes of sickness are not necessarily physical in nature. They could also be psychosomatic. Healing is not a magical act—it is a complicated process, in which the person participates with his whole nature, both soul and body.

The turning point in this entire episode is expressed in a phrase that is an incorrect grammatical construction in the original Greek, which was then incorrectly translated in most other languages: " 'But that ye may know that the Son of man hath power on earth to forgive sins,' (then saith he to the sick of the palsy), 'Arise, take up thy bed, and go unto thine house' " (Mt 9.6). Having begun this verse with a direct address to the scribes, but having not finished that phrase, Jesus then turned to the paralytic. Because of this grammatical construction in the original, which occurs in all three Synoptics, the attention of the reader is instantaneously transferred from the scribes to the paralytic at the exact moment when the miracle was about to occur.

The words "the Son of Man hath power on earth to forgive sins" resonate with the end of the account in Matthew: "Now when the multitudes saw it, they marveled and glorified God, who had given such power to men" (Mt 9.8). What is this "power"? The word ἐξουσία (exousia, "power") is constantly found applied to Jesus in the Gospels. People were amazed by the teaching of Jesus, because he taught them as "one having authority, and not as the scribes" (Mt 7.29). The power of Jesus here is directly opposed to the powerlessness of the scribes.

This opposition is especially evident in the account of the healing of the paralytic. Jesus has power that they do not. The nature of this power interested his opponents greatly: "What a word this is! For with authority and power he commandeth the unclean spirits, and they come out" (Lk 4.36).

In the Temple, the high priests and elders insistently asked him, "By what authority doest thou these things? And who gave thee this authority?" (Mt 21.23) Jesus did not give them a direct answer. As for the question, "Then answered the Jews and said unto him, 'What sign showest thou unto us, seeing that thou doest these things?' Jesus answered and said unto them, 'Destroy this temple, and in three days I will raise it up'" (Jn 2.18–19).

The Son of Man (Revelation), illustration from the Bamburgh Apocalypse. 11th century

Jesus purposely did not give direct answers to questions regarding his nature and power, because, from his perspective, it should be obvious. This power and authority come from God. Everyone who turned to Jesus with faith knew this, or at least intuited it; as for those who doubted his actions, the source of this authority was concealed, or they simply thought him to be a magician who "cast out demons . . . by Beelzebub the prince of the demons" (Mt 12.24).

Jesus spoke of his authority many times with his disciples, and they understood that he spoke of power received directly from God. In his prayer to the Father, he said, in the presence of the disciples, "As thou hast given him power over all flesh, that he should give eternal life to as many as thou hast given him" (Jn 17.2). After the resurrection, Jesus said to his disciples, "All power is given to me in heaven and in earth" (Mt 28.18). He shares this authority with them, even while he was still on this earth. To the twelve apostles, he "gave power and authority over all demons, and to cure diseases" (Lk 9.1). To the Seventy, he said, "Behold, I give unto you power to tread on serpents and scorpions, and over all the power of the enemy, and nothing shall by any means hurt you" (Lk 10.19). After his death and resurrection, he imparted this authority to his followers, concerning whom he said, "In my name shall they cast out demons; they shall speak with new tongues; shall take up serpents; and if they drink any deadly thing, it shall not hurt them; they shall lay hands on the sick, and they shall recover" (Mk 16.17–18). Jesus' authority has healing power, and he gives this power to his disciples.

In the case of the paralytic, this authority acted on him after Jesus turned to him. As soon as the man heard the command to rise up, take his bed, and walk home, "immediately he rose up before them, took up that whereon he lay, and departed to his own house, glorifying God" (Lk 5.25). He fulfilled Jesus' command literally.

The reaction of the eyewitnesses is described differently in the three Synoptics. Mark recorded their response: "We never saw it on this fashion!" Matthew ends his account with the following words: "But when the multitudes saw it, they marvelled, and glorified God, which had given such power unto men" (Mt 9.8). Luke ends it thus: "And they were all amazed, and they glorified God, and were filled with fear, saying, 'We have seen strange things to day'" (5.26). In all three versions, the people's amazement is recorded. Moreover, only Matthew has people speak of the power of God given to men—not to the specific figure of Jesus from Nazareth, but men in general. It is possible that they were speaking of the healing power that came both from Jesus and his disciples.

Healing the Paralytic at the Pool of Bethesda

Let us turn to another example of a healing of a paralyzed man, described in the Gospel according to John. The event occurred in Jerusalem, and in all other circumstances this event also differs from the previously-discussed healing of the paralytic. The only similarity is the phrase uttered by Jesus, as well as the reaction of the paralyzed man:

> After this there was a feast of the Jews; and Jesus went up to Jerusalem. Now there is at Jerusalem by the sheep market a pool, which is called in the Hebrew tongue Bethesda, having five porches. In these lay a great multitude of impotent folk, of blind, halt, withered, waiting for the moving of the water. *For an angel went down at a certain season into the pool, and troubled the water; whosoever then first after the troubling of the water stepped in was made whole of whatsoever disease he had.* And a certain man was there, which had an infirmity thirty and eight years.

When Jesus saw him lie, and knew that he had been now a long time in that case, he saith unto him, "Dost thou will to be made whole?" The impotent man answered him, "Sir, I have no man, when the water is troubled, to put me into the pool; but while I am coming, another steppeth down before me." Jesus saith unto him, "Rise, take up thy bed, and walk." And immediately the man was made whole, and took up his bed, and walked; and on the same day was the sabbath. (Jn 5.1–9)

The Evangelist John the Theologian in Silence, icon, 1679

The words that we offer here in italic typeface are missing in many old manuscripts, and so modern critical editions of the Gospel do not include this phrase. St Cyril of Jerusalem (fourth century), who dedicated an entire homily to the healing of the paralytic at the pool, never mentioned once that an angel occasionally entered the water and disturbed it. But his contemporary, John Chrysostom, does mention it,[39] and long before Chrysostom, Tertullian also cited this phrase.[40] It is possible that this phrase was a commentary by an ancient reviser of the Gospels, who wanted to explain what the paralytic's words "when the water is troubled" meant. But based on the witness of Tertullian and Chrysostom, this commentary was added to the text quite early.[41]

The miracles described here occurred during the early phase of Jesus' earthly ministry. In the Gospel according to John, it follows immediately after the healing of the son of the nobleman of Capernaum. The setting is described in great detail. The pool of Bethesda (according to one interpretation, the word comes from the Aramaic *bet hesda,* or "house of mercy") at the Sheep Gate in Jerusalem is known from other sources, including the scrolls from Qumram. Many authors mention this pool, including Cyril of

[39]John Chrysostom, *Homilies on the Gospel of John,* Homily 36.
[40]Tertullian, *On Baptism* 5 (ANF 3:671–72).
[41]Cf. Metzger, *A Textual Commentary on the Greek New Testament* (Stuttgart, 1971) 209. For an argument concerning the phrase's authenticity, see Z. C. Hodges, "The Angel at Bethesda," *Biblioteca Sacra* 136 (Jan.–March 1979), 25–39, at 39.

The Savior Heals the Paralytic at the Sheep's Pool, icon, 19th century

Jerusalem, Eusebius of Caesarea, Jerome, and Cyril of Alexandria. It comprised an entire complex of buildings, including cisterns and many bathing pools.[42]

According to the text, the paralytic had lain near the pool for thirty-eight years. In contrast to the paralytic in Capernaum, who is presented as not only immovable, but even without speech, the paralytic from Jerusalem can talk. But he does not show the initiative in this account—Jesus sees him, asks who he is, and asks whether or not he would like to be healed. The the paralyzed man's answer resembles other people who keep talking about the circumstances of earthly life while Jesus tries to raise their mind to more exalted truths. The conversations with Nicodemus and the Samaritan woman, which immediately precede this account, occur along the same lines.

Why did Jesus turn to this paralytic in particular, ignoring all the other sick, blind, lame, and wizened people who lay near him in great numbers? The evangelist does not say. Evidently, the answer must be sought in the fact that healing from physical diseases was not a goal in and of itself for Jesus; otherwise, he would have healed everyone who lay at that pool.[43] Moreover, Jesus usually healed people individually, even if in certain cases many sick people were brought before him at the same time. In this specific case, we do not know why Jesus came to the pool in the first place. We only know that his attention was drawn by a specific person who had lain near the pool for thirty-eight years.

This account presents us with a more general question—why does God choose only one person to show his mercy from among many who seem to be in exactly the same predicament? Why does God save some, but not

[42]L. A. Belyaev, "Vifezda" [Bethesda], in *Pravoslaavnaya entsiklopediya* [Orthodox encyclopedia] (Moscow, 2004), 8:595–96).

[43]H. Lockyer, *All the Miracles of the Bible* (Grand Rapids. MI: Zondervan Publishing House, 1961), 302.

others? This is an important question in Christian tradition, and it has not been definitively answered. An entire group of theologians for centuries insisted that God predestined some people for salvation, but others for damnation. Others, such as John Chrysostom, insisted that God predestined everyone for salvation—if someone is not saved, that means he chose not to answer God's call.

Without getting into a detailed analysis of the Christian understanding of predestination,[44] we remind the reader that in the Old Testament, God said to Moses, "I will make all my goodness pass before thee, and I will proclaim the name of the LORD before thee, and will be gracious to whom I will be gracious, and will shew mercy on whom I will shew mercy" (Ex 33.19). Commenting on this phrase, the Apostle Paul said, "So then it is not of him that willeth, nor of him that runneth, but of God that sheweth mercy. . . . Therefore hath he mercy on whom he will have mercy, and whom he will he hardeneth" (Rom 9.16, 18). It is God himself who is presented in Scripture as the one who takes the initiative to grant salvation and mercy to mankind, just as punishment and retribution likewise come from from God himself.

The Old Testament is filled with stories of God pouring forth mercy on the righteous, as well as harsh punishments, including on a mass scale, for sinners. The New Testament ushers in an outpouring of God's mercy on mankind that comes from God's own initiative. This mercy, however, does not come down on those who oppose God's will. For every specific person, the condition of accepting the gift of salvation is faith. Salvation occurs not en masse, but individually, and it cannot occur against man's own will.

Jesus often took the initiative himself. He chose the Twelve from among his followers. Concerning this choosing, Mark wrote, "And he goeth up into a mountain, and calleth unto him those whom he himself wanted, and they came unto him. And he ordained twelve" (Mk 3.13–14). He separated one group from the larger mass of his followers and took them with him up a mountain. From that smaller group, he then chose an even smaller one—those whom he chose, "that they should be with him, and that he might send them forth to preach, and to have power to heal sicknesses,

[44]A more detailed discussion of this topic is included in volume 1 of this series.

The Twelve Apostles, miniature from an illuminated manuscript, 13th century

and to cast out demons" (Mk 3.14–15). Evidently, he does not give all his followers this power, but only "those whom he himself wanted."

In this case, Jesus also takes the initiative and himself offers the paralytic an unexpected gift—healing after thirty-eight years of a debilitating illness. The paralytic still does not understand what is going on, and he begins to complain about his life, explaining his circumstances. The key words in this explanation are "I have no man." People depend on each other, and when one is in trouble, then others come to help. But this person had lain in one place for too long; he had passed from everyday life too long ago—there was no longer anyone he knew who could sit with him and patiently wait for the moment when the water would be disturbed.

In the person of Jesus, he found not merely a man who could help him. According to Gregory of Nazianzus, "Yesterday you were flung upon a bed, exhausted and paralyzed, and you had no one when the water should be troubled to put you into the pool. Today you have him who is in one person man and God, or rather God and man."[45] In the person of Jesus, God

---

[45]Gregory of Nazianzus, *Oration* 40.33 (NPNF[2] 7:372).

himself came to the paralyzed man's aid—He came by his own initiative, without any request from the paralytic.

Jesus did not listen long to the complaints of the paralytic. He uttered a formula similar to the one he used with the paralytic in Capernaum (here he tells him merely to "go," and not to his own home). The effect, however, is the same in both cases—immediate healing. The paralytic got up, took up his bed, and began to walk, in a single moment obtaining that bodily strength that he had lost many years ago.

We should mention that Jesus does not use water to perform his miracle. According to one New Testament scholar, his word does not act through the water, but becomes an alternative to it.[46] Thus, the healing of the paralytic is different form the healing of the blind man, whom Jesus sent to wash in the pool of Siloam (Jn 9.7).

The rest of the account deals with the issue of the Sabbath, a theme that constantly arises in all four Gospels. Since the healing occurred on a Sabbath day, the Jews say to the healed man:

> It is the sabbath day: it is not lawful for thee to carry thy bed. He answered them, "He that made me whole, the same said unto me, 'Take up thy bed, and walk.'" Then asked they him, "What man is that which said unto thee, 'Take up thy bed, and walk'?" And he that was healed knew not who it was; for Jesus had conveyed himself away, a multitude being in that place. Afterward Jesus findeth him in the temple, and said unto him, "Behold, thou art made whole: sin no more, lest a worse thing come unto thee." The man departed, and told the Jews that it was Jesus, which had made him whole. And therefore did the Jews persecute Jesus, and sought to slay him, because he had done these things on the sabbath day. (Jn 5.9–16)

The Jews' question "Who is the man?" resonates with the beginning of this narrative, when the paralytic mentioned that he had no man to help him. During the course of thirty-eight years, among the great multitudes who came to the temple in Jerusalem (the pool was in the immediate

---

[46]Craig Koester, *Symbolism in the Fourth Gospel: Meaning, Mystery, Community* (Minneapolis: Fortress Press, 1995), 172.

Christ Pantocrator,
icon, 13th century

vicinity of the temple), there was not a single person who paid any attention to the paralytic. And here such a Man was found—not only did he pay attention, but he pulled him up to his feet, and with his will alone, he delivered him from the cause of all his suffering. The Jews—those custodians of law and order—were neither moved by this miracle nor did they rejoice that a man paralyzed for so many years had received healing. They cared only about one thing—who dared violate the centuries-long proper order of things that dictated that paralytics must lie at the pool, and no one was to come help them! The only thing they paid any attention to was the violation of the Sabbath.

The argument between Jesus and the Pharisees concerning the Sabbath day rest was a battle to the death. Jesus' healings on the Sabbath ended with the following: "And the Pharisees went forth, and straightway took counsel with the Herodians against him, how they might destroy him" (Mk 3.6); "the Jews . . . sought to slay him, because he had done these things on the sabbath day" (Jn 5.16). During one of these meetings, the high priests and Pharisees actually condemned him to death (Mt 26.3–5; Jn 11.47–53, 57). During that time, only the Roman overlords could actually perform an execution; but Pilate's role was mostly a formality—those who initiatied Jesus' conviction were the Jewish high priests, the Pharisees, and the scribes; the Romans merely performed the act of crucifixion.

This is the proper context for interpreting these healing narratives that occurred on the Sabbath—the drama that ultimately ended with Jesus' arrest, judgment by the high priest, crucifixion, and death. These healings were connected, for him, with a risk of being killed. And even though he knew that he was to die violently, he avoided being captured until the appointed time. In this particular episode, when Jesus had healed the paralytic, he withdrew into the crowd.

After that, however, Jesus found the former paralytic in the temple. The word used, εὑρίσκει (*heuriskei*), means "to seek out," that is, the encounter was not accidental, but occurred by Jesus' initiative, as did the healing itself. This time, Jesus told him not to sin, lest something even worse happen to him. These words remind us of what Jesus said to the woman who was caught *in flagrante delicto*, after all her accusers had left: "Go, and sin no more" (Jn 8.11). But in this case, the context is somewhat different, and the point of Jesus' words is to emphasize the connection between sin and disease.

As Cyril of Jerusalem wrote, "He is a versatile doctor, sometimes healing the soul first, and then the body, sometimes following the reverse order."[47] In the case of the paralytic in Capernaum, Jesus first began speaking of the forgiveness of sin, and only then did he heal. In this case, the healed paralytic did not hear Jesus say the words, "Your sins are forgiven." The reminder about the connection between sickness and sin occurred during their second meeting. Having received healing, the former paralytic was not supposed to return to his previous sins; what sort of sins, we do not know.

We also do not know for what reason and under what circumstances the paralytic then announced to the Jews that it was Jesus who healed him. Did he do this with an evil intent in mind or not? According to some commentators, this deed was deliberate, that is, he revealed Jesus' name knowing of their negative reaction to him. According to other commentators, he continued "in the same right feeling . . . but when they continually advanced this seeming charge, he continually puts forward the defense, again declaring his healer, and seeking to attract and attach others to him. For he was not so unfeeling as after such a benefit and charge to betray his benefactor, and to speak as he did with an evil intention."[48]

Healing the Man with the Withered Hand

Let us now examine the account of the healing of the man with a withered hand. He is found in all three Synoptic Gospels, each of which adds its own accents. Here is Mark's account:

[47] Cyril of Jerusalem, "Homily on the Paralytic near the Pool," in *The Works of Saint Cyril of Jerusalem,* vol. 2, trans. Anthony A. Stephenson, The Fathers of the Church 64 (Washington, DC: The Catholic University of America Press, 1970), 209–22.

[48] John Chrysostom, *Homilies on the Gospel of John,* Homily 38 (NPNF[1] 14:132).

And he entered again into the synagogue; and there was a man there which had a withered hand. And they watched him, whether he would heal him on the sabbath day, that they might accuse him. And he saith unto the man which had the withered hand, "Stand forth." And he saith unto them, "Is it lawful to do good on the sabbath days, or to do evil? To save life, or to kill?" But they held their peace. And when he had looked round about on them with anger, being grieved for the hardness of their hearts, he saith unto the man, "Stretch forth thine hand." And he stretched it out, and his hand was restored whole as the other. (Mark 3.1–5)

In contrast with Matthew and Mark, who say nothing of who it was that was watching Jesus, Luke specifies that these were the scribes and Pharisees. He also mentions that Jesus commanded the man with a withered hand to stand up and walk to the middle of the crowd, because he knew their ill intentions. Moreover, Luke and Matthew both leave out what Mark says concerning Jesus' anger and his sorrow at their hardness of their hearts. In all other aspects, Luke follows Mark's version (Lk 6.6–10).

Matthew includes the expression: "Jesus knew their thoughts" (Mt 12.25). According to Matthew's version, the Jews were not simply watching out to see if Jesus would heal on the Sabbath, they "asked him, saying, 'Is it lawful to heal on the Sabbath?'" Mark and Luke depict Jesus initiating this conversation, while in Matthew, he answers their question. In Matthew, Jesus' answer is more complete: "What man shall there be among you, that shall have one sheep, and if it fall into a pit on the sabbath day, will he not lay hold on it, and lift it out? How much then is a man better than a sheep? Wherefore it is lawful to do well on the sabbath days." After these words, Jesus commands the sick man to extend his hand, "and it was restored whole, like as the other" (Mt 12.9–13).

The withered hand indicates complete paralysis of the hand. Only Luke mentions that the man had his right hand paralyzed, not his left (Luke in other such cases is generally more exact concerning issues of medicine). We do not know the reason for the paralysis. It could have been the result of a stroke or something else may have damaged his nervous system.

Judging by the fact that the sick man could get up by himself and walk to the middle of the room, the rest of his body was not similarly afflicted.

Jesus' words to the sick man are the same in all three Synoptics: "Stretch forth thine hand." With these words, Jesus asks the sick man to believe in something that just a moment ago was impossible. He could move his legs, he could use the other arm, but the paralyzed hand hung at his side, lifeless. He did not feel it, nor was he able to control it. The miracle occurs thanks to the healing power that flows from Jesus. But for the miracle to occur, the cooperation of the sick man is also necessary. This cooperation was expressed in the fact that the man, having believed Jesus, did the impossible.

The Healing of the Man with the Withered Hand, mosaic, 12th century

The healing occurs instantaneously and without Jesus' touch—merely through his word. Though everything occurs before the eyes of all, and Jesus brings the attention of his opponents to the fact that doing good is not forbidden on the Sabbath, Jesus did not perform this miracle with the purpose of justifying himself in the dispute about the Sabbath. The center of attention is not the scribes and Pharisees, but the sick man to whom Jesus speaks. Moreover, Jesus does not ask the man about his faith, as in some other cases, and the sick man says nothing at all during this entire scene. His answer to Jesus' words is an action—he stretched forth his hand, and it is healed.

The theme of the Sabbath is most important in this account. As in other similar cases, the miracle disturbs the Pharisees and scribes. According to Matthew, the Pharisees, "went out, and held a council against him, how they might destroy him. But when Jesus knew it, he withdrew himself from thence" (Mt 12.14). Mark mentions that the Herodians also took part in this event (Mk 3.6). According to Luke, the Pharisees "were filled with madness, and communed one with another what they might do to Jesus" (Lk 6.11).

The Healing of the Man with the Withered Hand, fresco, 16th century

We can ask why Jesus healed so often on the Sabbath. After healing the woman who was bent over, the leader of the Synagogue had said, "There are six days in which men ought to work; in them therefore come and be healed, and not on the sabbath day" (Lk 13.14). But the Sabbath was when people gathered in the Synagogue, and it was not infrequent that among those gathered there were people with illnesses. Jesus did not choose the Sabbath as his special "office hours." He healed on other days as well, but not in the Synagogues. But the gatherings in the Synagogues offered a regular opportunity for healing, since the sick approached him and asked to be healed.

In his commentary on this passage, St Jerome quotes "the Gospel that the Nazarenes and Ebionites use." This apocryphal gospel is one that Jerome himself translated from Hebrew to Greek. In it, the man with the withered hand is called a stonemason, who asked Jesus: "I was a stonema-son, seeking a livelihood with my hands; I plead with you, Jesus, that you restore soundness to me, that I might not have to beg for my food in base fashion."[49]

In contemporary Orthodox Judaism, the prohibition of prescribed forms of work on the Sabbath continues to be in effect to this day. All together, thirty-nine different tasks are forbidden, which cover the entire range of human activity. On the Sabbath, one can go to the Synagogue and prepare lunch, but one may not even tear a piece of paper.[50] One can use an elevator, but one cannot press the buttons. In Israel (and in some parts of the United States, where there is a large Jewish population), every building with many floors has a special arrangement that operates automatically every Sabbath: the elevator stops on every floor, the door opens for a short time, then it closes again and moves to the next floor. This allows a person to enter the elevator, ride on it, and leave it (all of which is allowed on the Sabbath), without pressing the buttons (which is forbidden).

Literalism, dogmatism, a relation to religion as nothing other than a certain number of rules that govern various spheres of human interac-tion—all this is profoundly contrary to the teaching that Jesus brought to earth, and to the acceptance of the word that he preached. One can do good at any time; there are no limits to good. He tried, without success, to make the Pharisees understand this, because they believed that one could only do good according to the rules that govern doing good. For them, good was not an end in itself; the most important thing was the ritual, fol-lowing the rules and laws of Moses, as well as the tradition of the elders.

For Jesus, the center of attention was always living man—anyone he met on the road, or in a house, or in the Synagogue, who might need his help here and now, not at some point in the future. Jesus did not walk past such people. If they turned to him, he immediately healed them. The Sab-bath was no obstacle to this.

---

[49]Jerome, *Commentary on Matthew* 2.12.13 (FOTC 117:140–41).
[50]See the Babylonian Talmud, concerning Shabbat.

6. Healing the Woman
with an Issue of Blood

The account of Jesus healing the woman who suffered from constant bleeding (an "issue of blood") is found in the three Synoptic Gospels, and in all
three cases, it is part of a larger account of the resurrection of Jairus' daughter. The account begins with one of the leaders of the Synagogue approaching Jesus and telling him that his daughter was on her deathbed. Jesus and
his disciples went with him; a mass of people followed Jesus, crowding
around him. Here a miracle occurs. Matthew describes it briefly:

> And, behold, a woman, which was diseased with an issue of blood
> twelve years, came behind him, and touched the hem of his garment.
> For she said within herself, "If I may but touch his garment, I shall be
> whole." But Jesus turned him about, and when he saw her, he said,
> "Daughter, be of good comfort; thy faith hath made thee whole." And
> the woman was made whole from that hour. (Matthew 9.18–19)

Mark gives a more detailed and emotionally full picture of the events:

> And a certain woman, which had an issue of blood twelve years, and
> had suffered many things of many physicians, and had spent all that
> she had, and was nothing bettered, but rather grew worse, when she
> had heard of Jesus, came in the press behind, and touched his garment.
> For she said, "If I may touch but his clothes, I shall be whole." And
> straightway the fountain of her blood was dried up; and she knew in
> her body that she was healed of that plague. And Jesus, immediately
> knowing in himself that virtue had gone out of him, turned him about
> in the press, and said, "Who touched my clothes?" And his disciples
> said unto him, "Thou seest the multitude thronging thee, and sayest
> thou, 'Who touched me?'" And he looked round about to see her that
> had done this thing. But the woman, fearing and trembling, knowing
> what was done in her, came and fell down before him, and told him all
> the truth. And he said unto her, "Daughter, thy faith hath made thee

whole; go in peace, and be whole of thy plague."
(Mark 5.21–24)

Luke, in his version, is close to Mark, though
he leaves out certain details (Lk 8.43–48). Furthermore, in Luke's version, Peter asks the question, not
"the disciples," and Jesus' perception of the power
flowing out of him is not recounted by the narrator
as in Mark, but in Jesus' direct answer to Peter's
question: "Somebody hath touched me; for I perceive that virtue is gone out of me."

*Healing the Woman with
an Issue of Blood*, icon,
19th century

In all the cases that we have written about in the
previous chapters, the healing had occurred by the will of Jesus. In some
cases, people approach him with requests, and the healing is an answer to
the request, while in others he himself found the person and healed him.
The miracle occurred either thanks to his touch or his word, and in some
cases it even occurred at a distance. In the story of the woman with an
issue of blood, we find the only account in all the Gospels when the healing seems to occur apart from from Jesus' will, by itself, as a consequence
of the power natural to him. He feels that the power flows out of him, and
he tries to find, in the mass of people who naturally crowd him and touch
him constantly, the one person who caused the power to flow out.

In spite of the mention of the many physicians on whom the woman
had wasted all her money, we know nothing concerning the cause of her
illness. Some ancient commentators hinted that the cause of the sickness
could have been some specific sin.[51] Some more contemporary commentators specify that the constant bleeding could have been a result of an
abortion performed at some point in the past.[52] Though abortion is not
specifically mentioned in the Law of Moses, in contrast to Greek literature,[53] that does not mean that ancient Israel knew nothing of abortion.

---

[51]Hilary of Poitiers calls the woman "dressed in blemished clothing and defiled by the spots
of her internal condition." *Commentary on the Gospel of Matthew* 9.6 (SC 254:210).

[52]Alexander Shargunov, *Evangelie dnya* [The Gospel of the day], 1:310.

[53]Among classical writers, Plato, in *Republic* 5.459b–461d, mentions abortion somewhat
favorably, but without using the word; Aristotle mentions it specifically and as a necessity under

The rabbinic literature of a later period does mention it.[54] At the same time, there is no mention in any of the Gospels that the woman's guilt was the cause of sickness.

Even without considering the guilt or the innocence of the woman in question, Jewish society of that time did consider bleeding to be a sign of impurity.[55] The laws concerning female impurity are described in detail in Leviticus 12.1–8. They refer to the period of time after birth and are connected first of all with the fact that during this period blood continues to flow out of the woman's body. In Jewish culture, the concept of feminine impurity spread to all forms of bleeding:

> And if a woman have an issue, and her issue in her flesh be blood, she shall be put apart seven days; and whosoever toucheth her shall be unclean until the evening. And every thing that she lieth upon in her separation shall be unclean; every thing also that she sitteth upon shall be unclean. And whosoever toucheth her bed shall wash his clothes, and bathe himself in water, and be unclean until the evening. And whosoever toucheth any thing that she sat upon shall wash his clothes, and bathe himself in water, and be unclean until the evening. And if it be on her bed, or on any thing whereon she sitteth, when he toucheth it, he shall be unclean until the even. And if any man lie with her at all, and her impurity be upon him, he shall be unclean seven days; and all the bed whereon he lieth shall be unclean. (Leviticus 15.19–24)

The Law of Moses touches on even those cases when "a woman has a discharge of blood for many days, other than at the time of her customary impurity or if it runs beyond her usual time of impurity." This is exactly the condition of the woman who touched Jesus. According to the Law, even the bed or anything that she sat on would be considered unclean, and "whosoever toucheth those things shall be unclean" (Lev. 15.25–27). If we

certain circumstances in his theory of the state, in *Politics* 7.14.10; and Ovid speaks of it as an evil in *Amores* 2.14.

[54]See the Mishna and Tosefta.

[55]The Evangelists say nothing about the nature of the bleeding, though it is assumed to be menstrual. See, for example, Nicole Wilkinson Duran, *The Power of Disorder: Ritual Elements in Mark's Passion Narrative* (London: T&T Clark, 2009), 90–91.

assume that the woman followed this law strictly, that would suggest she was isolated completely for more than a decade, and even her husband or near relatives could not touch her or anything that she touched. Naturally, that meant she herself was also forbidden from touching anyone, lest she become a cause of his or her impurity.[56]

Having touched Jesus' clothing, she broke the law in the most flagrant way. And when Jesus began to look for her in the crowd, she must have been extremely frightened, which is exactly what happened. She came up to him with fear and trembling. But fear and trembling are not merely emotional states that come from a feeling of guilt. In the Bible, these two words placed together often indicate a religious state that accompanies man's meeting with God. The emotional state of the woman could have resulted both from her fear at breaking the law and a profound religious experience.

The event could have remained unnoticed, if Jesus had not stopped. That flowing out of power was connected for both Jesus and the woman with an experience that Mark describes using two verbs with the same root. The woman ἔγνω τῷ σώματι (*egnō tō sōmati*), literally "knew with her body" that she had been healed from her sickness. Jesus began seeking the woman, ἐπιγνοὺς ἐν ἑαυτῷ (*epignous en heautō*) "having come to know within himself" that the power had come out of him. Both verbs come from the term γνῶσις (*gnōsis* "knowledge") and indicate in this context the kind of knowledge that has nothing to do with rational thought. In both cases, what occurs is an internal experience—it was on the basis of these feelings that Jesus and the woman shared a common experience.

The fact that power came out of Jesus as though contrary to his will has inspired various skeptical and even ironic speculation in the more rationalistic commentaries. For example, Strauss, in his *Life of Jesus*, compared the power flowing from Jesus with electrical current that passes from one body to another.[57]

---

[56]Subsequent Jewish tradition continued to write down the most detailed versions of the rules governing female impurity. If Leviticus dedicates half a chapter to this topic, in Maimonides' *Mishna Torah*, it takes over seventy-five pages.

[57]David Friedrich Strauss, *The Life of Jesus Critically Examined*, tr. Marian Evans, vol. 2 (New York: C. Blanchard, 1860), 508.

*The Woman with
an Issue of Blood
Begs for Healing,*
mosaic, 14th
century

However, this out-flowing of power from Jesus should not be under-stood as some kind of unwilling or even uncontrolled emanation of energy. Obviously, there were so many people crowding around Jesus that many touched him, and nothing happened to them. But the woman approached him with sincere faith, hope, or even conviction that the miracle would occur: "If I may touch but his clothes, I shall be whole" (Mk 5.28). In answer to this faith, the power of God poured out on her, and a miracle occurred: "A certain mystical transfer of life-giving power from the God-Man to the sick woman occurred."[58]

As in other cases, God acts together with man. A synergy of two forces—the healing power of God and the power of man's firm faith—per-forms the miracle. Speaking of this synergy, St Ephraim the Syrian wrote: "[The Lord] therefore sealed off the diseased flow of blood from her womb and the proclamation of her healing burst forth from her mouth. She drew near to his divinity and was healed by it, while his divinity drew near to her and was proclaimed by her."[59]

---

[58]Justin Popovich, *Tolkovanie na Evangelie ot Matfeya: Svyatosavvye kak filosofiya zhizni* [Commentary on the Gospel according to Matthew: The holy path of St Sava as a philosophy of life], in *Sobranie tvorenii prepodobnogo Iustina (Popovicha)* [Collected works of the Venerable Justin Popovich] (Moscow, 2014), 253 (translated by NK).

[59]St Ephraim the Syrian, *Commenary on Tatian's Diatessaron* 7.24. Translation in *Saint Ephrem's Commentary on Tatian's Diatessaron: An English Translation of Chester Beatty Syriac MS 709*, trans. Carmel McCarthy (Oxford: Oxford University Press, 1993), 140.

The power of Jesus had a quality different from the strength of someone like Sampson in the Old Testament, whose strength depended upon
the length of his hair (Judg 4.17–20). This power does not depend on any
external factor; as we have already said, it flowed from the divine nature of
Jesus, which was inextricably linked with his human nature.

Why did Jesus decide to seek out the woman and make public what
she had tried to conceal? It was hardly to demonstrate the miracle to others—he evidently wanted to see her. In some cases, as we have already
said, healing occurred in two stages. Here, the first stage was everything
that occurred up to the moment when Jesus saw the woman—that is, the
woman felt that she was healed from a long and difficult physical illness.
But Jesus wanted the second act to occur as well. Having received healing
from physical illness, she also had to receive from him a complete remis-
sion of that spiritual-moral state in which she had lived for twelve years.

The means by which she decided to pursue healing indicates how sick
she was in a psychological and moral sense as well. She touches Jesus in
secret, hoping to remain unnoticed. But he did not want her to walk away
from him with the sense that she had stolen her healing unlawfully. He
wanted to heal her of the sense of guilt and personal impurity that had lain
heavily on her during the time of her illness. As St John Chrysostom said,
"He puts an end to the woman's fear, lest being pricked by her conscience,
as having stolen the gift, she should abide in agony."[60]

In the Gospel according to Mark, the woman approaches Jesus with fear
and trembling, falls down before him and tells him the whole truth. Jesus
answers her, "Daughter, thy faith hath made thee whole; go in peace, and
be whole of thy plague" (Mk 5.33–34). Luke has the following: "And when
the woman saw that she was not hid, she came trembling, and falling down
before him, she declared unto him before all the people for what cause
she had touched him, and how she was healed immediately. And he said
unto her, 'Daughter, be of good comfort; thy faith hath made thee whole;
go in peace'" (Lk 8.47–48). He addresses the words "thy faith has made
thee whole" countless times to the ones he healed, but the expression "go

[60]John Chrysostom, *Homilies on Matthew*, Homily 31 (NPNF¹ 10:206).

in peace" happens only here and in one other place—when Jesus speaks to the woman who anointed his feet and wiped them with her hair (Lk 7.50).

In both cases, these words indicate the result that always occurs in people after an encounter with Jesus—inner peace is restored, the harmony of emotional and spiritual strength. The woman who was a sinner washed Jesus' feet with her tears. We can only guess what terrible sins she was repenting of and how great was her internal suffering. The woman with an issue of blood was also suffering and in fear when she walked up to Jesus, though the reason for these feelings was different. Jesus gave her the spiritual peace that, perhaps, she had before until the sickness afflicted her. It is quite likely, however, that he gives her this inner peace for the first time.

7. "The Blind See"

The Gospels mention many cases of healing blindness. Two similar accounts are found in the Gospel according to Matthew (Mt 9.27–31; 20.34). Matthew also mentions the healing of a possessed blind deaf-mute (Mt 12.22). Mark tells of a healing of a nameless blind man in Bethsaida (Mk 8.22–26) and Bartimeus in Jericho (Mk 10.46–52). The same healing in Jericho is described in Luke (Lk 18.35–43). In the Gospel according to John, there is a detailed account of the healing of the man who was blind from birth (Jn 9.1–7). Finally both Matthew and Luke mention that Jesus healed "many" blind people (Mt 15.31; 21.14; Lk 7.21).

The theme of blindness plays no significant role in the Old Testament. There is not a single example of the miraculous healing of blindness by God's power. But there are many mentions of blind people. God said to Moses, "Who hath made man's mouth? Or who maketh the dumb, or deaf, or the seeing, or the blind? Have not I the LORD?" (Ex 4.11) In the Psalter, it is said that "the Lord gives wisdom to the blind" (Ps 145.8). The prophet Isaiah promises the coming of the year of the New Covenant, the blessed day of the Lord, which is connected with healing of blindness: "In that day shall the deaf hear the words of the book, and the eyes of the blind shall see out of obscurity, and out of darkness" (Is 29.18); "The eyes of the blind shall be opened, and the ears of the deaf shall be unstopped" (Is 35.5).

According to some scholars, the Jews who awaited the Messiah for many centuries, did not think that he would be a healer. This assertion, however, is only partially true and can be disputed. One of the prophecies of Isaiah, which Matthew refers to Jesus (Mt 12.18–21), includes the promise of healing from blindness:

> "Behold my servant, whom I uphold, mine elect, in whom my soul delighteth; I have put my Spirit upon him; he shall bring forth judgment to the Gentiles. He shall not cry, nor lift up, nor cause his voice to be heard in the street. A bruised reed shall he not break, and the smoking flax shall he not quench; he shall bring forth judgment unto truth. He shall not fail nor be discouraged, till he have set judgment in the earth, and the isles shall wait for his law." Thus saith God the LORD, he that created the heavens, and stretched them out; he that spread forth the earth, and that which cometh out of it; he that giveth breath unto the people upon it, and spirit to them that walk therein: "I the LORD have called thee in righteousness, and will hold thine hand, and will keep thee, and give thee for a covenant of the people, for a light of the Gentiles, to open the blind eyes, to bring out the prisoners from the prison, and them that sit in darkness out of the prison house." (Is 42.1–7)

Of course, Isaiah speaks of healing spiritual blindness and the return of spiritual vision. But one cannot avoid the connection between the promises of the Old Testament and the miracle accounts that we find in the Gospels. This connection was evident to the evangelists, especially Matthew, who frequently brings the readers' attention to it. He offers quotations from Isaiah as a direct connection to the healings performed by Jesus, and in confirmation of the fact that he is the Son of David, the promised Messiah:

> But when Jesus knew it, he withdrew himself from thence; and great multitudes followed him, and he healed them all, and charged them

that they should not make him known, that it might be fulfilled which was spoken by Isaiah the prophet, saying, "Behold my servant, whom I have chosen, my beloved, in whom my soul is well pleased; I will put my spirit upon him, and he shall shew judgment to the Gentiles. He shall not strive, nor cry, neither shall any man hear his voice in the streets. A bruised reed shall he not break, and smoking flax shall he not quench, till he send forth judgment unto victory. And in his name shall the Gentiles trust." Then was brought unto him one possessed with a demon, blind and dumb; and he healed him, insomuch that the blind and dumb both spake and saw. And all the people were amazed, and said, "Is not this the son of David?" (Matthew 12.15–23)

Spiritual blindness is one of the most important themes of the entire Gospel narrative. Very often, Jesus accuses his opponents—the scribes and Pharisees—of spiritual blindness (Mt 15.14; 23.16, 17, 19; Lk 6.39). In the Gospel according to John, there is a direct parallel between the healing of physical blindness and freedom from spiritual blindness. Having begun his account about the healing of the man blind from birth, the evangelist then offers many utterances of Jesus concerning himself as Light: "For judgment I am come into this world, that they which see not might see, and that they which see might be made blind" (Jn 9.39); "I am come a light into the world, that whosoever believeth on me should not abide in darkness" (Jn 12.46).

From the many healing accounts in the Gospels, one belongs to the early period of Jesus' earthly ministry, even before the choosing of the Twelve. This is the healing of the two blind men. In the Gospel according to Matthew, it follows immediately after the account of the resurrection of Jairus' daughter and the healing of the woman with the issue of blood (Mt 9.27–31). The healing of the blind man in Bethsaida (Mk 8.22–26) occurs after the third Passover, but before Jesus' coming into Jerusalem for the Feast of Booths. The healing of the man blind from birth (Jn 9.1–41) takes place in Jerusalem during the Feast of Booths, and the healing of the blind man (or, in Matthew, two blind men) in Jericho (Mt 20:29–34; Mk 10.46–52; Lk 18.35–43) occurs immediately before Jesus' glorious entry into Jerusalem for his final Passover. This is the order in which we will examine these miracles.

Healing the Two Blind Men

The account of Jesus healing two blind men is only found in the Gospel according to Matthew. This miracle occurs on the way back from Jairus' house after Jesus brought his daughter back from the dead:

> And when Jesus departed thence, two blind men followed him, crying, and saying, "Thou son of David, have mercy on us." And when he was come into the house, the blind men came to him, and Jesus saith unto them, "Believe ye that I am able to do this?" They said unto him, "Yea, Lord." Then touched he their eyes, saying, "According to your faith be it unto you." And their eyes were opened; and Jesus straitly charged them, saying, "See that no man know it." But they, when they were departed, spread abroad his fame in all that country. (Matthew 9.27–31)

In this account, we must pay attention first of all to the way the blind men address Jesus. The expression "son of David" is found at the very beginning of the Gospel according to Matthew (Mt 1.1), where it indicates not so much Jesus' lineage as a descendant of David, but rather his status as the promised Messiah. In the Gospel according to Matthew, Jesus is frequently called the Son of David. The people asked: "Is this not the Son of David?" (Mt 12.23) The Canaanite woman addressed Jesus thus: "Have mercy on me, O Lord, thou son of David" (Mt 15.22). In Jericho, the blind men exclaimed, "Have mercy on us, O Lord, thou son of David" (20:30). As Jesus entered Jerusalem in triumph, the people greeted him with cried of: "Hosanna to the son of David" (21.9). The expression "Son of David" is also used in parallel passages of the other Synoptics.

On the one hand, we can see the expression simply as a respectful form of address; by doing so, those who greeted him would be underlining his royal lineage. On the other hand, the "Son of David" is an expression most often used when meaning the one whom Israel awaited with increasing impatience. Jesus' argument with the Jews concerning the meaning of the

*The Miracle
of Healing the
Two Blind Men,*
fresco, 14th
century

name "Son of David" (Mt 22.41; Mk 12.35–37; Lk 20.41–44) has a direct connection to the proper understanding of the role and significance of the Messiah. Consequently, by calling Jesus the Son of David, the people were admitting that he played a messianic role.[61]

In later commentaries that prefer allegorical readings of Scripture, the expression "Son of David" is explicitly opposed to the expression "Son of God." According to Origen, for example, the use of this expression indicates spiritual blindness that corresponds to physical blindness.[62] Mark the Ascetic follows this logic: "Blind is the person who cries and says, 'Son of David, have mercy on me!' (Lk 18.38), who prays superficially and does not yet possess spiritual knowledge. When the man who was blind recovered his sight and saw the Lord, he no longer venerated him as Son of David but confessed him to be Son of God."[63]

[61]For more on the connection between the understanding of the name "Son of David" as referring to the Messiah and healings per se, see Lidija Novakovic, *Messiah, Healer of the Sick: A Study of Jesus as the Son of David in the Gospel of Matthew* (Tübingen: Mohr Siebeck, 2003), 77–123.

[62]Cf. Origen's *Commentary on the Gospel of Matthew* 16.9 (PG 13:1403ff).

[63]Mark the Ascetic, *On the Spiritual Law* 11. Translation in Mark the Monk, *Counsels on the Spiritual Life*, trans. Tim Vivian, Popular Patristics Series 37 (Crestwood, NY: St Vladimir's Seminary Press, 2009), 93.

It should be noted, however, that in St Mark's commentary, two different people are combined into a single one (Mk 10.47–48 and Jn 9.35–38). Moreover, those who addressed Jesus in the hope of healing could have meant "Son of God" when they called him "Son of David," or at least something very close in meaning. Both expressions, from their perspective, assumed Jesus to be the Messiah. The Origenist tradition of understanding the term "Son of David," like many other strictly allegorical readings of events in the Gospel, is lacking in historical validity.

Why did Jesus not immediately pay attention to the two blind men who followed him along the way and called to him for help? It is possible that he did not want the miracle to become obvious to others. This is supported by the fact that as soon as he performed the miracle, he forbade them to speak about it. This miracle happened during the period of Jesus' ministry when he was still careful about limiting the spread of rumor about himself.

Having walked into the house, Jesus first of all determines whether or not the blind men believe in his ability to perform the miracle. Then he touches their eyes and says, "According to your faith be it unto you." The healing occurs through both word and touch.

After that, a similar event occurs to the aftermath of the healing of the leper. Jesus had said to him, "See thou say nothing to any man." But he, instead, "went out, and began to publish it much, and to blaze abroad the matter, insomuch that Jesus could no more openly enter into the city" (Mk 1.44–45). After healing the blind men, Jesus strictly tells them, "See that no man know it." But they "spread abroad his fame in all that country." As with the leper, the blind men could have acted without evil intent. They told everyone about the miracle because they themselves were astonished by it.

Healing the Blind Man in Bethsaida

The next event leaves the reader with many questions concerning Jesus' various methods of healing. It is found only in Mark:

> And he cometh to Bethsaida, and they bring a blind man unto him, and besought him to touch him. And he took the blind man by the hand, and led him out of the town; and when he had spit on his eyes,

and put his hands upon him, he asked him if he saw anything. And he looked up, and said, "I see men as trees, walking." After that he put his hands again upon his eyes, and made him look up; and he was restored, and saw every man clearly. And he sent him away to his house, saying, "Neither go into the town, nor tell it to any in the town." (Mark 8.22–26)

This event begins the second half of the Gospel according to Mark. If the first half is dominated by miracle narratives, the second has only three miracles, two of which are healings of blind men. The second of these occurs immediately before the triumphal entry into Jerusalem. The first is preceded by a series of questions that Jesus addresses to his disciples: "Why reason ye, because ye have no bread? Perceive ye not yet, neither understand? Have ye your heart yet hardened? Having eyes, see ye not? And having ears, hear ye not? And do ye not remember? (Mk 8.17–18). These questions introduce the theme of spiritual blindness that dominates in a section of this Gospel that is itself part of a thematic arc that includes both cases of healing from blindness.[64]

In this excerpt of the Gospel according to Mark we find the greatest number of dialogues between Jesus and his disciples, in which the disciples show no understanding of anything he says or does. Except for Peter, not a single one of them can give him a coherent answer to the question "Whom say ye that I am?" Even Peter responds to Jesus' prophecy of his coming passion and death with a vehement protest (Mk 8.31–33). Alone with the teacher, the disciples ask him why they could not expel the demon from the young man (Mk 9.28–29). His second prophecy concerning his death is once again met with lack of understanding (Mk 9.31–32). Then the disciples argue about which of them is greatest, but Jesus places a child before them and tells them that whoever wants to be first should become everyone's servant (Mk 9.33–37). John tells Jesus that the disciples forbade a certain person from using Jesus' name to expel demons, because he did not follow them; Jesus announces that they did so wrongly (Mk 9.38–40). The disciples are upset by his words concerning divorce, and he explains

[64]Joel Marcus, *Mark 8–16: A New Translation with Introduction and Commentary*, The Anchor Yale Bible Commentaries (New Haven: Yale University Press, 2009), 589. See also Narry Santos, *Slave of All* (London: Bloomsbury, 2003), 148–49.

his words (Mk 10.10–12). They are far more distressed by his words concerning the difficulty for rich men to be saved (Mk 10.23–27). Jesus then predicts his own death a third time, but the disciples are only terrified and remain in fear (Mk 10.32–34). Finally, the two sons of Zebedee come up with a request to have themselves placed on the right and left hand of his glory. The rest of the disciples are angry, while Jesus admonishes them.

All these episodes fit within the short space between two healings of physical blindness. And each of them in its own way develops the theme of spiritual blindness, from which the disciples are gradually being delivered, in stages, like the blind man in the first healing, who receives his healing in two stages. The miracle of the Transfiguration plays an important role in this process, and so it also fits within this thematic block in Mark (Mk 9.2–7). When he was transfigured before the apostles, Jesus gave them a glimpse of that glory that he has from the Father before the ages (Jn 17.5). In any case, their spiritual eyes were still not completely open, and they understood the glory they were to receive in a self-centered manner—or at least the two sons of Zebedee did (Mk 10.35–36).

Thus Jesus first of all takes the blind man by the hand and leads him out of the city. It is possible that he does this to avoid a public spectacle. The blind could not move around independently without someone to guide them, and so this blind man did not come by himself to Jesus; he was led. But now Jesus takes the role of guide and leads the man to the place where he will perform the miracle. Other than literal significance of this act, it also has a symbolic dimension: Jesus stands before us as the true "guide of the blind" (Rom 2.19), in contrast to those false guides whom Jesus admonishes, and the Apostle Paul after him (Rom 2.17–21).

The healing itself begins with the fact that Jesus spits on the eyes of the blind man. What is the meaning of this action, which is so strange to modern readers? In the Gospels, Jesus uses his saliva three times as a means of healing. The ancients thought that saliva had a certain softening or purifying quality to it, which could allow it to be used as a medicine in certain cases (the practice of licking an unexpected wound is universal and remains to this day). At the same time, saliva used to be understood as a carrier of energy, a substance capable of transferring the qualities of

Healing the Blind Man, El Greco, 16th century

the one to whom it belongs. In this sense, it can have both a positive or a negative effect.

In the Old Testament, any liquids flowing from the body of a human being were considered impure (Lev 15.1–18), and saliva, which was found in an impure place, was considered a carrier of impurity (Lev 15.8). In the New Testament, Jesus radically changed all notions about impurity. Being himself the bearer of purity and holiness, he gives it to others through touch, as well as through saliva, which is charged with his holiness and acts to destroy the power of the demons.[65]

Without getting into an overly detailed discussion of this theme, which has been examined thoroughly in scholarly literature,[66] we will only mention two major points. The first is the fact that in certain cases Jesus used saliva when the situation did not call for medical intervention of any kind. He did not use saliva merely as a substitute for medicine or salve or oil. Secondly, Jesus' use of saliva in this manner has nothing to do with any magical rites or practices widespread during his time.

We also cannot agree with the assertion that this action had merely a symbolic or pedagogical meaning.[67] In our opinion, Jesus periodically used

---

[65]Marcus, *Mark 8–16*, 473–74.

[66]Van der Loos, *The Miracles of Jesus*, 306–11.

[67]This was the opinion found in A. Jeremias, *Babylonisches im Neuen Testament* (Leipzig, 1905), 108.

saliva as one of the means to pass on his own energy, power, and holiness to the one being healed.

Jesus' question, in the majority of ancient manuscripts, is recounted as direct speech: "Dost thou see anything." The literal translation of the blind man's answer sounds like this: "I see men that, like trees, I see them walking" (Βλέπω τοὺς ἀνθρώπους ὅτι ὡς δένδρα ὁρῶ περιπατοῦντας [*Blepō tous anthrōpous hoti hōs dendra horō peripatountas*]). This grammatical construction does not accord with norms of Greek, and it is possible that the author is rendering an Aramaic idiom, the reconstruction of which would be merely hypothetical. But it is also not out of the realm of possibility that the syntax is purposely rendered thus to better give an idea of the confusion of the blind man during the moment when his vision begins to return to him but has not yet fully returned.

After Jesus lays his hands on the man's eyes a second time, his vision returns to him completely. The gradual return of the man's vision is rendered with five terms that follow one after another: ἀναβλέψας (*anablepsas*; "having looked up" or "having once again seen" that is, "having found his vision anew"), βλέπω (*blepō*; "I see"), ὁρῶ (*horō*; "I see"), διέβλεψεν (*dieblepsen*; "he looked" or possibly "be looked before himself" or "he saw clearly"), ἐνέβλεπεν (*eneblepen*; "he saw"). This carefully chosen series of terms having to do with sight underline the extraordinary nature of the event, as well as the fact that vision returned not all at once, but gradually.

Why did Jesus not immediately heal the blind man? Why was it necessary for him to lay hands on him twice, spit in his eyes, and then ask the question? Why did the blind man initially see people walking around like trees, and only begin to see clearly after a second touch? We cannot answer this question completely. But we must exclude any interpretation in which Jesus could not heal the man the first time around and requires a second attempt to finish the job, so to speak. The blind man's inability to see what surrounds him clearly is not lack of power on Jesus' part, but rather, there are subjective factors at play, connected with the unique qualities of the body of the man being healed. Just as in medicine, the body of a sick person sometimes does not initially react to medicine at all—or, by analogy, when someone first wakes up, at first he does not always see clearly—so too in this case, the healed man cannot clearly see the people around him. At first, they look like trees.

The gradual return of the man's vision could be compared with the state of a man who is released into the light after remaining for a long time in darkness and in bondage. Plato masterfully explains this state in his *Republic*:

> Take a man who is released and suddenly compelled to stand up, to turn his neck around, to walk and look up toward the light; and who, moreover, in doing all this is in pain and, because he is dazzled, is unable to make out those things whose shadows he saw before. What do you supposed he'd say if someone were to tell him that before he saw silly nothings, while now, because he is somewhat nearer to what is and more turned toward beings, he sees more correctly; and, in particular, showing him each of the things that pass by, were to compel the man to answer his questions about what they are? Do not you suppose he'd be at a loss and believe that what was seen before is truer than what is now shown? . . . And if he compelled him to look at the light itself, would his eyes hurt and would he flee, turning away to those things that he is able to make out and hold them to be really clearer than what he is being shown? . . . And if someone dragged him away from there by force along the rough, steep, upward way . . . would he be distressed? . . . And when he came to the light, wouldn't he have his eyes full of its beam and be unable to see even one of the things now said to be true? . . . Then I suppose he'd have to get accustomed, if he were going to see what's up above. At first he'd most easily make out the shadows; and after that the phantoms of the human beings and other things in water; and, later, the things themselves.[68]

The end of this account of the healing of the blind man sounds like this in the most authoritative ancient manuscripts: "And he sent him to his house, saying, 'Do not go in to the town'" (Mk 8.26).[69] This, evidently,

---

[68]Plato, *The Republic* 515c–516a. Translation in Plato, *The Republic of Plato*, 2nd ed., trans. Alan Bloom (New York: Basic Books, 1991), 194–95.

[69]*Novum Testamentum Graece*, 25th rev. ed. (Stuttgart: Deutsche Bibelgesellschaft, 1975), 116.

means that the blind man was not from Bethsaida, from where Jesus led him out by the hand. He no longer needed to enter Bethsaida. Now he could, under his own power, walk to his own home.

Healing the Man Blind from Birth in Jerusalem

The next healing to be discussed is described in the Gospel according to John. This Gospel contains the least number of miracles when compared to the other Gospels (only seven), and each of the miracles in put into a specific theological context. The account of the healing itself takes up a small part of chapter 9 (verses 1–7). But the rest of the chapter (verses 8–41) are a continuation of the healing narrative. Thus, the healing itself takes up only one-sixth of the chapter; everything else is theological commentary on the healing.

Some details of the account remind the reader of the episode we just analyzed from Mark:

> And as Jesus passed by, he saw a man which was blind from his birth. And his disciples asked him, saying, "Master, who did sin, this man, or his parents, that he was born blind?" Jesus answered, "Neither hath this man sinned, nor his parents, but that the works of God should be made manifest in him. I must work the works of him that sent me, while it is day; the night cometh, when no man can work. As long as I am in the world, I am the light of the world." When he had thus spoken, he spat on the ground, and made clay of the spittle, and he anointed the eyes of the blind man with the clay, and said unto him, "Go, wash in the pool of Siloam" (which is, by interpretation, "Sent"). He went his way therefore, and washed, and came seeing. (John 9.1–7)

First of all, we must note that this is the only mention of a man blind from birth in any of the Gospels. In other cases, we know no details about the blind men whom Christ heals—were they blind from birth or did they become blind because of some event in their life, and if so, what was it? We can assume that the blind man described by John is the only man blind from birth from all the blind men described in the Gospels. Therefore, this

The Healing of the Man Blind from Birth by Jesus Christ, V. I. Surikov, 1888

healing has special significance, which is reflected in the exalted language of the healed man himself: "Since the world began was it not heard that any man opened the eyes of one that was born blind" (verse 32).

The disciples' question reflects a widely-held assumption in the Jewish tradition of that time: that man's sickness can be a direct punishment for the sins of his parents or other ancestors. This assumption is partially based on Scripture: "I the LORD thy God am a jealous God, visiting the iniquity of the fathers upon the children unto the third and fourth generation of them that hate me" (Ex 20.5; cf. Ex 34.7; Num 14.18). But to correctly understand the meaning of these words, one should examine the context in which they were uttered. They are found in the second commandment of the Law of Moses, which concerned the prohibition against worshiping idols:

> Thou shalt not make unto thee any graven image, or any likeness of any thing that is in heaven above, or that is in the earth beneath, or that is in the water under the earth. Thou shalt not bow down thyself to them, nor serve them, for I the LORD thy God am a jealous God, visiting the iniquity of the fathers upon the children unto the third and fourth generation of them that hate me, and showing mercy unto thousands of them that love me, and keep my commandments. (Exodus 20.4–6)

From this text, it follows that the sins of one generation can be "paid off" by the next generation, just as the blessing of God is often passed on from one generation to another. As often happens in the Old Testament, there is no question here of the personal fate of this or that individual; here the fate of the nation is being discussed (children and fathers in this case are collective nouns referring to different generations).

Individualism, in general, is not characteristic of the biblical view concerning the world and man. A biblical worldview sees man not as an

*Christ and
the Scribes,*
Veronese, 1560

isolated individual, but part of a whole—his family, his lineage, his nation, mankind at large. People are connected to each other by many invisible bonds that also cross over into other generations. Each generation has its own inheritance—both good and bad. It was not by accident that Jesus rebuked his contemporaries, the scribes and Pharisees, for repeating the deeds of their fathers. The logic of these rebukes is sometimes difficult for us moderns to understand, since we were raised to assume that every person is responsible only for himself:

> "Woe unto you, scribes and Pharisees, hypocrites! Because ye build the tombs of the prophets, and garnish the sepulchres of the righteous, and say, 'If we had been in the days of our fathers, we would not have been partakers with them in the blood of the prophets.' Wherefore ye be witnesses unto yourselves, that ye are the children of them which killed the prophets. Fill ye up then the measure of your fathers." (Matthew 23.29–32)

These words clearly reflect the notion that the father's fault is passed to the children. But this only occurs in cases when the children repeat the sins of their fathers. Every new generation, having made the choice to do good, can throw off the burden of responsibility for the evil it received as an inheritance from its precedessors.

The disciples' question about why the man was born blind is fully within the limits of this worldview, which was formed under the influence of Jewish tradition, while also reflecting the universal question of the meaning

Christ's Argument with the Pharisees, Doré, 1860's

of suffering. Sooner or later, every human being asks this question, no matter what his ethnicity or epoch. How is he responsible for man's sickness and suffering, especially when he is born with this or that physical ailment. Many philosophical systems and movements have tried to find an answer to this question.

But Jesus shifts his disciples' attention from the question "Who is at fault?" to "What is to be done about it?" The reality of inequality in the world, including congenital diseases and all other things that by human standards seem unfair, is for Jesus not a reason for philosophical discourse, but rather a call to action. He answers his disciples with brevity. To understand the causes of illness, it is not necessary to find the guilty party; in fact, it is possible there is no guilty party. The disease may be a result of the fact that God has marked a person in a special way, so that he might reveal his works through that person.

In this case, the phrase "the works of God" refers to the healing that Jesus intends to perform. But the fact that the man was born blind is also one of the "works of God." God not only "killeth, and maketh alive; he bringeth down to the grave, and bringeth up. The LORD maketh poor, and maketh rich; he bringeth low, and lifteth up" (1 Sam 2.6–7). It is within his authority to send a man both sickness and release from it. This is exactly what happened with Job, whom God subjected to trials, including serious illness, so that the works of God could be revealed in him in a vivid manner. As we saw, Job understood very well who sent him these diseases, and from whom he should expect healing.

The following words of Jesus also contain a prophecy of his death: "while it is day" indicates the remaining time Jesus had on this earth, while "the night is coming" hint at the time of his suffering and death. We see a prophecy that is similar both in form and content in the Gospel according to Matthew: "Can the children of the bridechamber mourn, as long as the bridegroom is with them? But the days will come, when the bridegroom shall be taken from them, and then shall they fast" (Mt 9.15). In the Gospel according to Luke, Jesus said, "Behold, I cast out demons, and I do cures to day and to morrow, and the third day I shall be perfected" (Lk 13.32). Jesus had a clear understanding that he was given only a short time on this earth, and he constantly hinted and at times spoke openly about it to the apostles.

Jesus used these terms "day" and "night" in other places, especially in cryptic passages that confused the disciples, such as the words he spoke about Lazarus' sickness: "Are there not twelve hours in the day? If any man walk in the day, he stumbleth not, because he seeth the light of this world. But if a man walk in the night, he stumbleth, because there is no light in him" (Jn 11.9–10). Both in Lazarus' case and in the case of the man who was blind from birth, the terms "day" and "night" have the same metaphorical significance. They should be understood in terms of the theology of light that fills the Gospel according to John from beginning to end.

The theme of light is a motif found in all of John's writings, which include the Gospel and his three general epistles. John applies the term "light" to Jesus and to God. The fourth Gospel begins with a series of affirmations concerning the Word of God as light: "In him was life, and the life was the light of men. And the light shineth in darkness; and the darkness comprehended it not . . . That was the true Light, which lighteth every man that cometh into the world" (Jn 1.4–5, 9). Later, in the conversation with Nicodemus, Jesus said, "And this is the condemnation, that light is come into the world, and men loved darkness rather than light, because their deeds were evil" (Jn 3.19). In the Temple of Jerusalem, Jesus said to the people, "I am the light of the world; he that followeth me shall not walk in darkness, but shall have the light of life" (Jn 8.12). Six days before his last Passover, Jesus will say, "Yet a little while is the light with you. Walk while ye have the light, lest darkness come upon you; for he that walketh in darkness knoweth not whither he goeth. While ye have light, believe in the light, that ye may be the children of light. . . . I am come a light into the world, that whosoever believeth on me should not abide in darkness" (Jn 12.35–36, 46).

In his first general epistle, John writes, "This then is the message which we have heard of him, and declare unto you, that God is light, and in him is no darkness at all" (1 Jn 1.5). The last phrase is probably one the "sayings of Jesus" (λόγια Ἰησοῦ, *logia Iēsou*) that were remembered by the disciples and entered the New Testament canon. The form in which John gives this utterance shows that it belongs not to him, but to Jesus himself. The continuation of this same phrase may be a commentary by John: "If we say that we have fellowship with him, and walk in darkness, we lie, and do not the truth" (1 Jn 1.6).

In this world, darkness opposes the light, night opposes the day, evil opposes good, death opposes life, falsehood opposes truth, doubt opposes faith. Jesus is the bearer of light, and his opponents personify darkness. It is in this context that one should understand the healing of the man born blind, which is a powerful confirmation of everything that Jesus said concerning himself. Having announced that he is the light, he then turns to the man blind from birth and gives him light.

The method by which he healed the man born blind partially reminds us of the healing of blind Bartimaeus that Mark describes. There, Jesus spits on the eyes of the blind man, here he spits on the earth and makes "clay with the saliva," that is, a mixture of earth and his saliva. He wipes the eyes of the man with this improvised substance. But the healing does not occur immediately. Jesus sends the blind man to the pool of Siloam, and his vision returns to him there, after he washes in the pool.

"The waters of Shiloah that go softly" are mentioned by the prophet Isaiah (Is 8.6) The pool of Siloam was a reservoir that collected water from the stream of Gihon, found to the south-east of Jerusalem in the valley of Kedron. King Hezekiah commanded that a half-kilometer-long tunnel be dug from the stream to the pool of Siloam. The water of Siloam was used for ceremonial purposes (it was used to wash the altar during the Feast of Booths), as well as for ritual ablutions. It is possible that the water in the pool of Siloam was reputed to be wonderworking, as was the water in the pool of Bethesda, which is mentioned in connection with the healing of the paralytic (Jn 5.2).

Why did Jesus not heal the man immediately, but send him to the pool instead? To answer this question, we have to remember again that Jesus did not always heal people immediately; sometimes, he healed in several stages, and the final healing did not always occur in Jesus' presence (see Lk 17.14). It is possible that he acted thus to prevent the miracle from being widely talked about; it is possible there was some other reason. We can also indicate the typological similarity between the manner of healing the man born blind and the way the prophet Elisha healed Naaman the Syrian, who was also sent to wash in the Jordan, and after washing seven times, the leprosy disappeared (2 Kg 5.10–14).

This event also reflects another important theological theme in the Gospel of John—water as the source of life. This theme, which is especially evident in the first chapters of the fourth Gospel,[70] is most fully developed in the conversation with Nicodemus and the Samaritan woman. In the first conversation, Jesus speaks of the birth from water and the Spirit, that is, of baptism (Jn 3.5). In the second, he uses the symbol of water to develop the theme of eternal life, of which he himself is the source: "Whoever drinketh of the water that I shall give him shall never thirst; but the water that I shall give him shall be in him a well of water springing up into everlasting life" (Jn 4.13–14).

Not by coincidence, the Early Church saw the healing of the man who was blind from birth as a foreshadowing of baptism. Nine frescoes depicting this event survive in the Roman catacombs. This passage was included in the lectionary used to catechize those preparing for baptism.[71]

As with the case of the sole leper out of ten, the formerly blind man returned to give thanks. The words "came back seeing" do not tell us anything about where he went exactly—to Jesus, or to the place where he usually lived. His next meeting with Jesus would become the crowning moment of Christ's argument with the Jews, which the evangelist describes in great detail. Peripheral participants in the dispute include the parents of the man who was born blind, as well as some bystanders who have difficulty even recognizing the one who used to beg for alms in front of all the people:

---

[70]R. H. Lightfoot, *St. John's Gospel: a Commentary* (Oxford: Oxford University Press, 1956), 121.

[71]Brown, *The Gospel according to John (I–XII)*, 380–81.

*Healing the Man
Blind from Birth,*
V. P. Khudoiarov,
1860's

The neighbors therefore, and they which before had seen him that he was blind, said, "Is not this he that sat and begged?" Some said, "This is he"; others said, "He is like him"; but he said, "I am he." Therefore said they unto him, "How were thine eyes opened?" He answered and said, "A man that is called Jesus made clay, and anointed mine eyes, and said unto me, 'Go to the pool of Siloam, and wash.' And I went and washed, and I received sight." Then said they unto him, "Where is he?" He said, "I know not." They brought to the Pharisees him that aforetime was blind. And it was the sabbath day when Jesus made the clay, and opened his eyes. Then again the Pharisees also asked him how he had received his sight. He said unto them, "He put clay upon mine eyes, and I washed, and do see." Therefore said some of the Pharisees, "This man is not of God, because he keepeth not the sabbath day." Others said, "How can a man that is a sinner do such miracles?" And there was a division among them. They say unto the blind man again, "What sayest thou of him, that he hath opened thine eyes?" He said, "He is a prophet." But the Jews did not believe concerning him, that he had been blind, and received his sight, until they called the parents of him that had received his sight. And they asked them, saying, "Is this your son, who ye say was born blind? How then doth he now see?" His parents answered them and said, "We know that this is our son, and that he was born blind, but by what means he now seeth, we know not, or who hath opened his eyes, we know not. He is of age; ask him; he shall speak for himself." These words spoke his parents, because they feared the Jews: for the Jews had agreed already, that if any man did confess that he was Christ, he should be put out of the synagogue. Therefore said his parents, "He is of age; ask him." Then again called they the man that was blind, and said unto him, "Give God the praise; we know that this man is a sinner." He answered and said, "Whether he be a sinner or no, I know not; one thing I know, that, whereas I was blind, now I see." Then said they to him again, "What did he to thee? How opened he thine eyes?" He answered them, "I have told you already, and ye did not hear; wherefore would ye hear it again? Will ye also be his disciples?" Then they reviled him, and said, "Thou art his disciple; but we are Moses' disciples. We know that God spoke unto Moses; as for this fellow, we know not from whence he is." The man answered and said unto them, "Why herein is a marvellous thing, that ye know not from whence he is, and yet he hath opened mine eyes. Now we know that God heareth not sinners; but if any man be a worshipper of God, and doeth his will, him he heareth. Since the world began was it not heard that any man opened the eyes of one that was born blind. If this man were not of God, he could do nothing." They answered and said unto him, "Thou wast altogether born in sins, and dost thou teach us?" And they cast him out. Jesus heard that they had cast him out; and when he had found him, he said unto him, "Dost thou believe on the Son of God?" He answered and said, "Who is he, Lord, that I might believe on him?" And Jesus said unto him, "Thou hast both seen him, and it is he that talketh with thee." And he said, "Lord, I believe." And he worshipped him. (Jn 9.8–38)

This account is divided into five episodes. In the first episode, the formerly blind man speaks with those around him, in the third, his parents speak with the Pharisees. The second and fourth contain polemics with the Pharisees. Finally, in the fifth, he once again meets Jesus. The entire account, except for the third episode—in which the blind man is mentioned, though he takes no active part—is a detailed history of the gradual and step-by-step deliverance of the formerly blind man from spiritual blindness.

At first, when he speaks with his neighbors, he only establishes the fact of his healing, describing how it happened. He does not offer any interpretation to this fact. He describes the one who healed him using the words "The man called Jesus." He does not know this man, and he cannot say where he is.

Then, the blind man finds himself before the Pharisees, and he repeats the entire story of his healing in answer to their questions. They begin to argue amongst themselves—some of them say that this man cannot be from God, because he breaks the Sabbath; others ask how can a sinner perform such miracles? When they ask the formerly blind man what he thinks, he answers briefly and succinctly: "He is a prophet." Here we already see a specific, clearly articulated position. It is still distant from a confession of Jesus as the Son of God, but it no longer resembles what he had said to his neighbors. He formulates this position, clearly understanding that it would be unpopular with his interlocutors.

The next episode is interesting because it shows the reason why the polemic between the blind man and the Pharisees developed further. It also shows us the kind of family he belonged to. Here are those same parents—about whose guilt the disciples speculated— and they completely distance themselves from the events, twice saying that they know nothing, underlining their complete lack of participation in this event.

In the fourth episode, the Pharisees take a firmer position. There are no more arguments among them; they "know" that this man is a sinner. How do they know this? Because he breaks the Sabbath and because he does not look like them, the self-proclaimed disciples of Moses. They urge the formerly blind man to give thanks to God. How? Evidently by admitting publicly that Jesus is a sinner. But he answers, "Whether he be a sinner or no, I know not; one thing I know, that, whereas I was blind, now I see" (Jn 9.25). In this case, the first part of the phrase is most likely a rhetorical device. The words "I know not" sound very different coming from the blind man than from his parents. The accent here is on the second half of the phrase—the formerly blind man announced what to him seems an obvious and incontrovertible fact.

The Pharisees, though they took an intractable position, were still torn apart by doubts and therefore ask the formerly blind man more and more questions. Here, the blind man goes on the offensive—he told them everything already, but they would not listen. What else do they want from him? When he asks them if they want to become Jesus' disciples, it sounds like irritation—he is angry at their spiritual blindness. The Pharisees answer with even more irritation, rebuking the blind man for being a disciple of Jesus. The next answer of the blind man completes the picture. It has never before been recorded that someone opened the eyes of a man blind from birth; a typical sinner could never perform such a miracle. God only hears those who honor him and do his will.

The formerly blind man is only one step away from confessing Jesus to be the Son of God. But he does not make the final step by himself. Jesus himself finds him in the Temple to ask him the most important question, the answer to which would determine the future of this person, his fate in eternity: "Do you believe in the Son of God?" In the Greek text, this phrase is built in such a way that the accent falls on the word "you." Thus the meaning is as follows: they do not believe, but do you? The formerly blind man answers the question with a question, either not understanding the question or wanting to finally make clear who the Son of God was.

Jesus' answer sounds like this in a literal translation: "Thou hast both seen him, and it is he that talketh with thee." The word "have seen" refers to the first meeting. When addressed to the man blind from birth, it has an added meaning—Jesus is the first man Whom you have seen, after your sight was restored. It was he who gave you sight. The phrase "he that talketh with thee" points to the second meeting. Then, finally, the formerly blind person confesses Jesus to be the Lord, and he worships him.

In the grand scheme of Apostle John's theology, the words "I believe, Lord," when accompanied by worship, have only one meaning—an admission of Jesus as God. The Gospel according to John begins with a triumphant affirmation that Jesus is the Word of God, who was God from the beginning, and in the final chapters, he includes Thomas' confession: "My

Lord and my God" (Jn 20.28). Between these two statements of conviction, there are many moments that each in its own way reveal the truth that Jesus is the incarnate God.

The story of the healing of the man blind from birth is one of these moments. It demonstrates a sequential change within a person from spiritual blindness to complete illumination, expressed in the confession of Jesus as the Son of God, Lord and God. This is the confession that offers a key to understanding Jesus' words that begin this account: this man was born blind so that the works of God would be revealed in him.

In answer to Thomas' confession, Jesus said, "Because thou hast seen me, thou hast believed: blessed are they that have not seen, and yet have believed" (Jn 20.29). These words refer to the entire theology of the fourth Gospel, as well as to the account of the healing of the man blind from birth in particular. He was one who did not see, yet he believed. His opponents, on the contrary, did not merely remain in the state of spiritual blindness in which they had begun, but they became even more confirmed in it.

In parallel with the manner in which the formerly blind man is illumined, the Pharisees become more and more intractable in their opposition to Jesus. At first, it seems that they are merely interested in what happened. Then they begin to argue amongst themselves—they divide into those who reject Jesus and those who still wonder. At some point, they announce that they now know that Jesus is a sinner, but at the same time they continue to ask questions about the details of the healing process. Finally, they become completely confirmed in their blindness, announcing that they want to have nothing in common with Jesus, and they even cast out the formerly blind man with the words: "Thou wast altogether born in sins, and dost thou teach us?" All arguments are now pointless, for they have not been able to change the man's opinion. They have nothing left, but to accuse him of sins.

This entire account is a kind of parody of the juridical process. At the same time, it is a rehearsal for the judgment over Jesus. Like the Sanhedrin, the Pharisees gathered to interrogate a witness, but the interrogation is not impartial, and with every new cycle, they become more and more convinced that the man is a sinner (Jn 9.24). His most important sin is announced to the people to be the breaking of the Sabbath:

> That which followed the miraculous healing of the blind man truly reveals the worst and coldest darkness of the human mind and heart, which lies like a dark shadow under the bright light of the Sun, Christ. This is a frightening darkness of a Pharisaical, blind heart and mind. The Pharisees not only were not joyful that a poor blind man who sat near their Temple received his sight, but they even felt offended personally and became angry.

Giving Faith to Thomas,
fresco, 16th century

After all, their Temple had long become a watchtower of the Sabbath, just as their entire faith had transformed into the worship of the goddess named Sabbath. They do not ask the healed man with compassion: "How could you have lived so long in your blindness?" They crudely attack him, interrogating him as though he were a criminal: "How dare you receive your sight on the Sabbath? And how dare he who healed you do this on a Sabbath? This Man is not from God," they said, "because he does not keep the Sabbath." Thus, for them, this is the godly man—the one who spends his Sabbath sleeping, never leaving his room for fear of defiling himself with an extra step, action, or touch. Not the one who gave sight to the man born blind on the Sabbath! And by their moribund logic, the former shows honor to the Sabbath, but not the latter.[72]

We should note that the words "thou wast altogether born in sins" also constitute a kind of thematic arc of its own from the beginning of the account, when the disciples asked Jesus who was at fault that the man was born blind. This parallelism is meant to underline the fact that if the disciples received a complete answer to their question, the Pharisees, on the contrary, learned nothing from this event at all.

[72]Bishop Nikolai (Velimirovich), *Tvoreniya* [Collected works], 1:434–35 (translated by NK).

The Pharisees call themselves the disciples of Moses, and by doing this they set Jesus in opposition to Moses. But Jesus constantly mentions the name of Moses when speaking with the Jews. In one such conversation, he said to them, "Do not think that I will accuse you to the Father: there is one that accuseth you, even Moses, in whom ye trust. For had ye believed Moses, ye would have believed me; for he wrote of me. But if ye believe not his writings, how shall ye believe my words?" (Jn 5.45–47).

Jesus underlined the primacy of his teachings over the Law of Moses. In the Sermon on the Mount, he said, "Think not that I am come to destroy the law, or the prophets; I am not come to destroy, but to fulfil. For verily I say unto you, till heaven and earth pass, one jot or one tittle shall in no wise pass from the law, till all be fulfilled" (Mt 5.17–18). In one his parables, Abraham says to the rich man who is in hell and who asks for help for his brothers: "'They have Moses and the prophets; let them hear them.' And he said, 'Nay, father Abraham, but if one went unto them from the dead, they will repent.' And he said unto him, 'If they hear not Moses and the prophets, neither will they be persuaded, though one rose from the dead'" (Lk 16.29–31).

According to Jesus, the Pharisees' dependence on Moses has absolutely no validity. They are not his lawful descendants, because they have only assimilated the external aspects of the Law—the internal content of the Old Covenant is hidden from them. If they had been true followers of Moses and the prophets, they would have believed in Jesus. He returns to this theme again and again in his teachings and parables.

The account of the healing of the man born blind ends with Jesus' dialogue with the Pharisees, which summarizes the theological content of the entire account, which is one of the longest single episodes in the entire New Testament:

> And Jesus said, "For judgment I am come into this world, that they which see not might see, and that they which see might be made blind." And some of the Pharisees which were with him heard these words, and said unto him, "Are we blind also?" Jesus said unto them, "If ye were

blind, ye should have no sin; but now ye say, 'We see'; therefore your sin remaineth." (Jn 9.39–41)

Moses Destroying the Tablets of the Covenant, Rembrandt, 1659

Here Jesus uncovers not only the reason for the conflict between himself and the Jews, but he also considers the consequences of this conflict for them. Concerning himself, Jesus said, "I am the way, the truth, and the life." To the Jews, he said, "'And ye shall know the truth, and the truth shall make you free.' They answered him, 'We are Abraham's seed, and were never in bondage to any man; how sayest thou, "Ye shall be made free?"'" (Jn 8.32–33). They are sure that they know the truth and they are freed; they need no deliverer. The action of his grace does not spread to them, but not because he does not want this to happen, but because they do not want it: "Christ came to open the eyes and hearts of those who seek the truth. But those who are already sure that they abide in truth, that they know everything, though they do not know Christ, and so have nothing to learn from him—these remain in darkness. Their eyes and hearts are closed to God."[73]

The Son of God is shown in the Gospels not as a gentle healer who gives out good things to everyone in turn, and everyone receives them with joy. His coming into the world caused a fierce division between faith and disbelief, between light and darkness, between good and evil. Those who are on the side of good admit him first to be a prophet, then a messenger of God, and finally Lord and God. As for those who are on the side of evil, his preaching and miracles have only a negative effect—they become ever more confirmed in their stubbornness and lack of faith.

This theme constantly appears in various forms during Jesus' ministry. He said to his disciples, "Think not that I am come to send peace on earth; I came not to send peace, but a sword" (Mt 10.34). "Suppose ye that I am come to give peace on earth? I tell you, nay; but rather division. For from henceforth there shall be five in one house divided, three against two,

---

[73] Alexander Shargunov, *Evangelie dnya* [The Gospel of the day]. 1:129.

Christt before
Pilate,
M. Munkácsy,
1881

and two against three. The father shall be divided against the son, and the
son against the father; the mother against the daughter, and the daughter
against the mother; the mother-in-law against her daughter-in-law, and
the daughter-in-law against her mother-in-law" (Lk 12.51–53).

The history of the healing of the man born blind is only one of the many
examples confirming the truth of Jesus' words. In this event, the formerly
blind man and his parents find themselves on opposite sides of the divide.
They try to remain neutral, but there is no neutrality in matters of faith.
If a man find himself faced with a choice between the light and darkness,
between good and evil, between faith and disbelief, he cannot remain on
the sidelines. Like it or not, he will have to take a firm position one way
or the other.

Pontius Pilate did not want to rule officially on the guilt or innocence
of Jesus; he tried to distance himself from the decision, having washed his
hands. But this distance was only illusory; in fact, he took upon himself the
full responsibility for carrying out the sentence of death.

Jesus gives every person the right to choose. He never forces anyone
to act in a way he does not wish to. But as the bearer of absolute good and
absolute truth, he irrupts into this world where good is intermixed with
evil, and light with darkness, and he cleaves them in two by the sword of his
word. This word is "quick, and powerful, and sharper than any two-edged

sword, piercing even to the dividing asunder of soul and spirit, and of the joints and marrow, and is a discerner of the thoughts and intents of the heart" (Heb 4.12).

Jesus' miracles also become two-edged swords, for they act on people in the same way his word does. They bring some to faith, while others are confirmed in their lack of faith. Some are illumined by them, others, on the contrary, reveal their own blindness.

By coming into the world, the Son of God did not stop the activity of evil in the world and in people. The last chapter of the Revelation includes these words: "He that is unjust, let him be unjust still: and he which is filthy, let him be filthy still; and he that is righteous, let him be righteous still; and he that is holy, let him be holy still" (Rev 22.11). This, however, is not a call for everyone to act as he wills—that the good continue to be good, while the evil become worse in their evil. This is simply an admission of the fact that God is able to help people overcome evil within themselves only when they accept it. He can heal them from their sicknesses only if they desire it. He can open their spiritual eyes, but only if they cooperate with their own healing.

The Healing of Blind Bartimeus

The last healing of blindness mentioned in the Gospels occurs at the very end of Jesus' public ministry. It is written down in the three Synoptic Gospels. Here is Mark's version:

> And they came to Jericho; and as he went out of Jericho with his disciples and a great number of people, blind Bartimaeus, the son of Timaeus, sat by the highway side begging. And when he heard that it was Jesus of Nazareth, he began to cry out, and say, "Jesus, thou son of David, have mercy on me." And many charged him that he should hold his peace, but he cried the more a great deal, "Thou son of David, have mercy on me." And Jesus stood still, and commanded him to be called. And they call the blind man, saying unto him, "Be of good comfort, rise; he calleth thee." And he, casting away his garment, rose, and came to Jesus. And Jesus answered and said unto him, "What wilt thou that I

The Monastery
of the
Temptation near
Jericho

should do unto thee?" The blind man said unto him, "Lord, that I might receive my sight." And Jesus said unto him, "Go thy way; thy faith hath made thee whole." And immediately he received his sight, and followed Jesus in the way. (Mk 10.46–52)

In Luke, the blind man is nameless: "a certain blind man." He heard that the people were passing by him in a multitude, and he asked what it meant. "And they told him, 'Jesus of Nazareth passeth by.'" At this point, the man exclaimed, "Jesus, thou son of David, have mercy on me!" The rest of the account is almost exactly the same as in Mark. At the end, Luke adds that after the healing, "All the people, when they saw it, gave praise unto God" (Lk 18.35–43).

Matthew's version differs from Mark's and Luke's. In Matthew, there are two blind men—they both hear that Jesus is walking; they both begin to cry out for help; he stops, calls them both, and asks what they want; they answer that they wish to be healed. Then Jesus, having mercy on them, touches their eyes, and immediately they receive their sight and follow him (Mt 20.29–34).

Before us is another example of the so-called contradictions that some people like to point to when casting doubt on the authenticity of the Gospel narratives. If Mark and Luke wrote about a single blind man, while the parallel text in Matthew speaks of two, which is true?

To answer this question, we must remember, first of all, that the Gospel accounts are all based on eyewitness accounts. An eyewitness account is a distinct genre that has its own particularities. An eyewitness account always contains a certain degree of subjectivity; the person who is remembering tends to recall an event in his own particular way. If some time has passed between the event and the eyewitness account, then certain details may have fallen away from memory or have even changed. Recall is most often tinged with so-called mistakes of memory, and this is a standard reality of all eyewitness accounts. In addition, if a single event is remembered by several different people, then there will always be as many different versions of that event.

Second, if we have two eyewitness accounts of the same event, the presence of differences in details is most often not an indication that one is telling the truth, while the other is lying. It is simply a matter of each person remembering the event from his own perspective, in his own way. Usually the major aspects of the event are remembered in common by all, but with differences in the details.

Finally, secondary factors may influence eyewitness accounts, especially if some time has passed since the event in question. A single event in one's memory can become intertwined with another; one memory might develop details that were taken from another memory entirely. All this is clearly demonstrable, even in well-documented psychological studies, but they in no way lessen the veracity of an eye-witness account.

In this case, we have two accounts that are virtually identical—Mark's and Luke's. As for Matthew, in his account of the Gospel, in addition to this event, there is, another healing of blindness, and in that case, there are two blind men (Mt 9.27–31). That event occurred in the beginning of Christ's ministry; it took place on the way back from Jairus' house; and the blind men also exclaimed, "Have mercy on us, Jesus, thou son of David!" The healing also occurred as a result of Jesus touching their eyes. It is possible that both these events became conflated in Matthew's memory, and the second could have had certain details of the first added to it. For example, one blind man could have become two, and the touch of the eyes could have been added (it is missing in Luke and Mark).

Healing the Blind, miniature, Egypt, 17th century

Blessed Augustine gives a different interpretation. According to him, Jesus did heal two blind men, but Mark and Luke only mention one of them. Bartimeus was well known in the city for some reason; if he had not been, Mark would not have given his name or the name of his father. Some sort of calamity occurred with him that was commonly known:

Consequently there can be little doubt that this Bartimaeus, the son of Timaeus, had fallen from some position of great prosperity, and was now regarded as an object of the most notorious and the most remarkable wretchedness, because, in addition to being blind, he had also to sit begging. And this is also the reason, then, why Mark has chosen to mention only the one whose restoration to sight acquired for the miracle a fame as widespread as was the notoriety which the man's misfortune itself had gained.[74]

In other words, Mark and Luke only mention one blind man, because he was well known, while the other was not.

In any case, the second man remains a mere shadow, lacking all concrete characteristics, while Bartimeus comes across in Mark as someone who has all the characteristics of a historical character. We know both his name and the name of his father ("son of Timaeus" is a Greek translation of the name "Bartimaeus"). As a side note, we will mention that the name of the father of the blind man is neither Hebrew nor Aramaic, but Greek, and a rather common Greek name at that (Plato has an entire dialogue titled *Timaeus*).

We see how the blind man throws off his outer clothing—a detail that lends credence to the account. Why did he throw it off? Probably because it was preventing him from walking quickly to Jesus. At the same time, this detail also has a symbolic meaning. It is doubtful that a poor blind man who asked for alms on the side of the rode had much more than his outer

[74]Augustine, *On the Harmony of the Gospels* 2.65.125 (NPNF[1] 6:159).

The Healing of the Blind Man in Jericho, Egbert Psalter, 10th century

garments. It may have been all he owned on this earth. And yet he cast it off lightly, without even thinking about it, in order to follow Christ.

The crowd surrounding Jesus at first tried to force Bartimeus to be silent, but that only made him cry out louder. Jesus stopped and commanded them to call him. Here the people surrounding Bartimeus change their tune and say, "Be of good comfort, rise, he calleth" (Θάρσει, ἔγειρε, φωνεῖ σε; *Tharsei, egeire, phōnei se* [Mk 10.49]). The crowd's attitude toward Bartimeus changed as soon as Jesus stopped and paid attention to him. The word θάρσει (*tharsei*), which is sometimes translated as "fear not," literally means "be bold." This word is often used by Jesus when speaking to those he has healed (see Mt 9.2, 22). Here the crowd speaks the words.

In Mark's account, the blind man calls Jesus "Rabboni," in Luke "Lord." The request itself ("that I may receive my sight") shows us that he deserves the restoration of something that was lost—the verb ἀναβλέπω (*anablepō*) means "to see again." Thus Bartimeus was not blind from birth. In Mark, Jesus answers the blind man thus: "Go thy way; thy faith hath made thee whole." In Luke, he says, "Receive thy sight: thy faith hath saved thee" (or "made thee well"—σέσωκέν σε; *sesōken se* [Lk 18.42]). These words become the thematic center of the account—these same words are uttered by Jesus in several other accounts of healing.

Both in Mark and in Luke, the account ends with the blind man following Jesus (in Matthew, both blind men followed him). This important detail means that the blind man became, if not a disciple of Christ, then at least a follower. As a follower, he is a model for emulation.[75] As in other afore-mentioned cases of healing the blind, the man receives healing of physical blindness as well as spiritual blindness, which is necessary to believe in Christ as the Son of God.

The theme of spiritual blindness, which is revealed fully in the accounts we have examined, continues to be relevant in all times. At the end of the nineteenth century, St John of Kronstadt wrote the following:

> Speaking of the blind men in the Gospels and of their miraculous heal-ings by Jesus Christ because of their faith, I am carried by my thoughts to the blind men of a different kind, that is, the blind who are afflicted with spiritual blindness, which is much more dangerous, more disas-trous than physical blindness. First of all, this is the blindness of the ignorant or the completely overeducated people of our time, who do not see the hand of God, which created all and directs all, in the wise arrangement of the world. Instead, they consider it, as they do them-selves, entirely the product of chance, and they make their life into a kind of game or entertainment, and when this toy for whatever rea-son ceases to amuse them, they break it without pity, that is, they lay hands on themselves or they perform a series of evil acts on others and laugh over the misfortunes of mankind. . . . Reading the news every day concerning various events, we encounter murders, suicides, drunken-ness, debauchery, theft of public money, arson in cities and villages. Summarizing all this, we are forced to make the following conclusion: these people have turned away from God, from faith, from the Church of God. They are blind, they wander in darkness and do not know what their destination is or what will be the end of it all. . . . Where is the light of reason and conscience in these people? How have they lost the light of faith?[76]

---

[75]Concerning Bartimaeus as a "model follower" of Jesus, see J. F. Williams, *Other Follow-ers of Jesus: Minor Characters as Major Figures in Mark's Gospel* (Sheffield: Sheffield Academic Press, 1994), 152–66.

[76]St John of Kronstadt, *Homily on the Seventh Sunday after Pentecost* (translated by NK).

Jesus asked a similar question when he spoke of his second coming: "When the Son of man cometh, shall he find faith on the earth?" (Lk 18.8) Faith is that gift of God that opens man's spiritual eyes, allowing him to make a choice in favor of God, goodness, and light every moment of his life. But this gift can only be freely chosen; it cannot be forced on anyone, just as one cannot force healing on a blind person who believes he can see.

8. The Deaf Hear

In the Gospels, there are frequent mentions of Jesus healing the deaf (Mt 11.5; 15.30–31; Mk 7.37; Lk 7.22), but only one of them is described in any detail. There is also an account of Jesus healing a spirit of dumbness and deafness in a demoniac, which we will examine later in the chapter on exorcisms.

Here we will examine the account of Jesus healing a deaf man. It is recounted only in the Gospel according to Mark:

> And again, departing from the coasts of Tyre and Sidon, he came unto the sea of Galilee, through the midst of the coasts of Decapolis. And they bring unto him one that was deaf, and had an impediment in his speech; and they beseech him to put his hand upon him. And he took him aside from the multitude, and put his fingers into his ears, and he spit, and touched his tongue; and looking up to heaven, he sighed, and saith unto him, "Ephphatha," that is, "Be opened." And straightway his ears were opened, and the string of his tongue was loosed, and he spake plain. And he charged them that they should tell no man; but the more he charged them, so much the more a great deal they published it; and were beyond measure astonished, saying, "He hath done all things well; he maketh both the deaf to hear, and the dumb to speak." (Mk 7.31–37)

The Oldest
Extant Mosaic
Map of
Decapolis,
6th century

Decapolis is a region to the west of the Sea of Galilee—ten cities in a single region that was influenced by Greco-Roman culture. In the times of Jesus, there were many pagans living there, and it is quite likely that those who brought him the deaf man were pagan. Jesus came to this place not by accident—the direct route from Tyre and Sidon to the Sea of Galilee does not pass through Decapolis. Jesus visited the region because his preaching was intended to reach pagan lands as well.

The phrase "deaf, and had an impediment in his speech" could mean a congenital deafness, which then became the reason for the person's inability to speak normally. It could also mean that he was deaf and thus incapable of any speech whatsoever. Finally, it could mean that he was a deafmute, capable of only making indistinct sounds.

They brought the sick man to Jesus in the hope that he would lay hands on him. Instead of this, Jesus performed a whole series of actions. He took the man to the side, placed his fingers in the man's ears, spit, touched his tongue, looked up at heaven, sighed, and uttered the word: "open," which is rendered by Mark in the original Aramaic along with a Greek translation. Touching the organ that required healing is a means Jesus frequently used. We have already spoken at length of saliva (in this account, it is not clear where Jesus spit—on the earth or onto the afflicted organ).

Jesus also looked up to heaven before feeding the five thousand (Mt 14.19, etc.). Jesus' prayerful address to the Father (this is what looking up to

*The Healing of
the Deaf and
Dumb Man,*
fresco, 14th
century

heaven means) does not mean that Jesus as the Son of God lacks the power to perform the miracle without help. Rather, he saw his actions as the continuation of the Father's actions (Jn 5.17). Moreover, he insisted that "the Son can do nothing of himself, but what he seeth the Father do; for what things soever he doeth, these also doeth the Son likewise" (Jn 5.19–20).

To see what the Father does, the Son did not need to look up—here we are speaking of an inner, spiritual vision. In the person of Jesus, however, in his actions and gestures, both the spiritual and the physical, both the divine and the human were closely intertwined and mutually related. When he prayed, he turned his gaze to heaven, and he called his Father the heavenly Father.

The term "sighed" is sometimes interpreted in the sense that toward the end of his earthly ministry, Jesus was tired of performing miracles, tired of the crowds, and that he performed them as though forcing himself against an inner reticence. Some people find confirmation of this interpretation in the words that accompanied the healing of the demoniac youth: "O faithless and perverse generation, how long shall I be with you? How long shall I suffer you?" (Mt 17.17) But neither these words (which will be discussed at length later) nor Jesus' sigh are manifestations of exhaustion, sadness, or irritation. The word "sighed" should not be separated from the fact that he looked up into heaven—both of these actions are part of a whole. They both refer to a prayerful sigh, a sigh that accompanies the sacred communion of Jesus with his Father.[77]

Whom did Jesus forbid to speak about the miracle? Evidently, both the healed man and those who brought him. As in other such cases, however, the participants in the miracle did not obey Jesus' command.

The words that end the account—"He hath done all things well"—show us how the common people referred to Jesus. This sharply contrasts with the way the Pharisees and the scribes related to him, since every new miracle was taken as a new reason to accuse him. These words, it is possible, are an allusion to the creation account in Genesis, where every stage of creation ends with the words: "And God saw that it was good." Everything that God does is very good (Gen 1.31), and Jesus, who is continuing the work of God's creation on earth (Jn 5.17), "hath done all things well; he maketh both the deaf to hear, and the dumb to speak" (Mk 7.37).

Certain details of this account indicate its similarity to the healing of the blind man in Bethsaida, which is described in the same Gospel. In that case, Jesus also took the person aside, away from the crowd, spit, and touched the afflicted organ. After healing, he also commanded the healed man not to speak of the miracle.

---

[77]Van der Loos, *The Miracles of Jesus*, 327.

9. Healing the Woman Who Had a Spirit of Infirmity and the Man Sick of the Dropsy

The Woman Who with a Spirit of Infirmity

The Gospel according to Luke includes two cases of healing not found in the other Gospels. These two healings are similar in their outward context. Both miracles occurred on a Sabbath day, in both of them a "leader" plays an important role (in the first, he is a leader of the synagogue, in the second, a leader of the Pharisees). Both miracles offer Jesus the opportunity to speak concerning the Sabbath with a practical example from everyday life. We do not know the specifics of the place in either account. We know only that both of them occurred on the way to Jerusalem, as the other accounts told by Luke in the ten chapters between Jesus' desire to go to Jerusalem (Lk 9.51) and the triumphant entry into the city (Lk 19.35–44).

The first miracle occurs in the synagogue before many gathered people, in the presence of the leader of the synagogue:

> And he was teaching in one of the synagogues on the sabbath. And, behold, there was a woman which had a spirit of infirmity eighteen years, and was bowed together, and could in no wise lift up herself. And when Jesus saw her, he called her to him, and said unto her, "Woman, thou art loosed from thine infirmity." And he laid his hands on her, and immediately she was made straight, and glorified God. And the ruler of the synagogue answered with indignation, because Jesus had healed on the sabbath day, and said unto the people, "There are six days in which men ought to work; in them therefore come and be healed, and not on the sabbath day." The Lord then answered him, and said, "Thou hypocrite, doth not each one of you on the sabbath loose his ox or his ass from the stall, and lead him away to watering? And ought not this

woman, being a daughter of Abraham, whom Satan hath bound, lo, these eighteen years, be loosed from this bond on the sabbath day?" And when he had said these things, all his adversaries were ashamed; and all the people rejoiced for all the glorious things that were done by him. (Lk 13.10–17)

First of all, it is worth noting that, as in other cases, Jesus came to the synagogue not for the express purpose of healing someone, thereby transgressing the Sabbath by design, but in order to preach there. Custom allowed any man in the synagogue to read a passage from Scripture and to comment on it, and Jesus did exactly that. The word "teaching" indicates the lesson that followed the reading of the Scriptures, as occurred in the synagogue of Nazareth at the very beginning of his ministry (Lk 4.21).

The woman's sickness is described as "a spirit of infirmity" (πνεῦμα ἀσθενείας; *pneuma astheneias*). This expression has caused certain commentators to say that the woman was possessed, making the healing an exorcism.[78] But the expression "spirit of infirmity," in the opinion of some scholars, does not necessarily mean a demon possessed her and became the cause of her illness; rather, it could indicate the evil influence of the demons.[79] The word "spirit" is probably used here in a metaphorical sense, while the phrase "spirit of infirmity" is a typical Aramaism, similar to the expression "spirit of bondage" in the Apostle Paul (Rom 8.15).

The woman's sickness could have been an especially serious form of scoliosis or kyphosis, when the backbone is bent to a significant angle away from normal. We do not know the woman's age, but it is doubtful that this is a case of kyphosis, which is usually relegated to old age, and occurs as a result of the natural deterioration of the spinal disks. More likely, this woman was middle-aged, and her sickness was a serious anomaly.

As in certain other cases (Lk 7.13; Jn 5.6; 9.6; 11.11), Jesus performed the miracle without any request. He is the one to call the woman to himself. He does not ask her if she wants to be healed or not, or if she believes in his

---

[78]D. Lee, *Luke's Stories of Jesus: Theological Reading of the Gospel Narrative and the Legacy of Hans Frei* (Sheffield: Sheffield Academic Press, 1999), 324–25.

[79]M-J. Lagrange, *L'Evangile selon Saint Luc* (Paris: Victor LeCoffre, 1921), 382.

Healing the Woman with the Spirit of Infirmity, fresco, 14th century

ability to heal her or not. He simply announces that she is freed from her infirmity and lays hands on her; the woman immediately stands upright.

Jesus often uses the laying on of hands during his healing; Mark mentions this, for example, when speaking of how Jesus could not perform many miracles in his own country, "save that he laid his hands on a few sick folk, and healed them" (Mk 6.5). Jesus also lays hands on the blind man in Bethsaida (Mk 8.23). Jesus blesses the children by the laying on of hands (Mk 10.16; Mt 19.13–15). Luke, in his turn, tells of how "all they that had any sick with divers diseases brought them unto him; and he laid his hands on every one of them, and healed them" (Lk 4.40).

The rest of the account reminds us of the many dialogues Jesus had with the Pharisees concerning the keeping of the Sabbath. The difference in this case is the fact that the leader of the synagogue does not speak to Jesus directly. Instead, he speaks to all the people, intending for Jesus to hear his words as well: "There are six days in which men ought to work; in them therefore come and be healed, and not on the sabbath day" (Lk 13.14). He speaks as though there are receiving hours for healing. Before his very eyes, a healing occurred, the natural reaction to which should be wonder and gratitude to God. But the fate of the woman interests him little. He wants the miracles to occur according to a schedule, lest the order of services at the synagogue be disturbed by unusual actions of strange healers, who should probably move their activity to a different place:

There are six days in which you should work. . . . This is spoken by an angry son of the darkness. It is as though the demon who had left the woman had entered into him! This is self-love talking, accompanied by its constant companions: envy and wrath. Christ heals . . . and frees a human life from Satanic bonds, and he counts the days! Christ casts out an evil spirit from a sick woman, but he gets angry that the demon was cast out the wrong door! Christ opens the heavens for people and reveals the Living God, but he gets angry that the Lord opened heaven in the morning, not in the evening![80]

Jesus reacts sharply: in the presence of all gathered he turns directly to the leader of the synagogue and calls him a hypocrite. The woman he calls a daughter of Abraham, underlining that she belongs to the chosen nation of God, while he describes the cause of the sickness with the words "whom Satan has bound," indicating that the devil is the cause of the illness. The words "daughter of Abraham" are especially appropriate in the synagogue, where only the sons and daughters of Abraham—the chosen people of God—gathered. The woman bent over double did not end up there by accident—she came there to pray, that is, to meet God. And in the person of Jesus, she met the incarnate God, who freed her from her prolonged and heavy infirmity. Her reaction to the miracle was a reaction of a truly faithful person—having straightened out, she glorified God with her next breath.

We have already spoken of the fact that in the Old Testament we find the assumption that diseases were punishments that came directly from God. But in the Book of Job, the one who instigated all the calamities that strike the righteous man, including serious disease, is not God, but Satan. He did receive initial permission from God to afflict the flesh and bones of Job, but the action itself is described thus: "So went Satan forth from the presence of the LORD, and smote Job with sore boils from the sole of his foot unto his crown" (Job 2.7).

Byzantine theology later formulated a principle according to which the devil acts in the world only within the limits that are established by

[80]Bishop Nikolai (Velimirovich), *Tvoreniya* [Collected works], 2:424–26 (translated by DNK).

God. According to St John of Damascus (8th century), the devil and his demons "have no power or
strength against any one except what God in his
dispensation has conceded to them. . . . But when
God has made the concession they do prevail."[81]
In other words, God allows the devil to act within
the parameters that he has established through his
providence. Since God is not the source of evil, he
cannot be the source of sickness. But God allows
sickness within certain parameters.

Here it is appropriate to remember what Jesus
said to the disciples about the reasons why the man
who was blind from birth was born blind: "Neither
hath this man sinned, nor his parents; but that the
works of God should be made manifest in him" (Jn

St John of Damascus,
miniature, 11th century

9.3). In this case, the works of God revealed themselves in the woman bent
over double, and she stood straight thanks to the miracle.

The mention of Satan in this episode indicates that the evangelist
understood this as a victory in Jesus' war against Satan, which is reflected
on every page of every Gospel. Jesus' coming out in public to preach was
preceded by his personal encounter with Satan in the wilderness. There
he rejected the temptations, thereby declaring war on the devil. Many
episodes in the Gospels, including healings and exorcisms, are victories of
good over evil, God over Satan. The climax of this war is the story of the
passion, while the final and decisive victory is Jesus' resurrection.

In Christian exegetical tradition, the healing of the woman bent over
double is often interpreted allegorically, as an indication of man's deliverance from difficulties or sinful passions:

> You must also understand these miracles to refer to the inner man. The
> soul is bent over in infirmity whenever it inclines to earthly thoughts
> alone and imagines nothing that is heavenly and divine. It can truly
> be said that this soul has been infirm for eighteen years. For when a

[81]John of Damascus, *Exposition of the Orthodox Faith* 2.4 (NPNF[2] 9:20).

man is feeble in keeping the commandments of the divine law, which
are ten in number, and is weak in his hope of the eighth age, the age to
come, it can be said that he has been bent over for ten and eight years.
Is not that man indeed *bent over* who is attached to the earth, and who
always sins in disregard of the commandments, and who does not look
for the age to come?[82]

Thus, the woman bent over double, healed by the Savior, symbolizes
our own soul, twisted over with sins and by the devil. And what would
have happened to our souls if Christ did not come to earth to save the
race of man from the violence of the devil and the passions; what would
have happened if he did not save us constantly, breaking the bonds of
sin? We would all be like this twisted woman . . . we would slither on
the earth, looking only at the ground and would never look up to the
heavenly Father, and we would have no heavenly thought, desires, or
strivings, but would drown in earthly cares and labors.[83]

The Man Sick with the Dropsy

The healing of the man sick with dropsy is another example of healing on
the Sabbath. It occurred not in the synagogue, but in a house, perhaps after
Jesus returned from the service in the synagogue.

> And it came to pass, as he went into the house of one of the chief
> Pharisees to eat bread on the sabbath day, that they watched him. And,
> behold, there was a certain man before him which had the dropsy.
> And Jesus answering spoke unto the lawyers and Pharisees, saying, "Is
> it lawful to heal on the sabbath day?" And they held their peace. And
> he took him, and healed him, and let him go, and answered them, say-
> ing, "Which of you shall have an ass or an ox fallen into a pit, and will
> not straightway pull him out on the sabbath day?" And they could not
> answer him again to these things. (Lk 14.1–6)

[82]Blessed Theophylact of Ochrid, *The Explanation of the Holy Gospel According to Luke*,
trans. Christopher Stade (House Springs, MO: Chrysostom Press, 1997), 170.

[83]John of Kronstadt, *Pouchenie v nedelyu dvadtsat' sed'muyu po Pyatidesyatnitse* [Sermon
on Sunday of the twentieth week after Pentecost], 662 (translated by NK).

Healing the Man with Dropsy, Tetraevangelion, Athos, Iveron, 1300

Let us first note the similarity between this event and the healing of the man with the withered arm in Matthew. There, the Pharisees ask Jesus whether it is permissible to heal on the Sabbath, while he answers their question with a question: "What man shall there be among you, that shall have one sheep, and if it fall into a pit on the sabbath day, will he not lay hold on it, and lift it out?" (Mt 12.10–11). Here we see a somewhat different situation: Jesus himself asks the question about healing on the Sabbath. The answer becomes the healing itself, which is accompanied by a similar real-life example with slight variations. We also find an analogous expression in the story of the healing of the woman bent over double, which shows that Jesus used the same argument and similar images in similar cases.

According to Luke, Jesus frequently accepted invitations from the Pharisees to dine with them. In one case, "one of the Pharisees desired him that he would eat with him. And he went into the Pharisee's house, and sat down to meat" (Lk 7.36). In another, "a certain Pharisee besought him to dine with him; and he went in, and sat down to meat" (Lk 11.37). Despite the tense conflict between him and the Pharisees, Jesus did not avoid fellowship with certain members of that class. Moreover, even while dining in their homes, Jesus was not afraid of calling them hypocrites, unwise, whitewashed tombs, and other insulting names, accusing them of washing only the exterior, while leaving the interior "full of ravening and wickedness" (Lk 11.39).

Dropsy is a disease where liquid accumulates in the tissues and cavities under the skin. In fact, the illness is not so much a disease as a symptom that occurs as a result of various afflictions of the internal organs (such as the kidneys), as a result of which the person's body becomes puffy, making breathing difficult and making the body sweat profusely. Dropsy could afflict either the entire body or only certain parts of the body (such as the chest or the hands and legs). According to Josephus, Herod was afflicted with a series of serious illnesses, one of which was dropsy: "an aquaeous and transparent liquor also settled itself about his feet; and a like matter afflicted him at the bottom of his belly."[84]

Jesus healed the sick man, but not simply by touching his body: in this case, the participle ἐπιλαβόμενος (epilabomenos) is used, which could be translated as "having embraced" (from ἐπιλαμβάνω (epilambanō), to take, to grab, to embrace).

As he healed the man, Jesus did not utter any words. He then turns to the Pharisees immediately after the miracle, or immediately after the man's departure from the house (the word "then" after "he let him go" allows for both interpretations). Silence is the answer to his question about the permissibility of healing on the Sabbath. Neither did they have any retort concerning saving an animal from falling into a pit on the Sabbath.

---

[84]Josephus, *The Antiquities of the Jews* 17.6.5, in *The Works of Josephus, Complete and Unabridged*, tr. William Whiston (Peabody, MA: Hendrickson Publishers, 1987), 27–542, at 462.

Chapter 4

CASTING OUT DEMONS

Casting demons out of the possessed is a constantly repeated motif in the Synoptic Gospels. Unlike the Gospel according to John, which has no instances of exorcism at all, the Synoptics dedicate a considerable amount of attention to it. Several cases of exorcism are noted only in passing (Mt 4.24; Mk 1.34; 3.11; 16.9; Lk 4.41; 6.18; 7.21), while others are described in detail. When considering all the Synoptic accounts taken together, one must admit that exorcisms are one of the most important kinds of miracles that Jesus performed throughout his earthly ministry.

1. Exorcism and Demonology

In the New Testament, the power to cast out demons was ascribed not only to Jesus himself, but even to his name. This power he gave to his apostles (Mt 10.1, 8; Mk 6.7; 16.17; Lk 10.17–20). Even during Jesus' life, some people who did not belong to the company of his disciples were able to cast demons out in his name (Mk 9.38, Lk 9.49). After his death "certain of the vagabond Jews, exorcists, took upon them to call over them which had evil spirits the name of the Lord Jesus" (Acts 19.13).

This reference to Jewish exorcists indicates that exorcism was a common phenomenon in Judea during the times of Jesus. Josephus writes of "that skill which expels demons, which is a science useful and sanative to

Francis Borgia Casts Demons out of a Dying Man, Goya, 1788

men." He also mentions that "this method of cure is of great force unto this day," and describes exorcism as "incantations . . . by which distempers are alleviated . . . by which they drive away demons, so that they never return."[1]

Exorcism is a phenomenon well known in many different religious traditions. The practice of exorcism in different religions presupposes faith in the existence of evil spirits (demons) and in their ability to enter into a person's body. Exorcism is the act of casting out the demon from a possessed person, which is accomplished, as a rule, by uttering certain formulaic phrases. In many religions and cultures, exorcism is closely connected with magic and necromancy.

The Old Testament does not contain a firmly established demonology. But there is a sense of the possibility of a demon entering into a person and forcing him to evil actions. We see this in First Samuel, which recounts that the Spirit of the Lord left King Saul, and an evil spirit from the Lord disturbed him. Saul's servants recommend that he call a person who can play on the harp well, so that he might calm the king with his playing. David was the one to play this role in Saul's court: "And it came to pass, when the evil spirit from God was upon Saul, that David took an harp, and played with his hand; so Saul was refreshed, and was well, and the evil spirit departed from him" (1 Sam 16.23).

---

[1]Josephus, *The Antiquities of the Jews* 8.2.5, in *The Works of Josephus*, 214.

Saul Listens to David's Music, Josefson, 19th century

Is this comparison between the spirit that tormented Saul and the demons who are cast out by Jesus justified? As we see, in this case, the spirit that attacks Saul is called an evil spirit from the Lord or even merely a spirit from God. We can assume that it was a special spirit, sent by God, who inhabited Saul: "And it came to pass on the morrow, that the evil spirit from God came upon Saul, and he prophesied in the midst of the house; and David played with his hand, as at other times; and there was a javelin in Saul's hand. And Saul cast the javelin; for he said, 'I will smite David even to the wall with it.' And David avoided out of his presence twice" (1 Sam 18.10–11). Even though the word used here is "prophesied," it comes from the Hebrew *hitnabbe*, which can be translated "possessed." Nevertheless, the context of this account allows us to make the conclusion that the action of the spirit was demonic.

Stories involving the appearance of evil spirits inside people or their casting out are usually examined from two different, even diametrically opposed, points of view.

On the one hand, we have the Christian teaching concerning demons as fallen angels who were cast out of heaven following their leader, Satan. Initially created as good creatures, they disobeyed God (or, according to another interpretation, became proud), rose up against God, fell away from him, and became his enemies. Their most important goal is a constant antagonism to the good will of God. They are the bearer of absolute evil, completely lacking in the ability or the possibility of doing good. They act on people in different ways; they tempt them, turn them away from God, frighten them, incline them to sin, force them to commit insane actions. They can act on them both from without and from within, which includes inspiring a person to have sinful thoughts.

An evil spirit, according to the Christian worldview, can enter into a person and become his alter ego. Further, more than one demon may enter a person at a time. This idea is founded on such testimonies as the account of casting out the legion of demons from the Gadarene demoniac (Mk 5.9). It is also said that Jesus cast seven demons out of Mary Magdalene (Mk 16.9). The number seven also plays a role in the following words of Jesus, which cast light on the activity of demons with reference to mankind:

> When the unclean spirit is gone out of a man, he walketh through dry places, seeking rest, and findeth none. Then he saith, "I will return into my house from whence I came out"; and when he is come, he findeth it empty, swept, and garnished. Then goeth he, and taketh with himself seven other spirits more wicked than himself, and they enter in and dwell there; and the last state of that man is worse than the first. Even so shall it be also unto this wicked generation. (Mt 12.43–45)

The Gospel presents us with a world that is filled with demons that live among people and inside them, who are capable of entering them and of being cast out of them, who wander about wild places, seeking respite, but not finding it. They enter into dialogue with Jesus, make requests of him, and he sometimes even listens to their requests (for example, he allows the legion to enter a herd of swine). The reality of the existence of demons was never doubted—not by the evangelists, not by later commentators on the Gospels, not by the writers of Christian liturgical texts.[2]

On the other hand, the Gospels' accounts of casting out demons are frequently examined through the prism of rationalism and skepticism, which rejects the existence of demons based on the idea that their existence

---

[2]Cf. Klaus Berger, *Identity and Experience in the New Testament* (Minneapolis: Fortress Press, 2003), 45.

is incompatible with a faith based on reason. This is characteristic not only of the rationalists of the nineteenth century; the major existentialist philosopher Karl Jaspers concluded that belief in demons is incompatible with what he called "philosophical faith."[3]

In such a perspective, there are only two possible ways of interpreting Gospel accounts of exorcisms—either to completely reject these accounts as invented and untrue, or to try to ascribe some kind of rational explanation to this phenomenon. Most of the time, such explanations are sought in the realm of psychology or psychotherapy.

The Temptation of Christ,
Juan de Flandes,
16th century

In fact, many characteristics of possession as described in the Gospels are similar to the symptoms of various psychological or neurological illnesses, such as hysteria, paranoia, manic behavior, psychosis, epilepsy, and schizophrenia.

For example, in the Gospel according to Matthew, the father of the demoniac youth describes the symptoms of the boy's sickness thus: "he is lunatic, and sore vexed; for ofttimes he falleth into the fire, and oft into the water" (Mt 17.15). Some modern translations of the Gospel use the word "epileptic" or "moonstruck," which could be interpreted as a heavy form of somnambulism, when the actions of a sick man become aggressive during sleepwalking. In Mark's parallel account, other symptoms are indicated, which sound more like epilepsy proper: "Master, I have brought unto thee my son, which hath a dumb spirit; and wheresoever he taketh him, he teareth him; and he foameth, and gnasheth with his teeth, and pineth away" (Mk 9.17–18).

Concerning the Gadarene demoniac, Mark says, "he had been often bound with fetters and chains, and the chains had been plucked asunder by him, and the fetters broken in pieces; neither could any man tame him. And always, night and day, he was in the mountains, and in the tombs,

[3]Cf. Karl Jaspers, *Philosophical Faith and Revelation* (New York: Harper & Row, 1967).

Healing the Possessed Youth,
Raphael, 1519–20.

crying, and cutting himself with stones" (Mk 5.4–5). In these actions, one can see the symptoms of hysteria, psychosis, and manic disorder.

The demons often begin to speak with Jesus in exorcism accounts. This is described as though it is not the possessed man who speaks, but the demon inside him speaking through his mouth. This can be interpreted as multiple personality disorder, as described in the medical literature. The most important symptom of such a disorder is the existence of at least two personality or "ego-states" within the same person, so that the surrounding people might think that two personalities exist in a single body. Each of these personalities, who could differ in age, sex, emotion, worldview, or reactions, takes turns controlling the sick person. When the sick person is dominated by one personality, he cannot even remember what happened while he was dominated by the other. Research done on this illness in the 1980's has shown that in 99% of such cases, the "second personality" of the person associates itself with demons.[4]

One can characterize psychotherapy and demonology as two contiguous areas of study. This is very well known to any priest who has experience working with people who suffer from psychological disorders. Even a very experienced pastor cannot always distinguish psychological illness, which requires medical intervention, from possession, which could require the help of an experienced exorcist. Moreover, any mistake in this area is fraught with irreparable risk. Turning to an exorcist in cases when a person is mentally ill could worsen the illness considerably, even making it untreatable.

In our time, even the term "exorcist" is rarely found in the practice of Christian churches. In the ancient Church, the term ἐξορκιστής (*exorkistēs*; literally "one who invokes") referred to lower clergy whose duties included

[4]Haraldur Erlendsson, "Multiple Personality Disorder: Demons and Angels or Archetypal Aspects of the Inner Self." https://www.academia.edu/3065960/Multiple_Personality_Disorder_-_Demons_and_Angels_or_Archetypal_aspects_of_the_inner_self.

Healing the Gadarene Demoniac, Madgeburg ivories, 962–68

reading certain prayers over the possessed. In later times, the order of exorcists was practically eliminated, though the practice of reading prayers over demoniacs persisted (though in a rare, even marginal fashion). But even in our time, the casting out of demons from a possessed person is still practiced in certain communities, belonging to various confessions.

The author of this book had the opportunity to be in the Pskov Caves Monastery in the early 80's, where the famous spiritual father Adrian (Ulianov) practiced exorcisms. The possessed used to flock to him in great numbers from all over the Soviet Union. Their behavior was very reminiscent of the demoniacs described in the Synoptic Gospels; they fell to the ground, had fits, foamed at the mouth. A woman sometimes spoke or yelled in a male voice, making it seem like someone else was talking through her. This behavior became especially pronounced at the moment when Father Adrian appeared: they would become unpredictable or aggressive, screaming violently, even attacking Father Adrian physically.

Healing the Demoniac, fresco from the church of St Mary Magdalene in Magdala, 19th century

Modern man rarely sees such scenes. And so many begin to assume that possession either does not exist or is a phenomenon of the deep past, that is, they either ascribe the vast multitude of demoniacs in the Gospels to the imagination of the evangelists or to the specifics of a different cultural reality, within which Jesus lived and acted. The possession described in the Gospels is most often accepted in our times as a socio-cultural phenomenon—that is, in Jesus' time, people sincerely believed that they were surrounded by evil spirits, and so they assumed that various psychological disorders were actually the manifestation of evil powers.

In the Church, however, the persistent evidence of this phenomenon is not subject to doubt, which is made obvious by the continuing examples of exorcisms performed in our times. Or, more accurately, we maintain that same socio-cultural interpretation of this phenomenon that existed during Jesus' time and was lost in modern secular society.

On the other hand, Jaspers was not idly raising a red flag in the twentieth century concerning the rebirth of demonology. When we were discussing the miracle as a religious phenomenon in the beginning of this book, we mentioned that our time is characterized by a sudden rise in demand for various faith healers and psychics, an unhealthy interest in horoscopes, palm readings, and other superstitions. Popular culture is obsessed with the demonic, especially in films, where paranormal phenomena—which from a religious point of view are nothing other than demonic in nature—have become commonplace.

The major opponent of this obsession with the demonic and the occult in our current social reality is, as strange it may sound, not a rationalist worldview, atheism, or agnosticism, but the Church. For centuries, the Church has battled superstitions, warning people against them exactly because it sees in them an arena for the action of demonic forces, which present an actual threat not only to the spiritual life of a person, but to his mental state.

For the Church, as for Jesus, the existence of the devil in the world is just as obvious and indubitable as the existence of the soul in man. Moreover, the Church (in contrast to popular culture) not only does not seek to frighten people with the devil and demons, but on the contrary, calls us not to fear them at all. According to the Roman Christian writer of the third century named Lactantius,

> They [the demons] do indeed injure, but those only by whom they are feared, whom the powerful and lofty hand of God does not protect, who are uninitiated in the mystery of truth. But they fear the righteous, that is, the worshippers of God.[5]

We find this view expressed in the exorcism that immediately precedes baptism in the Orthodox Church. The one who is preparing for baptism must reject "Satan, all his works, all his angels, and his service, and all his pride," then he must blow on the devil and spit on him. This rite, which now often elicits either confusion or a smile and is often dismissed as a relic of the past, has a profound symbolic meaning—it shows us that the one who has accepted baptism has declared war on the devil, but at the same time he demonstrates his disdain of the devil, his conviction that the devil is powerless before the power that the believer receives directly from Christ.

Father Alexander Shmemann, when commenting on this rite, puts an accent on pride as a sickness by which the devil infects people, who often do not even realize who the source of that infection is:

> And the essence of the demonic is always *pride, pompa diaboli.* The truth about "modern man" is that whether a law-abiding conformist or a rebellious non-conformist, he is first of all a being full of pride, shaped by pride, worshiping pride and placing pride at the very top of his values.[6]

[5]Lactantius, *The Divine Institutes* 2.16 (ANF 7: 64–65).
[6]Alexander Schmemann, *Of Water and the Spirit: A Liturgical Study of Baptism* (Crestwood, NY: St Vladimir's Seminary Press, 1974), 29–30.

We should also note that in the rite of catechism, there are two invocations pronounced by the priest to cast out demons. These invocations are extremely ancient. They were written no later than the eighth century, and they reflect the practices of the Early Church. In the second of these exorcisms, there is a direct reference to one of Jesus' exorcisms:

> I charge you, most crafty, impure, vile, loathsome, and alien spirit, by the might of Jesus Christ, who has all power, both in heaven and on earth, who said to the deaf and dumb demon, "Come out of the man, and in nowise enter a second time into him"; depart! Acknowledge the futility of your might, which has not power even over swine.[7]

Reading these prayers over every person who approaches baptism, including babies, shows us that according to the faith of the Ancient Church, the impure spirit lives not only in the so-called demoniacs or the possessed. In any person who does not have Christ within himself there lives a "futile might" that is cast out by the power of God. This point of view does not come directly from the Evangelists' accounts of the casting out of demons; nevertheless, it is connected with them directly. In the baptismal experience of the Early Church, these accounts came alive every time a new member was accepted into the Church. He had to pass through a rite that reminded him and all present of the events described in the Gospels.

2. "What Have We To Do with You, Jesus of Nazareth?"

In the Gospel according to Mark, there is a long series of miracles that fill the majority of the first ten chapters. It begins with an account of Jesus healing

---

[7]Service of Baptism, Second Exorcism (available online: https://www.oca.org/files/PDF/Music/Baptism/baptism-service.pdf).

a demoniac. The placement of this account shows that Mark attributed special significance to the aspect of Jesus' service that is reflected in it:

> And they went into Capernaum; and straightway on the sabbath day he entered into the synagogue, and taught. And they were astonished at his doctrine: for he taught them as one that had authority, and not as the scribes. And there was in their synagogue a man with an unclean spirit; and he cried out, saying, "Let us alone; what have we to do with thee, thou Jesus of Nazareth? Art thou come to destroy us? I know thee who thou art, the Holy One of God."
>
> And Jesus rebuked him, saying, "Hold thy peace, and come out of him." And when the unclean spirit had torn him, and cried with a loud voice, he came out of him. And they were all amazed, insomuch that they questioned among themselves, saying, "What thing is this? What new doctrine is this? For with authority commandeth he even the unclean spirits, and they do obey him." And immediately his fame spread abroad throughout all the region round about Galilee. (Mk 1.21–28)

This same account is told in almost the same words by Luke, where it is also the first miracle performed by Jesus after his return from the desert (Lk 4.31–37). In both Gospels, the connection between this episode and the temptation in the desert is evident. There, Jesus rejected the temptation of the devil, thereby declaring war against the devil. Here, he takes the offensive in this war, which the Apostle Paul describes as a war "against the wiles of the devil. For we wrestle not against flesh and blood, but against principalities, against powers, against the rulers of the darkness of this world, against spiritual wickedness in high places" (Eph 6.11–12).

One of these spirits of wickedness, who had entered into a human being, stood before Jesus in the synagogue at Capernaum. In Mark's account, the demoniac is called ἄνθρωπος ἐν πνεύματι ἀκαθάρτου (*anthrōpos en pneumati akathartō*; literally "a man in an unclean spirit"). Luke uses a different expression: ἄνθρωπος ἔχων πνεῦμα δαιμονίου ἀκαθάρτῳ (*anthrōpos echōn pneuma daimoniou akathartou*; "a man, which had a spirit of an unclean demon") (Lk 4.33).

Healing the Demoniac in Capernaum, Les Tres Riches Heures du Duc de Berry, 1416

The framing device for this episode is the public preaching of Jesus. The account begins with Jesus entering the synagogue and teaching; all were amazed at his teaching, because he taught them not like the scribes, but "as one having authority." The account ends with the wonder of those who witnessed the miracle and a question that reads as follows in the most authoritative manuscripts: "What is this new teaching with authority? He commands the unclean spirits, and they listen to him!"[8] Both in the beginning and the end of the account, the term "teaching" (διδαχή; *didachē*) and "authority" (ἐξουσία; *exousia*) are used. However, if in the first case the term refers specifically to Jesus' teaching, in the second, both refer to the manifestation of power over the unclean spirits.

Later in his account, Mark will recount that when Jesus was in the Temple of Jerusalem the chief priests and elders of the people approached him with the question: "By what authority doest thou these things? And who gave thee this authority to do these things?" (Mk 11.28) Two other Synoptics have the same questions (Mt 21.23; Lk 20:2). In all three accounts, Jesus does not give a direct answer. But in Mark, the answer is obvious from the beginning—the authority that Jesus received comes directly from God. This authority is manifested both in how he speaks and what he does. Evidently, the evangelist does not divide the two aspects of Jesus' activity—His teaching is accompanied by miracles, which, in their turn, confirm the truth of his teaching.

The evangelist does not give specifics about the moment when the demon begins speaking with Jesus; did this occur after Jesus finished his teaching, or did the scream of the demon interrupt him? The latter seems more likely. At the same time, it is obvious that the demon did not reveal himself immediately upon Jesus' arrival in the synagogue; Jesus taught for some period of time, the people listened, and the demon remained silent.

[8] *Novum Testamentum Graece*, 86.

The words of the demon reveal him to be a creature with a certain amount of knowledge that, at least temporarily, is hidden from people. Even after Jesus became universally known, people were divided in their opinions about him. Some saw in him a resurrected prophet (either John the Baptist or one of the ancient prophets such as Elijah or Jeremiah [Mt 16.14; Mk 8.28; Lk 9.19]). In this account, the people are amazed at Jesus' teaching; they clearly do not know who he is; they may not even know his name. The demon, on the contrary, calls him by name and knows that Jesus of Nazareth is the Holy One of God.

In other examples from the Gospels, the demons also call Jesus by name, using the expression "Son of God" (Mt 8.29; Lk 4.41) and "Son of the Most High God" (Mk 5.7; Lk 8.28). Mark makes a point to indicate that "unclean spirits, when they saw him, fell down before him, and cried, saying, 'Thou art the Son of God.' And he straitly charged them that they should not make him known" (Mk 3.11–12). John Chrysostom mentions, "[while] the multitudes called him man, the demons came proclaiming his Godhead."[9] The demons, according to the Gospel, know Jesus' "secret," which at that time was hidden from most people.[10]

In Christian tradition, there is an established assumption that the demons believe in God. Apostle James writes, "Thou believest that there is one God; thou doest well: the demons also believe, and tremble" (Jas 2.19). But their faith is not salvific, and neither is the knowledge that they possess. According to St John of Damascus, the demons sometimes know more than people. However, if angels receive their knowledge through supernatural means from God, the demons acquire it by their own means:

Of the future both the angels of God and the demons are alike ignorant; yet they make predictions. God reveals the future to the angels and commands them to prophesy, and so what they say comes to pass. But the demons also make predictions, sometimes because they see what is happening at a distance, and sometimes merely making guesses;

[9]John Chrysostom, *Homilies on Matthew*, Homily 28.2 (NPNF[1] 10:191).
[10]Van der Loos, *The Miracles of Jesus*, 363.

*Healing Two
Demoniacs,*
fresco, 16th
century

hence much that they say is false and they should not be believed, even
although they do often, in the way we have said, tell what is true.[11]

In this scene, the demon speaks of himself as though a part of a large
group: "What have we to do with thee?" . . . Art thou come to destroy
us?" He speaks as a representative of a legion of demons that have been
disturbed by the presence of the Son of God. Jesus came to defeat "all the
power of the enemy" (Lk 10.19), that is, the entire host of the evil spirits,
with Satan at their head. Jesus' mission is to free people from their authority. Every concrete example of exorcism is but a battle in the war that he
wages against evil in all its manifestations.

Why does the demon announce himself, instead of remaining silent?
Why does this happen here and in other cases when it would seem to serve
the demons' benefit to remain inside the person in whom they had settled?
One possible explanation is that they experienced a kind of "fatal attrac-
tion" to him.[12] Jesus is attractive both to mankind and to the demons. But
if an encounter between man and Christ becomes healing and salvific, the

[11]John of Damascus, *An Exact Exposition of the Orthodox Faith* 2.4 (NPNF[2] 9:20).
[12]Joel Marcus, *Mark 1–8: A New Translation with Introduction and Commentary* (New
York: Doubleday, 2000), 192.

opposite is true for the demons—it always leads to their defeat. Like flies or moths who are fatally attracted to fire, the demons approach Jesus of their own initiative only to be destroyed by him.

Another explanation: the demons have no power to stop themselves when they are near Jesus, since the power inherent to him forces them to reveal themselves against their own will. According to St John Chrysostom, the demons admitted Jesus to be the Son of God only when they were being beaten and forced to do so. They would never do this by their own will.[13] According to Augustine, the devil speaks against his own will, being forced amid pain.[14]

This explanation comes from a consideration of the preaching and ministry of Christ at large. In the Gospel, he is one who did not merely come to do good to people, but also to render evil powerless and defeat it. Moreover, he does not defeat abstract evil, but wages concrete war against demons who have entered into people. In the same way, the good he brings is not abstract, but fully concrete—it is always addressed to a specific person, whether he is a publican, a sinner, a sick man, or a demoniac.

Jesus usually healed sick people in answer to a direct request. With demoniacs, however, the situation was slightly different—the demoniac was not able to ask for healing, because in the moment that he found himself before Jesus, his alter ego would predominate—that is, the demon inhabiting his body. It is always the demon that begins to speak with Jesus after completely subsuming the personality of the demoniac into his own.[15] Jesus frees the man's personality from the demon who enslaved him, thanks to a short commanding formula: "Hold thy peace, and come out of him." Jesus speaks of the possessed man in the third person, addressing the alter ego directly.

The impure spirit immediately reacts to the command. At the same time, the body of the man who is being freed from the demon also reacts. According to Mark, when the impure spirit came out of the man, he "had

---

[13]John Chrysostom, *Homilies on 1 Corinthians*, Homily 29.3 (NPNF¹ 12:170).

[14]Augustine, *Ten Homilies on the First Epistle of St John*, Homily 10.1 (NPNF¹ 7:520).

[15]Adof Deissmann, *Licht vom Osten: Das Neue Testament und die neuentdeckten Texte der Hellenistisch-Römischen Welt* (London: Forgotten Books [repr. ed.], 2017), 113.

torn him, and cried with a loud voice." According to Luke, "when the demon had thrown him in the midst, he came out of him, and hurt him not" (Lk 4.35).

The evangelist does not mention the further fate of the healed man. We do not know if the demon abandoned him forever or returned into him later. We have already offered Jesus' words concerning the evil spirit who goes "through dry places, seeking rest, and findeth none." If he finds his previous home "empty, swept, and garnished. Then goeth he, and taketh with himself seven other spirits more wicked than himself, and they enter in and dwell there; and the last state of that man is worse than the first. Even so shall it be also unto this wicked generation" (Mt 12.44–45).

These words indicate the possibility of repeated possession, even after exorcism. In what circumstances can such an event occur? If the healed man does not begin to live a virtuous life, but remains in sin:

> The possessed, says he, when delivered from that infirmity, should they be at all remiss, draw upon themselves their delusion more grievous than ever. . . . For when a man, being once delivered from his ills, fails to be corrected, he will suffer far worse than before. Yea, therefore he said, he finds no rest, to indicate, that positively and of necessity such a one will be overtaken by the ambush of the demons. Since surely by these two things he ought to have been sobered, by his former sufferings, and by his deliverance; or rather a third thing also is added, the threat of having still worse to endure. But yet by none of these were they made better.[16]

A demon who had once been cast out of a man can return and enter the person once again. This occurs when the sinner, who had repented and was forgiven by God, returns once again to his old sin. It shows that both sickness and possession can return, sometimes in an even worse form, if the person continues to sin after his healing.

We have already spoken about the connection between sickness and sin. Is there a connection between sin and possession? The evangelists do not indicate the circumstances or reasons for the possession in any of the

[16]John Chrysostom, *Homilies on Matthew*, Homily 43.4 (NPNF[1] 10:275–76).

exorcisms in the Gospel. Neither does Jesus speak about this topic in his preaching. However, he explains under what circumstances a demon can return into a person from whom he was cast out. He speaks about this metaphorically, in the form of a parable, but the meaning of the parable is clear enough, especially when we compare it with the words that he spoke to the former paralytic.

According to the Christian understanding, a demon cannot enter a person by the demon's own will without any kind of fault on that person's part. As a rule, the demon enters the inner house of the man, that is his soul, only if a person has opened some window or door for the demon. The path by which a demon enters into a person is a constantly repeated, intentional sin. Magic, necromancy, fortune-telling, and other superstitions also have an inherent danger, because with their help, a person may enter into direct contact with the demonic world.

As he cast out the impure spirit, Jesus completely freed the man from the demon's authority. Returning the man into his original identity, Jesus restores his personality in its former wholeness. But the fate of the healed man depends a great deal on his own actions. His deliverance from the demon occurred without his direct will, because that will was completely subjugated by the devil. But to protect his house against a second invasion of demonic powers, he will need faith and sobriety, according to the words of Apostle Peter:

> Be sober, be vigilant; because your adversary the devil walks about like a roaring lion, seeking whom he may devour. Resist him, steadfast in the faith, knowing that the same sufferings are experienced by your brotherhood in the world. (1 Pet 5.8–9)

3. "My Name is Legion"

The account of the exorcism of a legion of demons occurs in two different versions—in Mark, whom Luke follows almost exactly (Lk 8.26–39), and in Matthew (Mt 8.28–34). Mark's account, as is often the case, is much more detailed than Matthew's:

> And they came over unto the other side of the sea, into the country of the Gadarenes. And when he was come out of the ship, immediately there met him out of the tombs a man with an unclean spirit, who had his dwelling among the tombs; and no man could bind him, no, not with chains, because he had been often bound with fetters and chains, and the chains had been plucked asunder by him, and the fetters broken in pieces, neither could any man tame him. And always, night and day, he was in the mountains, and in the tombs, crying, and cutting himself with stones. But when he saw Jesus afar off, he ran and worshipped him, and cried with a loud voice, and said, "What have I to do with thee, Jesus, thou Son of the most high God? I adjure thee by God, that thou torment me not." (For he said unto him, "Come out of the man, thou unclean spirit.") And he asked him, "What is thy name?" And he answered, saying, "My name is Legion, for we are many." And he besought him much that he would not send them away out of the country. Now there was there nigh unto the mountains a great herd of swine feeding. And all the demons besought him, saying, "Send us into the swine, that we may enter into them." And forthwith Jesus gave them leave. And the unclean spirits went out, and entered into the swine, and the herd ran violently down a steep place into the sea (they were about two thousand), and were choked in the sea.
>
> And they that fed the swine fled, and told it in the city, and in the country. And they went out to see what it was that was done. And they come to Jesus, and see him that was possessed with the devil, and had the legion, sitting, and clothed, and in his right mind; and they were

afraid. And they that saw it told them how it befell to him that was possessed with the demons, and also concerning the swine. And they began to pray him to depart out of their coasts.

And when he was come into the ship, he that had been possessed with the demons prayed him that he might be with him. Howbeit Jesus suffered him not, but saith unto him, "Go home to thy friends, and tell them what great things the Lord hath done for thee, and hath had compassion on thee." And he departed, and began to publish in Decapolis what great things Jesus had done for him; and all men did marvel. (Mk 5.1–20)

Matthew's version omits many details. In Matthew's account, the place is called the country of the Gadarenes, while Mark and Luke speak of the country of the Gergesenes. But in a series of ancient manuscripts of the second and third Gospels, the place is called the country of the "Gerasenes."[17] The three different names come about as a result of three different cities that are close to one another. Gerasa (today's Jerash in Jordan) is far from the Sea of Galilee, where the pigs throw themselves after the demons enter into them. Gadara (toady's Umm Qais in Jordan) is rather close to the sea, and its region reaches the shores. Closest to the sea, built right on its shores, was Gergesa (which is called Kursi, in Israel). All these cities are part of the region known as Decapolis.

In Matthew, the demons' words are given as follows: "What have we to do with thee, Jesus, thou Son of God? Art thou come hither to torment us before the time?" (Mt 8.29). These words witness to the fact that the demons can foresee their final fate and admit the limitation of the time in which they will be able to act on humanity. They understood the Son of God's entry into the world as an early irruption of the power of God, into the world where they had, up to that point, won a certain amount of space and time for themselves.

The main difference between Mark and Matthew's versions is that Matthew speaks of two extremely violent demoniacs, while Mark and

---

[17]*Novum Testamentum Greace*, 95, 169.

Healing the
Gadarene
Demoniac,
mosaic, 12th
century

Luke speak only of one. We have already seen a similar "doubling" in the account of the blind man of Jericho.

There is no definitive explanation for this doubling. Augustine's argument in both cases is the same:

> Moreover, with respect to the circumstance that Matthew states that there were two men who were afflicted with the legion of devils which received permission to go into the swine, where as Mark and Luke instance only a single individual, we may suppose that one of these parties was a person of some kind of superior notability and repute, whose case was particularly lamented by that district, and for whose deliverance there was special anxiety.[18]

In this case, however, the argument sounds less convincing than in the case with blind Bartimeus. Augustine has a different interpretation that is more convincing, in which he argues that doubling of the demoniacs is somehow connected with the multiplicity of demons.

St John Chrysostom, like Augustine, believes that there were two demoniacs, not one:

> And though Luke and those who follow him say that it was one person, but this evangelist two, this does not exhibit any discrepancy at all. I

---

[18]Augustine, *On the Harmony of the Gospels* 2.24.56 (NPNF[1] 6:130).

Healing the Gadarene Demoniacs, miniature, 12th century

grant if they had said, there was only one, and no other, they would appear to disagree with Matthew; but if that spoke of the one, this of the two, the statement comes not of disagreement, but of a different manner of narration. That is, I for my part think, Luke singled out the fiercest one of them for his narrative, wherefore also in more tragical wise does he report their miserable case; as, for instance, that bursting his bonds and chains he used to wander about the wilderness. And Mark says that he also cut himself with the stones.[19]

It is possible that Matthew, when telling the story of the blind men of Jericho and the Gadarene demoniacs, used a different source or oral tradition than Luke or Mark.

Let us examine the version according to Mark. His account begins with Jesus' coming into the country of the Gergesenes and ends with the inhabitants of that country asking him to leave their country. Moreover, the demons ask that they not be sent out of that land. The mention of "country" (χώρα, *chōra*), in which the action takes place, and its limits, is possibly connected with the fact that Decapolis, which included Gadara and Gerasa both, was inhabited with pagans and was taken by the Jews to be a region of intense demonic presence. One should not forget that in the understanding of ancient Hebrews, pagan gods were nothing other

---

[19]John Chrysostom, *Homilies on Matthew,* Homily 28.2 (NPNF[1] 10:191).

than demons. In the Septuagint, the word for "idols" in Psalm 95 is actually rendered as "demons": "the gods of the nations are demons."

Mark describes the possessed man with the same words as in the first account of possession with the man "in an impure spirit" (ἄνθρωπος ἐν πνεύματι ἀκαθάρτῳ; *anthrōpos en pneumati akathartō*). If in the first case, however, the possessed man was more or less a member of human society, who could come into the synagogue and take part in the gatherings, in this case we have a situation where the demoniac is a complete pariah living among the tombs, that is, in caves that were used for burial. His interaction with people is limited only to their attempts to bind him with chains, but he always tore them apart, manifesting inhuman power (which was one of the activities of the demons possessing him).

Moreover, the demoniac in Capernaum was a Jew, while in this case the demoniac was most likely a pagan. This supposition is founded not only on the fact that Decapolis was inhabited primarily with pagans, but because the possessed man used the expression "Son of the Most High God." As a rule, "the Most High God" was expression used by pagans to indicate the God of Israel.[20] In the Acts of the Apostles, the pagan servant who was possessed with a spirit of prophecy called Paul and his fellow travelers the servants of the Most High God (Acts 16.17).

Living in the mountains, the possessed man had never before encountered Jesus and could not have known his name. But like the demoniac in Capernaum, he calls Jesus by name. More than that, he himself runs to Jesus and falls before him onto his knees—the word "worshipped" (προσεκύνησεν; *prosekynēsen*) has exactly that meaning in Mark. Luke, in a parallel passage, uses the verb "fell down" (προσέπεσεν; *prosepesen*), that is "fell at his feet." In this case, both uttering Jesus' name and bowing down before him are presented as actions of the demonic alter ego of the demoniac. It is the demon, attracted to Jesus by an intractable power, who runs to him and falls at his feet.

Here we cannot fail to remember that in the desert, the devil demanded that Jesus worship him (Mt 4.9). Jesus rejected the temptation. Now the

---

[20]D. E. Nineham, *The Gospel of Saint Mark (New Testament Commentary)* (New York: Penguin Books, 1964), 153.

devil, in the person of the demoniac, runs to Jesus and himself falls at his feet.

The casting out of the demon does not occur immediately, as it was with the case of the demoniac in Capernaum. Jesus commands the demon to leave the man, but the demon does not immediately come out. Why? Evidently, this is because there were many demons. "Legion" describes a subdivision of the Roman army that consisted of four or five thousand soldiers. In this case, the word "legion" is used figuratively—it indicates that there was a large number of demons inside a single man, probably similar to the total number of pigs who grazed there (around two thousand).

The most curious episode in this account is the possession of a flock of pigs by the same legion of demons. Some contemporary commentators see elements of comedic parody in this account, while they see a combination of religiosity and impudence in the demons' request to be allowed enter into the pigs.[21]

Ancient commentators, however, saw nothing grotesque or parodic about this episode. According to them, Jesus willingly accepted the seemingly absurd request of the demons. Chrysostom, for example, believed that Jesus allows the demons to enter the swine for three reasons: 1) to demonstrate to all people the flagrance of the evil being done to them; 2) to show that without his permission, the demons could not touch even a pig; 3) to make known that the demons would have done even worse things to them than to the pigs, if the providence of God had not protected every person, including the demoniac.[22]

Let us remember that swine, in Jewish tradition, were considered impure animals. The Law of Moses forbade the Jews from eating pork (Lev 11.7; Deut. 14.8). Keeping swine, consequently, was considered an unworthy, even godless, occupation. In Luke, the legion of demons beg Jesus "not [to] command them to go out into the deep" (Lk 8.31). The usual abode of the demons is the abyss, to which they have no desire to return. Evidently, their ability to remain on earth is only temporary, and whenever they lose

[21]Marcus, *Mark 1–8*, 350.
[22]John Chrysostom, *Homilies on Matthew*, Homily 28 (NPNF[1] 10:192).

God Gives Satan Permission to Test Job, France, 14th century

their earthly "home," they find no rest (Mt 12.43–45). They have no desire to return to the abyss.

The dialogue between Jesus and the legion of demons is part of the dramatic clash between God and the devil that constantly reveals itself in the pages of the Bible. This dialogue proceeds like a trade negotiation. The Book of Job describes an analogous negotiation: "the sons of God came to present themselves before the LORD, and Satan came also among them to present himself before the LORD" (Job 2.1). Thus, from the very beginning of the story, Satan pretends to be one of the sons of God. Then God asks him a series of questions: "From whence comest thou? Hast thou considered my servant Job?" (Job 2.2–3) Then Satan haggles with God, though it is clear that God begins the negotiation. Upon Satan's request, God allows the devil to touch everything that Job owned—in a single day, Job lost all his children and all his money. This was not the end of the negotiation. Satan offered God to test Job through sickness, and God gives Job's body to the hands of Satan.

The book of Job speaks of the interaction between God and Satan in the language of parable. But in the parabolic types we see two important theological affirmations: 1) Satan has direct access to God and has personal interaction with him; 2) Satan can act only within the limits that he can negotiate for himself from God. These two theological truths dominate in this account of the Synoptics. Here the demons also have personal contact with Jesus, they haggle with him, receive from him an answer to their request, and then act within the limits of that negotiation.

The following questions are often asked about the exorcism of the Gergesene demoniacs: Why did Jesus act so cruelly to animals? Why did he not think of the loss incurred by their owners? But neither of these questions has anything to do with the content of the story as told by the evangelists with a concrete symbolic and theological purpose.[23] The purpose of

[23]Cf. J. A. Fitzmyer, *The Gospel according to Luke (I-XI)* (New York: Doubleday and Co., 1981), 734.

the account is to show Jesus' authority over the demons and the saving act he performs for a person who is possessed by them. In this story, there are three main characters: Jesus, the possessed man, and the legion of demons, which in this account is always presented as a collective person. The pigs play no significant role—they interest the evangelists only insofar as they illustrate the power of the demons who inhabit a single man.

As for the fate of the possessed man, the evangelists are not indifferent at all. In contrast to the demoniac of Capernaum, who disappears immediately after the healing, the Gergesene demoniac remains a player in the story even after he was healed. The inhabitants of that country come to Jesus and find the former demoniac sitting at his feet, "sitting, and clothed, and in his right mind" (Mk 5.15). This should have inspired wonder or admiration in them, but they were much more concerned with the fate of the swine than the fate of a man. Earthly prosperity was most important to them, the fate of their fellow human being was not important in the least.

In addition to inflicting a crippling blow to their livelihood, Jesus also seriously terrified them with a sign like nothing they had ever encountered. The loss of the swine terrified them, but the miracle did not convince them of Jesus' divine power, and so they were not attracted to him.

But there is a different interpretation:

> Those who asked him to move on from their borders do this not out of pride (as some think) but out of humility. They judge themselves unworthy of the presence of the Lord, just as Peter did also at the catch of fish, when he fell down at the knees of the Savior and said: "Depart from me, Lord, for I am a sinful man."[24]

Thus, they ask Jesus to leave, and he agrees. The healed man, however, wants to remain with Jesus, but he does not allow him. In this rejection, we should not see any sign of lack of goodwill toward the healed man, just as in Jesus' agreement to leave the country we should not see any lack of goodwill toward the inhabitants of that country. More likely, the opposite

---

[24]Jerome, *Commentary on Matthew* 1.8.34 (FOTC 117:105).

The Temptation of Christ, fresco, 16th century

is true. By leaving a country where the people did not want to accept him, Jesus did what he commanded his disciples to do: "And whosoever shall not receive you, nor hear your words, when ye depart out of that house or city, shake off the dust of your feet. Verily I say unto you, it shall be more tolerable for the land of Sodom and Gomorrha in the day of judgment, than for that city" (Mt 10.14–15). At the same time, he does not leave the country without his attention, because he tells the healed man to return to his own people and to tell them everything that happened to him.

Jesus came to Decapolis to preach the Gospel. But if in Galilee and Judea he preached primarily to the Jews, in Decapolis he would have been preaching in a predominantly Gentile area. We know nothing of the content of that preaching—the evangelists only tell of one performed miracle in Decapolis. Nonetheless, the spread of the Good News did not stop after his departure—it continued in the preaching of the former demoniac.

In Luke's version, the account ends almost in the same was as in Mark:

> Now the man out of whom the demons were departed besought him that he might be with him: but Jesus sent him away, saying, "Return to thine own house, and show what great things God hath done unto thee." And he went his way, and published throughout the whole city what great things Jesus had done unto him. (Lk 8.38–39)

By commanding the healed man to preach about what God did for him, Jesus ascribes the miracle to God, while the healed man quite rightly ascribed it to Jesus. For the evangelist, there is no contradiction here, because Jesus is the incarnate God, and the miracle he performed vividly and convincingly proves his divinity. In the Gospel according to Mark, instead of the word "God," the word "Lord" is used, but the meaning is the same—as with Luke, Mark sees the miracle of the exorcism of the demoniac a manifestation of the power of God, which is the same as the power that comes from Jesus.

4. "He casts out demons by the power of Beelzebub, the prince of demons"

One of the Pharisees' main accusations against Jesus was that he cast out demons using demonic power. This accusation is found more than once in the Gospels, and Jesus answered it in different ways. For example, he spoke of this in a conversation with the twelve apostles, warning them that the same accusation would be brought against them: "The disciple is not above his master, nor the servant above his lord. It is enough for the disciple that he be as his master, and the servant as his lord. If they have called the master of the house Beelzebub, how much more shall they call them of his household?" (Mt 10.24–25).

We see an example of this earlier in the Gospel according to Matthew:

> As they went out, behold, they brought to him a dumb man possessed with a demon. And when the demon was cast out, the dumb spake; and the multitudes marvelled, saying, "It was never so seen in Israel." But the Pharisees said, "He casteth out demons through the prince of the demons." (Mt 9.32–34)

Here nothing is said about Jesus' answer to the accusation. We find a complete answer in a different account, when Jesus cast out a demon from a man who was both mute and blind:

> Then was brought unto him one possessed with a demon, blind, and dumb; and he healed him, insomuch that the blind and dumb both spoke and saw. And all the people were amazed, and said, "Is not this the son of David?" But when the Pharisees heard it, they said, "This fellow doth not cast out demons, but by Beelzebub the prince of the demons." And Jesus knew their thoughts, and said unto them, "Every kingdom divided against itself is brought to desolation; and every city or house divided against itself shall not stand, and if Satan cast out Satan, he is divided against himself; how shall then his kingdom stand? And if I by Beelzebub cast out demon, by whom do your children cast them out? Therefore they shall be your judges. But if I cast out demons by the Spirit of God, then the kingdom of God is come unto you. Or else how can one enter into a strong man's house, and spoil his goods, except he first bind the strong man? And then he will spoil his house. He that is not with me is against me; and he that gathereth not with me scattereth abroad. Wherefore I say unto you, all manner of sin and blasphemy shall be forgiven unto men; but the blasphemy against the Holy Spirit shall not be forgiven unto men. And whosoever speaketh a word

against the Son of man, it shall be forgiven him; but whosoever speaketh against the Holy Spirit, it shall not be forgiven him, neither in this world, neither in the world to come." (Mt 12.22–32)

Healing the Blind and Dumb Demoniac, G. Doré, 19th century

Luke describes the same event with similar expressions. In Luke, however, the demoniac is called mute, but nothing is said about his blindness (Lk 11.14–23). Scholars offer different explanations of how the mute man and the blind and mute man might be connected. These explanations are founded on the following: 1) the mute demoniac in Luke is identical to the mute demoniac from Matthew 9, but the continuation of the story (Jesus' answer) is taken from Matthew 12; 2) the mute man in Luke is the same as the one from Matthew 12, but Luke left out his blindness; 3) in the hypothetical primary source used by both Matthew and Luke, there was only one example of an exorcism of a mute man, but Matthew, who was prone to "doubling," divided it into two separate episodes, so that the single demoniac turned into two—a mute and a blind-mute.

We consider the third hypothesis to be impossible: Matthew has two exorcisms that occur in different places, times, and context. As for the first and second hypothesis, the more convincing seems to be the second, though the first may be possible as well.

Being blind or mute are not the same as possession. In the Gospels, there are many cases of Jesus healing both kinds of illness. Moreover, in one of them, being deaf and mute occurs after Jesus addresses the man (or the spirit inhabiting him): "dumb and deaf spirit, I charge thee, come out of him, and enter no more into him" (Mk 9.25). This makes the situation similar to other episodes in which Jesus spoke to the demons who had taken possession of people. In all other cases we have examined thus far, healings were performed for specific illnesses that Jesus healed with his word, touch, or both together.

In the case of the mute demoniac and the blind-mute demoniac we have cases not of simple illness, but of possession—the blindness and dumbness are mere side effects. We do not know exactly how physical illness is connected with possession; for example, it could have been that the person first became mute or blind and mute, and only later possessed. But the context of the account allows us to assume that the blindness and muteness in this case are direct results of the demon's influence over a person. Consequently, in contrast to physical blindness or muteness, which can afflict a person from birth or at a later point in life, any healing from such blindness or muteness requires not merely healing, but exorcism.

This is how the people assessed the event. Here, however, their opinions divide in two. Some of them see the exorcism as proof that Jesus is the Christ, the Son of David; others, on the contrary, accuse him of using demonic power. This accusation is also included in Mark, but in his account it is not connected to any specific exorcism. When speaking of the beginning of Christ's ministry, Mark writes about people's reaction to Jesus' activity—namely his family's and the scribes':

> And the multitude cometh together again, so that they could not so much as eat bread. And when his friends heard of it, they went out to lay hold on him, for they said, "He is beside himself." And the scribes which came down from Jerusalem said, "He hath Beelzebub, and by the prince of the demons casteth he out demons." (Mk 3.20–22)

Then Jesus answers (Mk 3.23–29), which is similar in content and in textual style to the analogous answers Jesus gives in Matthew and Luke. The account ends with the words "[this he said] because they said, 'He hath an unclean spirit.'" These words echo what the people say to Jesus in the Gospel according to John: "Thou hast a demon; who goeth about to kill thee?" (Jn 7.20).

Before us is an entire series of accounts with the same repeating motif. This motif appears in two variations: 1) Jesus is accused of using demonic power to exorcise; 2) Jesus is accused of being himself possessed by a demon. What is the nature of these accusations?

We have already said that the power by which Jesus performed healings and cast out demons had nothing in common with necromancy or magic. For eyewitnesses of his miracles, however, this was not always self-evident, and some of his actions could have been interpreted as connected with magic.[25] The external means that he used could have reminded some of the practices of popular exorcists who cast out demons with spells or magic formulas. Jesus also often used formulas, for example, "Hold thy peace, and come out of him!" (Mk 1.25) and "Come out of the man, thou unclean spirit!" (Mk 5.8). At the same time, he never used invocational spells as did other exorcists; he never called on an external or foreign power, separate from himself; he did not use any props as did exorcists (such as incense, amulets, or specially chosen music).

All these external differences, which are usually offered by scholars, only give a partial answer to the accusation of the Pharisees. The fullest answer is given by Jesus himself, which all three Synoptic evangelists recount. It should be noted that Jesus did not always answer all the accusations leveled against him. But he answered the accusation that he cast out demons by the power of the prince of the demons often and quite energetically.

The first argument that Jesus offers in his defense is as follows: if Satan casts out Satan, that means he is divided against himself. Satan opposes God; his kingdom stands against God's kingdom. Those who will inhabit the kingdom of Satan are in solidarity among themselves. This is proved, in part, by the episode with the legion of demons who all acted together, having a single will and power.

The second argument—"But if I by Beelzebub cast out devils, by whom do your sons cast them out? Therefore they shall be your judges" (Mt 12.27)—is a reference to the sons of those who accuse Jesus. These sons are sometimes understood to be the Jewish exorcists who acted during Jesus' time and are seen in other sources.[26] But it is much more likely that Jesus here is speaking of his disciples[27] to whom he gave authority over

---

[25]John Hull, *Hellenistic Magic and the Synoptic Tradition* (London: SCM Press, 1974), 142.

[26]Fitzmeyer, *The Gospel according to Luke (I-XI)*, 921–22.

[27]John Chrysostom, *Homilies on Matthew*, Homily 41.2 (NPNF[1] 10:265).

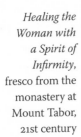

Healing the Woman with a Spirit of Infirmity, fresco from the monastery at Mount Tabor, 21st century

the unclean spirits (Mt 10.1; Mk 6.7). The generation of the apostles will be judges over their fathers who did not believe in Jesus despite his miracles and the miracles of his disciples.

The third argument is a reference to the Holy Spirit. Jesus knows—and he speaks of this to his critics—that the power that comes from him is nothing other than the Spirit of God. He utters strange words concerning the fact that blasphemy against the Son of Man is permissible, but blasphemy against the Holy Spirit is not permissible "neither in this world, nor in the world to come" (Mt 12.32). Blasphemy against the Holy Spirit is the accusation that he casts demons out by the power of Beelzebub. This is proven by the explanation made by Mark (Mk 3.30).

The claim that blasphemy against the Son of Man is permitted is usually interpreted to mean that until Jesus was glorified, while he remained in the humble form of man, any mistake concerning him was forgivable.[28] So, for example, Jesus was tolerant of any assertion that he was John the Baptist resurrected or one of the ancient prophets. He patiently endured the lack of understanding of those around him, including his disciples. But he categorically rejected anyone's right to accuse him of working through demonic power—this accusation he considered not blasphemy against himself, but against the Holy Spirit that acted through him:

[28]John Chrysostom. *Homily 41 on Matthew, chapter 3.*

Christ Harrowing Hades, fresco, Andrea di Bonaiuto da Firenze, 14th century

With a very grave qualification, he condemns the view of the Pharisees and the perversion of those who also think like them. He promises pardon of all sins but refuses pardon for blasphemy of the Spirit. While other words and deeds are treated with a generous pardon, there is no mercy if it is denied that God is in Christ. . . . For who is so completely beyond pardon as one who denies that Christ is of God, or repudiates that the substance of the Spirit of the Father resides in him [Mt 12.28]? Since Christ accomplishes every work by the Spirit of God, and the Lord himself is the Kingdom of God, and God is reconciling the world to himself in him [2 Cor 5.19], whatever sacrilege is directed against Christ is directed against God because God is in Christ and Christ is in God.[29]

Finally, Jesus offered yet another argument in parabolic form: in order to enter the house of a strong man and to steal his things, you must first bind the strong man. Here, the strong man is a symbol of Satan. To bind Satan, one must invade his kingdom—this is exactly what happens when Jesus invades the place where the devil had ruled without limit before his coming. Jesus' presence provokes a pained reaction from the demons—they cannot remain inside those whom they possessed; they are forced to reveal themselves; they try to oppose the power that comes from Jesus.

---

[29]St Hilary of Poitiers, *Commentary on Matthew*, trans. D. H. Williams, Fathers of the Church, Vol. 125 (Washington, DC: The Catholic University of America, 2012), 145–46.

Christ Frees the Righteous from the Maw of Hell, miniature from St Albans Psalter, 12th century

Every exorcism is described as a battle, a war. This war always ends with Satan's defeat and God's victory.

Luke gives this parable in a slightly different from, and the images taken from the military world come across more vividly than in Matthew or Mark:

When a strong man armed keepeth his palace, his goods are in peace, but when a stronger than he shall come upon him, and overcome him, he taketh from him all his armor wherein he trusted, and divideth his spoils. He that is not with me is against me; and he that gathereth not with me scattereth. (Lk 11.21–23)

Here, a strong man is opposed by a stronger man (ἰσχυρότερος; *ischyroteros*—"more powerful" [Lk 11.22]), who not only takes his "things" (σκεύη; *skeuē*, literally "vessels" [Mk 3.27]), but also all his arsenal of weapons (πανοπλίαν; *panoplian* [Lk 11.22]). He gives the picture of a kingdom completely destroyed and despoiled.

In the account of the healing of the woman bent over, Jesus told her that she was bound by Satan (Lk 13.16). Here Jesus speaks of the reality of the stronger man (Jesus) binding the strong man (Satan). The similarity between healing from physical illness and exorcism lies in the fact that in both cases Jesus frees someone from the bondage of Satan. Moreover, Satan himself ends up being the one who is defeated and bound.

By healing and casting out demons, Jesus destroys those islands of demonic presence on earth and in people, which the devil had negotiated for himself from God. But the earth is not the kingdom of the devil—he is merely here temporarily, trying to harm whomever he can, using all his strength and all the means available to him to oppose the fulfillment of the will of God on earth. In the biblical understanding, the proper home of the demons, the kingdom of Satan, is hell, that abyss that Jesus calls fiery Gehenna. This is the place where the souls of sinful, unrepentant,

Christ Leads the Righteous out of Hades through the Broken Gates, B. di Giovanni, 1491

and unfaithful people go. That is the constant dwelling-place of the devil and his demons.

Judging by the fact that the demons have no desire to return there, preferring to remain on the earth—if not inside people, then at least inside pigs—they are subjected to tortures in the abyss like the people who end up there. The heaviness of these tortures is expressed figuratively by Jesus in the form of a refrain: "everlasting fire, prepared for the devil and his angels" (Mt 25.41); "the furnace of fire" (Mt 13.50); "outer darkness" (Mt 8.12); "weeping and gnashing of teeth" (Mt 8.12); "the fire that shall never be quenched, where their worm dieth not, and the fire is not quenched" (Mk 9.43–44).

Jesus' final invasion of the kingdom of the devil will be his descent into hell after his death on the cross. The teaching of Jesus' descent into hell is part of Christian tradition from the time of the apostles. The apostle Paul speaks of Christ's victory over death and hell (1 Cor 15.54–57) and of Christ's "descent into the deep" (Rom 10.7). This teaching is most fully explored in the first general epistle of the apostle Peter, where he writes that "Christ also hath once suffered for sins, the just for the unjust, that he might bring us to God, being put to death in the flesh, but quickened by

The Harrowing of Hades, fresco, Fra Angelico, 1437–46

the Spirit, by which also he went and preached unto the spirits in prison" (1 Pet 3.18–19). In the same epistle, we read, "For for this cause was the gospel preached also to them that are dead, that they might be judged according to men in the flesh, but live according to God in the spirit" (1 Pet 4.6).

These words convery the teaching that during the three days that Jesus spent in the heart of the earth (Mt 12.40), when his body was in the tomb, his soul descended to hell, so that his preaching could be heard there as well. The most detailed description of this is the apocryphal "Gospel of Nicodemus," which did not enter the canon of the New Testament but was used by the Church as part of its liturgical tradition—its ideas and images became an inextricable part of Christian liturgy, influencing much of the services of Great and Holy Saturday.

The result of Christ's descent into hell is the exodus of the people who were suffering there—according to some, everyone was taken out, while others say it was only the Old Testament righteous ones.[30] As for the devil

[30]The author has written on this subject in greater detail in other books, not yet translated.

*The Harrowing of
Hades,*
A. Mantegna,
1470–75

and his demons, they were not freed from their prison. On the contrary, their tortures after Christ's descent into hell only worsened, since they were bound and imprisoned, while their treasures were despoiled. St John Chrysostom explains that these "treasures" were the people imprisoned by the devil:

> By his death, Christ bound the chief of robbers and the prison guard, that is, the devil and death, and transferred their treasures, that is, the entire human race, to the royal treasury. . . . The King himself came to the prisoners . . . and broke the doors, crushed the bars, vanquished hades, and stripped the prison.[31]

In the context of Christ's descent into hell, his words concerning the strong man bound by the stronger man acquire a prophetic dimension. In the same context, the exorcisms performed by Jesus acquire a deeper significance. They serve as a prelude to his final victory over the devil. That

[31]St John Chrysostom, *De coemeterio et de cruce* [On the cemetery and on the cross], PG 49:393–398. [This homily has not yet been translated into English in full, but excerpts can be found online: https://www.johnsanidopoulos.com/2011/05/st-john-chrysostoms-homily-on-cemetery.html. In the byzantine liturgical tradition, this homily is read the first Tuesday after Bright Week (i.e., the second Tuesday after Pascha), when memorial services first resume.—*Ed.*]

The Descent into Hell,
icon, 1408–10

victory will cost him his life, but the result will be complete freedom from the bondage of Satan for all who believe in him. As the demoniacs ran naked to Jesus and fell at his feet, in hell death itself—helpless, despoiled of its weapons, and naked—will run to him and will fall at his feet. And the devil will be "cast into the lake of fire and brimstone." There, he and his demons "shall be tormented day and night for ever and ever" (Rev 20.10).

In Matthew and Luke's versions of the casting out of the demon from the blind and mute man, we find the thematic center of the account: "He that is not with me is against me, and he that gathereth not with me scattereth abroad" (Mt 12.30). These words sound like one of the aphorisms that Jesus repeated in various situations. We see similar phrases in other places, such as "he that is not against us is for us" (Lk 9.50). Neutrality toward Jesus and his works is impossible—you must be either for him or against him. There is no third option.

Throughout the Gospels, we see how some people react positively to the words and miracles of Jesus, believe in him and follow him, while others, on the contrary, become more and more hardened the more they see his miracles and hear his words. The works and preaching of Jesus become a judgment upon the world. At this judgment, some will be justified, others condemned; some will find themselves on the right hand of Jesus, others on the left (Mt 25.33). Thanks to him, those who do not see obtain their sight, but those who think that they can see, if they do not accept him, are revealed to be blind (Jn 9.39). With faith in Jesus, the sick are healed, the possessed are freed from their possession; but those who do not believe take the side of the powers against whom Jesus battles, that it, the devil's side.

In the words we have examined, Jesus continues to use images from the military world. When battle rages, neutrality is impossible—man must fight either on one side or the other. In this case, this is left to the choice of each person. Every time a miracle is performed, Jesus puts a choice before his followers and eyewitnesses—to be with him or against him. This choice remains for every individual person; before entire groups of people (such as the scribes and Pharisees); it even stands before the entire Israelite nation when Jesus Christ stands before the judgment seat of Pilate.

5. "It Is Not Good to Take the Children's Bread and Throw It to the Dogs"

The Gospels of Matthew and Mark recount Jesus' casting out a demon from a possessed girl—or young woman or perhaps an older woman (we know nothing of her age)—at her mother's request. As with the healing of the servant of the centurion (Mt 8.5–13) and the son of the nobleman (Jn 4.46–53), the miracle occurs at a distance. Matthew describes this event thus:

> And, behold, a woman of Canaan came out of the same coasts, and cried unto him, saying, "Have mercy on me, O Lord, thou son of David; my daughter is grievously vexed with a demon." But he answered her not a word. And his disciples came and besought him, saying, "Send her away; for she crieth after us." But he answered and said, "I am not sent but unto the lost sheep of the house of Israel."
>
> Then came she and worshipped him, saying, "Lord, help me." But he answered and said, "It is not meet to take the children's bread, and to cast it to dogs." And she said, "Truth, Lord; yet the dogs eat of the crumbs which fall from their masters' table." Then Jesus answered and said unto her, "O woman, great is thy faith; be it unto thee even as thou wilt." And her daughter was made whole from that very hour. (Mt 15.20–28)

*The Healing of
the Daughter of
the Canaanite
Woman*, fresco,
16th century

Mark calls this woman a Syrophoenician[32] and a pagan (the word Ἑλληνίς [*Hellēnis*] literally means "Greek woman," but in this case it indicates religious identity, not ethnicity, in the same way that Paul uses the word "Greeks" in Romans and 1 Corinthians).[33] Mark does not recount Jesus' initial silence to the woman's screams or the disciples' initial reaction, as Matthew does. Jesus' words in Mark are rendered thus: "Let the children first be filled; for it is not meet to take the children's bread, and to cast it unto the dogs." Mark gives her answer thus: "Yes, Lord; yet the dogs under the table eat of the children's crumbs." Mark says nothing about her faith, but as in Matthew, Jesus praises her: "go thy way; the demon is gone out of thy daughter." This version ends with a detail that is missing in Matthew: "when she was come to her house, she found the demon gone out, and her daughter laid upon the bed" (Mk 7.24–30).

This account, identical in content in both evangelists, inspires many questions. Why did Jesus answer the woman so rudely, comparing her to

[32]These were inhabitants of Phoenicia, which in the Roman period belonged to the province of Syria. Phoenicia was found on the shore of the Mediterranean Sea, neighboring to Galilee. The majority of the inhabitants of that region were pagans, though there were Jewish villages. See also Gerd Theissen, *The Gospels in Context* (New York: T&T Clark, 1992), 66–68.

[33]On the meaning of the term Ἑλληνίς (*Hellēnis*) see Hans Leander, *Discourses of Empire: The Gospel of Mark from a Post-colonial Perspective* (Atlanta: Society for Biblical Literature, 2013), 225–30; V. Taylor, *The Gospel according to St. Mark* (Grand Rapids: Baker Book House, 1981), 349; Morna Hooker, *The Gospel according to St. Mark* (London: A&C Black, 1991), 183.

a dog? Why did he answer requests from pagans in other places (we call to mind the servant of the centurion and the son of the nobleman), while here it seems he rejects her solely because she does not belong to the chosen people? Why did he come to Tyre and Sidon at all, since it was filled with pagans, if he sought to avoid the latter entirely?

Ancient commentators had similar questions. Even St John Chrysostom wonders about it:

> For indeed it was a pitiful spectacle to see a woman crying aloud in so great affliction, and that woman a mother, and entreating for a daughter, and for a daughter in such evil case; she not even venturing to bring into the Master's sight her that was possessed, but leaving her to lie at home, and herself making the entreaty. And she tells her affliction only, and adds nothing more. . . . But he answered her not a word. What is this new and strange thing? The Jews in their perverseness he leads on, and blaspheming he entreats them, and tempting him he dismisses them not; but to her, running unto him, and entreating, and beseeching him, to her who had been educated neither in the law, nor in the prophets, and was exhibiting so great reverence; to her he does not vouchsafe so much as an answer. Whom would this not have offended, seeing the facts so opposite to the report? For whereas they had heard, that he went about the villages healing, her, when she had come to him, he utterly repels. And who would not have been moved by her affliction, and by the supplication she made for her daughter in such evil case? For not as one worthy, nor as demanding a due, not so did she approach him, but she entreated that she might find mercy, and merely gave a lamentable account of her own affliction; yet is she not counted worthy of so much as an answer.[34]

Chrysostom sees in Jesus' silence and his subsequent words—that the bread that is not to be given to dogs—his desire to make the faith of the woman obvious to all who surround her. Jesus sees her faith; he understands that she would not walk away from him; her answer was not

---

[34]John Chrysostom, *Homilies on Matthew*, Homily 52.2, 3 (NPNF[1] 10:321).

unexpected. He "knew that she would say this; for this reason did he deny the request, that he might exhibit her high self-command."[35] The event becomes, in its final form, yet another instructive lesson for the Jews. Jesus had them in mind when he said "many shall come from the east and west, and shall sit down with Abraham, and Isaac, and Jacob, in the kingdom of heaven. But the children of the kingdom shall be cast out into outer darkness; there shall be weeping and gnashing of teeth" (Mt 8.11–12).

Chrysostom's explanation only partially answers the questions, however. We should not forget that Jesus saw his mission first of all as directed at the Jews. The expansion of this mission to the gentiles has only an episodic character in the Gospels. To the disciples, he said, "Go not into the way of the Gentiles, and into any city of the Samaritans enter ye not; but go rather to the lost sheep of the house of Israel" (Mt 10.5–6). This may mean that the pagans should not be completely and principally excluded from the attention of Jesus and the apostles, but preaching among the Gentiles is not a priority for him.

In commenting on this passage, St Jerome notes that Jesus left the teaching of the salvation of the pagans to the time of his suffering and resurrection:

> This passage is not contrary to the command that is given later: "Go, teach all nations, baptizing them in the name of the Father and of the Son and of the Holy Spirit." For the former was commanded before

[35]Ibid.

the resurrection, but the latter was said after the resurrection. And it was necessary first to announce the advent of Christ to the Jews, lest they have a just excuse, claiming that they had rejected the Lord because he sent the apostles to the Gentiles and Samaritans. . . . [H] e was reserving the perfected salvation of the Gentiles for the time of his passion and resurrection. . . . He is not saying that he was not also sent to the Gentiles, but that he was sent first to Israel. In that way the transference to the Gentiles would be just, since Israel did not receive the Gospel.[36]

The widening of the Church's mission to include the pagans took place after his resurrection, and even that not immediately. The apostles remembered well Jesus' commandment not to go to the Gentiles; however, they quickly realized that the mission among the Jews had no future. It was under the influence of Paul that the apostolic community accepted the final decision during the council of Jerusalem to open the doors of the Church to the pagans, that circumcision was not required, and adherence to the Law of Moses was not necessary for salvation (Acts 15.1–29).

This decision was historical; it brought a radical change to the missionary strategy of the apostles. But it was prepared by events that had occurred during Jesus' life, such as the healing of the servant of the centurion and the daughter of the Canaanite woman. It was also prepared by the many teachings of Jesus in which he rebuked the Jews for their lack of faith, promising that the place that was originally prepared for the "sons" will be taken by those who are worthier.

The word translated as "dogs" is written in a diminutive form in Greek: κυνάρια (*kynaria*; literally "puppies"). In Greek, it sounds much less insulting than the "dogs" of older translations. In Mark, the word "daughter" is also given in a diminutive form: θυγάτριον (*thygatrion*; "little daughter") rather than Matthew's θυγάτηρ (*thygatēr*; "daughter").

This nuance, however, does little to soften the harshness of the impression the reader forms from Jesus' words. This answer must be understood in the context of the understanding that the Jews had of themselves and of

[36]Jerome, *Commentary on Matthew* 1.10.5–6, 2.15.23–24 (FOTC 117:116, 182–83).

the pagan peoples who surrounded them. Pagans were not simply people of a lesser sort; they were impure, no better than dogs. Jesus constantly attacked this pride in his preaching, underlining that what saves a person is faith, not being a member of God's chosen nation. In this case, as in many others, he once more underlined the priority of faith—her request is fulfilled because her faith was great.

Let us also note the difference in the thematic accents emphasized by both evangelists. In Matthew, who wrote his Gospel to the Jews, Jesus' words sound like a dogmatic assertion: "It is not meet to take the children's bread, and to cast it to dogs." But Mark, who wrote primarily for the pagans, this assertion is preceded with the phrase: "Let the children first be filled" (Mk 7.27). Thus Mark significantly softens Jesus' words. The word "first" (πρῶτον; *prōton*, literally "first of all") shows a certain proper order for the fulfillment of his ministry. First of all, it is addressed to the Jews, but secondly, it can include the Gentiles. This proper order is also evident in the order of events that Mark arranges—first Jesus feeds five thousand Jews with five loaves of breads (Mk 6.30–44), then four thousand Gentiles with seven loaves of breads (Mk 8.1–9).

The Apostle Paul says something similar to the Romans:

So, as much as in me is, I am ready to preach the gospel to you that are at Rome also. For I am not ashamed of the gospel of Christ, for it is the power of God unto salvation to every one that believeth; to the Jew first, and also to the Greek. (Rom 1.15–16)

The "Greeks" here are all Gentiles, who must receive the Gospel, according to Paul, after the Jews. In this epistle, Paul speaks of the Jews as the natural branches that have been broken off the cultivated tree, while the Gentiles are the wild engrafted olive branch that feeds from the original tree. The Jews fell away because of unbelief, and the Gentiles were grafted in by faith. But the Jews "if they abide not still in unbelief, shall be grafted in; for God is able to graft them in again" (Rom 11.23).

Faith is that key element that connects this passage from the Epistle to the Romans to Matthew's account of the Canaanite woman, and the theology of Paul in general with the preaching of Christ. Faith is necessary for

*Healing the
Woman with an
Issue of Blood*,
Veronese, 16th
century

healing. Through faith salvation is also granted—first of all to the Jews, and secondly to the Gentiles. The faith of the Gentiles is brought as an accusation against the unfaithful Jews, and the Canaanite woman stands in the same rank as the centurion and the grateful Samaritan (Lk 17.16) and other non-Jews who were saved by their faith.

If in all other accounts of exorcism, the evangelists describe the actual exorcism with more or fewer details, in this episode with the Canaanite woman, we do not see the actual casting out of the demon. We only hear about it in Mark's account, when we see that the woman, having returned home, found her daughter, from whom the demon had left, lying on her bed. In many other cases, rising from bed was the sign of healing: the mother-in-law of Peter got up and immediately served them food; the daughter of the leader of the synagogue got up and started to walk after being brought back to life; the paralytic got up, took his bed, and walked back home. Here, the daughter remains in bed, which does not indicate an incomplete healing. The words of Matthew: "And her daughter was made whole from that very hour" (Mt 15.28). leave no doubt that the healing occurred immediately, as soon as Jesus spoke, while Mark's words "the demon left" also witness to a full deliverance from possession.

In the Gospel according to Matthew, the healing of the Canaanite woman's daughter follows immediately after an episode in which the disciples of Jesus eat with unwashed hands, which leads to an argument between Jesus and the Pharisees. The core idea behind the argument was that impurity is not an external matter, but an internal one. It is not what enters a person's mouth that defiles him, but that which comes out of his mouth and heart—that is, evil words and thoughts and evil actions (Mt 15.1–20). St John Chrysostom noted the parallelism between these two events in Matthew and two episodes in the book of Acts in his fifty-second homily on the Gospel according to Matthew. In the first event, Peter refuses to eat, citing that he never ate anything unclean, but instead receives from God the following answer: "What God hath cleansed, that call not thou common" (Acts 10.15). Immediately afterward, the Roman centurion Cornelius sent his servants to Peter, asking for baptism. Peter comes to the centurion's home, and while he speaks, the Holy Spirit descends on all those who are present. Moreover, "they of the circumcision which believed were astonished, as many as came with Peter, because that on the Gentiles also was poured out the gift of the Holy Spirit" (Acts 10.1–45).

There is another parallel in the episode with the woman who had an issue of blood. This parallelism in Mark is underlined with similar phrases used in both cases. The Syrophoenician woman came to Jesus because she "heard of him" (Mk 7.25). The woman with an issue of blood also decided to seek healing "when she had heard of Jesus" (Mk 5.27). The Syrophoenician woman, "came and fell at his feet." The other woman "came and fell down before him" (Mk 5.33). Both women receive what they asked for—one is healed from a long and shameful illness, the other receives an exorcism for her daughter.

6. "This kind can come out by nothing but prayer and fasting"

The last case of casting out demons that we will examine is described by all three Synoptic evangelists after Jesus' transfiguration. In Matthew and Mark's accounts, this episode occurs immediately after Jesus comes down from the mountain, while Luke records that it happened the next day (Lk 9.37). In all three cases, the contrast between the two events is significant— on the mountain, the disciples saw Jesus in his divine glory; having come down from the mountain, they see how he encounters demonic forces, in all their ugliness and abomination, face to face.

As in many other accounts that we have already examined, the fullest and most detailed account is found in Mark. Luke offers a short version; Matthew's is even shorter and more lacking in detail. Here is Mark's account:

> And when he came to his disciples, he saw a great multitude about them, and the scribes questioning with them. And straightway all the people, when they beheld him, were greatly amazed, and running to him saluted him.
>
> And he asked the scribes, "What question ye with them?" And one of the multitude answered and said, "Master, I have brought unto thee my son, which hath a dumb spirit; and wheresoever he taketh him, he teareth him: and he foameth, and gnasheth with his teeth, and pineth away; and I spake to thy disciples that they should cast him out; and they could not." He answereth him, and saith, "O faithless generation, how long shall I be with you? How long shall I suffer you? Bring him unto me." And they brought him unto him; and when he saw him, straightway the spirit tore him; and he fell on the ground, and wallowed foaming.
>
> And he asked his father, "How long is it ago since this came unto him?" And he said, "Of a child. And ofttimes it hath cast him into the

fire, and into the waters, to destroy him; but if thou canst do any thing, have compassion on us, and help us." Jesus said unto him, "If thou canst believe, all things are possible to him that believeth." And straightway the father of the child cried out, and said with tears, "Lord, I believe; help thou mine unbelief."

When Jesus saw that the people came running together, he rebuked the foul spirit, saying unto him, "Thou dumb and deaf spirit, I charge thee, come out of him, and enter no more into him." And the spirit cried, and rent him sore, and came out of him; and he was as one dead; insomuch that many said, "He is dead." But Jesus took him by the hand, and lifted him up; and he arose. And when he was come into the house, his disciples asked him privately, "Why could not we cast him out?" And he said unto them, "This kind can come forth by nothing, but by prayer and fasting." (Mk 9.14–29)

The episode can be divided into four distinct scenes. In the first, Jesus, together with Peter, James and John, come down the mountain to the other disciples, who had remained below, while they were on the mountain. Approaching the disciples, he sees a crowd surrounding them, and that there is some kind of argument with the scribes, and he asks the scribes about the cause of the argument. This entire scene is missing in Luke and Matthew, who only in passing mention that Jesus approached the crowd (Mt 17.14) or that a crowd came to him (Lk 9.37).

The second scene includes Jesus' dialogue with the father of the possessed boy, who is not present. In Matthew, the father describes the symptoms in the following phrases: "he is lunatic [σεληνιάζεται; selēniazetai, literally "lunatic" or "moonstruck"] and sore vexed; for ofttimes he falleth into the fire, and oft into the water" (Mt 17.15). In Luke, the father says, "Master, I beseech thee, look upon my son; for he is mine only child. And, lo, a spirit taketh him, and he suddenly crieth out; and it teareth him that he foameth again, and bruising him hardly departeth from him" (Lk 9.38–39). Only Luke mentions that the boy is an only child. Jesus' answer is practically identical in all three Synoptic Gospels.

Healing the Demoniac, fresco, 14th century

In the third scene, the boy himself appears. He reacts to the presence of Jesus even before coming to him. According to Mark, "when he saw him, straightway the spirit tore him; and he fell on the ground, and wallowed foaming." According to Luke, "as he was yet coming, the demon threw him down, and tore him" (Lk 9.42). Matthew leaves out this detail entirely. Matthew and Luke also leave out Jesus' question about what time the symptoms of possession began, as well as the answer of the father. Also missing is the entire dialogue about faith and unbelief, which in Mark has a special thematic significance. The healing itself is also described without any details. Mathew limits himself to a single phrase "And Jesus rebuked the demon; and he departed out of him; and the child was cured from that very hour" (Mt 17.18). Luke also notes the reaction of the people: "Jesus rebuked the unclean spirit, and healed the child, and delivered him again to his father. And they were all amazed at the mighty power of God" (Lk 9.42–43).

Finally, the fourth scene is a postlude to the account. It is missing in Luke, while Mark and Matthew have it in two different versions. In Mark, as we have already seen, the disciples ask Jesus why they could not themselves cast the demon out of the boy, and they receive an answer that this kind of demon can only be cast out with prayer and fasting. In Matthew, the same question is answered differently: "Because of your unbelief." After that, Jesus teaches them about the kind of faith that can move mountains (Mt 17.20). We find an analogous teaching once more in Matthew in the passage where Jesus curses the fig tree (Mt 21.21) and in the parallel passage in Mark (11.22), while in Luke it is found as part of the teachings that Jesus utters on the way to Jerusalem (Lk 17.6).

As we have already said, the description of the boy's symptoms in Matthew can lead us to equate his condition with "moon sickness," while in Mark and Luke they are more like epilepsy. We must ask, however, whether it is appropriate to make any specific psychological or neurological diagnosis in this case.

In ancient times, "moon sickness" (somnambulism) was a name given to the various actions that a man might commit while asleep or half-asleep. This illness was usually ascribed to the power of the moon. In our current time, we do not equate somnambulism with the phases of the moon at all. This connection, it should be said, was always rejected by the Early Church, as shown by the homilies of St John Chrysostom on this episode in Matthew. Chrysostom ascribes the popular connection between sleepwalking and the power of the moon to the influence of demons who have given people the incorrect notion about this disease:

> And if he call him a lunatic, trouble not yourself at all, for it is the father of the possessed who speaks the word. How then says the evangelist also, he healed many that were lunatic? Naming them according to the impression of the multitude.[37]

---

[37]John Chrysostom, *Homilies on Matthew*, Homily 57.3 (NPNF[1] 10:355).

Matthew's expression: "for he is moonstruck" (older translations) cannot be understood to indicate that the boy suffered from somnambulism, because it is not normal for sleepwalkers to throw themselves into fire or water. More often, they simply walk around in a half-sleepy state. Their movements are slow, their actions are not generally aggressive.

Fyodor Dostoyevsky

As for epilepsy, this illness has many different forms, and its symptoms have been extensively studied. The famous Russian author Fyodor Dostoyevsky suffered from epilepsy, and he described the sense of falling into an epileptic fit very memorably through his character of Prince Myshkin in *The Idiot*. His friends and relatives were also frequent eyewitnesses of Dostoyevsky's fits:

> The fits occurred around once a month—that was their usual rhythm. But sometimes, though very rarely, they occurred more often; sometimes even two fits in a week. ... I was once a witness of a rather typical fit for Fyodor Mikhailovich. This was probably in 1863, right before Pascha. It was late, around eleven at night, when he came to visit me, and we had a very animated conversation. I can't remember the subject, but I know that it was a very important and academic topic. Fyodor Mikhailovich was very inspired and began to walk around the room, while I sat at the table. He spoke of something exalted and joyful; when I supported his thought with some kind of response, he turned to me with an inspired face, showing me that his exalted state had reached its highest point. He stopped for a moment, as though looking for the right words to express his thought. He had even opened his mouth already to speak. I looked at him with intense attention, feeling that he was about to say something extraordinary, that I would hear some kind of revelation. Suddenly, out of his opened mouth issued a strange, drawn-out, and meaningless groan, and he fell down senseless on the floor in the middle of the room. This time, the fit was not very severe.

Because of his convulsions, his body stretched out and foam appeared at the side of his mouth.[38]

The symptoms described here are similar to what we see in the Gospel according to Mark when the boy approached Jesus and "straightway the spirit tore him; and he fell on the ground, and wallowed foaming" (Mk 9.20). However, these same symptoms are also present in various other illnesses. For example, some people who are afflicted with somnambulism can also have fits like this.

From the perspective of the evangelists, these same symptoms can be manifestations of either physical illness or demonic possession. Blindness and muteness, for example, are some of the afflictions that Jesus healed, as well as the physical manifestations of possession that he also healed by exorcising the demon who produced these symptoms. One does not contradict the other. Both disease and demonic possession are anomalies, but they are anomalies of different kinds, stemming from different sources. Consequently, they require different approaches.

In this case, what we see is demonic possession, since Jesus, as in other cases of exorcism, speaks directly to the demon, calling him a deaf and dumb spirit and commanding him to come out of the boy and not to enter back into him. The immediate effect of this command is the departure of the demon, accompanied by a loud cry. The convulsions end, and the boy becomes still as death. Then Jesus takes him by the hand, as he took the daughter of Jairus (Mt 9.25; Mk 5.41; Lk 8.54), and the boy gets up.

Let us turn to the remark that the evangelist makes when speaking of the exorcism. Jesus performs his miracle when he "saw that the people came running together." This produces the impression that Jesus was prepared to continue the conversation with the father concerning faith and unbelief. The evangelist, it seems, tries to underline that Jesus' conversation with the father has no less significance than the miracle itself, and that the inner process of becoming freed from unbelief taking place in the

---

[38]Nikolai Strakhov, *Vospominanya o Fyodore Mikhailoviche Dostoyevskom* [Memories of Fyodor Mikhailovich Dostoevsky], in F. M. Doestoevsky, *Polnoe sobranie sochinenii* [Complete collected works], in fourteen volumes (St Petersburg, 1883), 1:169–329, at 213–214.

The Raising of Jairus' Daughter, I. Repin, 1871

soul of the father is no less important than the exorcism of the son. Two processes occur in parallel and end at the same moment.

The father plays an important role in the account, especially in Mark's version, and the dialogue between him and Jesus is offered with an unusual attention to detail. At first, the father tells Jesus of the symptoms of his son's illness. Then, answering Jesus' question, he speaks of the actions of the evil spirit on him. He addresses his request not only from himself, but on behalf of his son, whom he does not divide from himself: "But if thou canst do any thing, have compassion on us, and help us."

Jesus' words "O faithless generation" (Mark) or "faithless and perverse generation" (Matthew and Luke) allude to Deuteronomy, where the Israelite nation is called a "perverse and crooked generation" (Deut 32.5) and "a very froward generation, children in whom is no faith" (Deut 32.20). In the Septuagint, this last verse sounds like this: "for they are a perverse generation, sons in whom is no faith." The theme of faith is central in this conversation between Jesus and the father, and the allusion to Deuteronomy is intentional, because that passage is God's judgment over Israel for paganism and unbelief, which is echoed by Jesus' own words.

What do these words about the faithless and perverse generation have to do with the exorcism of the young man? To whom are they addressed? Who is this faithless and perverse generation exactly? Is it the nation of Israel in general, the disciples who were not able to cast out the demon, or the boy's father? Matthew and Luke do not provide an answer to this. In Mark, however, Jesus' words have a direct connection with the father's words. They sound like an immediate, spontaneous, and emotional reaction to the disciples' inability to cast out the demon. However, they also have a connection to what happens later when the father says to Jesus, "But if thou canst do any thing, have compassion on us, and help us." These words contain a poorly concealed doubt that Jesus is able to help them. It is as if the petitioner is asking, "Your disciples could not do it; can you?"

In many ancient manuscripts Jesus' answer sounds like this: "If you can, everything is possible to the man who believes."[39] The accent in terms of meaning is on the word "you." Jesus turns the doubt of the man back on himself. It turns out that the key element is not Jesus' ability to perform a miracle, but the faith of the petitioner, which is insufficient for the miracle to occur. For Jesus, there is nothing that is impossible; however, the unbelief of a person can make a miracle impossible.

Immediately afterward, the father of the boy answers in the first person singular: "Lord, I believe; help thou mine unbelief." He answers with tears, because he knows that his unbelief or weak faith can become the reason that his son will not be healed. His words reveal that he has entered a transitional state between unbelief and faith. It is as though he wants to believe, but cannot, and now he asks not for the miracle, but for Jesus to increase his faith. He stands at a crossroads—he is that kind of unbeliever who in the final analysis will probably reject Jesus, but at the same time, he hopes for the miracle of finding faith, which for him is connected with the possibility of his son's being freed from a horrifying affliction. In this, his unbelief is quite different from the unbelief of the Nazarenes (Mk 6.6). There, we have hidden and stubborn unbelief; here, a person reveals the depths of his soul to Jesus, repents of his unbelief, and asks for help in finding faith.[40]

While contemplating Jesus' words about the faithless and perverse generation, the contemporary Serbian theologian St Nikolai Velimirovich opposes these words to what Jesus says to the father of the boy:

> But look once more how the Lord wisely combines strictness and compassion. Though he fiercely rebukes unbelief, he speaks in general,

[39] *Novum Testamentum Graecae*, 111.

[40] C. D. Marshall, *Faith as a Theme in Mark's Narrative* (Cambridge: Cambridge University Press, 1989), 122.

awakening faith in all people, not humiliating anyone personally. Now, when he turns personally to the petitions, he speaks with him not strictly, but with attention and compassion: if you can only believe a little bit . . . Such care and compassion had their expected result. The father began to weep and exclaimed with tears: I believe, Lord! Help my unbelief. Nothing so melts the ice of unbelief like tears. In the hour when this man wept before the Lord, he repented of his lack of faith, and in the presence of God, his faith came rushing to him, like a river at high water. And then he uttered words that have remained a thundering instruction for all generations of mankind—I believe, Lord! Help my unbelief! These words show that without God's help, man cannot even acquire faith. With his own strength, man can only acquire weak faith, that is faith in good and evil, or, to say it in a different way, doubt both in good and evil. But the path from weak faith to true faith is long. And man cannot travel this path if the right hand of God does not support him.[41]

In a different place the disciples address Jesus with a similar request: "Increase our faith" (Lk 17.5). In the Gospel according to Luke, this request precedes words about faith that St Matthew gives at the conclusion of this account with the demoniac youth: "If ye had faith as a grain of mustard seed, ye might say unto this sycamine tree, 'Be thou plucked up by the root, and be thou planted in the sea,' and it should obey you" (Lk 17.6). In Matthew, these words are part of the answer to the disciples' question about the reason for their inability to cast out the demon:

> Then came the disciples to Jesus apart, and said, "Why could not we cast him out?"
>
> And Jesus said unto them, "Because of your unbelief; for verily I say unto you, if ye have faith as a grain of mustard seed, ye shall say unto this mountain, 'Remove hence to yonder place'; and it shall remove; and nothing shall be impossible unto you. Howbeit this kind goeth not out but by prayer and fasting." (Mt 17.19–21)

---

[41]Nikolai (Velimirovich), *Tvoreniya* [Collected works], 2:153–554 (translated by NK).

The theme of faith and unbelief is thus integral to the entire episode. Moreover, in Matthew, the rebuke is given to the disciples—their lack of faith is shown to be the main reason for their inability to cast out the demon. In Mark, on the contrary, the unbelief of the father is the thematic center of the account. Consequently, Jesus' words about the faithless and perverse generation can refer to all the participants in this drama—the father, the disciples, the crowd, the nation of Israel in general. For the father of the child, however, the miracle becomes a strong stimulus to find faith; thanks to the faith he received from Jesus as a gift together with the miracle, it is as though he ceases being part of the faithless and perverse generation.

We should also note that faith in Mark's version is interpreted as a gift, not as a personal acquisition or quality of a person. In other cases, Jesus asks those who wish to be healed, "Believe ye that I am able to do this?" (Mt 9.28) Moreover, it is as though it were assumed that they must already bear faith within themselves; they must find it before coming to Jesus. But this episode corrects a possible misunderstanding of this interpretation. Faith can be obtained at the moment of a person's encounter with Jesus, thanks to the encounter itself. Thus, it does not appear as a fruit of the person's own labors. He receives it as an unexpected and even undeserved gift.

Jesus' words at the conclusion of Mark's account deserve a more detailed analysis: "This kind goeth not out but by prayer and fasting." In modern critical editions of the New Testament, the phrase "and fasting" is missing. The reason for this excision is a lack of any mention of fasting in an entire series of ancient manuscripts. Some commentators even say that this phrase contradicts Jesus' teaching about fasting, given in answer to a rebuke from the disciples of John the Baptist: "Can the children of the bridechamber fast, while the bridegroom is with them? As long as they have the bridegroom with them, they cannot fast" (Mk 2.19). They also note that Jesus used the fasting of the Pharisees as an example of hypocrisy (Lk 18.12). Based on all these facts, some make the assumption that the Early Church, which purportedly introduced the idea of fasting

*Healing the
Possessed Youth*,
miniature,
13th century

contrary to Jesus' own teaching, added this phrase to the original Markian version.[42]

Because of this view, critical editions of the Gospel of Matthew completely leave out the phrase "This kind goeth not out but by prayer and fasting." Many scholars speculate that the Church first decided to add the reference to fasting to the Gospel according to Mark, then took the entire phrase in its edited form and added it to the Gospel according to Matthew.[43]

This opinion, however, is entirely based on an incomplete and one-sided understanding both of the realities of primary sources and the teachings of Christ himself. Many manuscripts that scholars agree are authoritative, including Codex Sinaiticus, include the words about fasting in both Mark and Matthew. As for Jesus' teachings concerning fasting, he did not speak about fasting only in answer to John's disciples. In the same reply, he says that his disciples will fast when the Bridegroom is taken away from them, that is, after his death (Mk 2.20). Moreover, he speaks about fasting in the Sermon on the Mount (Mt 6.16–18). From this it is entirely obvious that when he criticized the Pharisees' way of fasting, he was opposing true fasting to false, and to fasting "for show."

[42]Hooker, *The Gospel according to St. Mark*, 225; Metzger, *A Textual Commentary on the Greek New Testament*, 85; K. Aland and B. Aland, *The Text of the New Testament* (Grand Rapids: Wm. B. Eerdmans, and Co., 1987), 296.

[43]The textual tradition of the Gospel of Matthew is complex, but this is not the place for discussing it.

If the purported reviser of the Gospel according to Mark wanted to make the text of the given passage accord better with Jesus' answer to John's disciples, then it is more likely to assume that he would have left out the mention of fasting in his redaction entirely, not added it in.[44]

As for the Gospel according to Matthew, the words about fasting and prayer could have appeared there in the following ways: 1) they could have been taken from the Gospel according to Mark; 2) they could have been taken from the purported common source for both evangelists; 3) they could have been in the original version. In that case, the fact that they are missing in some early manuscripts could easily be ascribed to scribal error.

At the very least, in the fourth century, the words concerning prayer and fasting were assumed to be part of the original text of the Gospel according to Matthew, which is clear at least partially from the commentaries of the early Fathers. John Chrysostom had no doubt they were authentic.[45]

When speaking of the Sermon on the Mount, we have already mentioned that during Jesus' time fasting was understood as complete abstinence from food, not simply a temporary abstinence from certain types of food.[46] We also made the point that Jesus' own practices could differ from the practices of his disciples. He could fast, for example, while they did not. In one such episode, Jesus abstains from food when the disciples bring him some (Jn 4.31–32). In another, Jesus and his disciples came into a house, "And the multitude cometh together again, so that they could not so much as eat bread" (Mk 3.20). These words could be understood in the sense that the disciples wanted to eat, while Jesus was thinking of other things.

It is entirely possible that fasting as complete abstinence of food was one of the elements of Jesus' personal ascetical practice that was connected directly with his battle against the devil and his demons. Jesus' face-to-face encounter with the devil in the wilderness occurred, according to Matthew and Luke, only after Jesus had fasted for forty days. Evidently, abstinence from food was part of the preparation for the battle that Jesus

[44]Klutz, *The Exorcism Stories in Luke-Acts*, 203–4.

[45]John Chrysostom, *Homilies on Matthew*, Homily 57.4 (NPNF[1] 10:355).

[46]See Met. Hilarion Alfeyev, *Jesus Christ: His Life and Teaching*, vol. 2: *The Sermon on the Mount* (Yonkers, NY: St Vladimir's Seminary Press, 2020), 297–302.

Matthew Writing the Gospel, illuminated manuscript, 8–9th centuries

waged against the devil. The same can apply to Jesus' other battles against the demonic powers. If Jesus fasted, while his disciples did not fast, then the explanation that he gives them concerning their inability to cast out this demon is completely logical—they cannot do it because this sort of demon is cast out only by prayer and fasting.

The expression "this sort" indicates that demons have their own hierarchy and classification. Judging by the fact that in other cases the disciples managed to cast out demons without trouble, since the demons listened to them through the name of Jesus (Lk 10.17), then in this case they were dealing with a demon of a special kind, whose exorcism required a certain amount of ascetic effort on the part of the exorcist. Merely using the name of Jesus was not enough in this case.

To summarize everything we have said in this section, the miracle of the casting out the demon from the young man occurred thanks to the combination of three elements. The first and most important was the power of Jesus, which revealed itself in all cases of healing and exorcism that we read in the Gospels. The second element, which was an aid to the first, was the ascetical practice of Jesus himself, or rather his fasting, which the disciples did not do. The third element was the father's desire to find faith—he did not have it, or did not have it in full measure, but he trusted himself to Jesus and asked his help. This help came simultaneously to the father and the son—the father was healed of unbelief, and the son was delivered form demonic possession.

Chapter 5

MIRACLES CONNECTED WITH THE NATURAL WORLD

S everal miracles in the Gospels demonstrated Jesus' power over nature. To understand their significance, we must first examine the Old Testament teaching concerning the relationship between man and the natural world. We must also look at what role nature played in the life of Jesus and his disciples. Only within this broad context can we understand the full meaning of the miracles connected with the natural world.

1. Nature and Man in the Old Testament

The Bible begins with an account of God's creating the visible world. The epic narrative—the sequential revelation of God's creative potential through the creation of elements, luminaries, heaven and earth, water, creeping things, fish, birds, animals, and finally man—precedes the account of the history of the relationship between God and man, which comprises the majority of the Old Testament. As he created the world, God proceeded from simple to complex, from the elementary to the more complete. Man was the pinnacle of God's creative process, containing within himself elements of both the material and spiritual worlds; thanks to this, he became the connecting point between both worlds.

In contrast to the animals and other inhabitants of the material cosmos, man was created in God's image and likeness (Gen 1.26). The most important difference between man and the animals is reason, the ability to understand his surrounding reality. Most ancient commentators see this ability of man, his freedom and his power over the created world, as well as his creative potential, as the main aspects of God's image in him.[1]

The fact that man was created to be master over nature is demonstrated by the blessing that God gives to the first-created couple: "Be fruitful, and multiply, and replenish the earth, and subdue it; and have dominion over the fish of the sea, and over the fowl of the air, and over every living thing that moveth upon the earth" (Gen 1.28). Subjugation and dominion—these are the terms that initially explain the relationship between man and nature.

Another important biblical text that illustrates the same theme is found in the next chapter of Genesis, when God brought all animals and birds to Adam, "to see what he would call them: and whatsoever Adam called every living creature, that was the name thereof. And Adam gave names to all cattle, and to the fowl of the air, and to every beast of the field" (Gen 2.19–20). Having given man the right to give names to creatures, God placed man over them, making him their master, for to name something, in the biblical understanding, means to have power over it.[2]

By themselves they [the animals] are unnamed, as they are incapable of raising themselves into the light of self-comprehension; but the word of man knows and names them from the height of his light, and, thus, he dominates them in their innermost being from a higher point than they can themselves.[3]

"This happens, not that we may merely learn of his intelligence but that a symbol of his dominion may be provided through the imposition of the names." This is how John Chrysostom explains the significance of

[1]See Hilarion Alfeyev, *Orthodox Christianity, Vol. 1: The History and Canonical Structure of the Orthodox Church*, trans. Basil Bush (Yonkers, NY: St Vladimir's Seminary Press, 2015).

[2]L. Bue, *O Biblii i Evangelii* [On the Bible and the Gospel] (Brussels, 1980), 23.

[3]Hans Urs von Balthasar, *A Theological Anthropology* (Eugene, OR: Wipf & Stock, 1967), 220.

*Adam Names
the Beasts,
fresco, 1528*

the naming. Furthermore, he even mentions that re-naming continued to have significance in more recent history: "You see, with human beings also this normally constitutes a symbol of dominion when they buy slaves, to change their names. Hence God provides that Adam, too, as their master should give names to the brute beasts."[4]

The right to give names also shows man's ability to understand the nature of things, thereby becoming like God and cooperating with God in creation. According to Basil of Seleucia (fourth century), having given man the right to name the animals, it is as though God says to Adam, "Be the creator of names, since you cannot be the creator of living creatures. . . . We will share with you the glory of the wisdom of creation . . . Give names to those whom I gave life."[5]

The first two chapters of the Bible paint a picture of complete harmony between man and nature, as well as the absence of any predation in the animal world. Man was allowed to eat "every herb bearing seed, which is upon the face of all the earth, and every tree, in the which is the fruit of a tree yielding seed," while food for animals was "every green herb for food" (Gen 1.29–30). In this herbivorous world, there are no predators—no one eats anyone else, no one hunts anyone else, and no one looks at anyone else as potential food.

The entire system of man's relationship with nature changes after the fall. It turns out that obedience to God and abstinence from the fruit of

[4]John Chrysostom, *Homilies on Genesis*, Homily 14. *Homilies on Genesis, 1–17*, trans. Robert C. Hill, The Fathers of the Church, Vol. 74 (Washington, DC: The Catholic University of America Press, 1986), 190.

[5]Basil of Seleucia, *Homily 2 on Adam* (PG 85:40–41).

Expulsion from Eden, fresco by Masaccio, 15th century

the forbidden tree was necessary not only for the correct structure of man's relationship with God. Man's mastery over nature was contingent upon following the command of God. This power was given to man by God, but it was not given absolutely and without conditions—the main condition of its continuation was obedience to God. Together with the desire to hide from God, together with the sudden knowledge of their own nakedness, a new sensation appears in man—powerlessness before nature because of man's loss of authority over it. Explaining this new paradigm for man's relationship with nature after the fall, God says to Adam:

> Because thou hast hearkened unto the voice of thy wife, and hast eaten of the tree—of which I commanded thee, saying, "Thou shalt not eat of it"—cursed is the ground for thy sake; in sorrow shalt thou eat of it all the days of thy life; thorns also and thistles shall it bring forth to thee; and thou shalt eat the herb of the field. In the sweat of thy face shalt thou eat bread, till thou return unto the ground; for out of it wast thou taken; for dust thou art, and unto dust shalt thou return. (Gen 3.17–19)

Even the account of man's creation records that God created him out of the dust of the earth; but the text emphasized that God "breathed into his nostrils the breath of life" (Gen 2.7). This breath of God connected man with God and the invisible world. Now, God reminds man of his connection with the earth, with the material cosmos. These words are key: "Cursed is the ground for your sake." These words indicate that the earth, which was created for man to serve him and submit to him, now becomes a source of sorrow for him. It will give rise not only to grain, but to thorns and thistles. Man will have to eat bread "by the sweat of [his] face".

Nothing is said here about man's relationship with animals or of the relationship of animals with each other. But Gods' words to the serpent shed some light on that subject:

Thou art cursed above all cattle, and above every beast of the field; upon thy belly shalt thou go, and dust shalt thou eat all the days of thy life; and I will put enmity between thee and the woman, and between thy seed and her seed; it shall bruise thy head, and thou shalt bruise his heel. (Gen 3.14–15)

Cain Kills Abel, mosaic, 12th century

In this case, the serpent is not only a bearer of demonic power, but a representative of the animal world at large. Between it and man there is now an antagonistic relationship, and the original harmony of the animal world that did not allow animals to destroy each other disappeared.

From the moment of the fall, animals are divided into carnivores and herbivores, while man by his manner of life and diet belongs to the former. Even in the first generation of Adam's descendants, we see animal husbandry, which is personified by Abel, together with the agriculture of Cain. After Cain killed Abel, he hears yet another curse from God, which, like the previous curse addressed to Adam, refers to man's relationship with nature: "And now art thou cursed from the earth, which hath opened her mouth to receive thy brother's blood from thy hand; when thou tillest the ground, it shall not henceforth yield unto thee her strength; a fugitive and a vagabond shalt thou be in the earth" (Gen 4.11–12). If God told Adam that the earth was cursed because of him, then Cain is cursed from the earth. The earth itself, which absorbed the innocent blood of Abel, curses the killer and refuses to cede its power to him.

The first great natural disaster of human history is the flood, when by God's command, the water destroyed the entire first-created world, other than a single human family and the animals that Noah took with him into the ark—a pair of every kind of bird, reptile, and animal (Gen 7.8–9). The fate of the animal world is now completely connected to the fate of man— the earth was cursed because of man, and everything that filled the earth

*The Hebrews
Leave Egypt,*
D. Roberts, 1830

was destroyed, together with the old man, for his sins. But the covenant that God offered Moses after the Flood includes all of nature as well:

> And I, behold, I establish my covenant with you, and with your seed after you; and with every living creature that is with you, of the fowl, of the cattle, and of every beast of the earth with you, from all that go out of the ark, to every beast of the earth. (Gen 9.9–10)

In the miracles depicted by the Bible, nature often participates together with man. The plagues sent by God on Egypt through Moses and Aaron had a direct effect on nature: water turned into blood (Ex 7.19–20), the waters expelled frogs (Ex 8.6); there was a plague of biting insects (Ex 8.17); all the cattle in Egypt died (Ex 9.6); dust produced boils on both people and animals (Ex 9.10); hail destroyed crops and living creatures as well (Ex 9.25); locusts covered the face of the earth and ate everything that remained after the hail (Ex 10.15); thick darkness covered the land of Egypt for three days (Ex 10.22).

The history of Israel's exodus from Egypt is connected with miracles that also affected nature: they walked across the bottom of the parted Red Sea (Ex 14.21–28); the bitter waters turned sweet (Ex 16.13–35). Joshua's miracles, including stopping the sun over Gibeon, also directly affected nature (Josh 10.12–14).

Crossing the Red Sea, miniature from a Byzantine Psalter, 10th century

In the historical books of the Bible and the Law, man is shown to be an integral part of the natural world, while cattle are his constant companion. Often, mankind and cattle are mentioned in the same sentence (Num 20.4, 8, 11, 19; Ps 35.6, etc.). When calamity strikes people, it also affects the cattle (Ex 9.19). Whenever an enemy city was taken during the invasion of Canaan, all the cattle were destroyed together with the inhabitants of the city (Deut 13.15; Josh 6.20; Judg 20:48). Cattle not only passively participate in whatever happens with people, bearing the punishment for their sins; they are even capable of offering repentance for the sins of men. Having heard the preaching of Jonah, the king of Nineveh gives the following command:

> Let neither man nor beast, herd nor flock, taste any thing: let them not feed, nor drink water; but let man and beast be covered with sackcloth, and cry mightily unto God; yea, let them turn every one from his evil way, and from the violence that is in their hands. Who can tell if God

will turn and repent, and turn away from his fierce anger, that we perish not? (Jon 3.7–9)

According to the Psalmist, all of nature, including cattle, must take part in praising God along with man:

Praise the Lord from the heavens; praise him in the highest.
Praise him, all ye angels of his; praise him, all his hosts.
Praise him, sun and moon; praise him, all ye stars and light.
Praise him, ye heavens of heavens, and thou water above the heavens.
Let them praise the Name of the Lord; for he spoke, and they came
    to be; he commanded, and they were created.
He established them forever, yea, forever and ever; he made a decree,
    and it shall not pass away.
Praise the Lord from the earth, ye dragons, and all deeps,
fire and hail, snow and ice, stormy wind, performing his word,
Mountains and all hills, fruitful trees and all cedars,
beasts and all cattle, creeping things and winged birds,
kings of the earth, and all peoples; princes and all the judges of the
    earth;
young men and maidens, old men with the younger: let them praise
    the Name of the Lord, for his Name alone is exalted;
his praise is above earth and heaven, and he shall exalt the horn of
    his people. (Ps 148.1–14)

In spite of the fact that the primordial harmony between man and nature was destroyed by the fall, man continues to remain part of the natural world according to the Bible. The close connection between the fate of man and the fate of the world is clearly seen in the prophetic books. The eschatological expectation of a new heaven and a new earth (Is 65.17) is connected to the hope for the restoration of the lost harmony within the animal world: "The wolf and the lamb shall feed together, the lion shall eat straw like the bullock; and dust shall be the serpent's meat. They shall not hurt nor destroy in all my holy mountain, saith the LORD" (Is 65.25).

In summarizing everything that the Old Testament had to say about the relationship of man and nature (the created world), the Apostle Paul wrote:

> For the earnest expectation of the creature waiteth for the manifestation of the sons of God. For creation was made subject to vanity, not willingly, but by reason of him who hath subjected the same in hope, because creation itself also shall be delivered from the bondage of corruption into the glorious liberty of the children of God. For we know that the whole creation groaneth and travaileth in pain together until now. And not only they, but ourselves also, which have the firstfruits of the Spirit, even we ourselves groan within ourselves, waiting for the adoption, to wit, the redemption of our body. (Rom 8.19–23)

"The Liberator" is God, who from the beginning submitted nature to man's authority, then later, after his sin, declared the earth to be cursed because of man. The restoration of the lost harmony is possible only through the salvation and transfiguration of man, which will give rise to the salvation and transfiguration of the entire created world.

2. Jesus and Nature

Jesus and his disciples spent a significant amount of time in nature. Most of Jesus' miracles were performed outside, whether in the streets of cities or villages, or on roads connecting one city with another, or in deserted places, or on the shores of the Sea of Galilee, or in mountains and high places. Many of Jesus' teachings were also spoken outside—on an unknown hill in Galilee (Mt 5.1), on a plain when he came down from the mountain (Lk 6.17), from a boat, while people stood listening on the shore (Mt 13.2), or on the Mount of Olives (Mt 24.3).

In the sermons he spoke to his disciples and the people, Jesus often used images taken from the animal world. These images, however, are not

The Sea of Tiberias, V. D. Polenov, 1888

in and of themselves important—each of them becomes a symbol that reveals some spiritual truth. In the surrounding world, Jesus sees hints and direct indications of a spiritual world—he teaches his listeners to recognize this reality, to see beyond the phenomena of the material world to another, parallel reality that fills it and adds a spiritual dimension to it. He constantly raises the mental gaze of his listeners to this reality, tearing their mind away from what seems to them habitual and quotidian.

Nowhere in the Gospel do we find a sense of exaltation before nature, or any sort of wonder before the beauties of flora and fauna. We never see Jesus enjoying a view, or stopping to gaze at a sunset, or sitting down to pet a cat or dog, or smelling flowers. He has a calm and sober attitude toward nature. It comes from the fact that nature should first of all serve the needs of mankind. When he walks through fields of ripe wheat with his disciples on the Sabbath, the disciples tear off the stalks and eat them. Not only does he not condemn them for this, but he justifies their actions before the Pharisees (Mt 12.1; Mk 2.23; Lk 6.1). When he decides to enter Jerusalem in triumph, he takes the colt of a donkey, sits astride him, and rides thus into the city (Mk 11.7; Lk 19.35). In Matthew, Jesus sits on both the donkey and her colt (Mt 21.7).

Most events in the Gospels take place on the banks of the Sea of Galilee. In the Gospels of Matthew and Mark, this lake is called the Sea of Galilee,

Fishermen on the Sea of Galilee, lithograph, c. 1900

while in Luke it is called the Lake of Gennesaret, while John calls it the Sea of Galilee as well of the Sea of Tiberias. This last name comes from the city of Tiberias (Tveriah currently), built in the first century BC and named for Emperor Tiberias.

The most prevalent name of the lake comes from the city of Kinneret (Gennesaret in the Hellenized form). Flavius Josephus writes the following about the lake:

> Now this lake of Gennesareth is so called from the country adjoining it. Its breadth is forty furlongs, and its length one hundred and forty; its waters are sweet, and very agreeable for drinking, for they are finer than the thick waters of other fens; the lake is also pure, and on every side ends directly at the shores, and at the sand; it is also of a temperate nature when you draw it up, and of a more gentle nature than river or fountain water, and yet always cooler than one could expect in so diffuse a place as this is. Now when this water is kept in the open air, it is as cold as that snow which the country people are accustomed to make by night in summer. There are several kinds of fish in it, different both to the taste and the sight from those elsewhere. It is divided into two parts by the river Jordan.[6]

[6]Josephus, *The Wars of the Jews* 3.10.7, in *The Works of Josephus*, 662.

The Lake of Kinneret is the most important reservoir of fresh water for all of Palestine until this day. For many centuries, it served as the main source of fish for the inhabitants of the region. The river Jordan, the most important waterway of Israel, empties into the lake from the north and continues to flow from it to the south.

The four events that we will examine below occurred in connection with the Sea of Galilee: two miraculous catches of fish, calming a storm, and walking on water. Two more events in this chapter take place on the banks of the sea: the feeding of the five thousand with five loaves of bread and two fish, and the feeding of the four thousand with seven loaves of bread and a few fish.

---

3. Two Miraculous Catches of Fish

The Gospels according to Luke and John have two episodes with a similar miracle. The disciples catch an unnatural number of fish at Jesus' command. Because of the surface similarity of these two episodes, they are sometimes interpreted as the same event in two variants.[7] But the differences are too significant. In Luke, the episode occurs at the very beginning of Jesus' public ministry and is the first event to follow the healing of Peter's mother-in-law. In John, on the contrary, the miraculous catch of fish occurs after Jesus' resurrection from the dead and is the last miracle that concludes the entire Gospel. Evidently, we are dealing with two separate events that have a certain similarity between them, but they are certainly not identical.

In this chapter, we will concentrate on the first of the two miracles. The second will be examined only as it corresponds with the first. A more detailed examination of the second miracle, with all its characteristic traits

---

[7]Puig, *Jesus: a Biography*, 364, 389–90. Fitzmeyer, *The Gospel according to Luke (I-XI)*, 561. Raymond Brown, *The Gospel according to John (XIII–XXI)* (New Haven: Yale University Press, 2007), 1090–91.

The Miraculous Catch, Raphael 1515–16

as part of the Gospel according to John is only possible in conjunction with other accounts concerning the appearance of the risen Jesus to his disciples.

In the Gospel according to Luke, the account of the miraculous catch of fish in some ways fills the absence of an account of the calling of the first four apostles, which is found only in Matthew and Mark (Mt 4.18–22, Mk 1.16–20). Only in Luke, does Simon, one of the four, first appear in the episode where his mother-in-law is healed, while two others—James and John—first appear in this episode:

> And it came to pass, that, as the people pressed upon him to hear the word of God, he stood by the lake of Gennesaret, and saw two ships standing by the lake; but the fishermen were gone out of them, and were washing their nets. And he entered into one of the ships, which was Simon's, and prayed him that he would thrust out a little from the land. And he sat down, and taught the people out of the ship.
>
> Now when he had left speaking, he said unto Simon, "Launch out into the deep, and let down your nets for a draught." And Simon answering said unto him, "Master, we have toiled all the night, and have taken nothing; nevertheless at thy word I will let down the net."

And when they had this done, they inclosed a great multitude of fishes; and their net broke. And they beckoned unto their partners, which were in the other ship, that they should come and help them. And they came, and filled both the ships, so that they began to sink.

When Simon Peter saw it, he fell down at Jesus' knees, saying, "Depart from me; for I am a sinful man, O Lord." For he was astonished, and all that were with him, at the draught of the fishes which they had taken; and so was also James, and John, the sons of Zebedee, which were partners with Simon. And Jesus said unto Simon, "Fear not; from henceforth thou shalt catch men." And when they had brought their ships to land, they forsook all, and followed him. (Lk 5.1–11)

This account cannot be accepted merely as a version of the Synoptic account of the calling of the disciples, because Matthew and Mark leave out this miraculous catch completely. Evidently, we are dealing with an independent episode here, which occurred already after all four disciples were called by Jesus. At the same time, this account has a direct connection to the theme of election, which is made clear by its end, where Jesus speaks to Simon with words similar to what he said to Simon and Andrew in Mark and Matthew: "Follow me, and I will make you fishers of men" (Mt 4.19). In Luke, this event is thematically connected with the calling of the twelve apostles and their being sent out to preach the gospel (Lk 6.12–16).

Jesus' habit of teaching people from a boat is present in both Matthew and Mark in another episode (Mt 13.2; Mk 4.1). Evidently, Jesus used this method of communication more than once.

What does the expression "word of God" (λόγος τοῦ Θεοῦ; *logos tou Theou*) mean in Luke? This expression is present only once in each of the other Gospels (Mt 15.6; Mk 7.13; Jn 10.35), and in all cases it refers to the Old Testament revelation. In Luke, however, it appears four times in the Gospels (5.1; 8.11, 21; 11.28) and thirteen times in Acts (4.31; 6.2, 7; 8.14; 11.1; 12.24; 13.5, 7, 44, 46, 48; 16.32; 17.13; 18.11). In Acts, this expression indicates the Christian teaching of the apostles; in the Gospel it indicates Jesus' preaching. Consequently, this expression must not be understood to mean that Jesus was reading passages of the Old Testament to the people,

The Miraculous Catch of Fish,
A. P. Losenko,
1762

then offering commentary, as he did in the synagogue of Nazareth (Lk 4.16–21). Here and in other places of the Gospel according to Luke the "word of God" is the word of Jesus, his own teaching.

After the instruction ended, Jesus urged Simon to sail deeper into the sea and cast in his nets. Simon and everyone nearby accepted what happened next as a miracle—they were seized with terror at what they saw. Until this moment, Simon had been an eye-witness of only one miracle—the healing of his mother-in-law. Now, he sees in Jesus something that inspired trepidation. For him, a professional fisherman who knew the techniques of catching fish like the back of his hand—the amount of fish he caught was incredible—evidently, he had never before in his life caught so many at one time. All the more amazing was the event considering that he had been fishing for almost the entire night without catching a single fish.

Simon's words remind the reader of what Jesus heard in the country of the Gadarenes after he sent the legion of demons into the swine. The inhabitants of that lands asked Jesus to leave their country. In that case, Jesus listened to their request; in this case, he does not. The reason that similar requests produce opposite reactions is that Jesus took account

*The Calling
of Peter and
Andrew*, Duccio,
1308–11

of the motives of the people who made the requests. In the case of the
Gadarenes the request was inspired by avarice—the people regretted
losing the swine, and they were afraid that the newly-revealed prophet
would cause them even more financial losses. In the case of Simon, his
request was inspired by an overwhelming sense of his own sinfulness. He
felt himself unworthy to be in the same boat as a man who was capable of
performing such miracles.

The way Simon relates to Jesus changes throughout the account. In his
first answer, he calls Jesus "master" and speaks to him with a completely
different tone. His lack of faith then changes to fear, along with a sense of
his own sinfulness and a sense of reverence. This is one of several accounts
in the Gospels where faith is strengthened or found thanks to a miracle.

The words "from henceforth thou shalt catch men," which are spoken
to Peter, are reminiscent of similar images in the Old Testament (Jer 16.16;
Am 4.2; Hab 1.14–15). In the Old Testament, however, the image of the fishing line or the fishermen's net catching men has a frightening undertone
and refers to God's punishment of Israel for her unfaithfulness. In this case,
Jesus uses this image to show Simon that from now on his calling will be
not to catch fish but rather to preach to men. The net thrown into the sea
by the word of Jesus, which fills with a multitude, becomes a symbol of

the mission to which Jesus will call the apostles—to catch people in to the net of the word of God.

The words at the end Luke's account directly parallel the account in the other two Synoptics, where Peter and Andrew follow Jesus, having left their nets behind, and also the calluing of James and John, who left their father behind. Following Jesus and beginning a new life meant leaving behind everything that connected a person with his former life. For this reason, Jesus did not simply call the rich youth to follow him, but added, "Go and sell what thou hast, and give to the poor . . . and come and follow me" (Mt 19.21). He addressed an even more radical demand to the disciples: "If any man will come after me, let him deny himself, and take up his cross, and follow me" (Mt 16.24).

The miracle that John recounts—which belongs to the period after Jesus' resurrection—has the following similarities to the previous episode: 1) the disciples were fishing the whole night and caught nothing; 2) Simon and both sons of Zebedee are present (in the second episode, Thomas, Nathaniel, and two unnamed disciples join them); 3) Jesus commands the disciples to cast their nets into the water; 4) they catch such an abundance of fish that the only explanation is that a miracle occurred; 5) both accounts mention the state of the nets (in the first, they began to rip, in the second, the disciples are unable to pull the nets aboard because of their weight); 6) in both episodes, only Peter reacts to the miracle; 7) in both cases, Peter calls Jesus Lord; 8) the other participants say nothing in both accounts; 9) in both cases, the scene ends with the disciples following Jesus; 10) in both cases, Simon is called Simon Peter (a name found nowhere else in Luke).[8]

Nevertheless, there are also some significant differences. In the second episode, 1) Jesus is not in the boat with the disciples, but on shore; 2) the disciples do not immediately recognize Jesus; 3) Simon and the sons of Zebedee are in the same boat, not in different ones; 4) the nets do not break; 5) Peter does not ask Jesus to leave him, but jumps into the water to reach him more quickly; 6) the disciples pull the net with the fish to shore;

[8]Brown, *The Gospel according to John (XIII–XXI)*, 1090; Fitzmeyer, *The Gospel according to Luke (I–XI)*, 560–61.

7) Jesus commands them to bring the fish they caught, even though there are grilled fish on shore already; 8) they count the fish, and the evangelist gives an exact number; 10) no one dares ask "Who are you?" They know that this is the Lord.

It seems that the two miracles took place at the beginning and end of Jesus' earthly ministry by design, as though forming a thematic arc within which all the miracles of Jesus are contained, except for a few or the very earlierst miracles (e.g., healing Peter's mother-in-law and the miracle in Cana of Galilee). It is likely that after his resurrection Jesus performed this miracle in a way similar to the way he performed the miracle at the beginning of his ministry, so that Peter and the other disciples, having remembered the first miracle, would believe in his resurrection, just as two other disciples believed that the risen Jesus stood before them when they recognized him in the familiar gesture of breaking bread (Lk 24.30).

4. Calming the Storm

The next episode connected with the Sea of Galilee is the calming of the storm. It is included in all three Synoptic Gospels. As in many other cases, Matthew gives the shortest version, and the most detailed version is in Mark. In Mark, this event occurs after Jesus delivers a series of parables near the sea:

> And the same day, when the even was come, he saith unto them, "Let us pass over unto the other side." And when they had sent away the multitude, they took him even as he was in the ship. And there were also with him other little ships. And there arose a great storm of wind, and the waves beat into the ship, so that it was now full.
>
> And he was in the hinder part of the ship, asleep on a pillow; and they awake him, and say unto him, "Master, carest thou not that we perish?" And he arose, and rebuked the wind, and said unto the sea, "Peace, be still." And the wind ceased, and there was a great calm. And

*Calming the
Storm*, fresco,
16th century

he said unto them, "Why are ye so fearful? How is it that ye have no faith?" And they feared exceedingly, and said one to another, "What manner of man is this, that even the wind and the sea obey him?" (Mk 4.35–41)

Mark is the only one of the three Synoptics evangelists who mentions that there were other boats apart from the boat Jesus and the disciples were using. Whom does Jesus ask to sail to the other side of the lake? Mark frames the scene before Jesus enters the boat by saying: "But without a parable spake he not unto them; and when they were alone, he expounded all things to his disciples" (Mk 4.34). By the word "them" the evangelist means not the disciples, but the crowd at large. In Matthew and Luke, however, Jesus is clearly alone in the boat with his disciples. Moreover, if in Mark the disciples take Jesus with them (it is likely that he was using a boat that belonged to Peter and Andrew or the sons of Zebedee), then in Matthew, on the contrary, Jesus enters the boat and the disciples follow him (Mt 8.23). In Luke, Jesus enters the boat with his disciples (Lk 8.22).

What happens on the lake is called by Matthew a great storm (σεισμὸς μέγας; *seismos megas*). The term σεισμός (*seismos*) in Greek can also indicate an earthquake. Mark uses the expression λαῖλαψ μεγάλη ἀνέμου (*lailaps megalē anemou*), which can be translated as a "hurricane," "strong wind," or "strong storm with wind." All three evangelists mention that the boat began to take on water. Luke adds that they were in danger (Lk 8.23).

Despite the raging storm, Jesus slept. What can explain such a heavy sleep in such a violent storm? The traditional interpretation of the Holy Fathers is as follows: he tested his disciples, giving them time to feel fear and forcing them to sense the full seriousness of the situation. If he had been awake, the disciples would not have been as afraid and would not have called for his help. Therefore he slept to give them time to become truly afraid, so that their sense of what was happening would be sharper.[9]

Such an interpretation, however, lessens the reality of his human nature and contradicts the realism of the text itself. Such a point of view assumes that Jesus worked hard, but never became tired, did not need sleep, and if he slept, it was only to instruct his disciples. Doubtless, Jesus was a great teacher—all his words and many actions were pedagogical. Sometimes he did perform such acts to serve as examples. Having washed the feet of his disciples, he said to them, "If I then, your Lord and Master, have washed your feet; ye also ought to wash one another's feet" (Jn 13.14). In this case, however, his sleep was not instructive, but rather came about as a result of natural needs.

This miracle is one of many confirmations of the fact that Jesus had a complete human nature, which existed together with his divine nature:

> He was baptized as man—but he remitted sins as God. . . . He was tempted as a man, but He conquered as God. . . . He hungered—but he fed thousands. . . . He was wearied, but he is the rest of them that are weary and heavy laden. He was heavy with sleep, but he walked lightly over the sea. He rebuked the winds. . . . He is called . . . a demoniac, but the demons acknowledge him. He drives out demons, and sinks in the sea legions of foul spirits. . . . He prays, but he hears prayer. He weeps, but he causes tears to cease. He asks where Lazarus was laid, for he was man; but he raises Lazarus, for he was God.[10]

[9]Athanasius of Alexandria. *Paschal Homily 29* (*The Festal Letters of Athanasius*, 51); John Chrysostom, *Homily 28 on the Gospel of Matthew* (NPNF[1] 10:190); Cyril of Alexandria, *Commentary on the Gospel of Luke* 8:21 (PG 72:629B).

[10]Gregory the Theologian, Homily 29 (NPNF[2] 7:308–9).

The
*Enthronement
of Metropolitan
Hilarion,*
miniature from
the Radziwill
Chronicle,
13th century

In his "Homily on the Law and Grace," which was the first written work of Old Russian letters, the Metropolitan of Kiev, Hilarion, wrote the following:

> He was fully man by incarnation, not a phantom, but also God by divinity, not simply a man, having revealed on earth both the divine and the human. For as a man, he made his mother's womb heavy, but as God he was born without breaking the seal of virginity. . . . As man he was wrapped in swaddling clothes, but as God he led the magi by the star. As a man he lay in the manger, but as God he accepted the gifts and worship from the magi. As a man, he entered the water naked; as God he accepted the witness of the Father: "This is my beloved Son." As a man he fasted for forty days and became hungry, but as God he defeated the tempter. As a man he came to the marriage in Cana of Galilee, but as God he transformed the water into wine. As a man he slept in the ship, but as God he forbade the winds and the sea, and they listened to him.[11]

The Gospel paints Jesus as a true man, who naturally became tired (Jn 4.6), especially after a long and difficult day. They spent the entire day before they crossed the lake among crowds of people. Matthew, Mark, and Luke describe this day differently; moreover, it is not always clear from their accounts whether what they describe occurred over the course of a

---

[11]Metropolitan Hilarion of Kiev, "Homily on the Law and Grace" (translated by NK).

One of the First Historical Images of Jesus Christ with a Nimbus (Halo), detail from frescoes on catacomb walls, 4th century

single day or several. Based on Matthew's account, we can assume that in a single day, Jesus spoke the Sermon on the Mount, then came down from the hill and healed the leper, then came to Capernaum, where he healed the servant of the centurion; there he also healed the mother-in-law of Peter; finally, when the evening came, "they brought unto him many that were possessed with demons; and he cast out the spirits with his word, and healed all that were sick" (Mt 8.16). It is not surprising that after such a day, Jesus fell asleep in the boat and did not wake up, even when the storm began.

Only Mark mentions that Jesus slept "on a pillow." The term in Greek is προσκεφάλαιον (*proskephalaion*). According to some scholars, this was a special pillow used by fishermen when they did not participate in rowing.[12] According to others, this could have been something from the boat itself, such as a ballast bag[13] that Jesus used instead of a pillow.

How severe was the storm? Did the disciples exaggerate the danger? It may seem so, since we are speaking of a lake (though it was sometimes called a sea). But even today, a storm on the Sea of Galilee is no rare occurrence. Furthermore, because of the local climate, the storm may appear suddenly and be quite severe. The most likely time for such a storm is evening. A sudden storm can be caused by a sudden change in temperature. If we are to consider the quality of fishermen's boats during Jesus' time, then a storm in the middle of the sea in the dark was truly life-threatening.

All three evangelists mention that the disciples woke Jesus up, but only Mark gives their words a tone of rebuke. In Matthew, their words sound desperate: "Lord, save us; we perish" (Mt 8.25). Luke makes it sound as though they are screaming: "Master, master, we perish" (Lk 8.24). The

[12]G. Dalman, *Orte und Wege Jesu* (Gütersloh: Betelsman, 1924), 198.
[13]S. Wachsman, "The Galilee Boat: 2000 Year Old Hull Recovered," *Biblical Archaeology Review* 14 (1988): 18–33, at 33.

Jesus Sleeps during the Storm, Delacroix, 19th century

disciples were clearly quite upset and afraid. They saw their deliverance in Jesus alone, though they probably did not wake him up with the hope that he would stop the storm solely by his will. More likely, they hoped for his advice or some other form of help.

In Matthew, when Jesus wakes up he first admonishes the disciples for their weak faith and only then arises and forbids the winds and the sea. In Mark and Luke, he first gets up, calms the storm, and then, after silence falls, rebukes the disciples. Only Mark gives Jesus' words to the sea: "Peace, be still!" His words to the disciples are similar in all three versions. The most detailed version is found in Mark. Matthew's version reads: "Why are ye fearful, O ye of little faith?" (Mt 8.26) In Luke, he says, "Where is your faith?" (Lk 8.25)

The theme of faith is once again central, as in other miracle narratives. Jesus often rebukes weak faith directly. Sometimes he rebukes the crowd (Mt 6.30; Lk 12.28), sometimes all of his disciples (Mt 16.8), sometimes one of them (Mt 14.31). The term ὀλιγόπιστοι (*oligopistoi*, "those of little faith") indicates no small deficit of faith. In other cases, Jesus goes so far as to admonish them for "unbelief" (ὀλιγοπιστία; *oligopistia*, literally "little faith"; Mt 17.20).

This episode presents faith in two aspects.[14] On the one hand, Jesus' words can be interpreted as a reminder of faith in the omnipotence of God, who protects people even when they sleep: "When thou liest down, thou shalt not be afraid; yea, thou shalt lie down, and thy sleep shall be sweet. Be not afraid of sudden fear, neither of the desolation of the wicked, when it cometh. For the LORD shall be thy confidence, and shall keep thy foot from being taken" (Prov 3.24–26). On the other hand, here—as in many other cases of healing or exorcisms—faith may mean faith in Jesus himself, in his ability to perform the miracle, to protect the weak, to come to their aid, to save them from death.

Apparently, Mark records that those who had sailed together with Jesus and his disciples on other boats were struck with wonder at the miracle. In Matthew's version, up to this point there was no one present except for Jesus and his disciples; but he also speaks of people who "marvelled, saying, 'What manner of man is this, that even the winds and the sea obey him'" (Mt 8.27). In Luke, the wonder and awe is ascribed to the disciples directly, who say to each other, "What manner of man is this! For he commandeth even the winds and water, and they obey him" (Lk 8.25). These words sound similar to what the Pharisees who ate with Jesus said in the previous chapter: "Who is this that forgiveth sins also?" (Lk 7.49) In Luke's account, Jesus is gradually revealed through a series of events in which his actions inspire amazement.

Having examined this text in its three variants, we can ask the following question: What actually happened, and what is the meaning of the miracle? We will set aside the commentaries of the rationalists of the nineteenth century, who either reject the miracle outright or lessen the power of the storm, or consider that what happened was a typical change in weather, which the surrounding people ascribed to Jesus without any reason.[15] Such interpretations do not help understand the historical context or the theological meaning that the evangelists ascribed to it.

Much more useful for understanding this account is an examination of those Old Testament narratives that could be seen as foreshadowing the

---

[14]Marcus, *Mark 8–16*, 334.

[15]A survey of such opinions is present in Loos, *The Miracles of Jesus*, 639–41.

miracle. In the Old Testament, there is a special connection between God and the element of water. God's presence was often seen in natural disasters associated with water, and the cessation of such calamities was also associated with the hand of God: "The Lord hath his way in the whirlwind and in the storm, and the clouds are the dust of his feet. He rebuketh the sea, and maketh it dry, and drieth up all the rivers" (Nah 1.3–4). In the Psalms, God is called one who "troubles the depth of the sea. Who shall calm the noise of its waves?" (Ps 64.7). Before God, the waters tremble: "The waters saw thee, O God, the waters saw thee and were afraid; the depths were troubled. . . . Thy ways are in the sea, and thy paths in many waters" (Ps 76.16, 19). God created the waters (Ps 94.5). He "calleth for the waters of the sea, and poureth them out upon the face of the earth" (Am 5.8). Nevertheless, he is also able to stop their flow: "he withholdeth the waters, and they dry up; also he sendeth them out, and they overturn the earth" (Job 12.15).

In Exodus, Moses "stretched out his hand over the sea; and the LORD caused the sea to go back by a strong east wind all that night, and made the sea dry land, and the waters were divided. And the children of Israel went into the midst of the sea upon the dry ground; and the waters were a wall unto them on their right hand, and on their left" (Ex 14.21–22). Here many details are similar to the Synoptic accounts of Christ calming the waves: the miracle is ascribed to the direct intervention of God; the miracle occurs through the direct mediation of a specific person; there is strong wind mentioned in both; the miracle saves people from life-threatening danger. The Psalms describe the miracle in Exodus thus: "He rebuked the Red Sea also, and it was dried up; and he led them through the deep as through the wilderness. And he saved them from the hand of them that hated them, and redeemed them from the hand of the enemies. . . . They believed his word, and they sang his praise" (Ps 105.9–13). In other words, the miracle led those who were delivered to gain faith.

When the prophet Jonah wanted to flee from before the face of God:

> But the LORD sent out a great wind into the sea, and there was a mighty tempest in the sea, so that the ship was like to be broken. Then the

Crossing the Red Sea, B. D'Antonio, 16th century

mariners were afraid, and cried every man unto his god, and cast forth the wares that were in the ship into the sea, to lighten it of them. But Jonah was gone down into the sides of the ship; and he lay, and was fast asleep. So the shipmaster came to him, and said unto him, "What meanest thou, O sleeper? Arise, call upon thy God, if so be that God will think upon us, that we perish not."

And they said every one to his fellow, "Come, and let us cast lots, that we may know for whose cause this evil is upon us." So they cast lots, and the lot fell upon Jonah. Then said they unto him, "Tell us, we pray thee, for whose cause this evil is upon us; what is thine occupation? And whence comest thou? What is thy country? And of what people art thou?" And he said unto them, "I am a Hebrew; and I fear the LORD, the God of heaven, which hath made the sea and the dry land."

Then were the men exceedingly afraid, and said unto him, "Why hast thou done this?" For the men knew that he fled from the presence of the LORD, because he had told them. Then said they unto him, "What shall we do unto thee, that the sea may be calm unto us?" For the sea wrought, and was tempestuous. And he said unto them, "Take me up, and cast me forth into the sea; so shall the sea be calm unto you; for I know that for my sake this great tempest is upon you."

Nevertheless the men rowed hard to bring it to the land; but they could not; for the sea wrought, and was tempestuous against them.

Exodus, excerpt from the Nuremberg Chronicles, 1493

Wherefore they cried unto the LORD, and said, "We beseech thee, O LORD, we beseech thee, let us not perish for this man's life, and lay not upon us innocent blood; for thou, O LORD, hast done as it pleased thee."

So they took up Jonah, and cast him forth into the sea; and the sea ceased from her raging. Then the men feared the LORD exceedingly, and offered a sacrifice unto the LORD, and made vows. (Jon 1.4–16)

Again in this account there are many details reminiscent of the miracle of the calming of the storm: the storm at sea, the threat of death, the main character sleeping, his awakening, his companions rebuking him, the sudden cessation of the storm thanks to the direct intervention of God, fear of God expressed by those who witnessed the miracle.[16]

We may also mention that the words of Mark "and they feared exceedingly" are a Semitism and correspond to the words "the men feared the Lord exceedingly" in the Book of Jonah. In Mark, the expression "exceeding fear" echoes the phrases "great windstorm" and "great calm," which also appear in this episode. The triple use of the same adjective, on the one hand strengthens the contrast between the severity of the storm and the sudden calm; on the other hand, it also reflects the singular impression that was left in the hearts of the eyewitnesses.

[16]Cf. O. L. Cope, *Matthew: A Scribe Trained for the Kingdom of Heaven,* in The Catholic Biblical Quarterly Monograph Series, vol. 5 (Washington, DC: Catholic Biblical Association of America, 1976), 96–97.

These Old Testament accounts, as well as many other episodes where water reacts in a supernatural manner because of the direct action of God (Josh 3.14–17) or a prophet (2 Kg 2.8, 14), were well known to the evangelists. But it would have been extremely unlikely and unfair to suspect, as some scholars do, that its authors "modeled" the account of this particular New Testament miracle on Old Testament miracles. After all, this event was witnessed by many people, and the event left a strong impression on the evangelists themselves or on those eye-witnesses who provided the primary accounts for the evangelists who were not direct eyewitnesses to these events.

This reminder of the Old Testament miracles further shows the continuity of Christ's words and deeds with the Old Testament. In the Sermon on the Mount, he presented himself as the new Moses, who came not to destroy the Law, but to fulfill it (Mt 5.17), that is, to give it a new content, having renewed that covenant that God made with ancient Israel through Moses. The miracles of Jesus also reminded his contemporaries of the great prophets of ancient times and of the works of God that were accomplished through them. But if God acted through men in the history of the Exodus, then God and man still remained separate individuals. In this case, God and man act in a single person—Jesus Christ, the incarnate God. He performed both normal human actions (he grew tired, slept, awoke) and those that prove his divine essence (he stops the wind and calms the storm).

The first-created man was the master of nature, which was supposed to serve him and submit to his word without demur. After the fall, man lost that power. The God-Man Jesus, in his own person, restored the lost power of man over nature. He powerfully commands the wind and sea, and they submit to him immediately, just as demons submit to his word, and diseases are likewise healed by his word alone.

Moreover, in the Gospels, if demons and sicknesses represent the power of the evil one, from which Jesus frees mankind, nature and even natural disasters are not evil by their nature. Jesus' words "Peace, be still," could outwardly remind us of the words used to expel demons (see Mk 1.25; Lk 4.35); but this does not mean that Jesus treats the sea as a demonic power.

If every exorcism is presented as a battle between Jesus and the world of the demons, then here, on the contrary, we see the complete subjugation of the elements to the powerful word of Jesus. If the demons try to oppose his power, the sea and wind submit without complaining.

The calming of the storm was not a demonstration of Jesus' power or authority, just as his sleep was not a "teaching moment." If we are to assume that when they embarked, Jesus already knew that the storm would come, then the entire episode may appear as a carefully orchestrated event that was enacted according to a previously planned script. Instead, the evangelists paint a picture that gives the opposite impression—the storm came about sud-

The Storm at Sea, Gospel book belonging to Abbes Hilda of Meschede, 1020

denly, the disciples were not prepared for it, and the exhausted Jesus slept. His awakening and everything that followed was not a miracle for the sake of a miracle, it was not the sign that the Jews asked from him, which he did not give them. And though in answer to their request Jesus promised that they would see the sign of the prophet Jonah (Mt 16.1–4), that sign was completely different—the sign that Jesus was preparing for during the entire course of his earthly life, which he foretold to his disciples many times: his death and three-day burial in the womb of the earth.

In this account, Jesus looks not so much like Jonah as the Old Testament God. This similarity is seen first of all in the way he stopped the storm by his will alone, just as God "divideth the sea with his power, and by his understanding he smiteth through the proud" (Job 26.12). Even the fact that Jesus slept calls to mind the one who rested on the seventh day after all his work creating the world (Gen 2.2). The disciples' call is also similar to various exhortations of God found in the Psalms: "Arise, O Lord, save me, O my God!" (Psalm 3.8); "O Lord; keep not silence. O Lord, depart not from me" (Psalm 34.25); "Rise up, why sleepest thou, O Lord? Arise!" (Psalm 43.24).

Noah Releases a Dove from the Ark, detail of a mosaic, 12th century

The authors of the Old Testament books underline God's connection with water many times. The New Testament continues this theme in the mystical connection between Jesus and water—beginning with the waters of Jordan in which he was baptized, and ending with the waters of the Sea of Galilee, where many events of his life occurred. When Jesus was baptized by John, he sanctified the waters by descending into them, filling them with his divine presence. The Sea of Galilee, which witnessed so many of Jesus' miracles—a lake he crossed many times by boat, in which he caught fish together with his disciples—also absorbed into itself the wonder-working energy of his presence.

In contrast to Moses, Jesus never appeared on the banks of the Red Sea in the Gospels. The evangelists do not describe a single event connected with the Mediterranean Sea or its shoreline. Nor do they mention the Dead Sea, even though Jesus was in the area surrounding Jericho, which is quite close to it. The most important body of water—a kind of geographical center of Jesus' activity—was the Sea of Galilee.

This lake becomes a type of the baptismal font: all who enter the community of Jesus' disciples must descend into it. In the Gospels, many accounts connected with water foreshadow the theme of baptism—this is also true of the calming of the waves. As early as the late second century, Tertullian wrote of those (critically, it must be said) who believed that "the apostles then served the turn of baptism when in their little ship, [they] were sprinkled and covered with the waves."[17] Ancient Christianity often used the boat to symbolize the Church—the ark that, like Noah's ark, saves mankind from the surging waves of this world. According to Augustine, Noah is a type of Christ, and the ark is a type of the Church.[18]

---

[17]Tertullian, *On Baptism* 12 (ANF 3:675).

[18]Augustine, *Commentary on the Gospel of John* 9.11 (NPNF[1] 7:67) and *Letter* 108.7 (CSEL 34.2:633).

Ancient commentators reflect upon this rich series of images when they interpret the calming of the storm. But such interpretations are thematically distant from the text of the Gospels, since they transfer its content into the realm of symbols and allegory. Nevertheless, the symbolic significance of the miracles in the Gospels is revealed anew for every age. The question the disciples ask the sleeping Jesus reminds us of that universal question mankind asks God from the time of Jonah even to the present day, in various forms: "Why does God not take care of people when they are in trouble? Why does he sleep when the storm rages? Why does he allow evil, not cutting it off at the source?"

When Job, oppressed with sorrows and illness, asked God similar questions, God did not answer him for a long time. But then he suddenly answered in a frightening manner: "Who is this that darkeneth counsel by words without knowledge? Gird up now thy loins like a man; for I will demand of thee, and answer thou me" (Job 38.1–2). Instead of the answers that Job expected, God asks Job a series of questions:

Where wast thou when I laid the foundations of the earth? Declare, if thou hast understanding. Who hath laid the measures thereof, if thou knowest? Or who hath stretched the line upon it? Whereupon are the foundations thereof fastened? Or who laid the corner stone thereof, when the morning stars sang together, and all the sons of God shouted for joy? Or who shut up the sea with doors, when it broke forth, as if it had issued out of the womb? When I made the cloud the garment thereof, and thick darkness a swaddlingband for it, and broke up for it my decreed place, and set bars and doors, and said, "Hitherto shalt thou come, but no further, and here shall thy proud waves be stayed"? Hast thou commanded the morning since thy days, and caused the dayspring to know his place? Hast thou entered into the springs of the sea? Or hast thou walked in the search of the depth? Wilt thou also disannul my judgment? Wilt thou condemn me, that thou mayest be righteous? Hast thou an arm like God? Or canst thou thunder with a voice like him? (Job 38.4–12, 16; 40.8–9)

Job and His Friends,
Doré, 1860s

Job does not receive an answer to a single one of his questions. But he receives an answer to the most important question that summarized all of his other questions: why is God absent when man suffers? God is not absent. He is near. God's answer to all these questions is his presence in the life of man. Shaken by the fact that God appeared to him in person, Job said, "I have heard of thee by the hearing of the ear, but now mine eye seeth thee. Wherefore I abhor myself, and repent in dust and ashes" (Job 42.5–6).

In the Gospel account of the calming of the storm, we see a similar dialogue between men and God. They ask him: "Master, carest thou not that we perish?" And Jesus answers their question with a question: "Why are you so fearful? How can you have so little faith?" Man's most pressing calamity is not that God is absent, but that man does not notice his presence. Faith is the connective tissue between people and God, which helps them not to forget about God's constant presence in their lives. The fact that God is near, that he hears our prayers and answers them, that he actively participates in our lives and is always ready to come to our aid, that he loves us and has compassion on us—Jesus constantly reminds his disciples of all this both by his preaching and his actions.

God answers all mankind's questioning by sending his own Only-begotten Son to them. The people of the Old Testament lived in the hope that they would encounter God face to face. Job expresses this hope: "For I know that my redeemer liveth, and that he shall stand at the latter day upon the earth. And though after my skin worms destroy this body, yet in my flesh shall I see God, whom I shall see for myself, and mine eyes shall behold, and not another, though my reins be consumed within me" (Job 19.25–27). This hope is accomplished when the Redeemer—God in human form—comes to earth and people see him with their own eyes.

Jesus offered people direct access to God, without any intermediaries. To believe in God means to believe in Jesus as the Only-begotten Son sent by God, the one who has the same might, power, and majesty as his Father.

God is not far; he is near. God does not sleep; he is awake and remembers man. God is not powerless to deliver people from calamities, but this requires the cooperation of man; this requires faith. This is the good news that Jesus brought to earth directly from God. This is the answer that God gives in the Gospel to all of mankind's questions.

5. Feeding the Five Thousand

Only one of Christ's miracles is present in all four Gospels—the feeding of the five thousand men with five loaves of bread and two fish. Moreover, in three of the Gospels—Matthew, Mark, and John—another miracle immediately follows: Jesus walking on the Sea of Galilee. This is the best order in which to examine these two events, which are thematically connected.

The most complete version, which is filled with specific details, is found in Mark:

> And the apostles gathered themselves together unto Jesus, and told him all things, both what they had done, and what they had taught. And he said unto them, "Come ye yourselves apart into a desert place, and rest a while"; for there were many coming and going, and they had no leisure so much as to eat.
>
> And they departed into a desert place by ship privately. And the people saw them departing, and many knew him, and ran afoot thither out of all cities, and outwent them, and came together unto him. And Jesus, when he came out, saw much people, and was moved with compassion toward them, because they were as sheep not having a shepherd; and he began to teach them many things. And when the day was now far spent, his disciples came unto him, and said, "This is a desert place, and now the time is far passed. Send them away, that they may go into the country round about, and into the villages, and buy themselves bread, for they have nothing to eat."

The Church
of the
Multiplication
of the Loaves
in Israel (where
Jesus fed the five
thousand men)

He answered and said unto them, "Give ye them to eat." And they say unto him, "Shall we go and buy two hundred denarii of bread, and give them to eat?" He saith unto them, "How many loaves have ye? Go and see." And when they knew, they say, "Five, and two fish."

And he commanded them to make all sit down by companies upon the green grass. And they sat down in ranks, by hundreds, and by fifties. And when he had taken the five loaves and the two fish, he looked up to heaven, and blessed, and broke the loaves, and gave them to his disciples to set before them; and the two fishes divided he among them all. And they did all eat, and were filled. And they took up twelve baskets full of the fragments, and of the fish. And they that did eat of the loaves were about five thousand men. (Mk 6.30–44)

We can divide the account into three parts. The first is a kind of prelude: we read about the events preceding the miracle and the various extenuating circumstances. The second part is concentrated around the dialogue between Jesus and the disciples. The third is the actual account of the miracle. The insistent repetition of the word "many" and "much" underlines the large scale of the miracle and its prolonged nature. All these reminders have a dramatic effect on the reader and prepare him

Feeding the Multitude, A. Ivanov, 19th century

for the revelation of the total number of people who were present at the miracle: "about five thousand men," which does not include the women and children.

The beginning of the account is connected to the scene where Jesus "called unto him the twelve, and began to send them forth by two and two; and gave them power over unclean spirits." Having listened to his command, "they went out, and preached that men should repent. And they cast out many devils, and anointed with oil many that were sick, and healed them" (Mk 6.7, 12–13). We do not know how long this independent ministry of the apostles lasted; evidently, it was not very long. We also do not know what Jesus was doing while his disciples were absent.

And so they returned, and Jesus suggested they take their rest in a deserted place. The word "rest" can be understood only in one way—to rest from the crowd; after all, other kinds of rest are not possible in the middle of the desert. The remark that the apostles did not have time to eat reminds us of an earlier observation: "And the multitude cometh together again, so that they could not so much as eat bread" (Mk 3.20). It seems that the apostle whose story Mark recorded knew this particularity of Jesus' way of life—because of the multitude of the crowds, he and his disciples did not have time to eat. The sense of hunger was so keen that he remembered it years later, when, evidently, he told the evangelist about it.

The apostles go to a desert place by boat. Evidently, this deserted area was on the same shoreline, because the people ran after them along the banks of the sea. When the boat landed, the people, from whose company the apostles had planned to rest, were already there. Jesus was also there, though how he got there is not clear. It is possible he walked.

Matthew, Luke, and John paint a slightly different picture. According to Matthew, "When Jesus heard of it, he departed thence by ship into a desert place apart; and when the people had heard thereof, they followed him on foot out of the cities. And Jesus went forth, and saw a great multitude, and was moved with compassion toward them, and he healed their sick" (Mt 14.13–14). In Luke's version, as in Mark's, "The apostles, when they were returned, told him all that they had done. And he took them, and went aside privately into a desert place belonging to the city called Bethsaida. And the people, when they knew it, followed him; and he received them, and spake unto them of the kingdom of God, and healed them that had need of healing" (Lk 9.10–11).

Finally, in John's account, the beginning of the story differs from all Synoptics: "After these things Jesus went over the sea of Galilee, which is the sea of Tiberias. And a great multitude followed him, because they saw his miracles which he did on them that were diseased. And Jesus went up into a mountain, and there he sat with his disciples. And the passover, a feast of the Jews, was nigh" (Jn 6.1–4).[19] Thus, in John's version, this is the situation: a multitude was already with Jesus, and they did not want to leave.

If Matthew and Mark do not say anything about the place where this occurred, then Luke and John's versions have a slight discrepancy—Luke mentions a deserted place near Bethsaida, while John speaks of a hill near Tiberias.

The exact location of Bethsaida is a subject of contention among scholars; in current scholarship, however, there is a certain consensus that it was found near the place of the contemporary city of Et-Tell on the northern bank of the Sea of Galilee, to the right side of the Jordan.[20] Tiberias is found on the Western bank of the lake, quite a distance from Bethsaida.

[19]Some scholars consider the mention of the Passover as a parallel to Moses's sojourn in the desert. G. L. Borchert, *John 1–11: An Exegetical and Theological Exposition of Holy Scripture* (Nashville: Holmann Reference, 1996), 249.

[20]See M. A. Chancey, *Greco-Roman Culture and the Galilee of Jesus* (Cambridge: Cambridge University Press, 2008) 90–91, *The Myth of a Gentile Galilee*, 106–8.

*Feeding the
Five Thousand,
miniature,
1411–16*

It is difficult to harmonize the two accounts, though there have been many attempts. According to one theory, in Jesus' time there were two cities called Bethsaida.[21] Around 30 BC, the tetrarch Philip renamed Bethsaida "Julia" in honor of the daughter of Augustus Caesar.[22] This does not mean, however, that among Jewish society the city stopped being called Bethsaida, or that the name was transferred to a different city.

There is some tangential evidence not only in Luke, but also in John, to favor Bethsaida (as opposed to Tiberias) as the place where the multiplication of the loaves occurred. Only John mentions that Jesus "lifted up

[21]L. A. Belyaev, "Vifsaida" [Bethsaida], in *Pravoslavnaya entsiklopedia* [Orthodox encyclopedia] (Moscow, 2004), 8:606.

[22]Josephus, *The Antiquities of the Jews* 18.2.1, in *The Works of Josephus*, 478.

Bethsaida

his eyes, and saw a great company come unto him, [and] saith unto Philip, 'Whence shall we buy bread, that these may eat?' And this he said to prove him; for he himself knew what he would do" (Jn 6.5–6). Why does Jesus ask this question of Philip, and not some other disciple? Because Philip was from Bethsaida of Galilee (Jn 1.44), and it would have been natural to assume that Jesus would turn to Philip as an inhabitant of the city closest to where they were.

Another tangential piece of evidence is the mention of Andrew, the brother of Simon Peter, who, according to the Gospel, said to Jesus, "There is a lad here, which hath five barley loaves, and two small fishes, but what are they among so many?" (Jn 6.9) Andrew was also from Bethsaida, and it is likely that he knew of this boy because he knew the family of the boy who was at this moment in the crowd.

John's mention of Philip and Andrew could be a confirmation of the fact that in his Gospel Bethsaida was changed to Tiberias (perhaps because of some early scribal error).

In the Catholic tradition, the place where the loaves were multiplies is believed to be the village of Tabgha, on the Western shore of the sea of Galilee—there was a Christian church here as early as the fourth century. At the end of the fifth century, the original building was taken apart, and on its place a larger new church was built. A mosaic floor with the image of a basket holding five loaves of bread and two fish is extant from this church. This image was a symbol of the Eucharist, while at the same time reminding the assembled people of the miracle recounted in the Gospel.

As in Mark, Matthew mentions that Jesus, having seen the multitude of people, had compassion on them. But if in Mark the result of this compassion was that Jesus began to teach them many things, then in Matthew, Jesus expresses his compassion by healing their sick. Luke, saying nothing of Jesus' compassion, combined both versions by saying that "he received them, and spake unto them of the kingdom of God, and healed them that had need of healing" (Lk 9.11). Concerning Jesus' compassion for the people, Matthew places this passage elsewhere, using the same language that we find in Mark's account of the multiplication of the loaves:

> And Jesus went about all the cities and villages, teaching in their synagogues, and preaching the gospel of the kingdom, and healing every sickness and every disease among the people. But when he saw the multitudes, he was moved with compassion on them, because they fainted, and were scattered abroad, as sheep having no shepherd. Then saith he unto his disciples, "The harvest truly is plenteous, but the laborers are few. Pray ye therefore the Lord of the harvest, that he will send forth laborers into his harvest" (Mt 9.35–38)

The image of the harvest corresponds to the image of bread, which is central to this miracle. Seeing the crowd around him, Jesus thinks of them as a harvest for which workers are needed—the apostles must become these workers. At the same time, he compares these crowds to a flock with no shepherd. Only he can become such a shepherd. He is the Good Shepherd who gives his life for the sheep (Jn 10.11), "and the sheep hear his voice, and he calleth his own sheep by name, and leadeth them out. And when he putteth forth his own sheep, he goeth before them, and the sheep follow him; for they know his voice" (Jn 10.3–4).

The Synoptics agree that the disciples (Luke has them as "the twelve") asked Jesus to let the people go home because of the lateness of the hour, so that all the people could buy food. In answer, Jesus says, "Give ye them to eat" (Mt 14.16). The accent in this phrase is on the word "ye." Matthew and Luke leave out Mark's comment about the two hundred denarii needed to buy food for all these people. In John, it is Philip who mentions the two hundred denarii: "Two hundred pennyworth of bread is not sufficient for them, that every one of them may take a little" (Jn 6.7).

The denarius was a Roman silver coin corresponding to the daily wage of a day laborer—this is the meaning of the denarius in the parable with the owner of the vineyard (Mt 20:9–13). Two hundred denarii, consequently, was no small sum, one which the disciples would not have had available to them, even if they had saved some money in the moneybox (which Judas carried; see Jn 12.6). No moneybox would have had enough reserve to pay for food for such a multitude.

According to the Synoptics, the disciples answer Jesus that they have five loaves and two fish. Moreover, in Luke, the disciples add the following rejoinder: "except we should go and buy food for all this people" (Lk 9.13). In John's Gospel, as we have seen, Andrew answers Jesus concerning the five loaves and two fish belonging to a certain young man in the crowd (Jn 6.9). Only John mentions that the loaves of bread were made of barley. The word for "fish" in the three Synoptic Gospels is the classical Greek word ἰχθύς (ichthys; "fish")—the same that in the early Church was used as a cryptogram for "Jesus Christ, Son of God, Savior." John used the word ὀψάριον (opsarion), which is a double diminutive of the word ὄψον (opson), which in classical Greek meant "snack" or any dish made either from fish or meat that would be eaten with bread. In this case ὀψάριον (opsarion) clearly refers to salted or dried fish.[23]

As we see, the circumstances that preceded this miracle are different in all four Gospels. Moreover, the Synoptics' differences relate mostly to the amount of detail each gives to his version of the account; John differs from them in many details. The Synoptics do not single out any disciples by name; the disciples act as a single group. John, who in other cases paid attention to the remarks of individual disciples, names Andrew and Philip specifically. In Mark's version Jesus asks the disciples to go and see how much bread they have, in John, he does not ask the questions, because he knows in advance what he wants to do. If the synoptics have the disciples

---

[23]Brown, *The Gospel according to John (I–XII)*, 233.

request that Jesus let the people go, then in John's account, Jesus himself worries about how to satisfy their hunger.

The sequence of events for the miracle itself is described identically by all four evangelists. First, Jesus commands the disciples to seat the people in groups; he gives thanks to God; he breaks bread; he passes out the food; everyone eats and is filled; twelve full baskets of leftover bread remain.[24] John differs in certain details, however, while Mark has the most attention to detail among the Synoptics.

In Matthew, Jesus commands the disciples to bring him five loaves of bread and two fish, while he commands the people to sit on the grass (Mt 14.18–19). In Luke, Jesus commands the disciples to seat the people in rows of fifty (Lk 9.14–15). Mark twice uses a Semitic stylistic flourish in his account: he repeats the same word to indicate a multiplicity of objects or phenomena. In his account, Jesus commands the disciples to seat everyone συμπόσια-συμπόσια (*symposia-symposia*; literally "groups-groups"). In Greek, the word συμπόσιον (*symposion*), which comes from the prefix "together" and the verb "to drink," indicates a group of people who gather to sit together and eat and drink; this word can also mean a dinner or feast. In Mark, the people sit πρασιαὶ πρασιαὶ (*prasiai prasiai*; literally "rows-rows") by fifty and one hundred. In Classical Greek, the term πρασιά (*prasia*) indicates a seedbed, or in this case, a row. Mark is the only one to mention that the grass was green; John mentions "now there was much grass in the place" (Jn 6.10). This detail corresponds to the remark that it was before Passover, meaning that this occurred in spring, when the grass is still green and not burnt by the sun.

Matthew describes the thanksgiving that Jesus offers to God before breaking the bread with expressions similar to Mark's: "He . . . took the five loaves, and the two fish, and looking up to heaven, he blessed, and broke, and gave the loaves to his disciples, and the disciples to the multitude" (Mt 14.19). In Luke, the breaking of the bread is described in similar words (Lk 9.16). In John's account, "Jesus took the loaves; and when he had given

[24]Some scholars see a symbolic meaning in this number to suggest the twelve tribes of Israel. D. A. Carson, *The Gospel according to John* (Grand Rapids, MI: Wm. B. Eerdmans and Co., 1991), 271.

thanks, he distributed to the disciples, and the disciples to them that were set down; and likewise of the fishes as much as they would" (Jn 6.11). John is the only one who uses the participle εὐχαριστήσας (*eucharistēsas*; literally "having given thanks"), which in the early Church immediately calls the Eucharist to mind. All three terms: "break," "bless," and "give thanks" were only used by the Synoptics when describing the Mystical Supper.

Why did Jesus look up to heaven before breaking bread and giving it to the disciples? Commentators see in this an indication that he was giving honor to the Father without diminishing his equality with the Father, as well as an indication of the unity of will between Father and Son:

> Wherefore did he look up to heaven, and bless? It was to be believed of him, both that he is of the Father, and that he is equal to him. But the proofs of these things seemed to oppose one another. For while his equality was indicated by his doing all with authority, of his origin from the Father they could no otherwise be persuaded, than by his doing all with great lowliness, and with reference to him, and invoking him on his works. Wherefore we see that he neither did these actions only, nor those, that both might be confirmed; and now he works miracles with authority, now with prayer. Then again, that what he did might not seem an inconsistency, in the lesser things he looks up to heaven, but in the greater does all with authority; to teach you in the lesser also, that not as receiving power from elsewhere, but as honoring him that begot him, so he acts.[25]

Why did our Lord Jesus Christ look up at heaven? He did not act thus when he performed the great miracle—when he opened the eyes of the blind, purified lepers, cast out demons, forbid the sea and the winds, transformed water into wine, or even resurrected some of the dead. So why in this case did he look at heaven, turning his gaze to his heavenly Father? First of all, to show the unity of will between him and his father before such a multitude of people and thereby repudiate the hateful slander of the Pharisees who insisted that he performed all his miracles

[25]John Chrysostom, *Homilies on the Gospel of Matthew*, Homiliy 49 (NPNF[1] 10:304–5).

with the help of demonic power. Second, as the Son of Man, he did this to reveal to mankind a model of humility before God and gratitude for all good things that come from God. He gave them a similar example during the Mystical Supper: "Jesus took bread, blessed and broke it" (Mt 26.26), "then he took the cup, and gave thanks . . . and he took bread, gave thanks and broke it" (Lk 22.17, 19). He gave thanks to his heavenly Father and blessed the bread a gift of God . . . Third, as the Son of God, he showed the unity of the creative powers of the Trinity in unity, who creates in and of itself, by multiplying the loaves like a new act of creation. The Father, Son, and Holy Spirit—the Trinity one in essence and indivisible—is the Creator of all that is.[26]

The expression "they all ate and were filled" is found in all three Synoptic Gospels, as is the mention of the twelve baskets of leftovers. John's account notes that Jesus himself commanded the apostles to gather the leftovers. He also includes the reaction of the people: "When they were filled, he said unto his disciples, 'Gather up the fragments that remain, that nothing be lost.' Therefore they gathered them together, and filled twelve baskets with the fragments of the five barley loaves, which remained over and above unto them that had eaten. Then those men, when they had seen the miracle that Jesus did, said, 'This is of a truth that prophet that should come into the world'" (Jn 6.12–14).

In all four accounts, there are five thousand present at the miracle. Mark, Luke, and John add the detail that this count only included the men. Matthew expresses the same idea thus: "they that had eaten were about five thousand men, beside women and children" (Mt 14.21). If the men came with their wives and children, then we can estimate that there were far more than five thousand people present. At the very least, there is one child (παιδάριον; *paidarion* [Jn 6.9])—the one who had brought the barley loaves and fish—present in John's account. As for any other women and children, we know nothing definitive; but the fact that they are mentioned in Matthew and that all four evangelists use the word "men" in the

[26]St Nikolai Velimirovich, *Tvoreniya* [Collected works], 2:120–21 (translated by NK).

Christy and an Angel: The Eucharist, fresco, 14th century

specific, not general, sense, suggests that women were indeed present there as well.

The patriarchal culture of the Israel of that time did not allow for the possibility of women to gather in large crowds outside their homes, especially with their children, and to follow their husbands around. The modern tradition of family outings in nature appeared much later. During Jesus' time, women and children remained home for the most part, while the men worked and were active in society. In spite of this, however, we constantly see women in the crowds surrounding Jesus. Not long before this account of the multiplication of the loaves, Luke mentions that when Jesus "went throughout every city and village, preaching and showing the glad tidings of the kingdom of God, and the twelve were with him, and certain women, which had been healed of evil spirits and infirmities. . . . and many others, which ministered unto him of their substance" (Lk 8.1–3).

All four evangelists attribute special significance to this account, which is clear from the following: its inclusion in all four Gospels, Mark and John's attention to detail, and the use of eucharistic terminology in all four versions. In the early Church, the miracle of the multiplication of the loaves had significance not in and of itself, but first as a type of the Mystical Supper and a symbol of the Eucharist that Jesus commanded his disciples to perform in his remembrance. The Eucharist, after all, was the act of the ecclesiastical community that unified its members even before other unifying factors appeared, such as the canonical Gospels, a formalized dogmatic exposition of Christianity, or a system of universally accepted canons.

The Gospel according to John makes the connection between the miracle of the multiplication of the loaves and the Eucharist most obvious. John is the only evangelist who does not mention the act of breaking bread during the Mystical Supper. Nevertheless, he is also the only evangelist to relate Jesus' conversation with the Jews concerning the bread that came down from heaven. This conversation, which remained inscrutable to his listeners, is included in the same chapter of John as the miracle of the five loaves. It begins with the following words:

> Jesus answered them and said, "Verily, verily, I say unto you, ye seek me, not because ye saw the miracles, but because ye did eat of the loaves, and were filled. Labour not for the food which perisheth, but for that food which endureth unto everlasting life, which the Son of man shall give unto you; for him hath God the Father sealed." (6.26–27)

The Jews counter that their fathers ate manna in the wilderness (Ex 16.14–15), and they quote the Psalms: "bread of heaven did he give unto them" (Psalm 77.24):

> "Our fathers did eat manna in the desert; as it is written, 'He gave them bread from heaven to eat.'" Then Jesus said unto them, "Verily, verily, I say unto you, Moses gave you not that bread from heaven; but my Father giveth you the true bread from heaven. For the bread of God is he which cometh down from heaven, and giveth life unto the world." Then said they unto him, "Lord, evermore give us this bread." And Jesus said unto them, "I am the bread of life; he that cometh to me shall never hunger, and he that believeth on me shall never thirst." (Jn 6.32–35)

Thus, for John, the connection is obvious: the miracle of the feeding of the five thousand was performed by Jesus as a prelude to the Mystical Supper, which he would perform with his twelve disciples. At the Mystical Supper, the bread and wine were transformed into the Body and Blood of

The Last Supper,
Leonardo da
Vinci, 1495–98

Jesus. This miracle of miracles was also prefigured by another miracle—
the transformation of water into wine in Cana of Galilee. In John, these
two miracles become a double foreshadowing of the Eucharist. It is by
no means accidental that John begins his account of the multiplication of
the loaves with a note about the imminence of the Jewish Passover. The
Mystical Supper was also performed before Passover, and the Eucharist
was an event directly connected to the Passover feast, which for Christians
became filled with new meaning, "For Christ our passover is sacrificed for
us" (1 Cor 5.7).

For the Synoptics, this connection between the miracle and the Eucharist is also obvious. This is shown, at the very least, by the use of eucharistic
terms both during the description of the miracle of the five loaves and at the
Mystical Supper. The fact that only a small amount of bread was enough to
satisfy a huge mass of people was doubtless understood by the evangelists
as a symbol of the mystery that would unite the Church throughout the
whole cosmos. Having begun in a simple upper-story room, where Jesus
gathered with a few disciples before his passion, the Eucharist became an
event that gathered huge masses of people—at first thousands, then millions of Jesus' followers all over the planet. The rapid growth of the faith
began from the moment of Christ's resurrection, and by the time that the
Gospels were gathered in their final form, the Church was already a community spread out over many cities of the "oecumene" (οἰκουμένη)—the
Roman Empire. The most important thing that unified this community
was the Eucharist.

As a type of the Eucharist, the miracle of the feeding of the five thousand had its own types in the Old Testament. One of these was the story of Joseph, whose brothers wanted to kill him, but whom God saved in miraculous fashion and whom God raised up, so that eventually he was responsible for saving his own father Jacob and his brothers. In this story, bread holds a central place. When the young Joseph is thrown into the pit, his brothers sit together to eat bread. When they see a caravan of Ishmaelite merchants, they decide to sell Joseph into slavery instead of leaving him in the pit to die (Gen 37.23–28). In Egypt, Joseph quickly rises through the ranks in Pharaoh's court, and eventually Pharaoh puts him in charge of his entire kingdom. For seven years, Joseph gathered bread in granaries, and when famine came, he began to sell this bread to the starving Egyptians. When he heard that Egypt had bread, Jacob sent ten of his sons to buy bread; they came to Joseph, whom they did not initially recognize, and he sells them bread. When the famine worsened, they once again came to Joseph, this time with their youngest brother. At this point, Joseph reveals himself to them.

This entire drama covers nine chapters of the book of Genesis (Gen 37–45). The early Church viewed it as a foreshadowing of the death and resurrection of Christ. But the central theme of bread forces the reader also to consider it as a type of all the miracles in the New Testament that involve bread, including the miracle of multiplying the loaves, in which Jesus appears as a new Joseph, who feeds the hungry with bread.

The Second Book of Kings (LXX Fourth Kingdoms) contains a description of a miracle of the prophet Elisha. It also occurred during a famine:

> And there came a man from Baalshalisha, and brought the man of God bread of the firstfruits, twenty loaves of barley, and full ears of grain in the husk thereof. And he said, "Give unto the people, that they may eat." And his servitor said, "What, should I set this before an hundred men?" He said again, "Give the people, that they may eat; for thus saith the LORD, 'They shall eat, and shall leave thereof.'" So he set it before them, and they did eat, and left thereof, according to the word of the LORD. (2 Kg 4.42–44)

Collecting the Manna,
Tiepolo, 1738–40.

Without a doubt, this story was known to the evangelists when they wrote about Jesus' miracle. The parallels between the two stories are obvious. In both stories, bread plays a central role; there is not enough bread for everyone; the main character does not hand out the bread himself, but through his helpers; the helpers initially express doubt about the viability of the master's plan; the bread, having multiplied miraculously, satisfies everyone; moreover, there are leftovers. John strengthens the parallelism by mentioning that the loaves of bread were made of barley (in the Synoptic accounts, the loaves are assumed to be made of wheat).

The theme of hunger is one more connection between the Old Testament accounts and this miracle. Joseph fed the people with bread during a famine; Elisha performed a miracle during a famine; Moses fed the people who hungered in the desert, when God, responding to his intercession, sent the people manna—bread from heaven. It should be noted that even in the Old Testament, physical hunger is already a symbol for spiritual hunger, while bread is a symbol of the word of God: "And he humbled thee, and suffered thee to hunger, and fed thee with manna, which thou knewest not, neither did thy fathers know, that he might make thee know that man doth not live by bread only, but by every word that proceedeth out of the mouth of the LORD doth man live" (Deut 8.3). These are the exact words that Jesus quotes when he answered the devil, who tempted Jesus to turn stones into bread to satisfy his hunger after forty days of fasting in the wilderness (Mt 4.4).

The miracle of the multiplication of the loaves begins with a description of the crowd of people who followed Jesus. All four evangelists take time to describe this crowd. These people followed him into the desert, afflicted with spiritual hunger and not even thinking about the fact that there would be no place to buy bread in the wilderness. The thirst to hear the word of

God and to receive healing from diseases overcomes any natural need for food.

The disciples, however, do not forget about this need—as we see, they themselves often remained hungry when their master spent a long time talking to people (Mk 3.20). In this case, as we see in Mark's version, they actually interrupt Jesus, who had, in their opinion, talked too long to the people (Mk 6.34), and they suggested to him that it would be wise to pay attention to the physical needs of the people. Evidently, the disciples themselves had gotten hungry by this point. Jesus' answer was unexpected: "Give ye them to eat." Their surprise is evident in their answer: "Shall we go and buy two hundred denarii[27] of bread, and give them to eat?" (Mk 6.37) Jesus knew that they did not have such a sum of money; consequently, the question is tinged with sarcasm.

The disciples' behavior provides a strong contrast to the behavior of the crowd. The people had gathered (συνέδραμον; *synedramon* in Mark) from many different cities to be with Jesus; they patiently listened to his teaching, overcoming their own natural hunger. But the disciples, as often happened, did not understand the full significance of what was happening. It is possible they had already heard Jesus' teachings on the subject before—after all, Jesus often repeated himself—and thought it would not be at all out of place to eat something. So when he told them to feed the people, they did not understand what he expected of them. So he finally takes the initiative.

In Mark and Luke's version of this miracle, Jesus comes forward as one who simultaneously satisfies both physical and spiritual hunger. At first, he feeds the people with the words proceeding from God's mouth, by which man lives, and then he feeds them with physical bread necessary to uphold the strength of their bodies. In spite of the disciples' initial resistance, he performs the miracle by their hands—he only breaks the bread, but its miraculous multiplication occurs when the bread is in their hands. Thus, they unexpectedly become the agents of his command: "Give ye them to eat."

---

[27]For the value of a denarius, see above, p. 292.—*Ed.*

In this, one cannot fail to see the symbolism and eucharistic subtext. Jesus himself performed the mystery of the Eucharist one time at the Mystical supper, but that same Eucharist that is repeated again and again in the Christian community is performed by the hands of the apostles and their successors.

Earlier, when speaking of the other miracles of Jesus, we mentioned that in many cases, the evangelists made a point of emphasizing the people's participation in the performance of the miracle. This cooperation was expressed first of all in their faith in the possibility of the miracle, their faith in Jesus as the Savior. In this case, the miracle also occurred thanks to the faith of people. Even though nothing explicit is said about that faith, it is evident in the picture painted by the evangelists—if they did not have faith, they would not have gathered in such numbers from the surrounding cities.

The apostles also became participants in the miracle by working together with Jesus to bring it about. Earlier, he had given them power over unclean spirits (Mt 10.1). They took advantage of this power, fulfilled his command, and returned to tell him of all that they did and taught (Mk 6.30). Now, he gives them the opportunity to learn yet another important lesson—to see how in their own hands, by his command, bread multiplied in a miraculous manner. By doing this, he was preparing them for everything that awaited them after his death and resurrection, when not he, but they themselves would break bread and satisfy the spiritual hunger of thousands.

The earliest description of the mystery of the Eucharist outside the New Testament is found in the Didache, which dates either to the late first or early second century:

> Concerning the Eucharist, eucharistize thus:
> First, concerning the cup:
> We give you thanks, our Father,
> for the holy vine of your servant David which you revealed to us
> through your servant Jesus.
> To you is the glory forever.
> And concerning the broken loaf:

The Mystery of the Eucharist, V. Vasnetsov, 19th century

We give you thanks, our Father,
for the life and knowledge
which you revealed to us through your servant Jesus.
To you is the glory forever.
Just as this broken loaf was scattered over the hills,
and having been gathered together, became one;
in like fashion, may your church be gathered together
from the ends of the earth into your kingdom.
Because yours is the glory and the power through Jesus Christ
forever. . . .
And after being filled by the meal, give thanks thus:
We give you thanks, holy Father, for your holy name,
which you tabernacle in our hearts,
and for the knowledge and faith and immortality which you revealed
to us
through your servant Jesus.
To you is the glory forever.[28]

---

[28]*Didache* 9–10.2. Translation in *The Didache: Text, Translation, Analysis, and Commentary*, trans. Aaron Milavec (Collegeville, MN: Liturgical Press, 2003), 23–25.

*Christian
Frescoes in the
Catacombs of
Saints Peter and
Marcellinus,
1st century*

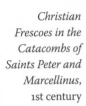

In this description of early Christian communion, we see a certain ter-
minological similarity with both the Synoptic accounts of the Mystical
Supper and John's version of the miracle with the five loaves. The use of the
verbs "give thanks," "break bread," and "gather together" further strengthen
this similarity.[29] The image of the hills (or mountains) in the Eucharistic
prayer from the Didache can be seen as an allusion to the mountain where
the multiplication of the loaves (in John's version) occurred. Finally, the formula "after being filled" (μετὰ δὲ τὸ ἐμπλησθῆσαι; *meta de to emplēsthēsai*)
reminds one of the phrase "when they were filled" (ὡς δὲ ἐνεπλήσθησαν;
hōs de eneplēsthēsan) in the Gospel according to John.

Because of this connection with the Eucharist, the miracle of the multiplication of the loaves was a very popular motif in the early iconography
of the Church. Beginning with the Roman catacombs, it became a constant
theme for artistic representation, while the basket with the loaves of bread
and two fish became a symbol of the Eucharist. The account of this miracle
entered the early lectionary—according to current liturgical practice, it is
read in Matthew's version on the eighth Sunday after Pentecost.

In the Gospel according to John, the account of this miracle ends with
a comment concerning the people's reaction:

> Then those men, when they had seen the miracle that Jesus did, said,
> "This is of a truth that prophet that should come into the world." When

---

[29]Margaret Barker, *King of the Jews: Temple Theology in John's Gospel* (London: SPCK Publishing, 2014), 52–55.

Bread and Fish, the Eucharist, Catacomb of St Kallistus, fresco, 1st century

Jesus therefore perceived that they would come and take him by force, to make him a king, he departed again into a mountain himself alone. (Jn 6.14–15)

Here we see two opinions concerning Jesus that were typical of his contemporaries, or at least as much as we can tell from the witness of the four Gospels. On the one hand, people saw him as a prophet; on the other, they thought of him as a potential king who would free the nation of Israel from the domination of the Romans. These two opinions often combined in people's minds, since the much-awaited, promised Messiah was supposed to contain within himself both the prophetic and kingly ministries, like David, his ancestor.

The words "the Prophet who is to come into the world" indicate not merely that the people equated Jesus with the ancient prophets (Elijah, Jeremiah) or a resurrected John the Baptist. This "Prophet" is the Messiah, and this miracle was taken by the crowd to be a confirmation of Jesus' Messianic dignity.

6. Walking on Water

The story that immediately follows the feeding of the five thousand in Matthew, Mark, and John is the miracle of Jesus walking on the water on the Sea of Galilee. Luke's version of the Gospel leaves this miracle out entirely. In contrast to most of the episodes we have examined earlier in this book, in this case, Matthew contains the most detailed version of the story:

> And straightway Jesus constrained his disciples to get into a ship, and to go before him unto the other side, while he sent the multitudes away. And when he had sent the multitudes away, he went up into a mountain apart to pray; and when the evening was come, he was there alone. But the ship was now in the midst of the sea, tossed with waves, for the wind was contrary. And in the fourth watch of the night Jesus went unto them, walking on the sea. And when the disciples saw him walking on the sea, they were troubled, saying, "It is a spirit," and they cried out for fear. But straightway Jesus spake unto them, saying, "Be of good cheer; it is I; be not afraid." And Peter answered him and said, "Lord, if it be thou, bid me come unto thee on the water." And he said, "Come." And when Peter was come down out of the ship, he walked on the water, to go to Jesus. But when he saw the wind boisterous, he was afraid; and beginning to sink, he cried, saying, "Lord, save me." And immediately Jesus stretched forth his hand, and caught him, and said unto him, "O thou of little faith, wherefore didst thou doubt?" And when they were come into the ship, the wind ceased. Then they that were in the ship came and worshipped him, saying, "Of a truth thou art the Son of God." (Mt 14.22–33)

In the Gospel according to Mark, we learn that the disciples went "to the other side before unto Bethsaida" at to Jesus' command. After Jesus sent the people away, he went up a mountain to pray. That evening, "the ship was in the midst of the sea, and he alone on the land. And he saw them toiling in rowing, for the wind was contrary unto them; and about the fourth watch of the night he cometh unto them, walking upon the sea,

*Walking
on Water,
miniature,
10th century*

and would have passed by them." The rest of Mark's account is the same as Matthew's—they thought he was a ghost, they were afraid and cried out, but he encouraged them. The episode with Peter coming out to Jesus over the waters is completely missing in Mark's account, which ends thus: "And he went up unto them into the ship; and the wind ceased: and they were sore amazed in themselves beyond measure, and wondered. For they considered not the miracle of the loaves: for their heart was hardened" (Mk 6.43–52).

John does not describe Peter walking on the water. His version differs from Matthew's and Mark's in several other details. According to John, the disciples' destination was Capernaum, not Bethsaida. They saw Jesus after they had sailed only about three or four miles. After they became afraid, he encouraged them, and "they willingly received him into the ship; and immediately the ship was at the land whither they went" (Jn 6.16–21).

In Mark's version Jesus had for some reason intended to walk past the disciples on the water, though he did approach them. It is possible that this was connected with the fact that the boat was already near the opposite coast (which would fit John's version as well). The author of *The Miracles of Jesus* offers a different answer. He believes that Jesus was to walk past the

Walking on Water,
Aivazovskii, 1888

disciples to meet them on the other bank, and they merely happened to notice him. Jesus, in intending to walk past them, wanted to test their faith; Jesus did not intend anyone to see him walking to the other side. This scholar believes that Mark's words can be interpreted to mean that Jesus did not want to merely walk by, but intended to reveal his presence to the disciples after having covered the same journey that they did, but on foot.[30]

Let us also mention the essential disagreement between Mark and Luke concerning the geography of the event. In Luke, the miracle of the feeding of the five thousand occurred near the city called Bethsaida, while in Mark's version, the miracle took place on the opposite shore from Bethsaida. Moreover, in both Mark and Matthew's versions, the journey ended in the land of Gennesaret (Mt 14.34; Mk 6.53). John's account does not add any details to resolve this apparent contradiction. In his version, the miracle of the feeding of the five thousand occurred near Tiberias, and then he depicts the miracle of Jesus walking on water:

> The day following, when the people which stood on the other side of the sea saw that there was none other boat there, save that one whereinto his disciples were entered, and that Jesus went not with his disciples into the boat, but that his disciples were gone away alone (howbeit there came other boats from Tiberias nigh unto the place where they did eat bread, after that the Lord had given thanks). When the people therefore saw that Jesus was not there, neither his disciples, they also took shipping, and came to Capernaum, seeking for Jesus. And when they had found him on the other side of the sea, they said unto him, "Rabbi, when camest thou hither?" (Jn 6.22–25)

In the Gospels, "the other side of the sea" usually indicates the eastern shore of the Sea of Galilee, not the western bank where Galilee is located.

[30]Loos, *The Miracles of Jesus,* 652–53.

The Greek text of this passage makes it clear that the people came from the place where the bread was multiplied. In Codex Sinaiticus, the word οὔσης (*ousēs*; "being") is added to the word ἐγγύς (*eggys*; "nearby"), and this means "from Tiberias, which is near the place where they ate bread." Thus we have the following picture: the multiplication of bread occurred near Tiberias (which is on the western bank of the sea); from there, the disciples sailed to the "other side" (the eastern side) without Jesus; late that same night, Jesus also walked to the same shore, but on foot over the waters; the journeys ended on the far side, in the land of Gennesaret.

So where does Capernaum fit, since it is located on the same shoreline as Tiberias (the western shoreline)? The only satisfactory answer is the following: the people, having come to Jesus to the place where he multiplied the loaves, saw that the disciples sailed away, and decided that the disciples had returned to Capernaum. The boats with the people, not having found Jesus or his disciples on the shore near the place where he had multiplied the loaves, then sailed to Capernaum, not knowing that the disciples had actually traveled across the sea to the opposite bank. Not having found Jesus and his disciples in Capernaum, they then sailed to the opposite side, and there, in the land of Gennesaret, they finally found them.

In John's account, a long teaching about the bread that comes down from heaven follows immediately (Jn 6.26–58). Jesus spoke this teaching, which was written as a dialogue, in a synagogue of Capernaum (Jn 6.59). How did he end up again in Capernaum if the people had found him on the opposite bank? Possibly, John means that Jesus once again traveled back to the western bank and returned to Capernaum, but he does not mention this fact. If so, then the first part of the conversation on the heavenly bread began on the eastern shore, and the second part, beginning with the words "Then said they unto him" (Jn 6.28) occurred in Capernaum after everyone—Jesus, the disciples, and the people—returned.

If that is so, then the meeting between Jesus and the people on the eastern shore, and the conversation about the heavenly bread, most of which occurred in the synagogue of Capernaum, are divided by several episodes that are relayed in the Synoptic Gospels, including the healing of the sick in the land of Gennesaret (Mt 14.34–36; Mk 6.53–56). Then, in

Walking on Water,
Luis Borrassa, 1411

Matthew and Mark, what follows is Jesus' conversation with the scribes who had come from Jerusalem (Mt 15.1–20; Mk 7.1–23). Then Jesus travels to the lands of Tyre and Sidon (Mt 15.21; Mk 7.24). Then Matthew has Jesus coming to the Sea of Galilee (Mt 15.21), while Mark mentions that he came to the sea through Decapolis (Mk 7.31). After this, Jesus travels by boat to Magdala (Mt 15.39) or Dalmanutha (Mk 8.10), which is found on the western bank near both Magdala and Capernaum. After that, Mark's version has him coming to Bethsaida (Mk 8.22), and then the two see him together with his disciples in the region of Caesarea Philippi (Mt 16.13; Mk 8.27).

Of all these places, the closest to Capernaum (where, according to John, Jesus continued his conversation with the people concerning the heavenly bread) is the region around Magdala and Dalmanutha. Evidently, his visit to those regions included this conversation about the bread that came down from heaven.

There is a different interpretation, however, according to which the boat appeared in Capernaum miraculously:

Whoever has been in Galilee can easily imagine how far the storm had carried the apostles of Christ. Bethsaida and Capernaum are on the northern bank of the sea. And the disciples, having entered the boat near Bethsaida, would have needed to simply sail along the shoreline. However, the Gospels tell us that because of a storm, they found themselves in the middle of the sea. Here, in the middle of the sea, our Lord Jesus Christ appeared to them. When the storm calmed, the boat had to sail from there back to the shoreline near Capernaum. Judging by the words of Matthew and Mark, the boat sailed there naturally, with the help of sails and oars; however, John's words suggest that the Lord performed another miracle by his invincible power, causing the boat to immediately appear at the shore, for "immediately the boat was at the land where they were going" (Jn 6.21). These accounts of the evangelists in no way contradict each other. For the one who could walk on water and forbid the wind and seas with his word and thought could without a doubt, if it were necessary, cause the boat to immediately appear at its destination.[31]

The account of the miracle of walking on water begins with Jesus (in Matthew and Mark) "constraining" (ἠνάγκασεν; *ēnagkasen*) the disciples to enter the boat and sail away. This verb indicates not simply a request or a command—it is best translated as "forced" or "insisted" or "compelled," and it assumes some level of resistance on the side of those who are being compelled.

So what are the evangelists trying to suggest with the use of this word? According to Chrysostom, "by saying 'he constrained them,' he indicates the very close attendance of the disciples. And his pretext indeed for dismissing them was the multitude, but he himself intended to go up into the mountain."[32] It is also possible that the word "constrained" indicates that the disciples needed to hurry to leave the place of the miracle, since Jesus had decided to depart, having found out that the people "would come and take him by force, to make him a king" (Jn 6.15). We can assume that this intention of the people became obvious to the disciples, which would explain their reticence to leave his side.

This habit of leaving the disciples and spending the night in prayer was typical for Jesus (see Mt 14.23; Mk 6.46; Lk 5.16; Lk 6.12; Jn 6.15; Jn 8.1). We can guess that in such cases the disciples were usually nearby or made plans beforehand to meet him somewhere the next morning. In this case, it seems, they remained unsure of how Jesus would make his way to the other side of the sea—perhaps this is also what caused their hesitation to enter the boat without him.

As in the episode with the storm at sea, here we also have a mention of waves and wind; but nothing is said concerning the waves actually threatening to sink the boat or that the disciples were in any danger.

---

[31]Nikolai Velimirovich, *Tvoreniya* [Collected works], 2:141–42 (translated by NK).
[32]John Chrysostom, *Homilies on Matthew*, Homily 49 (NPNF[1] 10:306).

*Walking on
Water,*
M. Vrubel, 1890

What sort of a boat would Jesus' disciples use—a sailboat or a rowboat? Mark's expression "He saw them straining at rowing" (Mk 6.48) indicates severe difficulties during rowing (the verb ἐλαύνειν [*elaunein*] means "to row"). In 1986, at the bottom of the sea of Galilee, a wooden fishing boat was discovered, dated to the period between the middle of the first century BC and the middle of the first century AD.[33] This boat had a flat bottom 8.27 meters (about 27 feet) in length, 2.3 meters (about 7.6 feet) in width, and was built from ten different kinds of wood. It was moved primarily by rowing with oars, but it also had a mast that allowed for the use of a sail. It is very likely that the disciples' boat was similar.

According to Matthew and Mark, Jesus came to the disciples in the fourth watch of the night, that is, between three and six in the morning, probably closer to three. For the Jews of that time (as for the Romans), the night and day were divided into four "watches," three hours each. The night was counted from the moment of sunset; the fourth watch was the time just before dawn. By this time, the disciples had sailed most of the way to the other side. According to John, it was around three or four miles.

---

[33]L. L.Winkler and R. Frenkel, *The Boat and the Sea of Galilee* (Jerusalem: Gefen Publishing House, 2010). The dating was based on radiological analysis both of the boat and pottery found inside the boat.

As we remember, Josephus gave the dimensions of the Sea of Galilee as around five miles wide and seventeen long.[34] Mark's words concerning the disciples being in the middle of the sea should not be understood literally; it is more likely, as John's version has it, that the disciples were almost at the other side already.

In the darkness before dawn, after a sleepless night, the figure of a person walking on water seemed ghostly to the disciples. The word φάντασμα (*phantasma*; "ghost") suggests a figment of the imagination. In the New Testament, this word is found only in this episode. Having seen something they thought was a spirit, the disciples were afraid and cried out.

In answer to this cry, Jesus turned to them with the words: "Be of good cheer. It is I; be not afraid" (Mk 6.50). In Matthew and John's accounts, the phrase "be of good cheer" is missing (θαρσεῖτε; *tharseite*, or literally "be daring" or "have courage"). The phrase "It is I" (ἐγώ εἰμι; *egō eimi*, or literally "I am") could be an allusion to the passage in Exodus where God reveals his name as Yahweh. According to the book of Exodus, before calling himself by that name, God said of himself, "I AM THAT I AM" (*ehye ašer ehye*). Then, he gives Moses a command: "Thus shalt thou say unto the children of Israel, I AM hath sent me unto you" (Ex 3.14). Here the word "HE WHO IS" is the translation of the Greek *ho Ōn* (ὁ Ὤν), which in turn translates the Hebrew *ehye*, which literally means "I AM."

The unity of context and the phonetic similarity (the name Yahweh most likely comes from the same root *hwy*, "to be") allow us to the see the phrase "I am" as an interpretation of the holy name of God. We can assume that Jesus used this formula with reference to himself as God, and on his lips it was intended to equate himself with God. The word "I AM" is also used in several important passages in the Old Testament, where they reveal the idea of divine omnipotence (together with the name Yahweh): Deut 32.39 (*ani ani hu*, "I, I am," here instead of the verb "to be" the pronoun "he" [hu] is used), Ex 43.11 (*anoki anoki Yahweh*, "I, I the Lord"). By saying to the disciples "I am," Jesus could have been not simply indicating himself; he could have been indicating his divine dignity as well.[35]

---

[34]Josephus, *The Wars of the Jews* 10.8.7, in *The Works of Josephus*, 662.
[35]For more on this topic, see Brown, *The Gospel according to John (I–XII)*, 533–38. However,

Walking on Water, A. A. Ivanov, 1850s

What is the historical value of the account of Jesus walking on water? Contemporary scholars answer this question in different ways. Some scholars prefer not to talk about the historicity of this event at all, concentrating instead on the analysis of the text itself. Others insist that the account is definitely historical. Still others believe that a certain event that had no miraculous element to it at all eventually was reinterpreted as a miracle. Yet others believe this episode has only symbolic meaning. Still others believe that this episode is a reworking of one of the events that followed Jesus' resurrection.[36] Finally, some believe that this entire episode is a hallucination because of the disciples' altered state of consciousness in the midst of the storm and its surrounding dangers.[37]

Without getting bogged down in analysis of any of these points of view, we will merely say that we reject any interpretation of this event that assumes it is not historically valid. We also reject any interpretation that tries to interpret these events through the terminology of psychological distress or hallucination. There are so many examples of Jesus' supernatural power in the Gospels that to reject the possibility that this was a miracle or to try to interpret this event through observable scientific

Barret and Carson, in their commentaries on this passage, consider the *egō eimi* to be nothing but Jesus indicating himself.

[36]P. Madden, *Jesus' Walking on the Sea* (Berlin and New York: Walter de Gruyter, 1997), 1.

[37]B. Malina, "Assessing the Historicity of Jesus' Walking on Water," 362–69 in *Authenticating the Activities of Jesus*, ed. B. Chilton and C. A. Evans (Leiden: Brill, 1999).

phenomena means to reject the historicity of the Jesus who appears in the pages of the Gospel. In this case, the only possible way out is to create another, alternate version of Jesus that reminds us of the one created by Hegel, Strauss, Renan, and Tolstoy. It is not our task to examine these versions of Jesus.

In Mark's version of this miracle and in John's, the episode ends with Jesus entering the boat. In Matthew's version, however, there is an additional episode with Peter, which becomes the thematic, emotional, and theological center of the entire event. This is the event that gives the essential key to understanding the significance of the miracle.

As in many other descriptions of miracles, the central theme is faith. Peter passionately answers Jesus' encouraging words because, first of all, he believed that it was Jesus, not a phantom, and secondly, he believed that Jesus is the Son of God. If he can walk on water himself, then the one who believes in him can do the same. Peter's reaction was emotional and spontaneous, as in other cases when he reacted to Jesus' words and actions before the other disciples. But at the same time, this action was not thought through; it was motivated by Peter's faith in Jesus as God, who is capable not only of performing miracles, but of giving the power to perform miracles to others as well.

Thus, Peter left the boat and walked on the water toward Jesus. But at a certain moment, seeing the strong wind, he became afraid and started fall into the water. The reason given was that he began to doubt. But in what? In the miraculous power of Jesus, or in his divine dignity? Or in his own ability to follow Jesus on the water? While Peter's actions were motivated by faith, he walked without fear on the waters; the moment faith began to waver in him, he lost the ability, newly received from Jesus, to miraculously overcome the laws of nature.

Being a fisherman, Peter of course knew how to swim, which is confirmed by a different episode when, seeing Jesus on the shore, he jumped into the water and swam while the others remained in the boat (Jn 21.7–8). Thus, it is unlikely that Peter would have drowned. More likely what we have here is an emotional reaction connected with the initial shock at seeing Jesus on the water, then strengthened by the increased fear from

*Walking on
Water,*
L. Borrassa, 1411

the strong wind and the supernatural character of the entire event. Jesus
extends his hand to Peter and saves him, simultaneously rebuking him for
his weak faith and doubt.

It is worth noting that there is a parallel between this episode in Mathew,
Mark, and John and the miracle of the calming of the storm in the Synoptic
Gospels (Mt 8.23–27; Mk 4.35–41; Lk 8.22–25). In both cases, the event
occurs at sea at night during a storm, when the disciples are in a boat. In
the first case, there is a strong wind, but Jesus is in the boat with the disciples; in the second, there is a strong wind and high waves, but Jesus is
not present with the disciples; in the first episode, the storm calms due to
the powerful word of Jesus; in the second, it calms after Jesus enters the
boat. In the first case, Jesus rebukes all the disciples for their lack of faith,

while in the second (according to Matthew), Jesus rebukes Peter alone. Both miracles show Jesus' mastery over nature.

If we examine the second miracle as a thematic continuation of the first, then the most important difference is found in the disciples' reactions. According to Luke, the first miracle ended with their frightened exclamation: "What manner of man is this! For he commandeth even the winds and water, and they obey him" (Lk 8.25). The second miracle, in Matthew, ends with the disciples coming up to Jesus, bowing before him, and saying, "Of a truth thou art the Son of God." This is the first time in the Gospel according to Matthew that the disciples confess their faith in Jesus as the Son of God. In Matthew's interpretation, consequently, the entire account becomes a lesson in faith that Jesus offers his disciples. The miracle, in which Peter was the first to confess his faith, ended with a triumphant confession of faith from all the disciples.

As with the account of the calming of the storm, this account was interpreted in the early Church as a foreshadowing of baptism. According to some scholars,[38] this interpretation is given further credence by the parallel between the miracle of walking on water in Mark and the resurrection of Jesus in Lk (24.36–41). The following common moments are seen in both accounts: 1) Jesus appeared suddenly and unexpectedly after parting with the disciples; 2) they are initially afraid; 3) they think he is a phantom (or "spirit"); 4) Jesus calms them; 5) Jesus says to them, "It is I" (or "I am"); 6) the disciples are amazed. Moreover, in both accounts, food is mentioned (Mk 6.52; Lk 24.41–43) and the hardness of the disciples' heart (or their confusion) is also mentioned.

The boat's destination was the land of Gennesaret. This was a large strip of shoreline on the Western side of the sea of Galilee between Tiberias and Capernaum, which was remarkable for its fertility. Josephus records:

> The country also that lies over against this lake hath the same name of Gennesareth; its nature is wonderful as well as its beauty; its soil is so fruitful that all sorts of trees can grow upon it, and the inhabitants accordingly plant all sorts of trees there; for the temper of the air is

---

[38]Marcus, *Mark 1–8*, 432–33.

so well mixed, that it agrees very well with those several sorts, particularly walnuts, which require the coldest air, flourish there in vast
plenty; there are palm trees also, which grow best in hot air; fig trees
also and olives grow near them, which yet require an air that is more
temperate. One may call this place the ambition of nature, where it
forces those plants that are naturally enemies to one another to agree
together; it is a happy contention of the seasons, as if every one of
them laid claim to this country; for it not only nourishes different
sorts of autumnal fruit beyond men's expectation, but preserves them
a great while; it supplies men with the principal fruits, with grapes and
figs continually, during ten months of the year and the rest of the fruits
as they become ripe together through the whole year; for besides the
good temperature of the air, it is also watered from a most fertile
fountain. The people of the country call it Capharnaum. Some have
thought it to be a vein of the Nile, because it produces the Coracin
fish as well as that lake does which is near to Alexandria. The length
of this country extends itself along the banks of this lake that bears
the same name for thirty furlongs, and is in breadth twenty, and this
is the nature of that place.[39]

But Jesus came to the land of Gennesaret not to enjoy its beauties
and the bounty of its nature. He came here for the same reasons that he
came to others places in Palestine. Mark describes this in more detail than
Matthew:

> And when they had passed over, they came into the land of Gen-
> nesaret, and drew to the shore. And when they were come out of the
> ship, straightway they knew him, and ran through that whole region
> round about, and began to carry about in beds those that were sick,
> where they heard he was. And whithersoever he entered, into villages,
> or cities, or country, they laid the sick in the streets, and besought him
> that they might touch if it were but the border of his garment; and as
> many as touched him were made whole. (Mk 6.53–56; cf. Mt 14.34–36)

[39]Josephus, *The War of the Jews* 3.10.8, in *The Works of Josephus*, 662.

Jesus Christ Walks on Water, mosaic, 12th century

This short excerpt can be divided into two parts, which can be read as a single account. In this case, the villages and towns are all part of the land of Gennesaret. We can also read the second half as an expansion referring to Jesus' ministry throughout Galilee, or even his ministry in general.

In the Gospel according to Mark, Jesus forces the disciples to enter the boat and travel to the other side to Bethsaida (Mk 6.45), which is on the eastern side, but in the final analysis they end up in the land of Gennesaret, which is on the west bank (Mk 6.53). This is sometimes explained away by the fact that the wind pushed them away from their original route.[40] But in John's version, from the beginning their destination was Capernaum (Jn 6.17), which is in the land of Gennesaret. This contradiction is explained by the fact that the place where the miracle of the multiplication of the loaves occurred differs in various accounts, which we have already discussed (John places it near Tiberias, Luke near Bethsaida).

[40]Henry Barclay Swete, *The Gospel according to St. Mark* (London: MacMillan, 1898), 129–30.

7. The Feeding of the Four Thousand

The account of the feeding of the four thousand with seven loaves of bread is found in Matthew and Mark, but not in Luke and John. In the scholarly literature, this miracle is sometimes interpreted as a variant of the miracle of the feeding of the five thousand.[41] But the evangelists see it otherwise. They describe this miracle with similar expressions as the previous one, but they place it in a different geographical location and separate it from the first by a period of time. Evidently, here we are dealing not with a repetition of a lesson, but a new instruction given by the teacher at a different time. This is especially evident if we read Mark's account:

> In those days the multitude being very great, and having nothing to eat, Jesus called his disciples unto him, and saith unto them, "I have compassion on the multitude, because they have now been with me three days, and have nothing to eat, and if I send them away fasting to their own houses, they will faint by the way, for many of them came from far."
>
> And his disciples answered him, "From whence can a man satisfy these men with bread here in the wilderness?"
>
> And he asked them, "How many loaves have ye?" And they said, "Seven."
>
> And he commanded the people to sit down on the ground: and he took the seven loaves, and gave thanks, and brake, and gave to his disciples to set before them; and they did set them before the people. And they had a few small fishes: and he blessed, and commanded to set them also before them. So they did eat, and were filled: and they took up of the broken meat that was left seven baskets. And they that had eaten were about four thousand: and he sent them away. (Mk 8.1–9)

A literal translation of the Greek at the beginning of this account reads as follows: "In those days once again [πάλιν; *palin*] a great multitude of

[41]Bultmann, *The History of the Synoptic Tradition* (Oxford, 1963), 217.

people gathered and, since they had nothing to eat, he called together the disciples and said to them . . ." This opening sequence shows that this event already had a precedent in the same Gospel. In Matthew's account (Mt 15.32–39), the miracle differs in almost no way, except for the different number of men present. Since there are two separate, but similar accounts in these Gospels, we may assume that such miracles occurred in Jesus' life more often than twice; it is very likely that thousands of people followed him into the desert frequently, and he would have had to use supernatural means to feed them.

Both in Matthew and Mark the feeding to the four thousand occurs on the shore of the Sea of Galilee after Jesus' return from the lands of Tyre and Sidon (in Mark, he returns through Decapolis). After this event, he travels by boat to the land near Magdala (in Mark, it is called the region of Dalmanutha). Consequently, the event itself took place on the Eastern shore of the lake, which was primarily inhabited by pagans. This is one of the largest points of difference between this event and the feeding of the five thousand.

Only in Mark's account does Jesus mention that some of those who came to him came "from afar." This expression, on the one hand, could underline the fact that some of the people here were pagans, but on the other hand, it could be a hidden allusion to the Old Testament account concerning the inhabitants of Gibeon, who came to Joshua with the words: "We have come from a far country." In that account, there is also mention of bread and "three days" (Josh 9.11–12, 16).

The fact that the people were with Jesus for three days means that they either followed him along the road for three days and then found themselves in the desert, or they had spent all three days with him in the desert, listening to him teach. By the third day, their food supply had run out, and yet they had no desire to leave. Then Jesus took it upon himself to care for their needs, both spiritual and physical. St John Chrysostom mentions that the people who had come to be healed did not dare to ask for bread; but Christ, the lover of mankind, gave them even what they did not ask for.[42]

---

[42]John Chrysostom, *Homilies on the Gospel of Matthew*, Homily 53 (NPNF[1] 10:326–27).

The Feeding of the Four Thousand, Doré, 1860s

In both Matthew's account and in Mark's, this entire episode serves as a prologue to Jesus' conversation with the Jews and his disciples after he arrived in the region of Dalmanutha:

> And the Pharisees came forth, and began to question with him, seeking of him a sign from heaven, tempting him. And he sighed deeply in his spirit, and saith, "Why doth this generation seek after a sign? Verily I say unto you, there shall no sign be given unto this generation."
>
> And he left them, and entering into the ship again departed to the other side. Now the disciples had forgotten to take bread, neither had they in the ship with them more than one loaf. And he charged them, saying, "Take heed, beware of the leaven of the Pharisees, and of the

leaven of Herod." And they reasoned among themselves, saying, "It is because we have no bread."

And when Jesus knew it, he saith unto them, "Why reason ye, because ye have no bread? Perceive ye not yet, neither understand? Have ye your heart yet hardened? Having eyes, see ye not? And having ears, hear ye not? And do ye not remember? When I broke the five loaves among five thousand, how many baskets full of fragments took ye up?" They say unto him, "Twelve." "And when the seven among four thousand, how many baskets full of fragments took ye up?" And they said, "Seven." And he said unto them, "How is it that ye do not understand?" (Mk 8.11–21)

This text, in our opinion, contains the answer to the question of why Jesus performed two similar miracles and why the evangelists decided to recount both of them. Other than the fact that the second miracle was performed for the same reasons as the first (the people were hungry and there was no food in the desert), there was yet another reason: the disciples did not learn their lesson after the first miracle. They did not believe in Jesus in the way that he expected of them. And so they receive a deserved rebuke for their hardness of heart, because they still do not understand the significance of what is happening right before their eyes.

The short dialogue with the Pharisees who sought a sign is placed between the two accounts, and it is a kind of thematic focal point for both. The "sign" in question is the one that the Pharisees often demanded from Jesus, which he refused to perform each time (Mt 12.38–39; 16.1; Lk 11.16; 11.29; 12.54–56; Jn 6.30). In Matthew, Jesus answers the Pharisees and Sadducees with an even sterner reply than in Mark:

The Pharisees also with the Sadducees came, and tempting desired him that he would show them a sign from heaven. He answered and said unto them, "When it is evening, ye say, 'It will be fair weather, for the sky is red.' And in the morning, 'It will be foul weather to day, for the sky is red and lowering.' O ye hypocrites, ye can discern the face of the sky, but can ye not discern the signs of the times? A wicked and adulterous generation seeketh after a sign, and there shall no sign be given unto it, but the sign of the prophet Jonah." And he left them, and departed. (Mt 16.1–4)

Jesus uses the phrase the "signs of the times" to indicate his own actions, which, in spite of the presence of signs and miracles, do not enlighten those whose hearts are hardened and whose eyes and ears and closed. This refers first of all to the Pharisees and Sadducees, and the scribes. But Jesus' disciples are also unable to understand the lessons that he offers them again and again. They continue to think exclusively in earthly categories, and they continue to worry about the fact that there is no bread in the desert, while they understand his words about the leaven of the Pharisees as if the Pharisees had brought actual, physical bread.

Taken together, these three episodes—the feeding of the four thousand, the dialogue with the Pharisees, and the dialogue with the disciples—form an account that is foreshadowed by the Exodus account in the Old Testament: "Would to God we had died by the hand of the LORD in the land of Egypt, when we sat by the flesh pots, and when we did eat bread to the full; for ye have brought us forth into this wilderness, to kill this whole assembly with hunger" (Ex 16.3). The Pharisees' request for a sign reminds us of the demands that the chosen people made of Moses, and of Moses's answer ("Why do ye tempt the Lord?"), and the miracle he performed when he struck the stone and water poured out (Ex 17.1–7). Jesus' words about the wicked and adulterous generation (especially in Matthew's version), along with the fact that Jesus walked away from those who required a sign, remind us of God's words concerning the nation of Israel: "I will hide my face from them, I will see what their end shall be; for they are a very perverse generation, children in whom is no faith" (Deut 32.20).

The dialogue about the leaven is an allusion to the feast of the Passover, when everything leavened was destroyed in every house (Ex 12.15, 19; 13.6–7). If we continue to seek such parallels, we can see an allusion to the twelve wells of water in Elim (Ex 15.27) in the twelve baskets of leftovers, while the seven leftover baskets could be an allusion to the seven days of the Passover feast and the feeding of the nation of Israel with manna for forty years.

All these echoes and allusions that scholars identify might seem far-fetched to a modern reader, but for the first-century readers of Matthew and Mark, this would not have been the case. Every number, especially sacred numbers like 3, 7, 12, 40, and their multiples, were reminders of some event in the sacred history of Israel. Numbers, just like codes or cyphers, hid information about the events of the past, which were understood by readers as types of the life of Jesus, his signs and miracles. All four evangelists follow this logic to a greater or lesser degree. This is especially true of Matthew, who constantly underlines that specific prophecies were fulfilled in the particular events of the Gospel's narrative.

In any case, as we have already seen, Jesus himself often pointed to specific Old Testament accounts, including the story of Jonah, as foreshadowings of New Testament realities. This is why he spoke of the sign of Jonah when discussing the most important sign that the Jews would see from him.

8. The Coin in the Mouth of the Fish

One episode that we find only in Matthew has all the appearance of a miracle. Nevertheless, it is often not included in the list of Jesus' miracles since the actual miraculous event is not directly narrated. The episode refers to the last visit to Capernaum that is mentioned in the Gospels:

> And when they were come to Capernaum, they that received tribute money came to Peter, and said, "Doth not your master pay tribute?" He saith, "Yes." And when he was come into the house, Jesus prevented him, saying, "What thinkest thou, Simon? Of whom do the kings of the earth take custom or tribute? Of their own children, or of strangers?" Peter saith unto him, "Of strangers." Jesus saith unto him, "Then are the children free. Notwithstanding, lest we should offend them, go thou to the sea, and cast an hook, and take up the fish that first cometh up; and

when thou hast opened his mouth, thou shalt find a piece of money: that take, and give unto them for me and thee." (Mt 17.24–27)

There is no sequel to this episode; consequently, we do not know if Peter did what Jesus commanded him to do. But it is assumed that he did, otherwise the evangelist would not have included this dialogue between Jesus and Peter.

We do not know the tone Jesus used when he said this to Peter. But it is difficult not to see a certain sense of humor in Jesus' words. The coin in the mouth of a fish seems more like a joke than one of the triumphant miracles that we have already seen. This entire episode strikingly differs in tone from Jesus' healings, exorcisms, or the calming of the storm.

In first-century Israel, the currency in use was mostly Greek or Roman. The temple tax was a silver coin worth two drachmas. Two such coins were called a τετράδραχμον (tetradrachmon). According to the law of Moses, every Israelite had to pay half a shekel as a ransom for his own life to the Lord; this money went to the upkeep of the Tabernacle (Ex 30.11–16). A shekel was worth four Attic drachmas.[43] Thus two drachmas was what every Israelite had to pay for the upkeep of the temple in Jesus' time.

When Jesus cleansed the Temple, he cast out the moneychangers, whose tables stood within the Temple itself (Mt 21.12; Mk 11.15; Jn 2.14). Their main job was to change various currencies into Tyrian shekels. These coins, which were minted in the Phoenician city of Tyre between 126 BC to 19 AD, were the ones most used in the Temple. In spite of the fact that Jesus was opposed to money changing in the Temple, he did not say anything negative about the practice of gathering taxes for the Temple.

Jesus never refused to pay taxes—neither the taxes required by the Roman authority, nor those that were required by Jewish law and custom. The first is confirmed by his answer to the question about paying taxes to Caesar (Mt 22.16–22). The second is confirmed by this episode.

[43]Josephus, The Antiquities of the Jews 3.82, in The Works of Josephus, 91.

Jesus did not have the necessary amount for the tax for himself and Peter; his non-acquisitiveness was absolute. But when the coin was needed, he devised a quick method of finding it.

He used this opportunity to increase the faith of his closest disciples. Peter, who was a fisherman, had already witnessed one miracle involving fish (Lk 5.1–11). Now, before his very eyes, another miracle occurred—he had never before pulled out a fish from the sea with a silver coin in its mouth.

Commentators offer different interpretations of this event. C. Venturini—one of those on the quest

Jesus Cleanses the Temple, Doré, 1860s.

for the "historical Jesus" in the nineteenth century—thought that Jesus commanded Peter to catch a fish, and then to pull the hook out of its mouth very carefully, after which he would be able to sell it for two drachmas.[44] Another rationalist commentator believed that Peter was supposed to keep catching fish until he found one that would be good enough to sell for two drachmas—as soon as he opened its mouth (that is, took the hook out), he could sell it and get the needed money.[45] All such interpretations are based on the desire to find a natural phenomenon at all costs, to pass off the supposed miracle as a misunderstanding or fabrication.

Ancient commentators, on the other hand, stress the unusual and supernatural nature of this event. St John Chrysostom sees it as the continuation of the other miracles of Jesus, especially the ones in which he shows mastery over nature:

> For wherefore does he not command him to give of what they have laid up? That, as I have said, herein also he might signify himself to be God of all, and the sea also to be under his rule. For he had indeed signified this even already, by his rebuke, and by his commanding this same Peter to walk on the waves; but he now again signifies the self-same thing, though in another way, yet so as to cause herein great amazement. For

[44]Quoted in A. Scheitzer, *Geschichte der Leben-Jesu Forschung* (Tübingen, 1933), 46.
[45]H. Paulus, *Exegetisches Handbuch,* II. S. 501–13.

A Shekel from Tyre
(two drachmas)

neither was it a small thing, to foretell that the first, who out of those depths should come in his way, would be the fish that would pay the tribute; and having cast forth his commandment like a net into that abyss, to bring up the one that bore the piece of money; but it was of a divine and unutterable power, thus to make even the sea bear gifts, and that its subjection to him should be shown on all hands, as well when in its madness it was silent, and when, though fierce, it received its fellow servant; as now again, when it makes payment in his behalf to them that are demanding it.[46]

Chrysostom interprets Jesus' words about the sons of the kingdom who are free from taxes as an indication that Jesus is the Son of God. This is how he understands them: "I am indeed free from paying tribute. For if the kings of the earth take it not of their sons, but of their subjects; much more ought I to be freed from this demand, I who am Son, not of an earthly king, but of the King of Heaven, and myself a King."[47] At the same time, he does not refuse to pay. Chrysostom goes on to say that Jesus speaks of his freedom from taxes not to confuse his disciples, and he pays the tax in order not to offend the tax collectors.

This entire episode should be understood in the general context of Jesus' relationship with the religious leaders of ancient Israel. During his entire life, he fulfilled all the dictates of the law, beginning with circumcision and ending with regular pilgrimage to Jerusalem for Passover and attendance at synagogue on the Sabbath. In the Gospel according to Matthew, he underlines his loyalty to the Law of Moses, which he came not to destroy but to fulfill (Mt 5.17). The Temple of Jerusalem is dear to him; from his childhood, he saw it as something that belongs to his Father (Lk 2.49), casting the moneychangers out of the Temple is contingent on his zeal for the house of God (Jn 2.17).

[46]John Chrysostom, *Homilies on Matthew*, Homily 58 (NPNF[1] 10:358).
[47]Ibid.

At the same time, he insisted on the secondary nature of those external rites, rules, and proscriptions that were called the tradition of the elders (Mt 15.2; Mk 7.3, 5). The religion that he preached was not connected either with the Temple or the cult of the Temple. He predicted that the Temple would soon be destroyed, and not even a stone would remain on top of another stone from the original edifice. To the Samaritan woman, he said:

> Jesus saith unto her, "Woman, believe me, the hour cometh, when ye shall neither in this mountain, nor yet at Jerusalem, worship the Father. Ye worship ye know not what; we know what we worship: for salvation is of the Jews. But the hour cometh, and now is, when the true worshippers shall worship the Father in spirit and in truth, for the Father seeketh such to worship him. God is a Spirit, and they that worship him must worship him in spirit and in truth." (Jn 4.21–24)

In these words, Jesus expressed the opposition between Jesus' teaching and the religion of ancient Israel. Comparing it to the cult of the Samaritans, he gives it preference. Moreover, he says that "salvation is of the Jews." The time will come, however, when this salvation will no longer be connected to any concrete place, or to the Jewish religious cult. The coming of the Son of God into the world inaugurates a new era in the relationship between God and man. God seeks not slaves who placate him with money, but sons who worship him in spirit and truth. Instead of a religion of laws, proscriptions, and rules, he preaches a religion of spirit and truth, which makes people sons and daughters of the Heavenly King.

9. Cursing the Fig Tree

Both Matthew and Mark record one of Jesus' strangest and most perplexing miracles, which took place in the last days of his earthly life. In Mark, this miracle occurs in two stages, before and after the episode with the

Cursing the Fig Tree, miniature, 14th century

moneychangers in the temple (Mk 11.15–19). The miracle itself takes place offstage. We only hear about its results:

> And on the morrow, when they were come from Bethany, he was hungry. And seeing a fig tree afar off having leaves, he came, if perhaps he might find any thing thereon, and when he came to it, he found nothing but leaves, for the time of figs was not yet. And Jesus answered and said unto it, "No man eat fruit of thee hereafter for ever." And his disciples heard it.
>
> And in the morning, as they passed by, they saw the fig tree dried up from the roots.
>
> And Peter calling to remembrance saith unto him, "Master, behold, the fig tree which thou cursedst is withered away."

And Jesus answering saith unto them, "Have faith in God. For verily I say unto you, that whosoever shall say unto this mountain, 'Be thou removed, and be thou cast into the sea,' and shall not doubt in his heart, but shall believe that those things which he saith shall come to pass, he shall have whatsoever he saith. Therefore I say unto you, what things soever ye desire, when ye pray, believe that ye receive them, and ye shall have them." (Mk 11.12–14, 20–24)

In Matthew's version, Jesus first casts out the money-changers from the temple (Mt 21.12), then the next morning, as he returned into the city, he found the fruitless fig tree. When he said, "Let no fruit grow on thee henceforward for ever," the fig tree immediately withered. Having seen this, the disciples ask, "How soon is the fig tree withered away!" In answer, they hear a lesson that is analogous to Mark's (Mt 21.18–22). Thus, in Matthew's version the miracle happens right before the eyes of the disciples.

We do not know which version of this account occurred first, which later. It is possible that Mark divided the account into two parts as a framing device for his account of the casting out of the money-changers from the temple.[48] Neither can we exclude the possibility of a certain level of literary dependence on an episode from the Book of Jonah, where a gourd grows over the head of the prophet, then withers the following day (Jon 4.6–8).

The fig tree is one of the most common types of trees in Palestine. People generally took care of fig trees and treasured them: "Whoso keepeth the fig tree shall eat the fruit thereof" (Prov 27.18). The appearance of buds on the fig tree was a sign of coming spring:

For, lo, the winter is past, the rain is over and gone; the flowers appear on the earth; the time of the singing of birds is come, and the voice of the turtle is heard in our land; the fig tree putteth forth her green figs, and the vines with the tender grape give a good smell. Arise, my love, my fair one, and come away. (Song 2.11–13)

---

[48]Marcus, *Mark 8–16*, 788.

*Cursing the Fig
Tree*, miniature,
16th century

The withering fig tree was thus a symbol of autumn, while a leafless fig
tree was symbolic of invasion: "He hath laid my vine waste, and barked my
fig tree; he hath made it clean bare, and cast it away; the branches thereof
are made white. . . . The vine is dried up, and the fig tree languisheth" (Joel
1.7, 12).

A well, a vineyard, and fig trees were nearly always present in house-
holds of that time:

> And Judah and Israel dwelt safely, every man under his vine and under
> his fig tree, from Dan even to Beersheba, all the days of Solomon.
> (1 Kg 4.25)

Then eat ye every man of his own vine, and every one of his fig tree, and drink ye every one the waters of his cistern. (2 Kg 18.31)

Then shall sit every man under his vine and under his fig tree; and none shall make them afraid. (Mic 4.4)

Jesus had neither his own home nor his own garden; therefore, he had no fig tree of his own. As we have seen, hunger was a frequent companion of the disciples. The fact that Jesus himself felt hunger was only mentioned twice in the Gospels: in the account of the devil tempting him (Mt 4.2, Lk 4.2) and in this account with the fig tree. These mentions, however, are more than enough to see that his hunger, as his exhaustion, did not merely serve a moral or pedagogical purpose for those surrounding him, as some commentators imagine. Blessed Augustine, for example, asks, "Did Christ truly want to eat when he sought the fruit on the tree? If he had found it, would he have started to eat it? . . . What else does Christ hunger or thirst for except our good deeds?"[49] The Gospels, however, give a different answer, presenting Jesus as a real person who felt a completely natural sense of hunger.

The words expressed by Jesus after he came to the fig tree and saw it had no fruit may seem like the emotional reaction of a hungry person when he had set his heart on eating something, but found nothing. Jesus did feel human emotions, including anger. It seems that placing this account in the same context as the casting out of the moneychangers from the temple is not an accident. In both cases, we see Jesus expressing human anger, which is a reflection of divine wrath. In the scene in the Temple, this wrath is poured out on those who made the house of God a marketplace; in the story with the fig tree, it pours out on a fruitless fig tree.

By withering the fig tree, Jesus reveals the same power over nature that he revealed earlier in calming the storm, walking on water, transforming water into wine. The primeval purpose of nature was to serve man. In paradise, God planted "the fruit tree yielding fruit after his kind" (Gen 1.11), and man was allowed to eat from all trees in the garden except the

[49]Augustine, *Commentary on the Psalms.* Quoted in *Ancient Christian Commentary on Scripture: Mark* (Downer's Grove, IL: InterVarsity Press, 2014), 150.

tree of the knowledge of good and evil (Gen 2.16–17). After man broke the commandment and ate the forbidden fruit, nature ceased to serve man or submit to his will without question. Jesus, as we have already said, restored the primeval harmony between man and nature in his person. But he did not simply expect silent submission from nature. The fig tree submitted to his word, but it could not give him the fruits that he expected of it. For this reason, it was punished.

The question that cannot fail to arise after reading Mark's version is this: what was the fault of the fig tree if it was not yet the fruit-bearing season? Jesus knew very well that a fig tree cannot give any fruit before summer (Mt 24.32; Mk 13.28). Moreover, he once taught by using a parable in which he offered the example of a person who took great care over his fruitless fig tree:

> He spake also this parable: "A certain man had a fig tree planted in his vineyard; and he came and sought fruit thereon, and found none. Then said he unto the dresser of his vineyard, 'Behold, these three years I come seeking fruit on this fig tree, and find none: cut it down; why cumbereth it the ground?'
>
> And he answering said unto him, 'Lord, let it alone this year also, till I shall dig about it, and dung it. And if it bear fruit, well; and if not, then after that thou shalt cut it down.'" (Lk 13.6–9)

Jesus himself, it seems, acts in a way contrary to this loving gardener. He knows that it is not yet time for figs, and yet he still curses the tree. Why? Evidently, we should not seek the answer in a strictly literal reading of this passage, but in the frequent symbolism of trees and growing things in Jesus' sermons.

The word "fruit" has a very specific symbolic meaning in the Bible. Even in the Old Testament, a righteous man was thus described: "He shall be like the tree planted by the streams of waters, which shall bring forth its fruit in its season; and its leaf shall not fall, and all whatsoever he may do shall prosper" (Ps 1.3). In the Psalms, fruitfulness is a symbol of righteousness: "The righteous shall flourish like a palm tree; he shall grow like the cedar in Lebanon. They that are planted in the house of the

Lord, shall flourish in the courts of our God. They shall still bring forth fruit in a ripe old age; and happy shall they be, that they may proclaim that upright is the Lord our God, and there is no unrighteousness in him" (Ps 91.12–15).

Likewise, a tree's lack of fruit is a symbol of spiritual fruitlessness. John the Baptist said, "And now also the axe is laid unto the root of the trees; therefore every tree which bringeth not forth good fruit is hewn down, and cast into the fire" (Mt 3.10). Jesus would repeat these words almost verbatim in the Sermon on the Mount, when speaking of false prophets:

Ye shall know them by their fruits. Do men gather grapes of thorns, or figs of thistles? Even so every good tree bringeth forth good fruit, but a corrupt tree bringeth forth evil fruit. A good tree cannot bring forth evil fruit, neither can a corrupt tree bring forth good fruit. Every tree that bringeth not forth good fruit is hewn down, and cast into the fire. Wherefore by their fruits ye shall know them. (Mt 7.16–20)

Jesus used the same images during the Mystical Supper, when he compared himself with the vine, and the disciples with its branches:

I am the true vine, and my Father is the husbandman. Every branch in me that beareth not fruit he taketh away, and every branch that beareth fruit, he purgeth it, that it may bring forth more fruit. . . . I am the vine, ye are the branches. He that abideth in me, and I in him, the same bringeth forth much fruit; for without me ye can do nothing. If a man abide not in me, he is cast forth as a branch, and is withered, and men gather them, and cast them into the fire, and they are burned. If ye abide in me, and my words abide in you, ye shall ask what ye will, and it shall be done unto you. Herein is my Father glorified, that ye bear much fruit; so shall ye be my disciples. (Jn 15.1–2, 5–8)

Jesus spoke these words on the eve of his death, only a few days after the incident with the fig tree, which was still very fresh in the disciples' memory. The constantly repeating motif of fruit and fruitlessness points to what Jesus expects from his disciples. This result, however, can only

The Mystical Supper, fresco, 13th century

be achieved in cases when they remain connected to the vine, that is, in unity with their Master. He is the source of the life-giving sap that feeds the entire tree of the Church and gives each member the chance to produce his own fruits.

The words "ye shall ask what ye will, and it shall be done unto you" in the passage from John echoes Jesus' words when he cursed the fig tree: "Whatsoever ye shall ask in prayer, believing, ye shall receive" (Mt 21.22). Evidently, during the last days of his earthly life, he thought much about the future of his disciples, seeking to strengthen their faith. Throughout his ministry, he spoke to them of faith, and he performed signs and miracles before their eyes. Now the time had come for for the final sign: the sign of the prophet Jonah (Mt 12.39). To help them understand its meaning, to help them endure the coming dark days, he gave them a much-needed reminder of the power of faith. This reminder was the incident with the fig tree. Jesus turned the incident into a lesson about faith.

After all, Jesus' words about faith are the thematic center of the entire episode. Jesus repeats almost word for word what he had already told his disciples at least twice. The first time, he answered their question about why they could not cast out the demon from the young demoniac: "Because of your unbelief; for verily I say unto you, if ye have faith as a grain of mustard seed, ye shall say unto this mountain, 'Remove hence to yonder place,' and it shall remove; and nothing shall be impossible unto you" (Mt 17.20). Another time, Jesus spoke similar words when answering their request to increase their faith (Lk 17.16). As a good teacher, Jesus repeated the same truths again and again, using the same imagery, so that the lesson would remain firmly in his disciples' memory. In this case, Jesus uses a vivid image—the withered tree that was punished for its fruitlessness.

When speaking of "this mountain," Jesus could have meant either the Mount of Olives or the Temple Mount; the latter is more likely, since he was walking in the direction of the temple. If he was pointing at the Temple Mount, then an entire series of associations with the Old Testament become possible. This mount is assumed in the following passage from Psalms: "They that trust in the Lord shall be as Mount Sion; he that dwells in Jerusalem shall never be moved" (Ps 124.1). The Temple Mount was also associated with the eschatological expectations of the nation of Israel:

And it shall come to pass in the last days, that the mountain of the LORD's house shall be established in the top of the mountains, and shall be exalted above the hills; and all nations shall flow unto it. And many people shall go and say, "Come ye, and let us go up to the mountain of the LORD, to the house of the God of Jacob; and he will teach us of his ways, and we will walk in his paths; for out of Zion shall go forth the law, and the word of the LORD from Jerusalem." (Is 2.2–3)

Nevertheless, Jesus underlines that neither the mount by itself, nor the temple standing on it, will save the nation of Israel if they do not bring the necessary fruits of faith. This subtext was noticed by early commentators:

It was not because Christ cursed it that the tree produced no fruit; instead, because the tree first produced no fruit, Christ cursed it to ensure that it would produce no leaves. Likewise, it was not because God abandoned them that the Jews squandered his righteousness; rather, because they failed to produce the fruits of righteousness, God

abandoned them to ensure that they would not have the appearance
or reputation of righteousness.[50]

St Jerome gives an elaborate allegorical interpretation of the miracle
with the fig tree, seeing in it an image of the judgments of God over his
chosen nation, which did not bring the necessary fruits:

> When he returned to the city, he was hungry. This shows both the real-
> ity of his human flesh and the fact that he was hungry for the salvation
> of believers. But he is seething over the unbelief of Israel. And when he
> had seen one tree, which we understand as the synagogue, the meeting
> place of the Jews, by the wayside (for though it had the Law, it was "by
> the wayside" because it did not believe in the Way), he went to it. This
> shows that it was standing there immobile and did not have the feet of
> the Gospel. And he found nothing on it except leaves only. This refers
> to the rustling of the promises, the Pharisaical traditions, their boasting
> in the Law, and the outer display of words without any fruit of truth.
> And this is why another evangelist says: "For it was not yet the time,"
> which refers either to the fact that the time of the salvation of Israel had
> not yet come, because the people of the Gentiles had not yet entered in,
> or that the time of faith had passed by, since, though he came to Israel
> first, he was spurned by them and passed on to the nations. "And he
> said to it: "May no fruit ever come from you,'" either "'in eternity'" or
> "in the age," for the Greek word αἰών [aiōn] signifies both." "And the fig
> tree withered." This means that it did not have the nourishment that
> the Lord desired when he was hungry. But the leaves withered in such
> a way that the trunk itself remained. And though the branches were
> broken off, the root was still alive. At the end of time, if they want to
> believe, this root will sprout the shoots of faith.[51]

The cursing of the fig tree was the last miracle recorded by the evangelists, if we do not count the healing the of the servant of the high priest after

[50]From an incomplete work on Matthew (PG 56:846). Translation in Manlio Simonetti,
ed., *Ancient Christian Commentary on Scripture, New Tastament 1b: Matthew 13–28* (Downers
Grove, IL: InterVarsity Press, 2002), 131.

[51]Jerome, *Commentary on Matthew* 3.21.18–20 (FOTC 117:239–240).

The Siege of Jerusalem, Hayez, 1867

one of the disciples cuts off his ear during Jesus' arrest (Lk 22.51). There is a thematic connection running through all the miracles from the first—the transformation of water into wine—to the last. But if the first miracle was a revelation of God's mercy, this last is a revelation of divine wrath.

This accords with the general mood of the last days of Jesus' earthly life, from the casting out of the money-changers to the prophecies concerning Jerusalem's destruction, to the terrifying warnings concerning the final judgment (Mt 24–25). When speaking of the day of judgment, Jesus offered the example of the fig tree:

> Now learn a parable of the fig tree: when his branch is yet tender, and putteth forth leaves, ye know that summer is nigh, so likewise ye, when ye shall see all these things, know that it is near, even at the doors! (Mt 24.32–33)

The fig tree that withered before the eyes of the disciples becomes a symbol of God's judgment over those who do not bring forth the necessary fruits. At the same time, it reminds us of God's intention for each object and creature he created:

> Everything in this world has its God-created purpose and function. The fig tree must give rise to figs. The angel must serve God. Man must

become like God. The bee must gather honey. If a creature does not follow its purpose, it falls under the curse of the Creator, whether in secret or openly. The God-Man came to the world, after all, to restore all to its divine, original purpose. He alone knows the function of every creature, every created thing. He alone has the power to give each created thing the power to fulfill its divine purpose. . . . The fig tree exists in the world to serve man. Man? To serve God. How does man serve God? By faith. Faith means this: to live by God, in God, for God with all your being, with all the strength of your existence. Only thus will human nature offer God the necessary fruit. In the opposite case, it will wither. . . . man's nature, not irrigated by the heavenly dew of grace, remaining outside the sun of divine power, withers, dries up, remains barren. . . . While man can graft himself to the God-Man by the labor of faith, and then the strength, the divine sap of the God-Man begins to flow through the nature of man, making him fruitful, and then human nature "bears much fruit" (Jn 15.5). . . . Faith deifies man and makes him a god by grace, and everything that he does will be divine, immortal, eternal.[52]

---

[52]Justin Popovich, *Tolkovanie na Evangelie ot Matfeya* [Commentary on the Gospel according to Matthew], 383–84 (translated by NK).

Chapter 6

THE
TRANSFIGURATION

M any contemporary scholars find the Transfiguration "an enigmatic
and difficult text."[1] In the scholarly literature dedicated to the miracles of Jesus, this event is usually missing, since it does not fit into one of
the four categories scholars generally use for all of his miracles: 1) healings,
2) exorcisms, 3) resurrections, and 4) events demonstrating mastery over
nature. Even this categorization is rather arbitrary, however, like the idea
that one can only consider an event miraculous that occurred as a result
of Jesus' desire to help a person or a group of people.

We should ask: Did Jesus intend to show his glory to the three disciples whom he took with him up the mountain, or did they simply see
him as he was transformed whenever he stood at prayer, conversing with
his Father? The tradition of the Church gives a clear answer—Jesus intentionally took the three disciples with him to strengthen their faith before
his passion. Soon they would have to see him humiliated and diminished
before other people, "a man of sorrows and acquainted with grief" (Is 53.3).
Jesus revealed his glory to them so that they would know that beneath this
human abasement the glory of his divine nature was concealed.

---

[1]Andrew P. Wilson, *Transfigured: A Derridean Rereading of the Markan Transfiguration*
(New York and London: T & T Clark, 2007), 56.

Transfiguration,
Raphael, 1519–20

1. Four Accounts of the Tranfiguration

In all three Synoptic Gospels, the Transfiguration is preceded by two accounts—Jesus' conversation with his disciples in Caesarea Philippi, when Peter confessed him to be the Son of God (Mt 16.13–20; Mk 8.27–30; Lk 9.18–21), and a conversation in which Jesus foretold his sufferings, death, and resurrection to his disciples (Mt 16.21–26; Mk 8.31–37; Lk 9.22–25). This second account also contains predictions concerning his second coming, when "the Son of man shall come in the glory of his Father with his angels; and then he shall reward every man according to his works" (Mt 16.27). The episode ended with Jesus' words: "Verily I say unto you, there be some standing here, which shall not taste of death, till they see the Son of man coming in his kingdom" (Mt 16.28).

The fact that all three evangelists put these events in the same order shows us that they saw a connection among all three of these events—the confession of Jesus as Son of God, the prophecy of his own death, and the Transfiguration. Moreover, his words concerning glory and the kingdom, which refer to the second coming, also help us to understand the Transfiguration, since this event, in its own turn, gives a foretaste of Jesus' glory that will be fully revealed in his second coming.

Let us turn to the Gospels themselves. They are almost all identical, differing only in minor details. Matthew's version reads thus:

> And after six days Jesus taketh Peter, James, and John his brother, and bringeth them up into an high mountain apart, and was transfigured before them; and his face did shine as the sun, and his raiment was white as the light. And, behold, there appeared unto them Moses and Elijah talking with him. Then answered Peter, and said unto Jesus, "Lord, it is good for us to be here; if thou wilt, let us make here three tabernacles; one for thee, and one for Moses, and one for Elias."

Transfiguration,
mosaic,
6th century

While he yet spake, behold, a bright cloud overshadowed them, and behold a voice out of the cloud, which said, "This is my beloved Son, in whom I am well pleased; hear ye him."

And when the disciples heard it, they fell on their face, and were sore afraid. And Jesus came and touched them, and said, "Arise, and be not afraid."

And when they had lifted up their eyes, they saw no man, save Jesus only. And as they came down from the mountain, Jesus charged them, saying, "Tell the vision to no man, until the Son of man be risen again from the dead." (Mt 17.1–9)

Mark ornaments his version with a few extra details. When he speaks about the clothing of the transfigured Jesus, he notes that they "became shining, exceeding white as snow, such as no fuller on earth can white them." Peter's words about the three tabernacles are given additional commentary: "For he knew not what to say; for they were sore afraid." But Mark also leaves out a series of details, including any mention of the fact that the disciples fell on their faces and that Jesus touched them and told them not to fear. As for the words coming from the cloud, Mark renders them thus: "This is my beloved Son: hear him." Mark also adds the following to Christ's prophecy about his resurrection from the dead: "And they kept that saying with themselves, questioning one with another what the rising from the dead should mean" (Mk 9.2–10).

Transfiguration,
mosaic,
St Catherine's
Monastery,
Mt Sinai,
A D 565–66

As for Luke, he omitted a series of details found in both Matthew and Mark, though he included some that they missed. His account begins thus: "About eight days after these sayings, he took Peter and John and James, and went up into a mountain to pray." Luke is the only evangelist to mention that Jesus went up on the mountain for the purpose of prayer, and that his transfiguration occurred when he was praying. Only Luke mentions that Moses and Elijah, "Who appeared in glory . . . spoke of his decease [literally, 'exodus'] which he should accomplish at Jerusalem." No one but Luke mentions that Peter and the others "were heavy with sleep," and that they saw the glory of Jesus and the other two men in the moment after waking up. Only Luke mentions that they all entered the cloud that came down over them. The voice from the cloud is given these words: "This is my beloved Son. Hear him!" Luke also has no mention that Jesus forbade his disciples to speak about the miracle until after the resurrection. His account ends with the following words: "And they kept it close, and told no man in those days any of those things which they had seen" (Lk 9.28–36).

After the Transfiguration, Matthew and Mark recount that the disciples ask Jesus a question, having in mind the prophecy about his resurrection: "Why then say the scribes that Elijah must first come?" (Mt 17.10) Jesus' answer in Matthew is as follows: "And Jesus answered and said unto them, Elias truly shall first come, and restore all things. But I say unto you, that Elijah is come already, and they knew him not, but have done unto him whatsoever they wanted. Likewise shall also the Son of man suffer from them" (Mt 17.11–12). Mark gives a similar version of this answer (Mk 9.12–13). Matthew also comments on this episode with a phrase missing in Mark: "Then the disciples understood that he spoke unto them of John the Baptist" (Mt 17.13).

In his second general epistle, Peter speaks of the Transfiguration as an eyewitness. In this letter, the apostle writes of the divine power of the Lord Jesus Christ that can make people "partakers of the divine nature" (2 Pet 1.4), as well as his eternal kingdom, whose entrance is revealed through an ever-greater confirmation of the faithful in their calling and election (1.10–11). In proof of the credibility of the Gospel he preached, Peter cited the Transfiguration:

> For we have not followed cunningly devised fables, when we made known unto you the power and coming of our Lord Jesus Christ, but were eyewitnesses of his majesty. For he received from God the Father honor and glory, when there came such a voice to him from the excellent glory, "This is my beloved Son, in whom I am well pleased." And this voice which came from heaven we heard, when we were with him in the holy mount. (2 Pet 1.16–18)

Thus, before us we have three full accounts of the event, and one direct reference to it.

All four authors are clear that the transfiguration occurred on a mountain. But none of them give the name of that mountain. Matthew and Mark call it a "high mountain," while Peter calls it "holy," evidently because that it was the place of Christ's Transfiguration, not that it was considered sacred before that event. In any case, he is clearly not speaking about any of the mountains that were considered holy in Jewish tradition (Sinai, Zion, Carmel), since none of them fit geographically in the Gospel accounts.

2. Tabor, Hermon, or Meron?

In Christian tradition, Tabor is considered the place where the Transfiguration occurred—a mountain about 588 meters tall, found in Galilee, about nine kilometers from Nazareth. It is likely that even by the fourth century, the first Christian temple on Tabor was built. Liturgical texts of the feast and the works of the Fathers of the Church mention Tabor as the place of the Transfiguration of the Lord. For example, St Cyril of Jerusalem writes that the Transfiguration occurred on Tabor in his catechetical lectures in the fourth century (12.16). Currently, there are two monasteries on top of the mountain—one Orthodox and the other Catholic. They are both dedicated to the Transfiguration.

At the same time, most contemporary scholars think that Hermon was the more likely place for the Transfiguration.[2] This mountain is 2813 meters high, found in northern Palestine. When gathering all the information available about both mountains, an Orthodox scholar of the mid-twentieth century writes the following:

> Tabor is not a very tall mountain found in southern Galilee. In the New Testament era, there was a fortress at the top of Tabor, which made the place not ideal for solitude. Contrary to the tradition, most scholars in our days lean toward Hermon as the more likely site. Hermon, which is tall (see Mt 17.1 for the expression "tall mountain"), and which is perfect for complete solitude. It is found to the North of Galilee. The region of Caesarea Philippi, where the disciples preached the teacher as the Messiah, lies at the foot of Mount Hermon. The chronology also fits Hermon as the site. Jesus' passage through Galilee that follows the Transfiguration (Mk 9.30) could naturally be understood as immediately preceding his path to Jerusalem, since it is a movement from north to south, not from Tabor to Hermon, but from Hermon

---

[2]See, for example, D. L Brake, and T. Bolen, *Jesus: A Visual History* (Grand Rapids, MI: Zondervan Academic, 2014) 120, 246.

Transfiguration, miniature from a Gospel book in Iveron Monastery, 11th century

to Tabor. However, this is not the only possible interpretation. It can also be disputed. But the total sum of available facts makes it much more preferable to the received tradition.[3]

In the Bible, Tabor is mentioned as the boundary between the lands of three tribes of Israel: Issachar, Zebulun, and Naphtali (Josh 19.22). At the foot of Tabor, one of the judges of Israel, Barak, defeated the armies of Sisera (Judg 4.1–24). The brothers of Gideon died at the hands of the kings of Midian Zebah and Zalmunna (Judg 8.18–19) on mount Tabor. In the Psalter, Tabor is mentioned together with Hermon: "Thou hast created the north and the south; Tabor and Hermon shall rejoice in thy name" (Ps 88.12). In the prophecy of Jeremiah, Nebuchadnezzar is compared to Mounts Tabor and Carmel: "Surely as Tabor is among the mountains, and as Carmel by the sea, so shall he come" (Jer 46.18).

As for Hermon, it is often mentioned in the Bible as the northern limit of the promised land (Josh 12.1; 13.2, 5, 8, 11). During the wars of conquest of the promised land by Joshua, Hermon belonged to Og, king of Bashan (Josh 12.4–5). He and Sihon, king of the Amorites, who ruled a neighboring territory (Josh 12.2), were killed by Moses, who then divided the lands among three tribes of Israel (Josh 12.5–6). This area was finally added to the Israelites during the time of King David.[4]

The argument in favor of Hermon as the tall mountain on which the Transfiguration occurred is further strengthened by the fact that the top of this mountain is covered in snow the whole year round. The comparison between the whiteness of Jesus' transfigured clothing and snow, which is present in many manuscripts of the Gospel according to Mark, seems more appropriate if the place was Hermon.

[3]Kassian (Bezobrazov), *Khristos i pervoe khristanskoe pokolenie* [Christ and the first Christian generation] (Moscow, 2001), 62.
[4]Y. M. Chekhanovets, *Hermon*, 676.

At the same time, several facts argue against Hermon as the site for the Transfiguration. First of all, to climb a mountain over 2800 meters high would have been rather difficult, especially if we consider that during Jesus' time, people wore light sandals on bare feet (even if we ignore this fact, climbing up this mountain and coming down again would have taken around two days of daylight). Second, it is unlikely that Jesus would have found a crowd awaiting him fifty kilometers away from the Sea of Galilee. Third, after the account of the Transfiguration and the subsequent exorcism of the young man, Mark writes, "they departed thence, and passed through Galilee" (Mk 9.30). These words could indicate that the place of the Transfiguration was outside Galilee, but it is more likely that it was either in Galilee or close to it.

Tabor, Catholic basilica of the Transfiguration

Because of these facts, scholars have recently offered a third hypothesis: the Transfiguration occurred on Mount Meron, which is thirteen kilometers north of the Sea of Galilee. This is the tallest mountain in Galilee (1208 meters), and it is found on the way from Caesarea Philippi to the Sea of Galilee.

We can affirm the following facts about the place of the Transfiguration:

1) The exact place remains unclear.

2) The arguments for Mount Meron are not yet well developed.

3) The arguments for Mount Hermon are not sufficient to completely disregard the received tradition, which began as early as the fourth century, and has firmly connected Tabor with the site of the Transfiguration.

Transfiguration,
icon, 12th
century

---

3. The Revelation of
the Glory of God

Matthew and Mark begin their accounts in the same way: "After six days had passed." In Luke, the beginning differs slightly: "about eight days after these sayings." Usually, this divergence is explained by the fact that Matthew and Mark only counted those days that elapsed between two events, while Luke included both events as two other days.[5] Note also that Luke uses the word ὡσεί (*hōsei*, "about"), indicating an imprecise count of days.

In Matthew and Mark, after Jesus ascended the mountain with three disciples, he was transfigured before them. In Luke, as we mentioned, Jesus ascended the mountain to pray, and "as he prayed, the fashion of his countenance was altered, and his raiment was white and glistering" (Lk 9.29) This difference seems significant. Matthew and Mark describe the event as though Jesus took the apostles to the top of the mountain specifically to show them his glory. Luke says something else—the disciples saw Jesus

---

[5]John Chrysostom, *Homilies on Matthew*, Homily 56 (NPNF¹ 10:345).

transfigured during prayer. Consequently, in this version, the Transfiguration was a revelation of his glory, but not a premeditated act on his part. The verb "transfigure" itself (μεταμορφόω; *metamorphoō*) is missing in Luke, as opposed to Mathew and Mark, who use exactly that word to describe the change that occurred with Jesus.

The Transfiguration affected, first of all, his face. According to Matthew, it began to "shine as the sun" (Mt 17.2). According to Luke, Jesus' face changed (literally "his face was altered"). Mark, however, says nothing about the change of Jesus' face. Second, Jesus' clothing also changed. According to Matthew, it became "white as the light." Mark men-

Transfiguration, icon from the workshop of Theophanes the Greek, c. 1403

tions that it became "shining, exceedingly white." Many manuscripts of the Gospel according to Mark also have the addition "like snow," and in some manuscripts of the Gospel according to Matthew, instead of "as the light," we read "as snow." In the Latin and Syriac translations the expression "as snow" is found in Matthew, as well as Mark, which indicates its presence in the Greek text from which these translations were made in the third century. Luke speaks of the clothing as "white and glistening" (Lk 9.29).

Only Luke mentions that Moses and Elijah appeared in glory and the apostles, "when they were awake, they saw his glory, and the two men that stood with him" (Lk 9.32). The term "glory" used here is also used in the second epistle of Peter, which refers to this event. In the Old Testament, this word indicated the presence of God in some visible form, including a cloud (Ex 16.7–10; 24.15–17; 40.34–35). All three evangelists also mention the cloud (Matthew calls it "bright"), which overshadows them, that is, it comes down on them like a light-bearing shadow (the verb ἐπεσκίαζεν [*epeskiazen*] comes from the word σκιά [*skia*], "shadow").

The term "glory" plays a special role in the Gospel according to John. The prologue of the fourth Gospel includes these words: "and we beheld his glory, the glory as of the only begotten of the Father . . . full of grace and truth" (Jn 1.14). Apparently, this does not refer to any particular event in

Transfiguration, icon from the series of icons on the 12 feasts in the Annunciation Cathedral of the Moscow Kremlin, 15th century

Jesus' life, such as the Transfiguration. More likely, it refers generally to the event of the incarnation of God, when the pre-eternal Logos of God became the Son of Man. On the other hand, the term "glory" in the same Gospel also refers to the existence of the Son of God before the Incarnation: "And now, O Father, glorify thou me with thine own self with the glory which I had with thee before the world was" (Jn 17.5). Finally, in John the term "glory" can also mean the revelation of God's power, which is directly related to concrete actions of Jesus. For example, before Lazarus' resurrection, Jesus says to Martha: "Said I not unto thee, that, if thou wouldest believe, thou shouldest see the glory of God?" (Jn 11.40) Here, "the glory of God" means an action leading to the resurrection of a dead man.

In the Gospel according to John, there is an episode that has some similarity to the Transfiguration. This episode occurred in the last period of Jesus' earthly life, after his triumphant entry into Jerusalem. John tells how during one of the conversations with the people, Jesus speaks of his imminent passion: "Now is my soul troubled; and what shall I say? 'Father, save me from this hour'? But for this cause came I unto this hour. Father, glorify thy name." This unexpected shift from conversing with the people to directly addressing God leads to God's immediate answer: "I have both glorified it, and will glorify it again" (Jn 12.27–28).

The voice of the Father appears in the Gospels only three times—during Jesus' baptism in the Jordan, in this event from John's Gospel, and in the Synoptics' accounts of the Transfiguration. The theme of glory serves as the connecting thread between this event in the Gospel according to John and the Transfiguration as recounted in Luke. In both events, there is a close connection between the glory of God, the voice of God, and the theme of Jesus' suffering and death, since it was concerning the passion, according to Luke, that he conversed with Moses and Elijah (Lk 9.31). The pre-eternal existence of the Word of God before his incarnation, the

Transfiguration, icon, 16th century

incarnation itself, and the passion and death of the Son of Man were all various aspects of that divine glory that was revealed to the world in the person of the Only-begotten Son of God.

Luke has his own understanding of the glory of God, which is a major theme throughout his Gospel. When Jesus was born in Bethlehem, angels of the Lord appeared before the shepherds, "and the glory of God shone round about them" (Lk 2.9). Then, the heavenly army itself appeared with the angels, and they cried out, "Glory to God in the highest, and on earth peace, good will toward men" (Lk 2.14). Simeon, when holding the Christ child in his arms, called him a light to enlighten the Gentiles and the glory of the people of Israel (Lk 2.32). From the first coming of the Son of Man, a connective thread extends all the way to his second coming, when "he shall come in his own glory, and in his Father's, and of the holy angels" (Lk 9.26). The Transfiguration becomes the connection between all these things, and it follows immediately after Jesus' words concerning his second coming. During Jesus' triumphant entry into Jerusalem, we hear words that echo the song of the angels at his birth: "Blessed be the king that cometh in the name of the Lord: peace in heaven, and glory in the highest!" (Lk 19.38). Finally, after his resurrection, Jesus appears to two disciples, though they do not recognize him. He asks them, "Ought not Christ to have suffered these things, and to enter into his glory?" (Lk 24.26).

4. Moses and Elijah

Why did Moses and Elijah appear on the mountain next to Jesus? St John Chrysostom gives several reasons:

1. And first of all this: because the multitudes said he was, some Elias, some Jeremias, some one of the old prophets, he brings the leaders of his choir, that they might see the difference even hereby between the servants and the Lord.

2. Men were continually accusing him of transgressing the law, and accounting him to be a blasphemer, as appropriating to himself a glory which belonged not to him, even the Father's . . . that both the charges might be shown to spring from envy, and he be proved not liable to either; and that neither is his conduct a transgression of the law, nor his calling himself equal to the Father an appropriation of glory not his own. . . .

Transfiguration, miniature from a Gospel in Iveron monastery, 11th century

3. To inform [the disciples] that he has power both of death and life, is ruler both above and beneath. For this cause he brings forward both him that had died, and him that never yet suffered this.

4. To show the glory of the cross, and to console Peter and the others in their dread of the passion, and to raise up their minds. Since having come, they by no means held their peace, but spoke, it is said, of the glory which he was to accomplish at Jerusalem; that is, of the passion, and the cross; for so they call it always.[6]

Often, even in scholarly literature, Moses and Elijah are interpreted as two symbolic figures that correspond to Jesus' frequently-used formula "the law and the prophets" (Mt 7.12; 22.40; Lk 16.16). Moses is a personification

[6]John Chrysostom, *Homilies on the Gospel of Matthew,* Homily 56 (NPNF[1] 10:346).

of the Law, Elijah of the prophets.[7] This interpretation originally comes from Origen, who insisted that Moses represents the Law, while Elijah represents not so much himself alone, as the choir of all the prophets.[8] Jerome follows Origen: "This passage points to the Law and the prophets, which by repeated utterances announced both the passion of the Lord and his resurrection."[9]

There is another formula to which this appearance corresponds, found in the Gospel according to Luke: "Moses and the prophets" (Lk 16.29, 31).[10] Jesus often stressed the primacy of his mission compared to the mission of Moses and the prophets. In the Sermon on the Mount, he said, "Think not that I am come to destroy the law, or the prophets. I am not come to destroy, but to fulfil. For verily I say unto you, till heaven and earth pass, one jot or one tittle shall in no wise pass from the law, till all be fulfilled" (Mt 5.17–18). At the same time, the main part of the Sermon on the Mount is built on the principle of opposition between the Jesus' teachings and what was written in the Law of Moses: "Ye have heard that it was said of them of old time . . . but I say unto you" (Mt 5.21–22, 27–28, 38–39, 43–44). Jesus' teaching is not at all a mere revision of or addition to the Law of Moses; it is a radical improvement over the Law of Moses, though at the same time it still preserves the essential aspects of continuity.

Jesus' reference to Moses is characterized by three factors. First of all, he insists on the worth of Moses's Law and the importance of fulfilling it. Second, he elaborates and adds to the Law, and in some cases, he changes or cancels certain of its tenets. Third, Jesus admits that Moses remains the most important authority for his opponents—the Pharisees and scribes, who consider themselves to be Moses' heirs (Jn 9.28). Therefore, in conversations with them, he appeals to Moses' authority, contrasting his understanding of what Moses said with theirs (for example, in Mt 19.7–8 and Mt 22.24–29).

[7] See, for example, Taylor, The Gospel according to St. Mark, 390; A. Plummer, A Critical and Exegetical Commentary on the Gospel according to St. Luke (New York: T&T Clark, 1960), 251; G. Schneider, Das Evangelim nach Lukas. (Würtzburg: Götersloher Verlagshaus, 1977), 216.

[8] Origen, Commentary on the Gospel of Matthew 12.38.

[9] Jerome, Commentary on Matthew 3.17.3 (FOTC 117:199).

[10] H. Schürmann, Das Lukasevangelium (Freiburg: Herder, 1969), 557.

Jesus rejects the scribes' and Pharisees' pretensions to be Moses' heirs and followers. He insists that they have unlawfully ascribed to themselves the right to speak in his name: "The scribes and the Pharisees sit in Moses' seat. All therefore whatsoever they bid you observe, that observe and do; but do not ye after their works: for they say, and do not" (Mt 23.2–3). Jesus claims to continue Moses' works, and he explains the Jews' lack of faith in his miracles as a lack of obedience to Moses himself: "If they hear not Moses and the prophets, neither will they be persuaded, though one rose from the dead" (Lk 16.31). Jesus sees Moses as his forerunner who witnessed to him coming: "Do not think that I will

Joshua and Aaron Hold Up Moses' Arms, John Everett Millais, 19th century

accuse you to the Father; there is one that accuseth you, even Moses, in whom ye trust. For had ye believed Moses, ye would have believed me; for he wrote of me. But if ye believe not his writings, how shall ye believe my words?" (Jn 5.45–47).

Moses' significance for Jesus is not limited by the fact that through him God gave the Israelite nation the law, which Jesus came to fulfill. Moses, doubtless, is important for Jesus not only as a giver of the law, but as a personality. During the Transfiguration, Moses appears to have come to Jesus to give his personal greeting, and the importance of this fact should not be minimized. The connection between Moses and Jesus should not be interpreted only in its pedagogic or missionary aspect, that is, one should not merely examine the connections between their teaching and mission. Rather, there was a profound connection between them, which is revealed in the Gospels through many references Jesus made to Moses, especially through his appearance during the Transfiguration.

This connection becomes further evident when comparing the Gospel account of the Transfiguration with Moses's encounter with God on Sinai (Ex 24.1–16).[11] In both cases, the event occurs on a mountain. Jesus ascends

[11]P-Y. Brandt, *L'identité de Jésus et l'identité de son disciple* (Göttingen: Vandenhoeck & Ruprecht, 2002), 256–58, 336.

Moses Descends from Mount Sinai, F. Bol, 17th century

the mountain with Peter, James, and John, while Moses approaches the summit with Aaron, Nadab, and Abihu. The Transfiguration occurs six days after Jesus' conversation with his disciples in Caesarea Philippi; for six days, Moses awaited the revelation of God's glory. On the mount of the Transfiguration, the disciples saw a cloud, and on Sinai the glory of God came down to the mountain in the form of a cloud. In both cases, the voice of God comes from the midst of the cloud.

Finally, the most evident and vivid parallel between the two events is the shining face of Moses, which was an immediate result of the experience of communion with God that he was given on Sinai:

> And it came to pass, when Moses came down from mount Sinai with the two tables of testimony in Moses' hand, when he came down from the mount, that Moses knew not that the skin of his face shone while he talked with him. And when Aaron and all the children of Israel saw Moses, behold, the skin of his face shone; and they were afraid to come nigh him. And Moses called unto them; and Aaron and all the rulers of the congregation returned unto him: and Moses talked with them.
>
> And afterward all the children of Israel came nigh; and he gave them in commandment all that the LORD had spoken with him in mount Sinai. And till Moses had done speaking with them, he put a veil on his face. But when Moses went in before the LORD to speak with him, he took the veil off, until he came out. And he came out, and spake unto the children of Israel that which he was commanded. And the children of Israel saw the face of Moses, that the skin of Moses' face shone; and Moses put the veil upon his face again, until he went in to speak with him. (Ex 34.29–35)

In the scholarly literature, the parallel between these two accounts is usually explained as a literary dependence of the latter event on the former. In other words, the event in Exodus served, as it were, a model for the account of the Transfiguration. Nevertheless, this literary interpretation is based either on an open or concealed admission that the entire scene of the Transfiguration serves nothing more than a literary function, imagined by the Evangelists or the hypothetical common author of some unknown primary source for all three Synoptics.

Both the three Synoptics and the apostle Peter in his general epistle cite the Transfiguration as an actual event; moreover, Peter stresses that he was a witness of this event. The presumption that the eyewitness accounts in the Gospels are true, which we stated at the beginning of this examination as the main tool of our analysis, excludes any possibility of such an interpretation, as though the evangelists invented particular events based

Transfiguration,
mosaic icon,
13th century.

on existing literary models. Consequently, any similarity between the two
events should be sought in the events themselves, not only in how they are
reflected in literary sources.

In both cases, we have an encounter of man with God face to face. In
the first case, Moses meets God, in the second, Jesus encounters his Father.
The difference between Jesus and Moses is clear—Jesus is the God-Man.
Moses is thus a type of Jesus (not a model at all, upon which the evangelists
purportedly invented the image of Jesus, transfigured on a mountain).

Another Old Testament foreshadowing of Jesus was Elijah, who communed with God on Mount Carmel (1 Kg 18.42). Elijah was raised to the

heavens on a fiery chariot (2 Kg 2.11), and, according to the prophecies, was supposed to return to the Israelite nation "before the coming of the great and dreadful day of the Lord" (Mal 4.5). It was not by accident that this is exactly what the disciples asked Jesus as they came down from the mountain: "Why then say the scribes that Elijah must first come?" And it was not by accident that Jesus answered that Elijah had already come, meaning John the Baptist (Mt 17.10–13).

Transfiguration, icon from the series of icons on the 12 feasts in the Dormition Cathedral of the Kirillo-Belozersk Monastery, 1497

In the disciples' question, we see a confusion of ideas typical of Jews of the time. The expectation of the Messiah had an eschatological character, and many thought that the Messiah would come at the end of times, before the end of history. Therefore all the prophecies about Elijah's return, which was supposed to happen before the day of the Lord (the end of days), was connected to the coming of the Messiah.[12] It was in the context of these assumptions, evidently, that the disciples of Jesus understood the presence of Elijah next to Jesus on mount of the transfiguration.

---

[12]Marcus, *Mark: 8–16*, 644–46.

5. Three Tents and the Voice from the Cloud

Peter's reaction to the mystical appearance of Moses and Elijah next to Jesus is described with significant variation in the three Synoptic Gospels. In Matthew, Peter calls Jesus "Lord" (κύριε, *kyrie*), in Mark, he calls him "rabbi," in Luke, he calls him "master" (ἐπιστάτα; *epistata*). The words "it is good for us to be here" illustrate a state of spiritual exaltation and ecstasy, which, evidently, all three disciples experienced. But as often happen in other such cases, only Peter is capable of expressing in words the state they shared in common.

The desire to put up three tents (or booths) can seem foolish. Mark adds the following phrase: "For he knew not what to say; for they were sore afraid" (Mk 9.6). Luke said, "not knowing what he said" (Lk 9.33). The Fathers of the Church often interpret the booths that Peter mentions in an allegorical fashion—as a symbol of those heavenly booths prepared for those who believe in Jesus,[13] or as a symbol of the three persons of the Holy Trinity, that is, "make three tabernacles, nay rather, make one for the Father and the Son and the Holy Spirit, so that there might be one tabernacle in your heart for those whose divinity is one."[14]

Some scholars suggest that the Gospel account of the Transfiguration shares a connection with the Jewish Feast of Booths, or Sukkoth. This autumn feast was established as a commemoration of the wandering of the Israelite people through the desert. According to tradition, one was supposed to leave one's house during the feast and live in tents or booths for seven days. Isaiah's prophecy was also connected with this feast: "And the LORD will create upon every dwelling place of mount Zion, and upon her assemblies, a cloud and smoke by day, and the shining of a flaming fire by night; for upon all the glory shall be a defense. And there shall be a tabernacle [*sukkah*, booth] for a shadow in the day time from the heat,

[13]John Chrysostom, *Homilies on the Gospel of Matthew*, Homiliy 56.3; Jerome, *Commentary on the Gospel of Mark* 6; Cyril of Alexandria, *Fragments* 200.

[14]Jerome, *Commentary on Matthew* 3.17.4 (FOTC 117:199).

Feast of Booths (Sukkoth), Marc Chagall, 20th century

and for a place of refuge, and for a covert from storm and from rain" (Is 4.5–6). This prophecy has certain aspects that are similar to the Transfiguration (the image of the mountain, the cloud, the shining, the booths). It is possible that when he offered Jesus to come abide in these booths with Moses and Elijah, Peter was consciously or subconsciously thinking of the traditional feast.

In any case, his words witness the desire to prolong that special spiritual state that he and the other two disciples experienced when they saw Jesus transfigured on the mountain. They probably should not be interpreted as some scholars do to mean that Peter placed Jesus, Moses, and Elijah on the same level.[15] If this were so, he would have addressed all of them at the same time, not Jesus alone, whom (and only whom) he had called Lord, Teacher, and Master.

The voice that came from the cloud uttered words identical to those that sounded forth at Jesus' baptism (Mt 3.17; Mk 1.11; Lk 3.22). These words the evangelists transmit with minor differences, based, it is possible, more on differences in translation into Greek of what the disciples heard in Hebrew or Aramaic. In Matthew and Mark, the Son of God is called "beloved" (ἀγαπητός; *agapētos*), while in Luke, according to a series of manuscripts,

---

[15]J. P. Heil, *The Transfiguration of Jesus* (Rome: Biblical Institute Press, 2000), 209.

The Baptism of Christ,
Verrocchio, *c.* 1472–75

he is called "chosen" (ἐκλελεγμένος; *eklelegme-nos*). The difficult expression ἐν ᾧ εὐδόκησα (*en hō eudokēsa*; literally "in whom I have good will," from εὐδοκέω (*eudokeō*), "I think well of someone," "I am happy with someone," "I approve of someone") is found only in Matthew.

Sometimes, the words "This is my Son" are interpreted as an allusion to the biblical account of Abraham's offering Isaac as a sacrifice to God—this account has always been interpreted in Christian tradition as a type of the passion of Christ. It begins with the words of God, addressed to Abraham: "Take now thy son, thine only son Isaac, whom thou lovest, and get thee into the land of Moriah; and offer him there for a burnt offering upon one of the mountains which I will tell thee of" (Gen 22.2). Here, there are several similarities with the account of the Transfiguration:

1) There is a son who must be offered as a sacrifice. 2) This is an only son. 3) This is a beloved son. 4) The action occurs on a mountain. God says to Abraham, "Lay not thine hand upon the lad, neither do thou any thing unto him; for now I know that thou fearest God, seeing thou hast not withheld thy son, thine only son from me" (Gen 22.12). And God the Father, according to the Apostle Paul, is the one "that spared not his own Son, but delivered him up for us all" (Rom 8.32). The entire scene of the Transfiguration directly evokes to the theme of sacrifice, which the Son of God must offer in his obedience to the Father. The words of the Father, uttered on the mountain of Transfiguration, develop a more profound meaning when considered within the larger context of the Son's relationship with the Father and of the passion of the Son of God.

The words "hear him" are included in all three Synoptic accounts. These words, bearing as they do the weight of a moral command, differentiate these words from what was heard during the baptism of Jesus in the Jordan. If there God the Father triumphantly announced to people that before them stands his beloved Son, here, he further calls the disciples to be obedient to him.

Let us note that it seems none of these three disciples who were present with Jesus on the Mountain of Transfiguration was a witness of Jesus' baptism by John; consequently, it is possible they did not hear the words of the Father then. Now, these words sound like a reminder of the fact that Jesus possesses the good will of the Father; therefore, the disciples must listen to him.

Such a reminder is especially necessary before the sufferings that Jesus discusses with Moses and Elijah and with the disciples themselves. On the cross, Jesus will exclaim to the Father, "My God, My God, why hast thou forsaken me?" (Mt 27.46). In answer to this cry, neither he, nor the surrounding people, will hear an answer. To prevent the disciples from thinking that Jesus had lost the good will of the Father in that moment, or that the Father himself had abandoned Jesus, they hear the encouraging and strengthening voice of God on the mountain of the Transfiguration. It reminds them that the disciples must remain obedient to Jesus, just as Jesus himself is fully obedient to the Father and "humbled himself, and became obedient unto death, even the death of the cross" (Phil 2.8).

All the evangelists, each in his own way, witness to the fear that the disciples felt when they witnessed the revelation of Jesus in his glory. Mark says that the disciples were seized by fear (ἔκφοβοι γὰρ ἐγένοντο; *ekphoboi gar egenonto*); Luke mentions that they were afraid (ἐφοβήθησαν; *ephobēthēsan*) as they entered the cloud; Matthew says that they fell on their face and were greatly afraid (ἐφοβήθησαν σφόδρα; *ephobēthēsan sphodra*). In all three cases, the evangelists use words derived from *phobos* (φόβος; "fear" or "terror"). In Greek, this indicates a very powerful kind of fear. But the same word is used in the Greek Bible to indicate "fear of God," that trepidation before God that is one of the most characteristic expressions of profound religious feeling.

The theme of fear in its religious aspect is present in all the Gospels, but especially in the Gospel according to Luke. When the angel appears to Zachariah, "he was troubled, and fear fell upon him. But the angel said unto him, 'Fear not'" (1.12–13). The angel who visited Mary saw that she was disturbed by his words, and so said, "Fear not, Mary" (Lk 1.30). After Zachariah announced that his son would be called John, "fear came on all

Transfiguration,
icon, 1685

that dwelt round about them" (Lk 1.65). An angel appeared before the shepherds in the field, "and the glory of the Lord shone round about them; and they were sore afraid. And the angel said unto them, 'Fear not'" (2.9–10). When Jesus healed the paralytic, "They were all amazed, and they glorified God, and were filled with fear, saying, 'We have seen strange things to day!'" (Lk 5.26). When he raised the son of the widow of Nain, there "came a fear on all, and they glorified God, saying, 'A great prophet is risen up among us', and, 'God hath visited his people'" (Lk 7.16).

The miracle of calming the storm inspires fear and wonder in the disciples (Lk 8.25). When the women came to the tomb of Jesus and did not find his body there, "Behold, two men stood by them in shining garments, and as they were afraid, and bowed down their faces to the earth, they said unto them, 'Why seek ye the living among the dead?'" (Lk 24.4–5).

The Transfiguration is part of a chain of events, all of which inspire fear—not only emotional fear, but religious fear. In answer to this fear, Jesus, according to Matthew, says to the disciples: "Arise, and be not afraid" (Mt 17.7). Having raised their heads, they no longer see anyone before them other than Jesus alone in his usual, familiar form—an earthly man.

When Jesus came down from the mountain with his disciples, he forbade them to speak of this vision to anyone until the Son of Man rose from the dead. These words establish a connection between the Transfiguration and the central point of the Gospel narrative—the resurrection of Jesus. On the mountain of Transfiguration, the disciples saw a face that was unknown to them before; they saw him in the glory that they only heard about from him previously. They had yet to become witnesses of his extreme humiliation, suffering, and death, but they would also see him resurrected. And they were going to recognize in the newly glorified, resurrected body of Jesus, the same face that they saw on the mountain of the Transfiguration.

The Transfiguration is also connected with the second coming of Jesus and with all that will follow it. The Apostle Paul writes the following:

"Behold, I show you a mystery: We shall not all sleep, but we shall all be changed, in a moment, in the twinkling of an eye, at the last trump; for the trumpet shall sound, and the dead shall be raised incorruptible, and we shall be changed. For this corruptible must put on incorruption, and this mortal must put on immortality" (1 Cor 15.51–53). The transfigured flesh of Jesus is the type and pledge of the incorruptibility and transformation that awaits all mankind after the last trumpet. Jesus himself spoke of this new state, when he said, "Then shall the righteous shine forth as the sun in the kingdom of their Father. Who hath ears to hear, let him hear" (Mt 13.43).

6. The Nature of the Divine Light

What is the nature of the light that the disciples saw on the mountain of the Transfiguration? Was this light an inner radiance that came from Jesus himself or did the light envelop him from an outside source, like the voice from the Father that came from outside him? The Gospel is very clear that Jesus himself was the source of the light that radiated from him and suffused his entire nature.[16] Jesus ascended the mountain in his human nature—the one that did not differ externally from other people's bodies. Then the disciples witnessed the transfiguration of Jesus' body. Moreover, not only Jesus' face is transfigured, but his clothing as well—this was simple clothing of cloth made by human hands, the same that he wore before this event.

Blessed Jerome examines the nature of this transformation in detail. He believes that the face of Jesus remained as recognizable as before, meaning the matter of his body did not change, but the disciples were given a glimpse of the form he would have during his second coming, when he comes with glory:

[16]D. Lee, *Transfiguration*. (London: Continuum, 2004), 17.

Transfiguration,
icon, 12th
century

When the splendor of the face is shown and the brilliance of the clothing is described, it is not that the substance is removed, but the glory is
changed. "His face shone like the sun." Surely, the Lord was transformed
into that glory with which he is going to come later in his kingdom. The
transformation added splendor; it did not make his face disapper.[17]

Was the light on Tabor natural or supernatural? Did the light that shone
from the face and clothing of Jesus differ from the light that radiated from
Moses' face after his encounter with God on Sinai? John Chrysostom
believes that the light that shone from Jesus was extraordinary—its comparison with the sun is only used because people do not know of a brighter
source of light than the sun; if the light of the Transfiguration was not
extraordinary, the disciples would have been able to bear it and would not
have fallen down.[18]

In the Eastern Christian tradition, a great deal of attention was devoted
to this topic. By developing the New Testament teaching that God is light
(1 Jn 1.5), St Gregory the Theologian said, "God is light: the highest, the
unapproachable, the ineffable, that can neither be conceived in the mind

[17]Jerome, *Commentary on Matthew* 3.17.2 (FOTC 117:198).
[18]John Chrysostom, *Homilies on the Gospel of Matthew,* Homily 56 (NPNF[1] 10:346).

nor uttered with the lips, that gives life to every reasoning creature. He is in the world of thought, what the sun is in the world of sense."[19] St Gregory sees the entire history of the Bible and the entire life of the Church, all the way to the eschatological entry into the kingdom of God, as an unbroken chain of God's revelation of himself through the appearance of divine light. One of the links in this chain is the Transfiguration:

> Light was also the firstborn commandment given to the firstborn man. . . . And a Light typical and proportionate to those who were its subjects was the written law, adumbrating the truth and the sacrament of the great Light, for Moses' face was made glorious by it. . . . It was Light that appeared out of Fire to Moses, when it burned the bush indeed, but did not consume it, to show its nature and to declare the power that was in it. And it was Light that was in the pillar of fire that led Israel and tamed the wilderness. It was Light that carried up Elijah in the car of fire, and yet did not burn him as it carried him. It was Light that shone round the Shepherds when the Eternal Light was mingled with the temporal. It was Light that was the beauty of the Star that went before to Bethlehem to guide the wise men's way, and to be the escort of the Light that is above us, when he came among us. Light was that Godhead which was shown upon the Mount to the disciples—and a little too strong for their eyes.[20]

In the eleventh century, the theme of the divine light was given especial attention by St Symeon the New Theologian, who not only theorized concerning the divine light, but described his personal experience of contemplating this light. He described his first vision of light, which happened in early youth, by using the third person:

> One day, as he stood repeating more in his intellect than with his mouth the words, "God, have mercy upon me, a sinner" (Lk 18.13), suddenly a profuse flood of divine light appeared above him and filled the whole room. As this happened the young man lost his bearings, forgetting

[19]St Gregory of Nazianzus, Oration 40.5 (NPNF[2] 7:361).
[20]Ibid.

St Symeon the New Theologian, icon, 20th century

whether he was in a house or under a roof; for he saw nothing but light around him and did not even know that he stood upon the earth. He had no fear of falling, or awareness of the world, nor did any of those things that beset men and bodily beings enter his mind. Instead he was wholly united to non-material light, so much so that it seemed to him that he himself had been transformed into light. Oblivious of all else, he was filled with tears and with inexpressible joy and gladness.[21]

In a different writing, after describing the first vision he had of the divine light,[22] Symeon speaks of a second vision when a ray of light appeared in his mind and light descended onto his head in the form of a small fiery cloud.[23] He described subsequent visions, revealing that during his life there were a great many:

> So I entered the place where I usually prayed and . . . I began to say, "Holy God." At once I was so greatly moved to tears and loving desire for God that I would be unable to decribe in words the joy and delight I then felt. I fell prostrate on the ground, and at once I saw, and behold, a great light was immaterially shining on me and seized hold of my whole mind and soul, so that I was struck with amazement at the unexpected marvel and I was, as it were, in ecstasy. Morevover I forgot the place where I stood, who I was, and where, and I could only cry out, "Lord, have mercy," so that when I came to mhyself I discovered that I was reciting this. . . . "Whether I was in the body, or outside the body" (2 Cor 12.2, 3), I conversed with this Light. The Light itself knows it; it

---

[21]Symeon the New Theologian, *Catechesis* 22. Translation in *The Philokalia*, Vol. 4, trans. G. E. H. Palmer, Philip Sherrard, and Kallistos Ware (London: Faber and Faber, 1995), 18. [In the Philokalia, this work is called "On Faith."—*Ed.*]

[22]Symeon the New Theologian, *Gratitude* 1:87–113.

[23]Ibid., 135–37.

scattered whatever mist there was in my soul and cast out every earthly care. It expelled from me all material denseness and bodily heaviness that made my members to be sluggish and numb. What an awesome marvel! It so invigorated and strengthened my limbs and muscles, which had been faint through great weariness, that it seemd to me as though I was stripping myself of the garment of corruption. Besides, there was poured into my soul in unutterable fashion a great spiritual joy and perception and a sweetness suprassing every taste of visible objects, together with a freedom and forgetfulness of all thoughts pertaining to this life. In a marvelous way there was granted to me and revealed to me the manner of depaure from this present life. Thus all the perceptions of my mind and my soul were wholly concentrated on the ineffable joy of that Light.[24]

The personal spiritual experience that Symeon describes included visions of the divine light that are similar to what the evangelists described. The divine light, in St Symeon's understanding, is not an angel or any other created thing or phenomenon.[25] According to Symeon, the divine light is God himself in his revelation to man.[26] Very often, Symeon also speaks of visions of Christ as light.[27] The light Symeon describes is not a physical or material phenomenon—Symeon himself indicates its immaterial nature,[28] "simple and formless, completely without composition, incorporeal, inseparable."[29] Symeon underlines that the divine light is beyond any material or formal categories, just as it is beyond the limits of human speech and comprehension. It is "a treasure inexpressible, unspeakable, without quality, quantity, or form, immaterial, shapeless, yet witform in beauty inexplicable, altogether simple, like light, him who transcends all light."[30]

[24]St Symeon, *The Discourses*, Discourse 16.3. Translation in Symeon the New Theologian, *The Discourses*, trans. C. J. deCatanzaro (Mahwah, NJ: Paulist Press, 1980), 200–201.

[25]Symeon the New Theologian. *Hymns* 17.238.

[26]Symeon the New Theologian, *Hymns* 45.6.

[27]Symeon the New Theologian, *Hymns* 51.15 and others.

[28]Symeon the New Theologian, *Hymns* 38, 64, 51, 141.

[29]Symeon the New Theologian, *Hymns* 13.41–42, in *Divine Eros: Hymns of Saint Symeon the New Theologian*, tr. Daniel K. Griggs, PPS 40 (Yonkers, NY: St Vladimir's Seminary Press, 1995), 75.

[30]Symeon the New Theologian, *Ethical Discourse* 11, St. Symeon the New Theologian, *On*

St Gregory Palamas,
icon, Nothern Greece,
15th century

In the fourteenth century, arguments arose concerning the nature of the divine light as described by Symeon the New Theologian and other ascetical writers. Barlaam of Calabria, a humanist monk who later became a Roman Catholic, believed that the light that monks saw during pure prayer was a material, created light. St Gregory Palamas, archbishop of Thessalonica, stepped forward with a refutation of this position. He proved that the divine light by its nature is immaterial, uncreated, and divine.

Palamas developed his teaching on the light of Tabor within the context of a the distinction between the essence and energies of God. According to Palamas, God by his nature is invisible and unattainable; thanks to his action in the world, however, he can be seen and apprehended by man. The divine light, according to Palamas, is the energy of God that transforms and transfigures man; in contemplation of the divine light, man sees God himself. Moreover, God continues to remain invisible in his essence:

> Now, this union with the illuminations—what is it, if not a vision? The rays are consequently visible to those worthy, although the divine essence is absolutely invisible, and these unoriginate and endless rays are a light without beginning or end. There exists, then, an eternal light, other than the divine essence; it is not itself an essence—far from it!— but an energy of the Supersessential. This light without beginning or end is neither sensible nor intelligible, in the proper sense. It is spiritual and divine, distinct from all creatures in its transcendence; and what is neither sensible nor intelligible does not fall within the scope of the senses as such, nor of the intellectual faculty considered in itself.[31]

the Mystical Life: The Ethical Discourses, vol. 2, tr. Alexander Golitzin, PPS 15 (Crestwood, NY: St Vladimir's Seminary Press, 1995), 135.

[31]Gregory Palamas, *Triads* 3.2.14. Translation in Gregory Palamasa, *The Triads*, trans. Nicholas Gendle (Mahwah, NJ: Paulist Press, 1983), 100.

It is not strange that in the arguments between Barlaam and Gregory Palamas a central theme was the interpretation of the evangelical account of the Transfiguration of Jesus Christ. St Gregory used this account as his main argument to support his teaching concerning the divine light. In his words, when Jesus was transfigured before his disciples, he opened a veil before their eyes, beyond which his divine essence was hidden, with the pre-eternal light natural to it.

He possessed the splendor of the divine nature hidden under his flesh. This light, then, is the light of the Godhead, and it is uncreated. According to the theologians, when Christ was transfigured he neither received anything different, nor was changed into anything different, but was revealed to his disciples as he was, opening their eyes and giving sight to the blind. Take note that eyes with natural vision are blind to that light. It is invisible, and those who behold it do so not simply with their bodily eyes, but with eyes transformed by the power of the Holy Spirit.[32]

Gregory Palamas notes that the divine light was revealed to the disciples during the time when Jesus prayed:

Thus while he was praying he became radiant and revealed this ineffable light in an indescribable way to the chosen disciples in the presence of the most excellent of the prophets, that he might show us that it is prayer which procures this blessed vision, and we might learn that this brilliance comes about and shines forth when we draw near to God through the virtues, and our minds are united with him. It is given to all who unceasingly reach up towards God by means of perfect good works and fervent prayer, and is visible to them.[33]

In conclusion, the Eastern Fathers of the Church teach the following concerning the nature of the light revealed to the disciples at the time of the Transfiguration:

---

[32]Gregory Palamas, *Homily* 34.13 (*On the Transfiguration*); English in St Gregory Palamas, *The Homilies*, 2nd rev. ed., trans. Christopher Veniamin (Dalton, PA: Mount Thabor Publishing, 2016), 272.

[33]Gregory Palamas, *Homily* 34.10, ibid., 270.

1) God in his nature is light.

2) The light natural to God has both an uncreated and an immaterial material character.

3) This light is part of his nature, his essence.

4) The divine light seen by people is an energy of God (an action of God), which has a supernatural character.

5) This light is compared with the sun only by analogy; it is brighter than the light of the sun and has a different nature.

6) When he was transfigured before his disciples, Jesus allowed them to see the light that was pre-eternally natural to him as the pre-eternal Word of God.

7) This light, natural to his divine essence, was also a quality of his human nature because of the indivisible union of the two natures within him.

8) In everyday life, this light was veiled by the curtain of flesh, but in the moment of the Transfiguration it was revealed to the disciples.

9) Moreover, Jesus was not changed in any way, and did not become something he was not before—this change was only with respect to the witnesses of the miracle, who had their spiritual eyes opened, because of which they saw what was before hidden from them.

10) The face of Moses shone with a reflected light, while the face of Jesus revealed his own, essential light.

7. The Transfiguration of the God-man and the Deification of Man

The Transfiguration played an important role in the formation of the Church's teaching on the deification of man.

Though the term "deification" is not found in the Holy Scriptures, the Eastern Christian tradition describes salvation not only as deliverance from the consequences of sin and the power of the devil, but first of all as the actualization of the goal for which man was created and called as the one created in God's image and likeness. To describe both the goal and the means for accomplishing it, the Greek Fathers used the term deification or *theōsis*. At the foundation of this teaching concerning theosis is nothing other than the doctrine of salvation, expressed in the tongue of the Eastern tradition of theology.

The theme of theosis has its roots in the New Testament teaching of mankind's calling to become "partakers of the divine nature" (2 Pet 1.4), as well as Christ's words, in which he called all people "gods" (Jn 10.34). In addition, St John the Theologian's words concerning God adopting us as children (Jn 1.12) and God's likeness in man (1 Jn 3.2) also form the backbone of this teaching, as well as many texts of the Apostle Paul, in which he develops the biblical teaching concerning the image and likeness of God in man (Rom 8.29; 1 Cor 15.49; 2 Cor 3.18; Col 3.10), the teaching of the adoption of mankind as sons (Gal 3.26; Rom 4.5), of man as the temple of God (1 Cor 3.16), of the glorified state of mankind after the resurrection, when all men are to be transfigured and raised up again under their head—Christ (Rom 8.18–23; Eph 1.10), and when God is "all in all" (1 Cor 15.28).

The doctrine of theosis played an important role in fourth-century polemics with the Arians. The classical formula expressing man's theosis is found in St Athanasius: "For he was incarnate that we might be made god."[34] In another place, Athanasius says, "For he has become man, that he might deify us in himself."[35] For Athanasius, as for other fathers of the era of the Ecumenical Councils, the only foundation for man's deification is the incarnation of the Son of God. Athanasius underlines the ontological distinction between our becoming sons of God by adoption and theosis, on the one hand, and the sonship and divinity of Christ on the other hand. In theosis, we become sons not in essence and not in direct sense, but by the grace of the one who called us.[36]

How does the Transfiguration of Christ confirm this teaching? It shows that human flesh is capable of containing God within itself, so that the material cells of the body can be filled, as it were, or pierced through with divine presence. Jesus Christ is the pre-eternal divine Logos, who become flesh (Jn 1.14). When he was transfigured before his disciples, Christ did not appear to them in some other form (it is not by accident that Jerome underlines that his body and face remained his own, but were filled with divine glory). He remained in the same body in which he was born and lived among men. But this flesh became capable of complete Transfiguration, and through it, the divine light was revealed to mankind.

Christ's human flesh did not differ from the flesh of any other person. According to Orthodox teaching, man, when united with God, can become transfigured just as Christ was. St Justin (Popovich), a recent theologian, wrote:

> God became man, became a body, lived in the body, shone from that body, to show that the body and matter itself is for God. . . . By his Transfiguration, the Lord showed that the body is created to be the dwelling place and conduit of the eternal and uncreated light of God, that God lives in it completely, through it, and by it. As the New Adam, the Lord showed us that the human body was created for God to live in it, and so it shines and radiates, as the Lord transfigures it from power to power and from glory to glory. The Lord Christ became man so that

---

[34]Athanasius, *On the Incarnation* 54 (PPS 44a:167).
[35]Athanasius, *Letter* 60.4 (NPNF² 4:576).
[36]Athanasius, *Contra Arianos* 3.19 (PG 26:361).

Transfiguration,
D. Bellini, c. 1490

by himself as the God-Man . . . he would transfigure mankind into the God-Man by grace. How is this possible? Through the holy mysteries and holy virtues, all of human nature is enveloped by God, filled with God, pierced through with divine light, deified. This occurs with every faithful person in the Church, which is the body of the God-Man and as such is always filled with the power to transfigure, always radiated from itself and through itself the divine light, by which it transfigures, "Christifies," "theanthropizes" the members of the Church. . . . The Church constantly lives by the God-Man and through everything that belongs to him, for he completely, and all which belongs to him, continues in the Church through the ages of ages, even the Transfiguration itself. Despite the fact that this was a personal experience of the Savior, the Transfiguration becomes a communal event in the Church.[37]

The Fathers of the Church witness to the fact that the transfiguration of human nature through union with Christ is an experience within the reach of every human being in this earthly life. For St Symeon the New Theologian, the vision of the divine light is an expression of the experience of theosis, which mankind reaches through the communion of the body and blood of Christ and through holiness of life. Just as the body and blood

[37]St Justin (Popovich), *Tolkovanie na Evangelie ot Matfeya* [Commentary on the Gospel according to Matthew], 343 (translated by NK).

of Communion enter into the nature of man, into the cells of his body, the divine light not only illumines man from outside or from above, but fills his body, transfiguring him entirely:

> We are made members of Christ, and Christ becomes our
>   members, (1 Cor 6.15)
> and Christ becomes my hand and the foot of all-wretched me,
> and wretched I become the hand of Christ and the foot of
>   Christ.
> I move my hand and my hand is Christ entire.
> For, understand me, the divine divinity is indivisible!
> I put my foot in motion and behold, it flashes as himself.
> Do not say that I blaspheme, but accept these things
> and fall down and worship Christ who makes you like this!
> For if you also wish, you shall become his member,
> and thus every member of each one of us
> shall become a member of Christ, and Christ our members,
> and he shall make all shameful things decent (1 Cor 12.23–24)
> by the beauty of his divinity and by his glory he shall adorn
>   them,
> and when we are united to God we shall at the same time
>   become gods.[38]

According to Symeon, the divine light is not only visible, but physically apprehensible. One can be united with it not only intellectually or spiritually, but physically. Moreover, Symeon does not consider his experience to be extraordinary—he is sure that everyone who so desires can have such an experience, if he believes in Jesus, communes of his body and blood, and leads a virtuous life.[39]

This fact—that such a spiritual experience can belong not only to saints but to simple faithful, is proved by the conversation of St Seraphim of Sarov

---

[38]St Symeon the New Theologian, *Hymns*, Hymn 15.141–54 (*Divine Eros*, PPS 40:87).

[39]Abp Basil Krivocheine, *In the Light of Christ: Saint Symeon the New Theologian (949–1022), Life–Spirituality–Doctrine*, trans. Anthony P. Gythiel (Crestwood, NY: St Vladimir's Seminary Press, 1986), 103–23.

with the nobleman Nikolai Motovilov. During this
conversation, the holy man was transfigured before
his visitor like Jesus, transfigured before the apostles. Motovilov remembered later:

> When I (Motovilov) asked him, the great elder
> Seraphim, "How and in what way shall I know that
> I am in the Holy Spirit or not?"
>
> He, putting his hands on my shoulders, said,
> "Look, Lover of God, you and I are both now in the
> fullness of the Holy Spirit. Why do you not look at
> me, poor Seraphim, in the eyes?"

St Seraphim of Sarov,
portrait, late 19th century

> I answered, "I cannot, because lightning flashes from them, and it
> hurts my eyes. I cannot look at you, Father Seraphim because you are
> brighter than the sun."
>
> And he said to me, "But there is no sun and the day is cloudy; so
> what is it?"
>
> I answered, "I know that there is no sun and that it is a cloudy day,
> but your face becomes brighter than the sun and my eyes are hurting;
> this light is burning them and I cannot look at you."
>
> And he answered, bending his head over my right ear, "You also are
> in the same gracious light, otherwise you would not be able to see me,
> nor I you, in this light."[40]

In the Orthodox tradition, the Transfiguration of the Lord is considered one of the twelve major feasts of the Church. The liturgical texts of
this feast develop the theme of theosis. The Transfiguration is taken as
proof of the deification of human nature, which occurred in the person
of Christ thanks to the union of his divine nature with his human nature.
Deification is passed on to all mankind, since thanks to the incarnation,
every person has the ability to reach this state:

---

[40] *The Aim of Christian Life: The Conversation of St Seraphim of Sarov with N. A. Motovilov,*
trans. John Phillips (Cambridge: Saints Alive Press, 2010), 33.

Transfiguration,
miniature,
13th century

Today Christ on Mount Tabor has changed the darkened nature of Adam, and filling it with brightness he has made it godlike.[41]

Thou hast put Adam on entire, O Christ, and changing the nature grown dark in past times, thou hast filled it with glory and made it godlike by the alteration of thy form.[42]

When the infinite Light that knows no evening, even the brightness of the Father that give splendor to creation, ineffably appeared in unapproachable glory on Mount Tabor, it made men godlike as they sang: "O all ye works of the Lord, bless ye the Lord."[43]

The Transfiguration of Christ is examined in the hymnography as a foreshadowing of that change that awaits all the faithful at the second coming, according to St Paul (1 Cor 15.51–52):

Thou wast transfigured upon Mount Tabor, showing the exchange mortal men will make with thy glory at thy second and fearful coming, O Savior. Elijah and Moses talked with thee, and thou didst call the

---

[41]Service for the Feast of the Transfiguration of our Lord and God and Savior Jesus Christ, Small Vespers, Aposticha. Translation in *The Festal Menaion*, trans. Mother Mary and Archim. Kallistos Ware (South Canaan, PA: St Tikhon's Seminary Press, 1998), 469.

[42]Ibid, Matins, First Canon, Ode 3, Troparion 1. Ibid, 483.

[43]Ibid, Matins, First Canon, Ode 8, Troparion 2. Ibid, 491.

three disciples to be with thee. As they gazed upon thy glory, O Master, they were struck with wonder at thy blinding brightness. Do thou who then didst shine upon them with thy light, give light now to our souls.[44]

Thus, for the Orthodox Church, the feast of the Transfiguration is not simply a remembrance of one of several important events in the Gospels, but also a reason to remind the faithful that such an event can occur within each one of them: "He that believeth on me, the works that I do shall he do also, and greater works than these shall he do, because I go unto my Father" (Jn 14.12). The experiences of Jesus, including the miracles he performed, can be repeated by those who believe in him. The history of the Church is filled with examples that prove this assertion.

[44]Ibid, Matins, First Sessional Hymn, ibid., 478 [slightly edited].

Chapter 7

RESURRECTION FROM THE DEAD

The healings Jesus performed became proof of his power over illnesses. Exorcisms became proof of his power over the realm of the bodiless spirits. Walking on water, calming storms, feeding the five and four thousand—these proved Christ's mastery over nature. The Transfiguration revealed the divine face of Jesus and his glory to the disciples, who up to that moment saw in him only the form of an earthly man.

But there is another category of miracles, proving his power over life and death. In the Gospels, three miracles belong to this category: the raising of Jairus' daughter, the raising of the son of the widow of Nain, and the raising of Lazarus. All three have a direct thematic connection to the most important event in the Gospels—the resurrection of Jesus Christ.

Before examining each in detail, we will explain how death and resurrection were understood in the Old Testament.

1. Biblical Assumptions concerning Death and Resurrection

In the first-created world, there was no death. Both animals and man received from God the same blessing—to be fruitful and multiply (Gen 1.22, 28), but nothing is said about the limit to this process of multiplication.

The Tree of the Knowledge of Good and Evil, Michaelangelo, Sistine Chapel, 1508–12

Living beings became not only the bearers of life, received from God, but the source of life for their own progeny.

In the first-created world, death was present only in potential, as a threat. Having created man, God allowed him to eat of all the fruits in the garden of Eden, except for the tree of the knowledge of good and evil, from which he was not allowed to eat, "for in the day that thou eatest thereof thou shalt surely die" (Gen 2.17). Man was supposed to fulfil this commandment and walk by the forbidden tree. He could eat his fill of the fruits of all other trees, including the tree of life, which meant he could be immortal. But he had to abstain from eating evil, because as soon as he tasted evil, he would lose the immortality that he had as created in the image of God.

Death, according to the Old Testament, was not created by God, and man was originally intended for eternal life. Death entered the world by the action of the devil: "For God created man to be immortal, and made him to be an image of his own eternity. Nevertheless, through the envy of the devil, death came into the world" (Wis 2.23–24). These words are a summary of the first three chapters of Genesis, which recounts how Adam and Eve transgressed the command of God by listening to the counsel of the evil serpent. For transgressing the commandment, Adam was cursed by God: "In the sweat of thy face shalt thou eat bread, till thou return unto the ground; for out of it wast thou taken; for dust thou art, and unto dust shalt thou return" (Gen 3.19). If before the fall God spoke to man only about the process of life continuing to following generations, then after the fall, he spoke of life's return to the dust, that is, death. From that moment, mankind's life on earth was no longer endless.

From the perspective of the Old Testament, death is an evil, while deliverance from death, even temporarily, is a good. God is capable of delivering people from death (Job 5.20; Ps 55.13), while men cannot: "A brother does not redeem, shall a man redeem? He shall not give to God a ransom for himself, nor the price of the redemption of his soul, though he labored forever, and shall live unto the end. For he shall not see corruption" (Ps 48.7–9). Psalm 48 contains various thoughts concerning death and the fate of the human soul after death. These thoughts reflect the widely-help belief in Jewish tradition that the souls of all people end up in Sheol (hades), a place of darkness:

> The fool and the mindless shall perish together, and shall leave their wealth to others.
>
> Their graves are their homes forever, their dwelling place from generation to generation; they have called their lands after their own names.
>
> And man, being in honor, did not understand; he is compared to the mindless cattle and is become like unto them.
>
> This way of theirs is a stumbling block for them, yet afterwards they will please with their mouth.
>
> Like sheep they are laid in hell; death shall be their shepherd; and the upright shall have dominion over them in the morning,
>
> and their help shall wax old in hell; they have been exiled from their glory.
>
> But God will redeem my soul from the hand of hell, when he shall receive me.

The Fall, mosaic,
12th century

> Be not afraid when a man is made rich, and when the glory of his
>   house is increased.
> For when he dies he shall carry nothing away; and his glory shall not
>   descend after him.
> For his soul shall be blessed in his life; he shall acknowledge thee
>   when thou doest good unto him.
> He shall enter the generation of his fathers; nevermore shall he see
>   light.
> And man, being in honor, did not understand; he is compared to the
>   mindless cattle, and is become like unto them. (Psalm 48.10–20)

The idea that man was created from dust and must return to dust fills
the pages of the Old Testament. As for any assumptions about the fate of

mankind and animals after death, the authors of the Old Testament books had only a dim view. The Preacher wrote:

> For that which befalleth the sons of men befalleth beasts; even one thing befalleth them: as the one dieth, so dieth the other; yea, they have all one breath, so that a man hath no preeminence above a beast: for all is vanity. All go unto one place; all are of the dust, and all turn to dust again. Who knoweth the spirit of man that goeth upward, and the spirit of the beast that goeth downward to the earth? (Eccl 3.19–21)

At the same time, in Ecclesiastes we find other words that the soul of man returns to God after death:

> Man goeth to his long home, and the mourners go about the streets. Then shall the dust return to the earth as it was, and the spirit shall return unto God who gave it. (Eccl 12.5, 7)

The laws concerning how a dead body was to be handled also shed light on the Old Testament understanding of death. As soon as a person died, his body became impure, and to touch it was considered defilement. Even being in the same building as a dead body made a person impure:

> He that toucheth the dead body of any man shall be unclean seven days. Whosoever toucheth the dead body of any man that is dead, and purifieth not himself, defileth the tabernacle of the LORD; and that soul shall be cut off from Israel: because the water of separation was not sprinkled upon him, he shall be unclean; his uncleanness is yet upon him. This is the law, when a man dieth in a tent: all that come into the tent, and all that is in the tent, shall be unclean seven days. And every open vessel, which hath no covering bound upon it, is unclean. And whosoever toucheth one that is slain with a sword in the open fields, or a dead body, or a bone of a man, or a grave, shall be unclean seven days. (Num 19.11, 13–16)

In the Old Testament, one does find the idea of the universal resurrection, but it is difficult to separate it from the hope of the restoration of the might of the Israelite nation, which fills the books the of the prophets.

Isaiah, detail from the
Maestà of Duccio, 1311

While prophesying the total annihilation of death, Isaiah still concentrated not so much on the universal aspect of resurrection and the restoration of communion with God, but rather on what effect this would have on the state of the Israelite nation with respect to other nations:

> And in this mountain shall the LORD of hosts make unto all people a feast of fat things, a feast of wines on the lees, of fat things full of marrow, of wines on the lees well refined. And he will destroy in this mountain the face of the covering cast over all people, and the veil that is spread over all nations. He will swallow up death in victory; and the Lord GOD will wipe away tears from off all faces; and the rebuke of his people shall he take away from off all the earth, for the LORD hath spoken it. (Is 25.6–8)

By "this mountain," Isaiah means Mount Zion, and the description of God taking away "the rebuke of his people" are the central theme of the entire passage.

The same is true of the prophecy traditionally understood as a reference to the universal resurrection: "Thy dead men shall live, together with my dead body shall they arise. Awake and sing, ye that dwell in dust; for thy dew is as the dew of herbs, and the earth shall cast out the dead" (Is 26.19). Here, it seems, the prophecy refers to the fate of the entire human race. However, in the very next verse, the prophet speaks to the Israelite nation: "Come, my people, enter thou into thy chambers, and shut thy doors about thee; hide thyself as it were for a little moment, until the indignation be overpast. For, behold, the LORD cometh out of his place to punish the inhabitants of the earth for their iniquity; the earth also shall disclose her blood, and shall no more cover her slain" (Is 26.20–21). Once again, the people of God are contrasted to "inhabitants of the earth," whom God will punish for their sins, while the sons of Israel will escape the wrath of God.

The most vivid prophecy of the universal resurrection is found in the book of Ezekiel:

> The hand of the LORD was upon me, and carried me out in the spirit of the LORD, and set me down in the midst of the valley which was full of bones, and caused me to pass by them round about, and, behold, there were very many in the open valley; and, lo, they were very dry. And he said unto me, "Son of man, can these bones live?" And I answered, "O Lord GOD, thou knowest."
>
> Again he said unto me, "Prophesy upon these bones, and say unto them, 'O ye dry bones, hear the word of the LORD. Thus saith the Lord GOD unto these bones: "Behold, I will cause breath to enter into you, and ye shall live; and I will lay sinews upon you, and will bring up flesh upon you, and cover you with skin, and put breath in you, and ye shall live; and ye shall know that I am the LORD.'"
>
> So I prophesied as I was commanded; and as I prophesied, there was a noise, and behold a shaking, and the bones came together, bone to his bone. And when I beheld, lo, the sinews and the flesh came up upon them, and the skin covered them above: but there was no breath in them.
>
> So I prophesied as he commanded me, and the breath came into them, and they lived, and stood up upon their feet, an exceeding great army. Then he said unto me, "Son of man, these bones are the whole house of Israel; behold, they say, 'Our bones are dried, and our hope is lost; we are cut off for our parts.'" (Ezek 37.1–8, 10–11)

In Christian tradition, this prophecy has come to be accepted as universal in character, referring to the resurrection of all mankind. Moreover, the words "house of Israel" are understood more broadly as indicating all mankind, especially the New Israel, the Church. The author of the book, however, and his readers in the times before Christ, as well as the Jews of Christ's time, would not have interpreted the prophecy in that way. The house of Israel is the nation of Israel, and the vision was first of all offered

Jeremiah, mosaic,
13th century

as a symbolic description of the restoration of the glory of this nation, which was almost universally associated with the coming of the Messiah. The coming of the Messiah was not thought of by the Jewish people as a universalm phenomenon—they saw him first of all as their leader, who would justify all their hopes and expectations, who would remove their humiliation, and restore their glory and power.

It is in this context that one should understand the words of Isaiah about the annihilation of death. It is unlikely that Isaiah meant it in the universal sense given to it later by Christian commentators. If the author did intend such a reading, it was not clear to the readers and listeners of his own time.

The prophets Isaiah and Ezekiel are separated from the time of Christ by more than seven and six centuries respectively. Moreover, in later times, closer to Jesus, in the age of the Seleucids (c. 124 BC), the Second Book of Maccabees was written, where an understanding of the universal resurrection differs quite substantially from the early prophets.

This book describes the martyrdom of seven brothers and their mother, who refused to obey the command of the pagan king, which required them to break the laws of their fathers. One of the brothers, as he was dying, said to the king: "Thou like a fury takest us out of this present life, but the King of the world shall raise us up, who have died for his laws, unto everlasting life" (2 Macc. 7.9). Another, when commanded to extend his hands to be chopped off, said, "These I had from heaven; and for his laws I despise them; and from him I hope to receive them again" (2 Macc. 7.11). Yet another brother said, "It is good, being put to death by men, to look for hope from God to be raised up again by him" (2 Macc. 7.14). Their mother, encouraging them, said:

I cannot tell how ye came into my womb: for I neither gave you breath nor life, neither was it I that formed the members of every one of you; but doubtless the Creator of the world, who formed the generation of man, and found out the beginning of all things, will also of his own mercy give you breath and life again, as ye now regard not your own selves for his laws' sake. (2 Macc. 7.22–23)

All seven were executed after severe tortures. The mother died after her sons.

Here we see a direct connection between the universal resurrection and the restoration of the might of the house of Israel. As she encouraged her sons, the mother reminded them not of the past glories of the Israelite nation, but of the creation of the world and man. It was from this event that a connection is established all the way to the resurrection, which is now thought of as universal, that is, referring to all who were created by God. Moreover, faithfulness to his laws is taken as the pledge not only of resurrection, but the eternal life that will follow it.

Other than the texts that speak of universal resurrection, the historical accounts of people being raised from the dead by the prophets are of special interest. There are only two such accounts in the Old Testament— one was performed by Elijah, the other by Elisha. Both episodes occurred around nine centuries before the coming of Christ.

Jesus directly refers to one of the miracles Elijah performed for the widow of Zarephath in his preaching at the synagogue of Nazareth (Lk 4.26). The same widow was the beneficiary of a second miracle, which is one of the most paradigmatic episodes of the entire Old Testament:

And it came to pass after these things, that the son of the woman, the mistress of the house, fell sick; and his sickness was so sore, that there was no breath left in him. And she said unto Elijah, "What have I to do with thee, O thou man of God? Art thou come unto me to call my sin to remembrance, and to slay my son?"

And he said unto her, "Give me thy son." And he took him out of her bosom, and carried him up into a loft, where he abode, and laid him upon his own bed. And he cried unto the LORD, and said, "O LORD

Elijah Receives Bread from the Widow of Zarephath, L. Giovanni, 17th century

my God, hast thou also brought evil upon the widow with whom I sojourn, by slaying her son?" And he stretched himself upon the child three times, and cried unto the LORD, and said, "O LORD my God, I pray thee, let this child's soul come into him again."

And the LORD heard the voice of Elijah; and the soul of the child came into him again, and he revived. And Elijah took the child, and brought him down out of the chamber into the house, and delivered him unto his mother; and Elijah said, "See, thy son liveth."

And the woman said to Elijah, "Now by this I know that thou art a man of God, and that the word of the LORD in thy mouth is truth." (1 Kg 17.17–24)

Another similar miracle is ascribed to the prophet Elisha. He also had a patroness, a rich woman who gave him bread whenever he was in the area. He even had his own room in her house. The husband of the woman was old, and they had no son. When he learned this from his servant, the prophet foretold that in a year she would hold her own son in her hands; she then became pregnant and gave birth to a boy.

*Elisha Raises the
Son of the Widow
of Zarephath,*
Pleshanov, 1854

Later, when the boy was older (his exact age is not indicated, but the context makes clear that he was still a small boy), he came to his father, complaining of a severe headache. The father commanded his servant to carry the boy to his mother; she held him in her arms for half the day, until he died. The woman left to see the prophet, grabbed his legs and told him of her sorrow. At first, the prophet sent his servant to lay his staff on the boy, but then he himself followed after her. The servant's attempts bore no fruit; the boy remained dead. Then Elisha walked into the house:

> Behold, the child was dead, and laid upon his bed. He went in therefore, and shut the door upon them twice, and prayed unto the LORD. And he went up, and lay upon the child, and put his mouth upon his mouth, and his eyes upon his eyes, and his hands upon his hands, and stretched himself upon the child, and the flesh of the child waxed warm. Then he returned, and walked in the house to and fro, and went up, and stretched himself upon him; and the child sneezed seven times, and the child opened his eyes. (2 Kg 4.32–35)

After this, Elisha called the woman and gave her her resurrected son. She "went in, and fell at his feet, and bowed herself to the ground, and took up her son, and went out" (2 Kg 4.37).

The name of Elisha is associated with another miracle that bears some significance for our theme. The year after Elisha's death, a host of Moabites invaded the land of Israel. At that time, a burial was taking place. Seeing the enemy army, the gravediggers threw the body into the tomb of Elisha, and "when the man was let down, and touched the bones of Elisha, he revived, and stood up on his feet" (2 Kg 13.21).

All these episodes were well known to Jesus' contemporaries. Parents told these stories to their children; the leaders of synagogues read the passages during services in synagogues, then they would provide commentary. Jesus himself mentioned both of these prophets, and not by accident, when he preached in the synagogue in Nazareth, since these prophets were the ones associated with the most famous, universally known biblical accounts. Therefore, it was no accident that when Jesus began to perform similar miracles, he became associated in the public mind with Elijah, Jeremiah, or one of the ancient prophets (Mt 16.14; Mk 8.28; Lk 9.19). With their miracles, the prophets laid the spiritual and moral paradigms that would lie at the foundation of how subsequent generations of Jews would relate to miracles, including Jesus' contemporaries.

2. The Resurrection of the Daughter of Jairus

The account of the resurrection of Jairus's daughter is included in all three Synoptic Gospels. As in many other cases, the most detailed version is found in Mark. In his Gospel, this miracle occurs immediately after the exorcism of the Gadarene demoniac:

> And when Jesus was passed over again by ship unto the other side, much people gathered unto him, and he was nigh unto the sea. And,

The Raising of the Jairus' Daughter, Polenov, 1871

behold, there cometh one of the rulers of the synagogue, Jairus by name; and when he saw him, he fell at his feet, and besought him greatly, saying, "My little daughter lieth at the point of death. I pray thee, come and lay thy hands on her, that she may be healed, and she shall live." And Jesus went with him; and much people followed him, and thronged him. (Mk 5.21–24)

In this account, as in the two other Synoptics, the episode is interrupted by the healing of the woman with an issue of blood. The account ends with the words of Jesus, directed to the woman: "Daughter, thy faith hath made thee whole; go in peace, and be whole of thy plague" (Mk 5.34). After this, the evangelist returns to the account of Jesus raising the daughter of Jairus:

While he yet spoke, there came from the ruler of the synagogue's house certain who said, "Thy daughter is dead. Why troublest thou the master any further?" As soon as Jesus heard the word that was spoken, he saith unto the ruler of the synagogue, "Be not afraid, only believe."

And he suffered no man to follow him, save Peter, and James, and John the brother of James. And he cometh to the house of the ruler of the synagogue, and seeth the tumult, and them that wept and wailed greatly. And when he was come in, he saith unto them, "Why make ye this ado, and weep? The damsel is not dead, but sleepeth." And they

*The Raising of
Jairus' Daughter,*
G. Max,
19th century

laughed him to scorn. But when he had put them all out, he taketh the
father and the mother of the damsel, and them that were with him, and
entereth in where the damsel was lying. And he took the damsel by the
hand, and said unto her, *"Talitha cumi,"* which is, being interpreted,
"Damsel, I say unto thee, arise."

And straightway the damsel arose, and walked, for she was of the
age of twelve years. And they were astonished with a great astonish-
ment. And he charged them straitly that no man should know it; and
commanded that something should be given her to eat. (Mk 5.35–43)

In Matthew, this episode is given in a much shorter form. A certain
"ruler" came to Jesus and said, "My daughter is even now dead; but come
and lay thy hand upon her, and she shall live." Jesus, getting up, follows him
with the disciples. Then, after the healing of the woman with an issue of
blood, Matthew omits all details about the people coming to tell the leader
of his daughter's death. When Jesus comes he sees "the minstrels and the
people making a noise, [and] he said unto them, 'Give place, for the maid
is not dead, but sleepeth.'" Then they all laugh at him. When they sent all
the people out, he walks into the room where the girl is lying dead, takes
her by the hand, and she gets up. "And the fame hereof went abroad into
all that land" (Mt 9.18–26).

Luke's version is almost the same as Mark's, except for one detail: Jairus' daughter is described as being an only daughter, aged twelve, lying on her deathbed. This is reminiscent of the account of the exorcism of the young man, where only Luke offers the father's words: "He is mine only child" (Lk 9.38). The other evangelists leave this detail out, just as in this case also they do not mention that Jairus had only one daughter. It should be noted that in an age when most families had many children, such details were not unimportant. A single child would have been the object of a great deal of affection and care. We should also mention that none of the evangelists, other than Luke, speak of the raising of the son of the widow of Nain, which is another case of an only child (Lk 7.21).

Jairus is one of a very few characters in the characters in the Gospels whom two evangelists call by name (Mark and Luke). However, this does not mean that we should look for some hidden meaning in his Jewish name. More likely, he was called by name because he was known in the early Christian community; possibly, after the resurrection of his daughter, he became a follower of Jesus.

The expression "one of the rulers of the synagogue" means that Jairus was not a priest or a Levite. He was a layperson who was given the administration of the prayer-gatherings in the local synagogue. Each synagogue had several such laypeople. Since the services at synagogue were not connected with the Levitical priesthood and it was nothing more than an assembly of laypeople, it was natural for a layperson to lead it.[1]

In Matthew and Luke, Jairus calls his daughter θυγάτηρ (*thygatēr*; "daughter"), while in Mark, we find the diminutive θυγάτριόν (*thygatrion*; "little daughter"). When he addresses Jesus, his daughter is still alive, though on her deathbed. Mark's expression ἐσχάτως ἔχει (*eschatōs echei*) is hard to literally translate; the closest translation is "was at her last breath." Matthew uses the expression ἄρτι ἐτελεύτησεν (*arti eteleutēsen*; "is now

[1]In today's Judaism, the leader of a synagogue is, by rule, a rabbi. Contrary to widespread misapprehension, a rabbi is not a cleric—he is a teacher who has the right to lead a community and to serve in the synagogue (in this sense, the rabbi is similar to the lay leaders in certain old believer communities that have no priests). Those who have descended from the Levitical priesthood have the last name "Cohen," but after the destruction of the Temple, the Cohens lost the majority of their ritual functions and have no role in modern Judaism.

dying"), while in Luke the girl ἀπέθνῃσκεν (*apethnēsken*; "was on the point of death"). Consequently, the girl's father hoped not merely for healing, but for return to life.

Jairus asks Jesus to put his hands on the girl. As we have already said in our commentary on the healing of the woman who was bent over, Jesus often used the laying on of hands when healing. The leader of the synagogue hoped that in this case Jesus would perform the miracle by laying his hand on his daughter, bringing her back to life.

In the meantime, while Jesus spoke with the woman with an issue of blood, people are sent to tell Jairus that his daughter has died. From their point of view, there was no more point in bothering the Rabbi—the final line had been crossed. They knew Jesus as a healer, but until this moment, he had not yet raised anyone from the dead. Therefore, it seemed obvious that he could do nothing more.

The evangelists do not give us the father's reaction to the news of his daughter's death. We can only guess at his reaction based on Jesus' words to him: "Do not be afraid; only believe."

Jesus did not take anyone with him, other than the three disciples who were closest to him. Matthew leaves this detail out, but it is present in Mark and Luke. Peter, James, and John are Jesus' closest disciples, whom he set apart even from the rank of the Twelve. They are the only ones he took to the mountain of the Transfiguration (Mt 17.6); they alone were near him in the garden of Gethsemane (Mt 26.37), when he prayed with a bloody sweat (Lk 22.44). In this case, the fact that he took only these three shows the importance of the coming event.

By the time Jesus came to the house of Jairus, the first part of the funeral ceremony was already beginning. Those who "wailed loudly" in Mark are professionals who were hired to take part in the burial. These are the professionals that the Preacher mentions in the passage from Ecclesiastes mentioned above (Eccl. 12.5). The job of the professional wailers was to sing and loudly lament, as well as to accompany their singing with certain movements and clapping, to help create an atmosphere of sorrow and to inspire tears in those who were present. Jeremiah spoke of the mastery of

*The Raising of
Jairus' Daughter,*
I. Repin, 1871

the wailers and their professional preparations in a passage that is connected with the image of death:

> Thus saith the LORD of hosts, "Consider ye, and call for the mourning women, that they may come; and send for cunning women, that they may come. And let them make haste, and take up a wailing for us, that our eyes may run down with tears, and our eyelids gush out with waters. For a voice of wailing is heard out of Zion, 'How are we spoiled! We are greatly confounded, because we have forsaken the land, because our dwellings have cast us out.' Yet hear the word of the LORD, O ye women, and let your ear receive the word of his mouth, and teach your daughters wailing, and every one her neighbor lamentation. For death is come up into our windows, and is entered into our palaces, to cut off the children from without, and the young men from the streets."
> (Jer 9.17–21)

Matthew mentions "flute players"—these were also a necessary element of any funeral. The word αὐλητής (*aulētēs*; "flautist"), comes from the word αὐλός (*aulos*), which is an ancient Greek musical instrument probably more similar to an oboe than a flute. The musician held the *aulos* vertically (not horizontally, as a flute). As a rule, the *aulos* was a wooden (sometimes bone) tube with holes bored into it. The *aulos* was used for simple melodies as an accompaniment to a vocal soloist. There are analogous instruments in the Bible: Khalil (Is 5.12), *ugab* (Gen 4.21), *mashrokita*

(Dan 3.5, 7, 15). These were all used both in the Temple ceremonies and in other cases, including funerals.

Jesus' words are given by each of the evangelists with insignificant differences, and the meaning of all is the same: the girl is not dead, but asleep. These are the words that immediately allow rationalist commentators to insist that this is a case of healing from a comatose state, not resurrection. But a whole series of details contradicts such an interpretation. First of all, the funeral rites had already begun by the time Jesus had come. Second, Jesus spoke these words even before he walked into the room and saw the girl. Third, the girl had been on her death bed for a while already (the different terms used by the evangelists all mean essentially the same thing). Fourth, the reaction of the people to Jesus' words is a final proof.

The picture painted by the evangelists is intended to stress exactly this fact—this is not a case of a coma, but death. As for Jesus' words, they can be understood in two ways—either he wanted to minimize the significance of the miracle, lest it be talked about too much (this event occurred during the early period of his ministry, when he still tried to minimize the spread of his fame), or he was giving a new understanding to the concept of death itself, which should be accepted as nothing more than sleep. This latter interpretation is the consensus among the Fathers. St John Chrysostom wrote that Jesus here is "teaching us not to fear death; for that it is not death, but is henceforth become a sleep. Thus, since he himself was to die, he does in the persons of others prepare his disciples beforehand to be of good courage, and to bear the end meekly. Since in truth, when he had come, death was from that time forward a sleep."[2]

The reaction of the surrounding people might seem unexpected—how could they suddenly start laughing when they had just been wailing? The answer is rather simple—professional wailers can very easily go from weeping to laughter, just as they can go quickly from equanimity to weeping. Moreover, the verb καταγελάω [katagelaō], which Mark uses to indicate laughter, is not used for merriment or joy, but for ridicule, that is, making a joke at someone's expense. The death of the girl was so obvious to everyone that Jesus' words seemed foolish and absurd.

[2]John Chrysostom, *Homilies on Matthew*, Homily 31.3 (NPNF[1] 10:207).

The Raising of Jairus' Daughter, fresco, 14th century

The professional wailers and the others who had assembled for the funeral could not possibly fully understand the significance of what was about to happen. Perhaps this is why Jesus sent them out, leaving only the three disciples and the father near him. Having entered the room, he takes the girl by the hand. We remember that when he took Peter's mother-in-law by the hand, she stood up from the bed (Mk 1.31); when he took the demoniac youth by the hand when he had fallen as though dead after the exorcism, the boy got up (Mk 9.27). In this case, the same thing occurs. The girl comes back to life and stands up.

The words Jesus spoke as he raised her to life are rendered by Mark in their original Aramaic as *"Talitha, cumi,"* followed by a Greek translation. Why did Mark consider it necessary to give the Aramaic original? Most likely, this is the way the apostle Peter retold the account to him personally. It is possible that the event was vivid in the apostle's memory, including the specific words of Jesus. As for the tradition that Mark was the disciple of Peter, it is known even from the New Testament (1 Pet 5.13) and can be found in the writings of the fathers as early as Papius of Hierapolis (early second century). This event, in which Peter is a silent witness, confirms this tradition.

Luke describes the miracle of resurrection in the following words: "And her spirit came again, and she arose straightway: and he commanded to give her food. And her parents were astonished; but he charged them that they should tell no man what was done" (Lk 8.55–56). The expression "her spirit came again," which is missing in the other evangelists, could indicate that the girl began to breathe (the term πνεῦμα [*pneuma*] can mean both spirit and breath), and it also shows Luke's desire to give absolute medical exactness when describing the return to life. At the same time, it is more likely that the return of the spirit refers to resurrection:

> Behold! Death is but a dream! Her spirit returned. The spirit left the body and went to the place where the spirits of the dead awaited. By his touch and his words, the Lord performed two miracles. First, he healed the body; second, he returned the spirit from the spiritual world into the healthy body. For if he had not healed the body, what benefit would there have been for the girl, when the spirit would have returned into a sickly body? She would have come back to life only to get sick and die again! Such an incomplete resurrection would not have been a resurrection, but torture. But the Lord does not give partial gifts—only complete ones. He does not give imperfect gifts, only perfect ones. He returned to the blind men not only a single eye, but both. He gave hearing not only to one ear of the deaf, but to both; to the paralytics he gave not one good leg, but two. The same is true here. He returns the spirit into a healthy body, not a sick one, so that the whole person would be alive and healthy.[3]

The fact that Jesus commanded she be given something to eat is also included in Mark's account. It shows Jesus' care for the physical needs of the girl. The shocked parents (Luke speaks of their wonder, Mark speaks of the great wonder of all who saw the miracle) could have completely forgotten about such a mundane (but important) detail. A twelve-year-old girl who had been gravely ill for a long time and then died would have needed some food.

---

[3]Nikolai Velimirovich, *Tvoreniya* [Collected works], 2:381 (translated by NK).

3. Raising the Son of the Widow of Nain

A second case of Jesus raising someone from the dead is found only in the Gospel according to Luke. If, when reading the account of the resurrection of the daughter of Jairus, some scholars had the unsupported idea that the girl did not die but was in a coma, then in this case, there are even fewer reasons to think anything of the sort, because here we have a case of an actual funeral procession (the next stage of the funeral rites after inviting the professional wailers into the home):

> And it came to pass the day after, that he went into a city called Nain; and many of his disciples went with him, and much people. Now when he came nigh to the gate of the city, behold, there was a dead man carried out, the only son of his mother, and she was a widow, and much people of the city was with her.
>
> And when the Lord saw her, he had compassion on her, and said unto her, "Weep not."
>
> And he came and touched the bier, and they that bore him stood still. And he said, "Young man, I say unto thee, arise."
>
> And he that was dead sat up, and began to speak. And he delivered him to his mother. And there came a fear on all; and they glorified God, saying, "A great prophet is risen up among us," and, "God hath visited his people." (Lk 7.11–16)

This account is the only one in the New Testament that mentions a city Nain (Nein today). The city is found to the southwest of Nazareth, a significant distance (over 40 kilometers) from Capernaum, where the previous episode (the healing of the servant of the centurion) occurred. Consequently, the two events did not occur on the same day.

As in the other two cases of only children already mentioned (Lk 8.42 and Lk 9.38), Luke uses the term *monogenēs* (literally "only-begotten"), which is used in the Johannine corpus only with reference to Jesus as the Only-begotten Son of God (Jn 1.14; 3.16, 18; 1 Jn 4.9). The mention of the fact that the woman was a widow is further proof of Luke's attention to detail concerning the lives of the people who turned to Jesus for help.

Here we find Jesus addressed as "Lord" for the first time in the narrative sections of St Luke's Gospel. From this moment, the name "Lord" will be found in Luke another thirteen times, replacing the more common "Jesus," which is used in all narrative sections of the four Gospels, including Luke.

The expression "had compassion on her" reminds us of other events when Jesus' actions are inspired by compassion (Mt 9.36; 14.14; Mk 6.34). The theme of pity is also present in the parables—the merciful Samaritan had compassion on the man who had been robbed (Lk 10.33); the father had compassion on the prodigal son when he saw him returning and ran out to meet him (Lk 15.20). Compassion and co-suffering—these are the most important reasons why Jesus stopped the funeral procession without anyone asking him to do anything.

In contrast to other miracles, performed by the request of others, here the miracles occur only because of Jesus' compassion toward the weeping woman. Some time before, she had lost her husband, and now she was bidding farewell to the only one she had left—her "only-begotten" son. The Only-begotten Son of God stopped the procession because his heart answered the sorrow of another human being. Jesus acted according to the dictates of his co-suffering human heart. In this action, however, his divine nature is also completely present.

In contrast to the daughter of Jairus, who was described as twelve years old, we know nothing about the age of the young man. However, the word νεανίσκος (*neaniskos*) in Greek means not a youth, but a young man who has reached the age of adulthood. This same term is used to describe the rich young man who did not want to follow Jesus, as well as the young man who followed Jesus "having a linen cloth cast about his naked body" (Mk 14.51).

Jesus touches the bed on which the dead body lies; evidently, this is not to help raise the young man from the dead (in such a case, he would have touched the body itself), but to stop the procession. The return of the dead man to life occurred thanks to the words of Jesus, addressed to the

*The Raising of
the Widow's Son
of Nain,* V. A.
Kotarbinskii,
1879

young man, which are similar to ones we see in many miracle narratives. Jesus used the word "arise" with the paralytic (Mt 9.6 and others) and the daughter of Jairus (Lk 8.54).

After the commanding word of Jesus, the young man sat and began to speak. Those surrounding him were seized by fear. In the meantime, Jesus "presented him to his mother." Here the evangelist repeats words from the account of the prophet Elijah raising the son of the widow of Zarephath (1 Kg 17.23). Evidently, Luke used the expression on purpose, to remind the reader of the ancient prophet's miracle.

The words "a great prophet has risen up among us" could indicate the widespread idea that Jesus was Elijah or Jeremiah risen again. But they could also show faith in Jesus as the eschatological Prophet-Messiah, whose coming was awaited by the Hebrew nation.

The words "God has visited his people" connect the account of the resurrection of the son of the widow of Nain with the first chapters of the Gospel according to Luke, where Mary said that God "hath helped his servant Israel, in remembrance of his mercy; as he spoke to our fathers, to Abraham, and to his seed for ever" (Lk 1.54–55). Then, Zechariah also proclaimed that God visited his people (Lk 1.68). Finally, Simeon, while holding the child Jesus in his arms, spoke of him as the light to enlighten all the gentiles and the glory of the people Israel (Lk 2.32). The coming of the

Only-begotten Son of God constitutes a special mercy of God to the nation of Israel. At the same time, Jesus is the light to enlighten the Gentiles. His mission has a universal dimension.

In the Gospel according to Luke, the account of the resurrection of the son of the widow of Nain immediately follows the account of the healing of the centurion's servant (Lk 7.1–11) and precedes an episode where John the Baptist sends two disciples to Jesus to ask him: "Art thou he that should come? Or look we for another?" (Lk 7.20). The question is obviously connected with the fact that witnesses of the resurrection had spread word around concerning the great prophet. Both these words and the question of John's disciples reflect messianic expectations.

Jesus answered the disciples: "Go your way, and tell John what things ye have seen and heard; how that the blind see, the lame walk, the lepers are cleansed, the deaf hear, the dead are raised, to the poor the gospel is preached. And blessed is he, whosoever shall not be offended in me" (Lk 7.22–23). We find an analogous answer in Matthew (Mt 11.5–6), but there it comes before the only resurrection account in that Gospel (Mt 9.18–19, 23–26), while in Luke it follows the resurrection of the son of the widow of Nain.

Christian tradition takes the account of this resurrection as one of the most vivid examples of God's omnipotence. If God has the power to give man life, then there is nothing impossible in him returning the dead to life. One of the greatest Orthodox theologians of the twentieth century writes the following:

This miracle occurred not by the faith of the mother, as was the case with Jairus. . . . No, the miracle occurred not by the faith of anyone or by anyone's expectation, but only by the powerful word of our Lord Jesus Christ. "So he who was dead sat up and began to speak. And he presented him to his mother." The creation heard its Creator and heeded his command. That same divine power that once blew the breath of life into the dust of earth and created man from the dust is now active again, bringing to life the dust of death, forcing the blood to flow, the eyes to see, the ears to hear, the tongue to speak, the bones and flesh to move. Wherever the soul of the young man was, it heard the voice of its master and immediately returned to the body to fulfill his command together with the body. The servant hears the voice of his King and called out. . . . The Lord takes his hand with his own hand and gives him to his mother to show her that now he gives him to her as a gift in the same way that he did when she gave birth to him. Life is a gift of God. The life of any person is given by the hand of God. And God does not despise to take by the hand any man he created and to direct him in this earthly, temporary life . . . Look at how much beauty and love is in every word and gesture of the Lord and Savior! In this case, as in all—both before and afterward—he shows not only that every gift of God is perfect, but that the method God uses to give it is also perfect.[4]

4. The Resurrection of Lazarus

The miracle of Lazarus' resurrection holds a central place in the entire Gospel story. This miracle indicates not only the factual end and culmination of a long series of miracles accomplished by Jesus during his earthly ministry, but a transition to the Passion narrative.[5] The culmination of this story, in turn, is the resurrection of Christ, which shares a thematic connection with the resurrection of Lazarus.

In the Gospel according to John, the account of this event is placed in the exact middle of the story, as though separating it into two halves. Being the "mathematical center" of the fourth Gospel, the account of Lazarus' resurrection is also a "moral center" of the Gospel—it is simultaneously a culmination and a transitional point.[6] The chapters that precede the eleventh chapter (which is completely dedicated to the resurrection

[4]Nikolai Velimirovich, *Tvoreniya* [Collected works], 2:321–22 (translated by NK).

[5]R. Hakola, "A Character Resurrected: Lazarus in the Fourth Gospel and Afterwards," in *Characterization in the Gospels: Reconceiving Narrative Criticism*, ed. D. Rhoads and K. Syreeni (Sheffield: Sheffield Academic Press, 1999), 223–263, at 228–29.

[6]F. R. M. Hitchcock, "Is the Fourth Gospel a Drama?" *Theology* 7 (1923): 307–17.

The Resurrection of Lazarus, late 14th to early 15th century

of Lazarus) contain the entire earthly ministry of Jesus over the course of more than three years—from his meeting with John the Baptist (Jn 1.29) to the return to the place where John used to baptize (Jn 10.40). The ten chapters that follow the resurrection of Lazarus record the events of the last days of the earthly life of Jesus, his suffering, death, and resurrection. Thematic links connect this event with both the beginning and the end of the Gospel, and the account itself becomes the most important type of the most important event in the Gospels—the resurrection of Jesus Christ.

So why, if it is so incredibly important, is this story completely missing from the Synoptic Gospels? This question has bothered scholars since the inception of modern biblical criticism:

> Around the resurrection of Lazarus the critics are ranked in battle array, like an army round a beleaguered fortress . . . The fact that the

Synoptics do not report this miracle seems to many to be reason enough to doubt its factuality. Moreover, there is the still unanswered question of the outlook and the purpose of the fourth Evangelist. Some think that the historical form of the miracle story serves only to illustrate the idea that Jesus is the Life and the Giver of life. It is believed that the discussion which Jesus had with Martha and Mary was expanded into a miracle story. Or it is considered that the story is a composite one, made up from what Luke tells about Martha and Mary and the parable of the beggar Lazarus. In any case, it is thought, the solution must be sought in symbolism and not in history.[7]

The silence of the Synoptics concerning such an important miracle is indeed difficult to explain. At the same time, the majority of the accounts described in the Synoptic Gospels are missing in John. Usually, this is explained by the fact that he wrote after all the others, knew of what they wrote, and did not want to repeat their accounts. Evidently, this is the truth. On the other hand, the Synoptic accounts are also not monolithic— even if we postulate common sources, every evangelist has some unique content. For example, the account of the resurrection of the son of the widow of Nain is present only in Luke.

Whether or not to accept the historicity of the resurrection of Laza-rus—this seems to depend entirely on the personal opinion of each scholar, in the same way that many of them simply choose to believe or to doubt Jesus' resurrection from the dead. The historicity of the resurrection of Lazarus is generally rejected by those scholars who deny the historicity of the miracle of the multiplication of the loaves, in spite of the fact that all four evangelists speak of this miracle. The resurrection of Jesus is also recounted in all four Gospels, and yet, whoever chooses not to believe in it, does not believe in it, just as the Pharisees and Saducees also chose not believe. Concerning such people, Jesus said, "If they hear not Moses and the prophets, neither will they be persuaded, though one rose from the dead" (Lk 16.31).

---

[7]H. van der Loos, *The Miracles of Jesus*, 576–77.

We will not provide arguments for the historicity of the resurrection of Lazarus here, since these arguments, echoed many times by scholars, will still not convince the skeptics. But we cannot fail to note that this narrative contains one of the most detailed episodes in the entire corpus of the New Testament. As in other miracle narratives, Jesus is presented here as both God and man. At the same time, his human qualities are described with special care, and his divine power is shown with unusual vividness. For a proper understanding of New Testament Christology—the teaching of how the divine and human natures are united in a single hypostasis (or person) of Jesus Christ—this chapter provides rich material.

The validity of the account of Lazarus' resurrection is proven not only by the consistency of external factors. This episode has that unique internal consistency that allows us to separate the account of an actual historical event from its literary function, or history from fiction. It was this internal consistency that allowed Dostoyevsky to make the account of Lazaraus' resurrection the thematic center of the novel *Crime and Punishment.* The novel begins with the chilling murder of an elderly female moneylender by the student Raskolnikov, as well as the second murder of another innocent woman, and it ends with the murderer's spiritual rebirth. The turning point of the novel occurs when Sonia Marmeladova reads the account of the resurrection of Lazarus aloud. It was this scene, in which the text of the Gospel account appears in its complete form, that also divided the narrative of the novel in half, just as it does in the Gospel according to John. In the conclusion of the novel, the Gospel—the same book from which Sonia read to Raskolinkov about the resurrection of Lazarus—is next to the criminal on his prison bunk, and from this moment, "A new story begins, the story of the gradual renewal of a man, the story of his gradual rebirth, the gradual transition from one world into another, an acquaintance with a new reality, heretofore unknown."[8]

---

[8]Fyodor Dostoyevsky, *Crime and Punishment* (translated by NK).

Jesus Learns of Lazarus' Death

The story of the resurrection of Lazarus is written like a three-act drama. The first act seems to take place beyond the Jordan (Jn 10.40) According to John, Jesus had returned from Jerusalem after the winter feast of Hanukkah:

> Now a certain man was sick, named Lazarus, of Bethany, the town of Mary and her sister Martha. (It was that Mary which anointed the Lord with ointment, and wiped his feet with her hair, whose brother Lazarus was sick.) Therefore his sisters sent unto him, saying, "Lord, behold, he whom thou lovest is sick." When Jesus heard that, he said, "This sickness is not unto death, but for the glory of God, that the Son of God might be glorified thereby."
>
> Now Jesus loved Martha, and her sister, and Lazarus. When he had heard therefore that he was sick, he abode two days still in the same place where he was. Then after that saith he to his disciples, "Let us go into Judaea again." His disciples say unto him, "Master, the Jews of late sought to stone thee; and goest thou thither again?" Jesus answered, "Are there not twelve hours in the day? If any man walk in the day, he stumbleth not, because he seeth the light of this world. But if a man walk in the night, he stumbleth, because there is no light in him."
>
> These things said he, and after that he saith unto them, "Our friend Lazarus sleepeth, but I go, that I may awake him out of sleep." Then said his disciples, "Lord, if he sleep, he shall do well." Howbeit Jesus spoke of his death, but they thought that he had spoken of taking of rest in sleep. Then said Jesus unto them plainly, "Lazarus is dead. And I am glad for your sakes that I was not there, to the intent ye may believe; nevertheless let us go unto him." Then said Thomas, which is called Didymus, unto his fellow disciples, "Let us also go, that we may die with him." (Jn 11.1–16)

The expression "a certain man Lazarus" indicates that the person has not yet appeared in the Gospel according to John. He was the brother of Martha and Mary; but they had not yet been mentioned in this Gospel

*The Resurrection
of Lazarus,*
Van Gogh, 1890

either. Thus, this account introduces three new characters into the fourth Gospel. They were members of a single family that played an important role in the life of Jesus.

The Gospel according to Luke mentions the sisters Martha and Mary:

> [Jesus] entered into a certain village, and a certain woman named Martha received him into her house. And she had a sister called Mary, which also sat at Jesus' feet, and heard his word. But Martha was cumbered about much serving, and came to him, and said, "Lord, dost thou not care that my sister hath left me to serve alone? Bid her therefore that she help me."
>
> And Jesus answered and said unto her, "Martha, Martha, thou art worried and troubled about many things, but one thing is needful, and Mary hath chosen that good part, which shall not be taken away from her." (Lk 10.38–42)

It is very likely that this event was known to the author of the fourth Gospel, since he speaks of Martha and Mary as though the reader is already acquainted with them. Moreover, the clarification that "it was Mary who anointed the Lord with fragrant oil and wiped his feet with her hair" could refer not only to the event that John will recount later in the twelfth chapter, but also to two analogous events in the Synoptic Gospels. One of them is contained in the Gospel according to Luke. There, a woman who was a sinner, "when she knew that Jesus sat at meat in the Pharisee's house, brought an alabaster box of ointment, and stood at his feet behind him weeping, and began to wash his feet with tears, and did wipe them with the hairs of her head, and kissed his feet, and anointed them with the ointment" (Lk 7.37–38). This particular event occurred in Galilee during the period of time between Christ's second and third Passover. Matthew and Mark record another event, which refers to the time immediately before the fourth Passover—in this account, Jesus reclines at table in Bethany in the home of Simon the leper; a woman approaches him with a vessel of expensive myrrh and pours it on his head (Mt 26.6–7; Mk 14.3).

If John had one of these other events in mind, it was probably the latter more than the former, since it fits better into the chronology of Jesus' life as presented in his own Gospel account. In this case, the clarification about Mary in John's account could have the following meaning: the event did indeed happen in Bethany, and the woman who had anointed Jesus was named Mary. Moreover, it is quite likely that John did not have any of the Synoptic accounts in mind and was recounting different events altogether.

The sisters inform Jesus of Lazarus' illness, but Jesus answers with words similar to those he used about the man born blind: "Neither hath this man sinned, nor his parents, but that the works of God should be made manifest in him" (Jn 9.3). As in that case, his disciples see the event only from the perspective of this temporal life, while he sees it *sub specie aeternitatis* (from the perspective of eternity), a perspective that first of all considers not the event of human history, but the action of God that is revealed or acts through this event.

Though the news that the sisters send to Jesus was also a request for him to come heal the sick man, he did not hurry to respond to their request and remained where he was for another two days. This delay is not a consequence of indifference. As the narrator takes pains to emphasize, Jesus loved both Lazarus and his sisters. In this case, the word used for "love" is ἀγαπάω (*agapaō*), which indicates a powerful and fiery love, contrasting to the verb φιλέω (*phileō*), which may indicate a calm, friendly attachment.

The latter verb is used in these expressions: "He whom thou lovest is sick" (11.3) and "Behold how he loved him" (Jn 11.36).

John uses the verb ἀγαπάω (*agapaō*) and the noun that derives from it (ἀγάπη; *agapē*) when he describes the love of God for mankind or the love of Jesus for his disciples. In his Gospel the theme of love is central. The very coming of the Son of God into the world is a consequence of divine love: "For God so loved the world, that he gave his only begotten Son, that whosoever believeth in him should not perish, but have everlasting life" (Jn 3.16). During the mystical supper, in John's account, "When Jesus knew that his hour was come that he should depart out of this world unto the Father, having loved his own which were in the world, he loved them unto the end" (Jn 13.1). The washing of his disciples' feet (Jn 13.5) as well as the subsequent discussion in which Jesus gave his disciples a new command-ment of love (Jn 13.34) continue this theme, which reaches its high point in Jesus' death on the Cross.

Why does John emphasize the love that Jesus feels for Lazarus' family? Evidently, here we are not speaking of the kind of love that Jesus, being God, had for all mankind. Since this narrative constantly emphasizes the personal qualities of Jesus, here John speaks of love as human attachment. This was love and friendship at the same time—Jesus calls Lazarus "our friend," meaning that the disciples were also acquainted with him. Judging by the episode with Marth and Mary in Luke, the house of Lazarus and his sisters was a place that Jesus and his disciples had visited several times.

At first, the conversation between Jesus and his disciples is not con-nected with Lazarus. Jesus announced his intention to return to Judea; the disciples remind him that the Jews had only recently tried to stone him to death (Jn 10.31). But Jesus answered by speaking about the light of this world and about darkness, continuing his words spoken during the healing of the man blind from birth: "I am the light of the world: he that followeth me shall not walk in darkness, but shall have the light of life" (Jn 8.12). These words in themselves are also an allusion to the Old Testament: "Give glory to the LORD your God, before he cause darkness, and before your feet stumble upon the dark mountains, and, while ye look for light, he turn it into the shadow of death, and make it gross darkness" (Jer 13.16).

As in other conversations in the Gospel according to John (with Nicodemus and the Samaritan woman, for example), the people with whom Jesus speaks are on a level of perception different from the one to which he is trying to raise them. Therefore, this conversation does not sound like a dialogue based on a strict logical progression. Quite the opposite: Jesus says one thing; the disciples hear something else entirely. Jesus says that Lazarus fell asleep, but they answer that since he fell asleep that means he will get better. Finally, Jesus openly announces Lazarus' death, though no one had yet informed him of it. Moreover, he lets them know that his delay in visiting Lazarus is intentional—it is necessary for the disciples to come to believe in him.

Thomas' retort proves that the disciples, though they sensed the tragic conclusion for which Jesus had been preparing them with frequent prophecies of his own death, though they tried to hinder his return to Judea, they were still internally ready to follow him. At the very least, this is true of Thomas, who is mentioned by name three times in the Gospel according to John. The first time was during the resurrection of Lazarus, the second was during the mystical supper (Jn 14.5), and the third was after Jesus' resurrection (Jn 20.24–28).

Jesus Goes to the Tomb of Lazarus

The second act of the drama occurs at the entrance to the village where Martha and Mary lived. Lazarus, by that time, had been buried:

> Then when Jesus came, he found that he had lain in the grave four days already. Now Bethany was nigh unto Jerusalem, about fifteen furlongs off, and many of the Jews came to Martha and Mary, to comfort them concerning their brother. Then Martha, as soon as she heard that Jesus was coming, went and met him; but Mary sat still in the house.
>
> Then said Martha unto Jesus, "Lord, if thou hadst been here, my brother had not died. But I know, that even now, whatsoever thou wilt ask of God, God will give it thee." Jesus saith unto her, "Thy brother shall rise again." Martha saith unto him, "I know that he shall rise again in the resurrection at the last day." Jesus said unto her, "I am the resurrection,

and the life: he that believeth in me, though he were dead, yet shall he live; and whosoever liveth and believeth in me shall never die. Believest thou this?" She saith unto him, "Yea, Lord, I believe that thou art the Christ, the Son of God, which should come into the world." And when she had so said, she went her way, and called Mary her sister secretly, saying, "The Master is come, and calleth for thee."

As soon as she heard that, she arose quickly, and came unto him. Now Jesus was not yet come into the town, but was in that place where Martha met him. The Jews then which were with her in the house, and comforted her, when they saw Mary, that she rose up hastily and went out, followed her, saying, "She goeth unto the grave to weep there." Then when Mary was come where Jesus was, and saw him, she fell down at his feet, saying unto him, "Lord, if thou hadst been here, my brother had not died." When Jesus therefore saw her weeping, and the Jews also weeping which came with her, he groaned in the spirit, and was troubled. And said, "Where have ye laid him?" They said unto him, "Lord, come and see."

Jesus wept. Then said the Jews, "Behold how he loved him!" And some of them said, "Could not this man, which opened the eyes of the blind, have caused that even this man should not have died?" (Jn 11.17–37)

The second act of the drama is divided into two scenes. In the first scene, Jesus approaches the village and finds out that Lazarus had already been buried for four days. According to ancient Jewish belief, during the first three days after death, the soul remains next to the body, trying to enter back into it, but then it leaves it behind for all time.[9] The reference to four days in this context is used to underline that the death of Lazarus was complete and irrevocable. Further, this reference shows that at least four days had passed since he told his disciples about the death of Lazarus.

Jews did not have a tradition of burying their dead on the second or third day—a dead body was taken to a tomb soon after death. This tomb

---

[9]This belief is at least partially reflected in the Jerusalem Talmud. See X. Léon-Dufour, *Life and Death in the New Testament: The Teachings of Jesus and Paul* (New York: HarperCollins, 1986), 15, 44.

was usually a cave cut out of a cliffside. Such cave-tombs were found beyond the borders of cities and villages, though within walking distance.

Martha's words to Christ have a note of rebuke to them: we called you, but you did not come. Yet the woman still hopes that Jesus can help, since God hears his prayers. She accepts him as a mediator between God and man, though it is doubtful that she thought he was to raise her brother, who had died four days earlier.

Before, in a conversation with the Jews after healing the paralytic, Jesus said:

> Verily, verily, I say unto you, the hour is coming, and now is, when the dead shall hear the voice of the Son of God, and they that hear shall live. For as the Father hath life in himself, so hath he given to the Son to have life in himself, and hath given him authority to execute judgment also, because he is the Son of man. Marvel not at this, for the hour is coming, in which all that are in the graves shall hear his voice, and shall come forth: they that have done good, unto the resurrection of life, and they that have done evil, unto the resurrection of damnation. (Jn 5.25–29)

Here he spoke of the final judgment and the universal resurrection that will follow. The belief in a universal resurrection appeared among the Jews relatively late—evidently the Pharisees believed it, but the Sadducees did not (Mt 22.23; Mk 12.8; Lk 20.27; Acts 23.8). The words "the hour is coming, and now is" (we find an analogous expression in John 4.23 when Jesus speaks to the Samaritan woman), however, indicate that a distant perspective now enters this temporal frame, within which the event occurs. This conflation of two temporal perspectives occurs several times in Jesus' words. For example, his prophecy concerning the destruction of Jerusalem grows into the picture of the universal judgment (Mt 24.1–44). Such conflation of different temporal perspectives is also common in the prophetic books.

We should also note that Jesus speaks of two kinds of resurrection—the resurrection of life and the resurrection of condemnation. Resurrection is an event that will touch all mankind, but it will not mean life for all people. The word "life" in this case indicates the eternal life that those who believe in Jesus will inherit. Resurrection and life, in this way, are not completely synonymous, and the words of Jesus to Martha emphasize that distinction.

The event that will occur in Bethany in some way corresponds to the universal resurrection; perhaps the resurrection of Lazarus will become its type or its beginning. Another type of the general resurrection is the event that Matthew recounts: "And, behold, the veil of the temple was rent in twain from the top to the bottom; and the earth did quake, and the rocks rent, and the graves were opened; and many bodies of the saints which slept arose, and came out of the graves after his resurrection, and went into the holy city, and appeared unto many" (Mt 27.51–53).

Martha, however, knows none of this, and so she understands Jesus' words about her brother's resurrection as though it were a reminder of the universal resurrection on the last day, which the prophets Isaiah and Ezekiel described in the passages quoted earlier. But this is not the consolation that she wants from Jesus. Then Jesus utters a saying that begins with the words "I am," through which he reveals the significance of his ministry: "I am the resurrection and the life."

His words concerning the fact that those who believe in him will not die, and if they do die, will come back to life, have a general meaning and refer to eternal life—to the salvation that Jesus will bring to all people. But in this specific situation they also refer to a specific person who will be raised to life by Jesus. This resurrection will become a type not only of the universal resurrection, but eternal life as well—that kingdom of heaven whose approach Jesus announced at the beginning of his earthly ministry.

The next part of the dialogue between Jesus and Martha reminds us of many conversations that preceded Jesus' miracles. The theme of the conversation was faith. As often happens in John, a thematic word is repeated several times in a single passage: 1) He who believes (ὁ πιστεύων; *ho pisteuōn*) in me shall never die; 2) Do you believe (πιστεύεις; *pisteueis*) this? 3) I believe (πεπίστευκα; *pepisteuka*). In the third case, the word πεπίστευκα (*pepisteuka*) is the active perfect form of the verb πιστεύω (*pisteuō*; to believe)—this form indicates an action that has begun in the past and that is continuing constantly. Consequently, the words of Martha can be interpreted thus: "I have believed and I do believe in the fact that thou art the Christ, the Son of the God who is come into the world." Evidently, Martha means that she had believed even before the gift of close friendship with Jesus, and she continues to believe now.

As in other cases, when the evangelists mention a vacillation between faith and doubt (e.g., Mk 9.24), here we see an example of fiery and emotional faith that remains incomplete and unstable. This is a feminine faith that comes from a secret hope in a miracle, but not the faith that Jesus preached to his disciples. This is not the faith that can move mountains. At some point in her life, Martha came to believe in Christ, and she confesses him to be the Son of God; nevertheless, she still does not understand how that faith can grow into an actual miracle.

Martha returned to her sister, and Jesus remained in place, not coming into the village. As before, he does not hurry. Mary, having run to him, fell at his feet and utters the same exact words as Martha. Evidently, both sisters were sure that had Jesus come in time, nothing would have happened as it had. This time, Jesus does not answer. It is interesting to note that in the episode described by Luke, only a conversation with Martha is recorded; Jesus does not say a word to Mary (Lk 10.41–42).[10]

In John's account of Lazarus' resurrection, Martha and Mary are described somewhat differently. We hear Martha speak three times, Mary only once, and when she does speak, all she does is repeat Martha's exact words. Martha came to meet Jesus, and then she went and called Mary in secret. Mary, as soon as she heard, got up quickly and came to Jesus, then fell at his feet. Jesus reacted to Martha with his own words, but his reaction to Mary's grief was different: "He groaned in the spirit and was

---

[10]The behavior of both sisters in John's account generally corresponds to their characterization in Luke. There, Martha is worried about preparing food, while Mary "sat at Jesus' feet." Here, Martha speaks with Jesus, but Mary remains seated at home, when she hears of his arrival, she quickly gets up, goes to him and falls to his feet. For a more detailed comparison of the characters of the sisters in both Gospels, see W. O. Walker, Jr., "Martha and Mary in the Third and Fourth Gospels: An Exercise in Source Criticism," in *Resourcing New Testament Studies*, Festshcrift for D. L. Dungan, ed. A. J. McNicol, D. B. Peabody, and J. S. Subramanian (New York: T&T Clark, 2009), 126–34.

troubled." Martha is presented as calmer and more rational. Mary is more emotional—her state is conveyed not only through her words, but even more through gesture and emotion.[11]

The next scene is the emotional climax of the entire drama. Jesus, seeing the mourners that came with Mary, "groaned in the spirit and was troubled" (ἐνεβριμήσατο τῷ πνεύματι καὶ ἐτάραξεν ἑαυτόν; *enebrimēsato tō pneumati kai etaraxen eauton*) The verb ἐνεβριμήσατο (*enebrimēsato*) derives from βριμάομαι (*brimaomai*; "to be in a state of fierce anger"). In other cases, this verb indicates anger (Dan 11.30 LXX), strict interdiction (Mt 9.30, Mk 1.43), or complaining (Mk 14.5). Some interpreters believe that Jesus was angered by the Jews' lack of faith,[12] others think that phenomenon of death itself was the source of his anger.[13] In the greater context of the passage, however, this expression is better understood as indicating not so much anger as very strong internal emotion. John Chrysostom interprets the expression ἐνεβριμήσατο τῷ πνεύματι (*enebrimēsato tō pneumati*) as an internal cessation of weeping:

He only acts measurably and condescends; and to prove his human nature, weeps in silence, and defers the miracle for the present . . . then rebuking those feelings (for "he groaned in spirit" means restrained his trouble), he asked, "Where have ye laid him?" so that the question might not be attended with lamentation.[14]

The expression ταράσσω ἑαυτόν (*tarassō heauton*) has many meanings: "to be shaken," "to be overwhelmed," "to be upset," "to be angry," "to be overcome with emotion." In this case, it also indicates profound emotional stress.

---

[11]Ruben Zimmerman, "The Narrative Hermeneutics of John 11: Learning with Lazarus How to Understand Death, Life, and Resurrection," in *The Resurrection of Jesus in the Gospel of John,* ed. Craig R. Koester and Reimund Beiringer (Tübingen: Mohr/Siebeck, 2008), 97.

[12]R. Schnakenburg, *The Gospel according to St. John Volume II* (New York: Crossroad Pub. Co., 1990), 336.

[13]J. Kremer, *Lazarus: Die Geschichte einer Auferstehung.* (Stuttgart: Verlag Katholisches Bibelwerk GmbH, 1985), 73.

[14]John Chrysostom, *Homilies on the Gospel According to John,* Homily 63.1 (NPNF[2] 14:232).

The sentence "Jesus wept" is one of only two mentions of Jesus' tears in all four Gospels. The only other time Jesus wept was for Jerusalem, when he foretold its destruction (Lk 19.41–44). Outside the Gospels, his tears are mentioned only one other time, but in a completely different context: "Who, in the days of his flesh, when he had offered up prayers and supplications, with vehement cries and tears to him who was able to save him from death, and was heard because of his godly fear" (Heb 5.7). This is likely a reference to the prayer in the garden

The Resurrection of Lazarus,
fresco, Giotto, 14th century

of Gethsemane (Mt 26.36–44; Mk 14.32–42; Lk 22.39–46), though not a single evangelist, when describing this event, mentions tears.

John uses two different verbs when he speaks of the tears of Martha and the Jews and the weeping of Jesus: κλαίω and δακρύω (*klaiō* and *dakryō*). They are in fact synonymous (accordingly, the King James Version translates them all with the same word: weep, weeping, and wept in vv. 31, 33, and 35). Some interpreters believe the weeping of Jesus to be allegorical—that is, that his weeping referred not to Lazarus, but to the Jews (e.g., St Andrew of Crete), but commentators of a more literal bent interpret this manifestation of strong emotional distress to be a strong witness of the reality of Jesus' human nature:

> He comes then to the tomb; and again rebukes his feelings. Why does the Evangelist carefully in several places mention that he wept, and that he groaned? That you may learn that he had of a truth put on our nature … Therefore at the passion they [the other evangelists] attribute to him much that is human, to show the reality of the dispensation. And Matthew proves this by the agony, the trouble, the trembling, and the sweat; but John by his sorrow. For had he not been of our nature, he would not once and again have been mastered by grief.[15]

---

[15]John Chrysostom, *Homilies on the Gospel According to John*, Homily 63.2 (NPNF[2] 14:233).

Jesus Resurrects the Dead Man

The emotional distress that Jesus felt, which the evangelist imparts with the help of several expressions of synonymous meaning, became obvious to those who were in attendance. Some seem to sympathize with him, while others, on the contrary, find it a reason to rebuke him for not healing his friend in time.

Finally, the third act of the drama comes, containing the denouement of the entire story, its climax, and its logical conclusion:

> Jesus therefore again groaning in himself cometh to the grave. It was a cave, and a stone lay upon it. Jesus said, "Take ye away the stone." Martha, the sister of him that was dead, saith unto him, "Lord, by this time he stinketh; for he hath been dead four days." Jesus saith unto her, "Said I not unto thee, that, if thou wouldest believe, thou shouldest see the glory of God?"
>
> Then they took away the stone from the place where the dead was laid. And Jesus lifted up his eyes, and said, "Father, I thank thee that thou hast heard me. And I knew that thou hearest me always, but because of the people which stand by I said it, that they may believe that thou hast sent me." And when he thus had spoken, he cried with a loud voice, "Lazarus, come forth." And he that was dead came forth, bound hand and foot with graveclothes, and his face was bound about with a cloth. Jesus saith unto them, "Loose him, and let him go." (Jn 11.38–44)

The expression "groaning in himself" (πάλιν ἐμβριμώμενος ἐν ἑαυτῷ; *palin embrimōmenos en heauet*) once again indicates the profound emotional distress that accompanies this entire episode.

The entrance of the cave where they had buried Lazarus was covered, as was customary, with a stone. Jesus commanded that the stone be moved away from the tomb. Martha, who had only a moment ago expressed her faith that Jesus would receive everything that he might ask from God, now carefully reminds him that the body of the dead man had already begun to smell, since it had been lying in the tomb for four days. Jesus, in answer, repeated his words: If you believe, you will see the Glory of God. These words were not recounted directly by John in the previous conversation. Either this was part of an "off-screen" conversation or Jesus simply summarizes his previous words to Martha in a simpler expression. Once again, the conversation is about faith, and Jesus, who intends to accomplish a miracle, wants to test the faith of the sister of the dead man, to free her from any remaining internal doubts or wavering.

Before performing the miracle, Jesus turns to his Father with a prayer, as though confirming what Martha had said before: "Whatsoever thou wilt ask of God, God will give it thee." In this prayer, he does not ask anything of God—he thanks God for hearing Him. N. T. Wright, a famous British commentator, explains that John likely wants us to understand that there was no smell. Jesus knows that his prayer for Lazarus' incorruptibility was heard.[16]

But we cannot agree with such an interpretation. This prayer, as follows from the context, refers to the miracle yet to come—it has not yet occurred, but Jesus' conviction that it will happen is certain, as is his conviction of his complete oneness of mind with the Father. Moreover, Jesus adds that he prayed aloud precisely for the sake of the people—"that they may believe." He could, naturally, have raised Lazarus without an audible prayer to the Father, since he performed this miracle with his own power. This is something that John Chrysostom energetically emphasizes in his polemic with the Arians:

> Let us then ask the heretic: Did he receive an impulse from the prayer, and so raise the dead man? How then did he work other miracles without prayer? Saying, "Thou evil spirit, I charge thee, come out of him"; and, "I will, be thou clean"; and, "Arise, take up thy bed"; and, "Thy sins be forgiven thee"; and to the sea, "Peace, be still." . . . But let us see what the prayer was, "I thank thee that thou hast heard me." Who now ever prayed in this manner? Before uttering any prayer, he says, "I thank thee," showing that he needed not prayer. "And I knew that thou hearest

---

[16]N. T. Wright, *The Resurrection of the Son of God* (Minneapolis, MN: Fortress Press, 2003), 483.

me always." This he said not as though he himself were powerless, but to show that his will and the Father's is one. . . . "And I knew that thou hearest me always," that is, "In order that my will be done I need no prayer, except to persuade men that to thee and me belongs one will." "Why then prayest Thou?" for the sake of the weak and grosser sort. And when he had thus spoken, he cried with a loud voice. Why said he not, "In the name of my Father come forth?" Or why said he not, "Father, raise him up?" "Lazarus, come forth." For, that you might not think that he received the power of working from another, he taught you this before, and gave proof by deeds, and said not, "Arise," but, "Come forth," conversing with the dead man as though living. What can be equal to this authority?[17]

The miracle itself occurred after Jesus commanded the dead man with a short formula—one of those that he used in other situations as well: "Arise, take up thy bed, and go unto thine house" (Mt 9.6); "Stretch forth thine hand" (Mt 12.13); "Damsel, I say unto thee, arise" (Mk 5.41); "Be opened" (Mk 7.34). But the resurrection of Lazarus is the only miracle in the Gospels during which Jesus used someone's proper name in the commanding formula. This is also the only miracle in which Jesus did not merely speak, but "cried out with a loud voice" (the verb κραυγάζω [kraugazō] means "to yell"). The next time anyone will hear Jesus cry out in a loud voice will be from the cross (Mt 26.47, 50; Mk 15.34; Lk 23.46).

Lazarus comes out of the tomb, wrapped head to foot in a burial shroud. In ancient Israel, the bodies of the dead were wrapped in a shroud before burial (κειρίαι; keiriai), while the head was wrapped in a separate shawl (σουδάριον [soudarion], from the Latin sudarium). Jesus commanded that the dead man be unwrapped, so that he could walk freely.

As in other miracle narratives, the evangelist here emphasizes the reaction of the witnesses: "Then many of the Jews which came to Mary, and had seen the things which Jesus did, believed on him. But some of them went their ways to the Pharisees, and told them what things Jesus had

[17]John Chrysostom, *Homilies on the Gospel according to John*, Homily 64.2–3 (NPNF² 14:237–38).

done" (Jn 11.45–46). When the Pharisees found out about the miracle, they called a meeting in which the high priest Caiaphas took part. At this meeting, after what seems to have been a long and contentious argument, they "took counsel together for to put him to death" (Jn 11.53). Thus, the resurrection of Lazarus became one of the most important reasons for their decision to kill Jesus.

The story of the death and resurrection of Lazarus is a prologue to the account of the suffering, death, and resurrection of Jesus Christ. Lazarus remained in the tomb for four days, Jesus for three.

The Resurrection of Lazarus,
Carl Bloch, 1875

Lazarus walked out of his tomb, wrapped in a burial shroud and his head wrapped in linen. After his Jesus' resurrection, the burial shroud was found lying in the tomb, with the head wrapping laid aside in a separate place. In both accounts, the Pharisees, Caiaphas, and the crowd are involved. In both stories, a special place is given to the women who were present.

Yet there is an important difference between the two accounts as well, found in the quality of the event itself. Lazarus returns to the life from which he was taken four days earlier. The evangelist says nothing about the way he looked, but evidently the same body came out of the tomb that was put into it. Some time later, Lazarus appears again, and we see him reclining at table next to Jesus. Lazarus was raised from the dead not so that he would never die again. He would live some time on the earth, and then die again.

After the resurrection of Jesus, his body disappeared from the tomb. When he began appearing to the woman and apostles, they did not recognize him. Mary thought he was the gardener (Jn 20.15); two disciples thought he was merely a traveler (Lk 24.13–35); of the eleven apostles, some bowed to him, others doubted who he was (Mt 28.17). All this shows that the body of the risen Jesus looked different from the one in which he was known before his crucifixion.

Lazarus returned to the place from which he was taken; Jesus, soon after his resurrection, returned to the place from which he had come. He rose not to remain on earth, but to ascend bodily into heaven (Lk 24.51; Acts 1.9) and to remain there, indivisible from his Father. "He was received up into heaven, and sat on the right hand of God" (Mk 16.19), while he left his disciples on the earth, so that they "went forth, and preached every where, the Lord working with them, and confirming the word with signs following" (Mk 16.20).

The meaning of the resurrection of Lazarus is revealed in the larger context of the development of St John's theological thought in the fourth Gospel. Beginning with the triumphant proclamation of the truth concerning the Logos' eternal abiding with God, that "All things were made by him; and without him was not any thing made that was made" (Jn 1.3). The evangelist then leads the reader through a series of encounters and conversations that the incarnate Word of God has with various people, and several of the miracles he performed. The Gospel leads us to the most important miracle—the resurrection of a man who was four days dead. This miracle confirms that the Word of God not only took part in the creation of the world, but is the source of life for all that is created, having power of life and death. Not long before the resurrection of Lazarus, Jesus said to the Jews: "I lay down my life, that I might take it again. No man taketh it from me, but I lay it down of myself. I have power to lay it down, and I have power to take it up again" (Jn 10.17–18). The subsequent account confirms this authority of the incarnate Word of God not only over the lives of others, but over his own life as well.

All four Gospels contain narrative sections (the events of the life and miracles of Christ) and sections recording Christ's direct speech (teachings, parables, responses in dialogues). Every evangelist constructs a unique relationship between these two, but in all four Gospels, Jesus' actions serve as confirmation of his words, and his words explain his actions. In John, every miracle confirms one of the theological truths that Jesus expressed concerning himself: "I am the bread of life" (Jn 6.35, 48); "I am the light of the world" (Jn 8.12); "I am the door" (Jn 10.9); "I am the way, the truth, and the life" (Jn 14.6); "I am the vine" (Jn 15.5). Through this series of descriptions, Jesus reveals his identity, but each of these descriptions is further strengthened by his actions. The raising of Lazarus becomes a practical expression of what he explained to Martha: "I am the resurrection, and the life" (Jn 11.25). Jesus is the source of life (Jn 4.10, 14). He, like the Father, has life in himself (Jn 5.6).

The story of Lazarus' resurrection confirms the unbreakable unity between Father and Son, which is announced in the prologue of the Gospel according to John (Jn 1.1–2) and in Jesus' many conversations with the Jews. The refrain of all these conversations is the same: "As the Father knoweth me, even so know I the Father" (Jn 10.15); "I and my Father are one" (Jn 10.30); "I am in the Father, and the Father in me" (Jn 14.11). These assertions do not remain only in word; Jesus confirms words with deeds— his signs and miracles.

By raising Lazarus, Jesus acted both as God and as the messenger of God—he turns his gaze to God and gives thanks to him, but not because this is required to perform the miracle, but because by this he reveals his complete unity with the Father. The words "I can of mine own self do nothing" (Jn 5.30) are not an indication of the dependence of the Son on the Father or his powerlessness to perform the miracle without the will of the Father. Rather, they indicate the complete unity of will between the Father and the Son, and the impossibility, even theoretically, that the will of the Son could be contrary to the will of the Father or that the Son could do anything by himself without the Father.

At the same time, the resurrection of Lazarus, like no other miracle in the Gospels, reveals Jesus as a real, earthly man, having the fullness of human nature. The realism and the details that describe Jesus' emotional state in this account are unprecedented in the entire corpus of the Gospels outside of his passion. But if in the account of his passion, his sorrows come from his own suffering, here it is a consequence of co-suffering with the sorrow of others:

> Never does life seem so precious as when it is threatened with death.
> The dead body of Lazarus is surrounded by the cries of his dear ones.
> The Lord himself weeps for the loss of his friend—this is how profoundly

The Resurrection of Lazarus,
Carravaggio, 1609

he enters into human sorrow. He is so fully human that he takes on himself all the sorrow that surrounds him. He weeps over every dead man every time that death holds its temporary victory. All the more so does he weep when it seems that this is a victory of death over the soul of a person. And these are not simply tears—the Lord is ready to pay with his own life for every soul over which he weeps.[18]

When we explored the stories of God's miracles in the Old Testament, we mentioned that the God of the Bible has little in common with the god of the deists, who is far from the world and does not interfere with human life. The God whose face is revealed in the pages of the New Testament is even further from this deistic speculation concerning the first principle at the foundation of the world's orderliness. In the New Testament, God reveals himself through his Son—the God-Man, Jesus Christ. In his face, God enters into the everyday parts of human history, revealing not simply a desire to help man, to save him, but the highest degree of love for him; God suffered for him, felt solidarity with him, expressed in the complete identification of his own self with the life, sorrows, sicknesses, sufferings, and death of man. In the face of Jesus Christ, God lives a human life from cradle to the grave. This life ends with resurrection—the passage into a new life, a new state, both physically and spiritually.

The Old Testament speaks of life as a vale of tears and labor, and of death as a return to that from which man was taken: "In the sweat of thy face shalt thou eat bread, till thou return unto the ground; for out of it wast thou taken: for dust thou art, and unto dust shalt thou return" (Gen 3.19). There is a certain parallel between the beginning and the end of life. The life of man begins from conception and the time in the womb, and it ends with a return to the earth and our time in the womb of the earth. The earth becomes the motherly bosom that takes in all the dead.

[18]Alexander Shargunov, *Evangelie dnya* [The Gospel of the day], 2:353–54.

The New Testament reveals the meaning of life and death anew through the teaching of the resurrection. In light of this teaching, death is understood also as a return, but not to the primal dust from which man was created, but to God, by whose hands man was created, and by whose will man was brought to life. If in the Old Testament death was first of all conceived of as a punishment for sins, a necessary consequence of the fall to sin, in the New Testament, it becomes a door leading into another quality of life—the same life that Jesus called eternal life. Life itself, then, is understood no longer as "labor and sorrow" (Ps 89.10) in an earthly existence, but also as the possibility of tasting eternal life as a life, "more abundant" (Jn 10.10) life, flowing from the very source of life himself (Jn 4.10, 14).

* * *

In our own days, death is understood primarily as a sorrowful and tragic event; people prefer not to talk or think about it. When it occurs, the funeral is usually accompanied by an extremely sorrowful ritual. The most depressing and dispiriting of these is the nonreligious funeral, performed over a person who did not believe in the afterlife and did not belong to any religious confession. Similar unbelievers gather at this ceremony, which carries no consolation or tranquility to those who remain on earth.

The Orthodox funeral is pierced through with a completely different spirit. It is performed not in the black vestments of mourning, but the white of resurrection. It begins with an exclamation: "Blessed is our God!" and it includes a multitude of prayers and hymns that are filled with the conviction that the one for whom the entire Christian community prays will rise again. There is a sense of hope for his rest in a place "where there is neither sickness nor sorrow nor sighing, but life everlasting." The acceptance of death as a feast, a passage into a better life, imbues the Christian worldview, and this is fully reflected in the words of the hymns of the Orthodox funeral. Their triumphant, joyful, and life-affirming character speaks for itself.

If we were to compare the Christian understanding of death with the way that ancient religious traditions—whether Jewish, Egyptian, Greek, or Roman—related to death, we will find such a stark fundamental difference

The Resurrection of Christ,
Piero della Francesca, 1458

that one can speak of a complete reassessment of the conceptual framework regarding dying, death, and burial. Early Christian theology and the art of the catacombs—the place where the dead were buried *en masse*—reflect this reassessment. The bright, simple, triumphant, and joyful images on the walls of the catacombs might seem initially to contrast severely with the atmosphere of underground chambers, caves, and ossuaries filled with the bodies of the dead. But what seems paradoxical and difficult to explain to modern man was natural for early Christians—they understood death to be a feast, while the bodies of the dead were only temporarily in residence under the earth, awaiting the universal resurrection.

The sense of a dead body as something unclean, an idea that pervades the Old Testament, is completely foreign to Christianity. Even in the early Church, reverence for the dead body was typical, and the entire burial rite was performed in the immediate vicinity of the body. The final parting with the dead occurred—and continues to occur—through a final kiss. The remains of martyrs were treated with special reverence—they were considered holy objects, they were touched for their healing power, and liturgies were performed on the tombs of the martyrs. The idea that the body is the temple of the Holy Spirit (1 Cor 6.19) extended even to the dead body.

To many people, life seems pointless. Having all sorts of material goods, they still do not understand why they live. The lack of meaning in their life often becomes a reason for suicide—a phenomenon that has never in history been so pervasive as it is today. Recent records in Russia alone indicate that nearly a million people commit suicide each year; among them are many young people and even children. The unofficial number may be much higher (often the reason for death is listed as "accidental," or "overdose," "falling from a great height," or "accidental misfire of a gun," and so on). The reasons for this tragic and pervasive phenomenon are numerous—from personal or professional problems to severe mental disease. But one of the main reasons remains a lack of meaning in life.

It is impossible to find a meaning in life without seeing a meaning in death. And all efforts to find such meaning outside a religious perspective (for example in the call to live for future generations) led to an inescapable philosophical dead end. If the life of man is limited to a short span of time, and if in that life there are no higher goals or if a perspective of eternal life is missing, one's very existence on earth can appear to be pointless and even unnecessary.

Christianity reveals other horizons before man and teaches us to look at temporal life from the perspective of eternity. In this perspective, suffering itself becomes meaningful (and suffering is inevitable in any life), as does life and death. Faith in the resurrection is what gives meaning and justification to death. If there were no such faith, the Apostle Paul says, then Christianity would be a lie: "But if there be no resurrection of the dead, then is Christ not risen; if Christ be not risen, then is our preaching vain, and your faith is also vain" (1 Cor 15.13–14).

The central event of the history of the Gospels is the resurrection of Jesus Christ. But in and of itself this event would have had no decisive significance if the possibility of victory over death were not also extended to all mankind. This possibility becomes available through faith in Jesus Christ as God and Savior, through the communion of his body and blood, through participation in the life of the Church he established, and through the fulfillment of his commandments. In an ineffable, supernatural way, a man can be grafted into Christ like a branch into a tree, being filled by him with that life-creating sap that is capable of returning life even to a dried and dead branch.

This is the ultimate message of the Gospels, especially in the narratives concerning Christ raising people from the dead. All three people that Christ raised returned back to this temporal life, and after the passage of time, they once again died. But these three miracles became a foreshadowing of the universal resurrection, and the hope for this ultimate reality flows from Christ's resurrection.

CONCLUSION

As the nineteenth century gave way to the twentieth, the words of Fr John Ilyich Sergiev sounded throughout all of Russia. He was a simple parish priest from Kronstadt. But his activity was accompanied by many miracles documented and attested by eyewitnesses. The healings that he performed occurred before the eyes of thousands of people, newspapers wrote about them, journalists wrote stories about them. John of Kronstadt had many admirers and followers throughout the country, including a group of people who were so fanatically dedicated to him that they formed a sectarian cult.

The wonderworker of Kronstadt lived in an age of quickly spreading nihilism and rationalism, when the Church was under attack from the intelligentsia, including such refined examples as Leo Tolstoy. St John considered Tolstoy to be his archnemesis and an enemy of Russia, rebuking him in many sermons, articles, and notes in his journal. Tolstoy's relationship with St John was far from loving.[1]

The atmosphere that gathered around St John of Kronstadt was in some ways reminiscent of certain scenes in the Gospels. The same crowds of people thirsted to hear a word from the pastor, to touch his clothing, to be healed of diseases, to receive consolation in sorrows, to stand on the path of a virtuous life. And the same uncompromising opposition from skeptics, rationalists, liberals, and the intelligentsia, whom St John called the Pharisees and Sadducees of the new age.[2] Naturally, these latter were convinced neither by his teaching nor by the wonderworker's miracles.

---

[1] P. Basinsky, *Svatoi protiv L'va* [A saint versus Leo] (Moscow, 2013), 480–81 (translated by NK).

[2] John of Kronstadt, *Zhivoi kolos s dukhovnoi nivy: Vypiski iz dnevnika prot. Ioanna Il'icha Sergieva* [A living ear from the spiritual field: Extracts from the diary of archpriest Ioannn Ilych Sergiev] (St Petersburg, 1909), 94 (translated by NK).

St John of Kronstadt,
icon, 20th century

History repeats itself, and the phenomenon of the miracle continues to be a stumbling block for many. A miracle is capable of bringing people together and inspiring them, but it is also capable of separating them, factionalizing them and dividing them along strict ideological lines. In the Russian society of the early twentieth century, the Church and the liberal intelligentsia found themselves on opposite sides of ideological barricades. Even though the miracles of St John brought many to faith, they did not convince those who had decided to retain their rationalistic and positivistic position to the end. The ideological warfare between Jesus and the Jews of his time was no less severe, and his miracles could not shake the unbelief of those who would not accept in principle what he said or did.

In this book, we have seen the great panorama of the miracles of Jesus Christ—from the first miracle of transforming the water into wine in Cana of Galilee to the last miracle of the raising of Lazarus. We have seen different people—blind, deaf, dumb, bent over, bleeding, paralyzed completely or in part—healed by the divine power of Jesus. We saw demoniacs whom he returned to a normal life. We saw the dead whom he raised. We saw how he was transfigured before the eyes of the apostles and how the otherworldly light of his divinity showed through his human flesh. We saw how nature obeyed his divine word.

All these accounts, which constitute a major portion of the Gospels, were written either by direct witnesses and participants in these events, or by those who heard eyewitnesses speak of them.

When Jesus stood before the judgment seat, these witnesses were not found necessary. He was condemned the night before Passover, in haste—the Jews did not want to ruin their feast by his presence, which had become abhorrent to them. But the judgment of history was different, and two thousand years later, these eyewitness accounts are read with reverence by millions of people all over the world. The most unfair condemnation in the history of the human race became the most decisive victory over injustice, unrighteousness, and evil. A shameful execution became the greatest victory over death.

This victory has significance for all humanity and for every person. But the fruits of this victory are only available through faith in Jesus Christ as God and Savior, a faith that helps people endure sickness, overcome earthly difficulties, and trample the fear of death.

Every miracle described in the Gospels was a victory for Jesus—a victory over sickness or possession, lack of faith or weak faith, physical or spiritual death. Jesus' miracles showed his ability not only to overcome natural laws, but even to give other people this ability (it was not by accident that Peter walked on water toward Jesus). The experience of all people whom Jesus healed or raised from the dead, whom he exorcised or before whom he commanded the forces of nature, was unique. But this experience continued through the lives of the apostles and many other Christians after them, to whom Jesus gave the power to perform miracles.

Let us remember once more the words that Jesus spoke to his disciples before his death: "Verily, verily, I say unto you, he that believeth on me, the works that I do shall he do also; and greater works than these shall he do, because I go unto my Father" (Jn 14.12). What works is he speaking of here? Those that he would list in his final conversation with his disciples after his resurrection:

> And these signs shall follow them that believe. In my name shall they cast out devils; they shall speak with new tongues; they shall take up serpents; and if they drink any deadly thing, it shall not hurt them; they shall lay hands on the sick, and they shall recover. (Mk 16.17–18)

This promise was fulfilled in the Church he founded, and is continually fulfilled for over twenty centuries, and thousands of miracles performed by his servants and followers have been documented in the history of the Church, in the lives of the saints—both ancient and modern.

Miracles continue in our times. People write about them rarely, and the TV news as a rule do not talk about them. But they are being carefully gathered, as in a bank, by the memory of the Church, so that future generations can know what occurred with their fathers and grandfathers.

St Matrona of Moscow,
icon, 20th century

Let us offer another example. In the first half of the twentieth century, a simple woman lived in Moscow, named Matrona. She was blind from birth, and when she was seventeen, she lost the use of her legs. But from youth, she was remarkable for many spiritual gifts, including clairvoyance and healing others from sickness. Throughout her entire life, Matrona lived in different apartments, either living in a separate room or in the corner of a room belonging to her friends or distant relatives. The time was horrible, the height of Soviet power, and religious persecutions raged all over the country. No one could dream of any public announcements concerning the good of religion. If one were to follow normal human logic, she should simply have been forgotten after her death, in the same way all invalids who were burdens to their family are, when their deaths lead to nothing but a sigh of relief.

Yet nothing of the sort happened. The steady stream of pilgrims to visit Matronushka's grave (that is what they lovingly called her) continued throughout the second half of the twentieth century, and in the 90's, it turned into a raging torrent of many thousands of people. In 1998, her body was exhumed from her grave, and the next year she was canonized. Her relics rest in the Monastery of the Protection in Moscow, and thousands of pilgrims stand in lines for hours every day to pray at her tomb, to receive healing from their sicknesses, resolution of family and everyday problems, and strengthening of their faith. The chronicle of healings that has been recorded at her grave includes hundreds of stories that make absolutely no sense from the perspective of natural laws.

Of course, in our own times, there are many rationalists and skeptics who simply do not want to believe in miracles even when given all sorts of proof, and so they explain away the mass pilgrimages to the relics of wonderworkers by using words like "mass psychosis," "psychological manipulation," "marketing," "superstition," or other such things. If a person does not want to believe in a miracle, there is no way to force him.

Someone might ask: why do we need miracles at all? Can't we live without miracles? The answer is simple: yes, it is possible. And many people live lives that outwardly seem to pass completely within the bounds of natural laws. But there are situations in life when a miracle suddenly becomes the only possible way out of a situation. For example, a person may be gravely ill and the doctors can do nothing to help him. In such cases, people still say "It would take a miracle."

And two possible outcomes are possible—either the miracle does not occur and the person dies, or the miracle does happen—by the prayers of his relatives, by his own fervent prayers, by the intercession of the saints, by the direct action of God, or for some other reasons. If a miracle does occur, and the sick person unexpectedly gets better, the believer sees the hand of God and gives thanks to God. The unbeliever will ascribe the miracle to nothing more than a chance series of events.

We return to the question with which this book began: the theme of the interpretation of miracles. A person who thinks within the paradigm formulated by the rationalist philosophers of the seventeenth to the nineteenth centuries (Spinoza, Kant, Hegel), which has infiltrated the consciousness of millions of people, will explain any miracle either with natural explanations or will reject it outright. To such a person, the miracles of Jesus Christ seem no more than legends created by the early Christian Church, myths bereft of any historical basis. And no one will be able to convince such a person, unless he himself becomes the recipient of a miracle that will force him to believe—not merely in some abstract concept of God who does not get involved in the affairs of men, but in the God of the Bible, of whom it is said: "Who is so great a God as our God? Thou art the God who doest wonders" (Ps 76.14).

There can be many kinds of miracles—obvious miracles seen by thousands of people or barely noticeable ones that are only significant for a single person. Concerning such "insignificant" miracles, some people are even ashamed to speak of them, since their supernatural character is evident only to him.

During the course of the entire Gospel, in the examples of many people's lives, the great miracle of the transfiguration of the human soul is revealed. This miracle took place thanks to people's encounter with the God who came to them in human flesh. Very often, it was connected with healings from incurable diseases or other supernatural events of similar nature. But not always. In an entire series of events, the presence of Jesus alone was enough for a person to completely change his manner of living or his way of thinking. This came to pass with such "heroes" of the Gospels as Zaccheus (Lk 19.2–10), the sinful woman who anointed the feet of Jesus (Lk 7.37–50), and the thief on the cross (Lk 23.40–43).

Such miracles occur in the Church constantly. Drug addicts and alcoholics come to the Church, villains and criminals, debauchers and adulterers, those who have lost hope in salvation and who have lost their humanity. And gradually, right in front of the eyes of the priest and the parish, the spiritual rebirth of these people takes place through faith and repentance, through participation in the mysteries of the Church and virtuous deeds, which they begin to perform not by some command from above but by the inner call of the heart, because Christ himself calls them.

When he was asked, Christ himself refused to perform a miracle merely for the sake of a miracle. Miracles were not Jesus' primary work on this earth—he came not to heal physical illnesses and return the dead to earthly life, but to save human souls and give people eternal life. And though his miracles were an important witness of his power (both for those who were healed and for the disciples), the Gospel does not place its primary stress on miracles, but on the salvation of the human soul through the death and resurrection of Jesus Christ.

The most important miracle of Christian history is Jesus Christ himself—God who became man. And his resurrection is the miracle that he promised the Jews instead of the sign that they demanded. All four Gospels lead their narratives toward this single greatest miracle. In the light of this miracle, the entire story of the Gospels begins to make sense, and it is the resurrection that gives Christianity the uniqueness and singularity that radically separates it from any other philosophical movement or religious tradition.

ABBREVIATIONS

ANF   The Ante-Nicene Fathers. Edited by Alexander Roberts and James Donaldson. Buffalo, 1885–1887. 10 vols. Repr., Peabody, MA: Hendrickson, 1994.

CSEL   Corpus Scriptorum Ecclesiasticorum Latinorum. Vienna, 1866–2012. Berlin: De Gruyter, 2012–.

NPNF¹   The Nicene and Post-Nicene Fathers, Series 1. Edited by Philip Schaff. New York, 1886–1889. 14 vols. Repr., Peabody, MA: Hendrickson, 1994.

NPNF²   The Nicene and Post-Nicene Fathers, Series 2. Edited by Philip Schaff and Henry Wace. New York, 1890. 14 vols. Repr., Peabody, MA: Hendrickson, 1994.

PG   Patrologia Graeca. Edited by J.-P. Migne. 162 vols. Paris, 1857–1886.

PL   Patrologia Latina. Edited by J.-P. Migne. 217 vols. Paris, 1844–1864.

PPS   Popular Patristics Series. Crestwood, NY [Yonkers, NY]: St Vladimir's Seminary Press, 1996–

SC   Sources chrétiennes. Paris: Les Éditions du Cerf. 1942–

BIBLIOGRAPHY

1. The Old and New Testaments

Biblia Hebraica Stuttgartensia. 4th ed. Karl Elliger and Wilhelm Rudolph, eds. Stuttgart: Deutsche Bibelgesellschaft, 1990.

The Holy Bible: King James Version. Standard text ed. Cambridge: Cambridge University Press, 1995.

Novum Testamentum Graece. 28th rev. ed. Eberhard Nestle, Erwin Nestle, and Kurt Aland, eds. Stuttgart: Württembergische Bibelanstalt, 1963.

Septuaginta: id est, Vetus Testamentum graece iuxta LXX interpretes. Editio minor. Alfred Rahlfs, ed. Stuttgart: Deutsche Bibelgesellschaft, 1979.

Synopsis Quattor Evangeliorum: Locis parallelis evangeliorum apocryphorum et partum adhibitis. 13th rev. ed. Kurt Aland, ed. Stuttgart: Deutsche Bibelgesellschaft, 1988.

2. Works of the Fathers and Teachers of the Church

Andrew of Caesarea. *Commentarius in Apocalypsin Divi Joannis*. PG 106:207–458. In English: *Commentary on the Apocaplypse*. English in *Greek Commentaries on Revelation: Oecumenius and Andrew of Caesarea*. Translated by William C. Weinrich. Downers Grove, IL: InterVarsity Press, 2011.

Athanasius of Alexandria. *Contra Arianos*. PG 26:361. In English: *Four Discourses against the Arians*. NPNF² 4:306–447.

_____. *De incarnatione*. St Athanasius the Great of Alexandria. *On the Incarnation*. Greek original and English translation. Translation and Introduction by John Behr. Popular Patristics Series 44A. Yonkers, NY: St Vladimir's Seminary Press, 2011.

_____. *Epistulae festales*. English: *The Festal Letters of Athanasius*. Edited by W. Cureton. Loondon: Society for the Publication of Oriental Texts, 1848.

_____. *Letters of Athanasius with Two Chronicles of His Life*. NPNF² 4:495–581.

Augustine. *De consensu evangelistarum.* PL 34:1041–1230. English: *On the Harmony of the Gospels.* NPNF[1] 6:77–236.

———. *Ennarationes in Psalmos.* PL 36 and PL 37. *Commentary on the Psalms.* Quoted in *Ancient Christian Commentary on Scripture: Mark.* Downer's Grove, IL: InterVarsity Press, 2014.

———. *Epistolae.* PL 33. Selected letters in English in NPNF[1] 1:211–593.

———. *In Ioannis Evangelium.* PL 35. English: *Commentary on the Gospel of John.* NPNF[1] 7:7–452.

———. *Ten Homilies on the First Epistle of John.* NPNF[1] 7:455–530.

Basil of Seleucia. *Homily 2 on Adam.* PG 85:37–50.

Cyril of Alexandria, *Fragments* 200. PG 72:476–943.

———. *Commentary on John.* Translated by E. B. Pusey. *A Library of the Fathers of the Holy Catholic Church: Commentary on the Gospel according to S. John, by S. Cyril, Patriarch of Alexandria,* Volume I: Saint John I–VIII. Oxford: James Parker and Co., 1874.

———. *Commentary on the Gospel of Luke.* PG 72:475–950.

Cyril of Jerusalem. "Homily on the Paralytic near the Pool." In *The Works of Saint Cyril of Jerusalem,* vol. 2. Translated by Anthony A. Stephenson. The Fathers of the Church 64:209–22. Washington, DC: The Catholic University of America Press, 1970.

Didache. The Didache: Text, Translation, Analysis, and Commentary. Translated by Aaron Milavec. Collegeville, MN: Liturgical Press, 2003.

Ephraim the Syrian. *Saint Ephrem's Commentary on Tatian's Diatessaron: An English Translation of Chester Beatty Syriac MS 709.* Translated by Carmel McCarthy. Oxford: Oxford University Press, 1993.

Eusebius of Caesarea. *Ecclesiastical History.* NPNF[2] 1:81–387.

———. *The Treatise of Eusebius, the Son of Pamphilus, against the Life of Apollonius of Tyana Written by Philostratus, Occasioned by the Parallel Drawn by Hierocles between Him and Christ.* In *Philostratus. The Life of Apollonius of Tyana, the Epistles of Apollonius, and the Treatise of Eusebius.* Translated by F. C. Conybeare, in two volumes, 2:485–605. Loeb Classical Library 17. Cambridge, MA: Harvard University Press, 2005.

Gregory of Nazianzus, the Theologian. *Lettres.* Edited by P. Gallay. 2 vols. Paris: Les Belles Lettres. 1967.

_____. Oration 30. In St Gregory of Nazianzus. *On God and Christ: The Five Theological Orations and Two Letters to Cledonius.* Popular Patristics Series 23:93–116. Crestwood, NY: St Vladimir's Seminary Press, 2002.

Gregory Palamas. *The Triads.* Translated by Nicholas Gendle. Mahwah, NJ: Paulist Press, 1983.

_____. *The Homilies,* 2nd rev. ed. Translated by Christopher Veniamin. Dalton, PA: Mount Thabor Publishing, 2016.

Hilary of Poitiers. *Commentary on Matthew.* Translated by D. H. Williams. Fathers of the Church, Vol. 125. Washington, DC: The Catholic University of America Press, 2012.

Hippolytus of Rome. *Demonstratio de Christo et Antichristo* [On Christ and the Antichrist]. PG 10:725–788.

Irenaeus of Lyons, *Against Heresies.* ANF 1:315–567.

Isaac the Syrian. *Ascetical Homilies II /9.5.* In Hilarion Alfeyev. *The Spiritual World of Isaac the Syrian.* Cistercian Studies Series 175. Kalamazoo, MI: Cistercian Publications, 2000.

John Chrysostom. *De coemeterio et de cruce* [On the cemetery and on the cross]. PG 49:393–398.

_____. *Homilies on First Epistle of St Paul the Apostle to the Corinthians.* NPNF[1] 12:3–269.

_____. *Homilies on the Epistle of St Paul to the Colossians.* NPNF[1] 13:257–321.

_____. *Homilies on the Gospel according to St John.* NPNF[1] 14:1–334.

_____. *Homilies on the Gospel according to St Matthew.* NPNF[1] 10:1–534.

_____. *Homilies on Genesis 1–17.* Translated by Robert C. Hill. The Fathers of the Church, Vol. 74. Washington, DC: The Catholic University of America Press, 1986.

John of Damascus. *An Exact Exposition of the Orthodox Faith.* NPNF[2] 9b:1–101.

John of Kronstadt. *Pouchenie v nedelyu dvadtsat' sed'muyu po Pyatidesyatnitse* [Sermon on Sunday of the twentieth week after Pentecost]. In *Polnoe sobranie sochinenii* [Complete collected works], 2:661–664. St Petersburg, 1894.

_____. *Pouchenie v nedelyu sed'muyu po Pyatidesyatnitse* [Homily on the seventh Sunday after Pentecost]. In *Polnoe sobranie sochinenii* [Complete collected works], 2:382–385. St Petersburg, 1894.

_____. *Zhivoi kolos s dukhovnoi nivy: Vypiski iz dnevnika prot. Ioanna Il'icha Sergieva* [A living ear from the spiritual field: Extracts from the diary of archpriest Ioann Ilych Sergiev]. St Petersburg, 1909.

Justin Martyr. *Dialogue with Trypho*. ANF 1:194–270.

Mark the Ascetic. *On the Spiritual Law*. In Mark the Monk. *Counsels on the Spiritual Life*. Two volumes in one, 1:92–111. Translated by Tim Vivian. Popular Patristics Series 37. Crestwood, NY : St Vladimir's Seminary Press, 2009.

Methodius of Patara. *The Banquet of the Ten Virgins*. ANF 6:309–355.

Origen. *Commentary on the Gospel of Matthew*. PG 13:829–1600; SC 162.

Symeon the New Theologian, *Catechesis 22*. English in *The Philokalia*. Translated by G. E. H. Palmer, Philip Sherrard, and Kallistos Ware, 4:16–24. London: Faber and Faber, 1995. [In the *Philokalia*, this work is called "On Faith."—Ed.]

_____. *Divine Eros: Hymns of Saint Symeon the New Theologian*. Translated by Daniel K. Griggs. Popular Patristics Series 40. Yonkers, NY: St Vladimir's Seminary Press, 2010.

_____. *Gratitude*. SC 113:304–356.

_____. *On the Mystical Life: The Ethical Discourses*. 3 vols. Translated and introduced by Alexander Golitzin. Popular Patristics Series 14, 15, and 16. Crestwood, NY: St Vladimir's Seminary Press, 1995–1997.

_____. *The Discourses*. Translated by C. J. deCatanzaro. Mahwah, NJ: Paulist Press, 1980.

Tertullian. *On Baptism*. ANF 3:669–680.

Theophylact of Ochrid. *The Explanation of the Holy Gospel According to St. Luke*. Translated by Christopher Stade. House Springs, MO: Chrysostom Press, 1997.

3. Other Sources

Achtenmeier, Paul J. *Jesus and the Miracle Tradition*. Eugene, OR: Cascade Books, 2008.

Aim of Christian Life, The. The Conversation of St Seraphim of Sarov with N. A. Motovilov. Translated by John Phillips. Cambridge: Saints Alive Press, 2010.

Aland, K., and B. Aland. *The Text of the New Testament*. Grand Rapids and Leiden, 1987.

Alfeyev, Metropolitan Hilarion. *Christ the Conqueror of Hell: The Descent into Hell from an Orthodox Perspective*. Yonkers, NY: St Vladimir's Seminary Press, 2009.

_____. *Jesus Christ: His Life and Teaching. Vol. 1: The Beginning of the Gospel*. Yonkers, NY: St Vladimir's Seminary Press, 2018.

_____. *Jesus Christ: His Life and Teaching. Vol. 2: The Sermon on the Mount.* Yonkers, NY: St Vladimir's Seminary Press, 2019.

_____. *Orthodox Christianity. Vol. 1: The History and Canonical Structure of the Orthodox Church.* Yonkers, NY: St Vladimir's Seminary Press, 2011.

_____. *The Spiritual World of Isaac the Syrian.* Cistercian Studies 175. Kalamazoo, MI: Cistercian Publications, 2000.

Aristotle. *Politics.* Translated by H. Rackham, M.A. Loeb Classical Library 264. London: William Heinemann, Ltd, and Cambridge, MA: Harvard University Press, 1959.

Ashton, John. *Understanding the Fourth Gospel.* Oxford: Oxford University Press, 2007.

Barker, Margaret. *King of the Jews: Temple Theology in John's Gospel.* London: SPCK Publishing, 2014.

Basinsky, P. *Svyatoi protiv L'va* [A saint versus Leo]. Moscow, 2013.

Bauckham, Richard. *Jesus and the Eyewitnesses. The Gospels as Eyewitness Testimony.* Grand Rapids, MI: William B. Eerdmans Publishing Co., 2003.

Beasley-Murray, G. R. "John." In *Word Biblical Commentary* 1:36. Nashville, TN: Thomas Nelson, Inc. 1999.

Belyaev, L .A. "Vifezda" [Bethesda]. In *Pravoslavnaya entsiklopediya* [Orthodox encyclopedia], 8:595–96. Moscow, 2004.

_____. "Vifsaida" [Bethsaida]. In *Pravoslavnaya entsiklopediya* [Orthodox encyclopedia], 8:606. Moscow, 2004.

Berger, Klaus. *Identity and Experience in the New Testament.* Minneapolis: Fortress Press, 2003.

Bezobrazov, Bishop Kassian. *Khristos i pervoe khristianskoe pokolenie* [Christ and the first Christian generation]. Moscow, 2001.

Blomberg, Craig L. "The Miracles as Parables." In *Gospel Perspectives, vol. 6: The Miracles of Jesus.* Edited by David Wenham and Craig Blomberg. Eugene, OR: Wipf and Stock, 1986.

_____. *The Miracles as Parables.* Sheffield: JSOT Press, 1986.

Borchert, G. L. *John 1–11: An Exegetical and Theological Exposition of Holy Scripture.* Nashville: Holmann Reference, 1996.

Bornkamm, Günther, G. Barth, and H. J. Held. *Tradition and Interpretation in Matthew.* Louisville, KY: Westminster Press, 1963.

Brake, D. L., and T. Bolen. *Jesus. A Visual History.* Grand Rapids, MI: Zondervan Academic, 2014.

Brandt, P.-Y. *L'identité de Jesus et l'identité de son disciple: Le recit de la Transfiguration comme clef de lecture de l'Evangile de Marc.* Göttingen: Vandenhoeck & Ruprecht, 2002.

Brown, Raymond. E. *The Gospel according to John (I-XII): Introduction, Translation and Notes.* New Haven: Yale University Press, 2007.

_____. *The Gospel according to John (XIII-XXI): Introduction, Translation and Notes.* New Haven: Yale University Press, 2007.

Bruce, Alexander. B. *The Miraculous Element in the Gospels.* New York: A. C. Armstrong & Son, 1886.

Bue, L. *O Biblii i Evangelii* [On the Bible and the Gospel]. Brussels, 1980.

Bultmann, Rudolf. *Das Evangelium des Johannes: Kritisch-exegetischer Kommentar über das Neue Testament.* 2nd edition. Göttingen, 1952.

_____. *The History of the Synoptic Tradition.* Oxford, 1963.

_____. *The New Testament and Mythology & Other Basic Writings.* Philadelphia: Fortress Press, 1984.

Carson, D. A. *The Gospel according to John.* Grand Rapids, MI: William B. Eerdmans and Co., 1991.

Chancey, Mark A. *Greco-Roman Culture and the Galilee of Jesus.* Cambridge: Cambridge University Press, 2008.

_____. *The Myth of a Gentile Galilee.* Cambridge: Cambridge University Press, 2004.

Chekhanovets, Ya. M. "Ermon" [Hermon]. In *Pravoslavnaya entsikolpediya* [Orthodox encyclopedia], 18:676–677. Moscow, 2008.

Cicero. *On divination.* In Cicero: *De senectute, De amicitia, De divinatione,* translated by William Armistead Falconer, 222–539. Loeb Classical Library 154. Cambridge, MA: Harvard University Press and London: William Heinemann, Ltd, 1923, 1964.

Cope, O. L. *Matthew: A Scribe Trained for the Kingdom of Heaven.* The Catholic Biblical Quarterly Monograph Series 5. Washington, DC: Catholic Biblical Association of America, 1976.

Cotter, Wendy J. *The Christ of the Miracle Stories: Portrait through Encounter.* Grand Rapids, MI: Baker Academic, 2010.

Crane, Thomas E. *The Synoptics. Mark, Matthew and Luke Interpret the Gospel.* London: Sheed and Ward, Ltd., 1999.

Culpepper, R. Alan. *Anatomy of the Fourth Gospel: A Study in Literary Design.* Minneapolis: Fortress Press, 1987.

Dalman, Gustaf. *Orte und Wege Jesu.* Gütersloh: Betelsman, 1924.

Davies, Stevan. L. *Jesus the Healer: Possession, Trance and the Origins of Christianity.* New York: Continuum International Publishing Group, 1995.

Deissmann, A. *Licht vom Osten: Das Neue Testament und die neuentdeckten Texte der hellenistisch-römischen Welt.* Tübingen: Mohr (Paul Siebeck), 1923; London: Forgotten Books [reprint edn], 2017.

Dibelius, Martin. *Die Formgeschichte des Evangeliums.* 2nd edition. Tübingen: Mohr (Paul Siebeck), 1933.

Dodd, C. H. *Historical Tradition in the Fourth Gospel.* Cambridge: Cambridge University Press, 1963, 1999.

_____. *The Interpretation of the Fourth Gospel.* Cambridge: Cambridge university Press, 1953, 1998.

Dostoevsky, Fyodor. M. *Prestuplenie i nakazanie* [Crime and punishment]. Volume 5 in *Sobranie sochinenii* [Collected works] in 15 volumes. Leningrad: 1989.

Erlendsson, Haraldur. "Multiple Personality Disorder—Demons and Angels or Archetypal aspects of the inner self." https://www.academia.edu/3065960/Multiple_Personality_Disorder_-_Demons_and_Angels_or_Archetypal_aspects_of_the_inner_self.

Eusebius of Caesarea. *The Treatise of Eusebius, the Son of Pamphilus, against the Life of Apollonius of Tyana Written by Philostratus, Occasioned by the Parallel Drawn by Hierocles between Him and Christ.* In *Philostratus. The Life of Apollonius of Tyana, the Epistles of Apollonius, and the Treatise of Eusebius.* Translated by F. C. Conybeare, in Two volumes, 2:485–605. Loeb Classical Library 17. Cambridge, MA: Harvard University Press, 2005.

Evans, Craig A. *Jesus and His Contemporaries: Comparative Studies.* Boston: Brill Academic Publishers, Inc., 2001.

Fitzmyer, J. A. *The Gospel according to Luke (I-IX): Introduction, Translation and Notes.* New York: Doubleday and Co., 1981.

Flew, Anthony N. "Neo-Humean Arguments about the Miraculous." In *In Defence of Miracles. A Comprehensive Case for God's Action in History,* edited by R. Douglas Geivett and G. R. Habermas, 49–51. Downers Grove, IL: InterVarsity Press, 1997.

Frank, Frederick. *Days with Albert Schweitzer: A Lambaréné Landscape.* New York: Henry Holt and Company, 1959.

Gaiser, Frederick J. *Healing in the Bible: Theological Insight for Christian Ministry*. Grand Rapids, MI: Baker Academic, 2010.

Galbiati, E., and Alessandro Piazza. *Pagine difficili dell'Antico Testamento*. Genoa: Bevilacqua & Solari, 1951. [In Russian as *Trudnye stranitsy Biblii. Vetkhii Zavet*. Moscow, 1992.]

Hakola, R. "A Character Resurrected: Lazarus in the Fourth Gospel and Afterwards." In *Characterization in the Gospels: Reconceiving Narrative Criticism*, edited by D. Rhoads and K. Syreeni, 223–263. Sheffield: Sheffield Academic Press, 1999.

Hegel, G. W. F. *Three Essays, 1793–1795: The Tübingen Essay, Berne Fragments, The Life of Jesus*. Notre Dame, IN: University of Notre Dame Press, 1984.

Heil, J. P. *The Transfiguration of Jesus: Narrative Meaning and Function of Mark 9:2–8, Matt 17:1–8 and Luke 9:28–36*. Rome: Pontifical Biblical Institute, 2000.

Hitchcock, F. R. M. "Is the Fourth Gospel a Drama?" *Theology* 7 (1923): 307–17.

Hodges, Z. C. "The Angel at Bethesda—John 5:4." *Bibliotheca sacra* 136 (1979): 25–39.

Hooker, Morna D. *The Gospel according to Saint Mark*. London: A&C Black, 1991.

Horsley, R. A. *Jesus and the Spiral of Violence: Popular Jewish Resistance in Roman Palestine*. Minneapolis: Fortress Press. 1993.

Hull, John M. *Hellenistic Magic and the Synoptic Tradition*. London: SCM Press, 1974.

Hume, David. *An Enquiry concerning Human Understanding*. Chicago: The Open Court Publishing Co., 1900.

Humphrey, Edith M. "God and Angels." In *Jesus among Friends and Enemies: A Historical and Literary Introduction to Jesus in the Gospels*, edited by Chris Keith and Larry W. Hurtado, 46–49. Grand Rapids, MI: Baker Academic, 2011.

Jaspers, Karl. *Philosophical Faith and Revelation*. New York: Harper & Row, 1967.

Jefferson, Lee M. *Christ the Miracle Worker in Early Christian Art*. Minneapolis: Fortress Press, 2014.

Jeremias, A. *Babylonisches im Neuen Testament*. Leipzig, 1905.

Josephus (Flavius Josephus). *The Antiquities of the Jews*. In *The Works of Josephus, Complete and Unaridged: New Updated Edition*. Translated by William Whiston, 27–542. Peabody, MA: Hendrickson Publishers, 1987.

_____. *The Wars of the Jews.* In *The Works of Josephus,* Complete and Unaridged: New Updated Edition. Translated by William Whiston, 543–772. Peabody, MA: Hendrickson Publishers, 1987.

_____. *The Works of Josephus Complete and Unabridged: New Updated Edition.* Translated by William Whiston. Peabody, MA: Hendrickson Publishers, 1987. [The translation was first published in 1736.]

Kant, Immanuel. *Religion within the Boundaries of Pure Reason.* Translated by J. W. Semple. Edinburgh: Thomas Allen & Co., 1838.

Keener, Craig. S. *Miracles: The Credibility of the New Testament Accounts.* 2 vols. Grand Rapids, MI: Baker Academic, 2001.

Kertelge, K. Die *Wunder Jesu im Markusevangelium: Eine redaktionsgeschichtliche Untersuchung.* Munich: Kösel, 1970.

Kim, S. S. *The Miracles of Jesus according to John: Their Christological and Eschatological Significance.* Eugene, OR: Wipf & Stock, 2010.

Klutz, T. *The Exorcism Stories in Luke-Acts: A Socio-Stylistic Reading.* Cambridge: Cambridge University Press, 2004.

Knight, J. *Jesus. An Historical and Theological Investigation.* London: T&T Clarke International, 2004.

Koester, Craig. R. *Symbolism in the Fourth Gospel: Meaning, Mystery, Community.* Minneapolis: Fortress Press, 1995.

Kostenberger, A. J. *John.* Grand Rapids, MI: Baker Academic, 2004.

Kremer, J. *Lazarus: Die Geschichte einer Auferstehung.* Stuttgart: Verlag Katholisches Bibelwerk GmbH, 1985.

Krivocheine, Archbishop Basil. *In the Light of Christ: Saint Symeon the New Theologian (949–1022): Life–Spirituality–Doctrine.* Translated by Anthony P. Gythiel. Crestwood, NY: St Vladimir's Seminary Press, 1986.

Lactantius. *The Divine Institutes.* ANF 7: 9–222.

Lagrange, M.-J. *L'Evangile selon saint Luc.* Paris, 1921.

Leander, Hans. *Discourses of Empire. The Gospel of Mark from a Post-colonial Perspective.* Atlanta: Society for Biblical Literature, 2013.

Lee, D. *Luke's Stories of Jesus: Theological Reading of the Gospel Narrative and the Legacy of Hans Frei.* Sheffield: Sheffield Academic Press, 1999.

_____. *Transfiguration.* London; New York, 2004.

Léon-Dufour, X. *Life and Death in the New Testament: The Teachings of Jesus and Paul.* New York: Harper Collins, 1986.

Lightfoot, R. H. *St. John's Gospel: A Commentary*. Oxford: Oxford University Press, 1956.

Lindars, B. "Elijah, Elisha and the Gospel Miracles." In *Miracles: Cambridge Studies in Their Philosophy and History*, edited by C. P. D. Moule, 61–79. London: Bowbray, 1965.

Lockyer, H. *All the Miracles of the Bible*. Grand Rapids, MI: Zondervan Publishing House, 1961.

Loos, H. van der. *The Miracles of Jesus*. Leiden: E. J. Brill, 1965.

Madden, P. *Jesus' Walking on the Sea: An Investigation of the Origin of the Narrative Account*. Berlin and New York: Walter de Gruyter, 1997.

Malina, B. "Assessing the Historicity of Jesus' Walking on the Sea." In *Authenticating the Activities of Jesus*, edited by B. Chilton and C. A. Evans, 351–371. Leiden: Brill, 1999.

Marcus, Joel. *Mark 1–8: A New Translation with Introduction and Commentary*. The Anchor Yale Bible Commentaries. New Haven, CT: Yale University Press, 2000.

———. *Mark 8–16: A New Translation with Introduction and Commentary*. The Anchor Yale Bible Commentaries. New Haven, CT: Yale University Press, 2009.

Marshall, C. D. *Faith as a Theme in Mark's Narrative*. Cambridge: Cambridge Unisesity Press, 1989.

Meier, J. P. *A Marginal Jew: Rethinking the Historical Jesus. Vol. 2: Mentor, Message and Miracles*. New York: Doubleday, 1994.

Metzger B. *The New Testament: Its Background, Growth, and Content*. Nashville, TN: Abingdon Press, 2003.

———. *A Textual Commentary on the Greek New Testament*. Stuttgart, 1971.

Meyendorff, John. *Marriage: An Orthodox Perspective*. Crestwood, NY: St Vladimir's Seminary Press, 1975.

Moshe ben Maimon (Maimonides). *Mishneh Torah*. Book "Holiness."

Nineham, D. E. *The Gospel of Saint Mark (New Testament Commentary)*. New York: Penguin Books, 1964.

Novakovic, L. *Messiah, the Healer of the Sick: A Study of Jesus as the Son of David in the Gospel of Matthew*. Tübingen: Mohr Siebeck, 2003.

O'Collins, G. *Jesus: A Portrait*. London: Dartman, Longman and Todd, Ltd, 2008.

Ovid. *Heroides* and *Amores*, with an English Translation by Grant Showerman. Loeb Classical Library 141. London: William Heinemann, and New York: The Macmillan Co., 1914.

Paulus, H. E. G. *Exegetisches Handbuch über die drei ersten Evangelien.* New York: Wentworth Press, 2018.

_____. *Philologisch-kritischer und historischer Kommentar über das neue Testament.* Vol. 4.1. Lübeck, 1804.

Petzke, G. *Die* Traditionen *über Apollonius von Tyana und das Neue Testament.* Boston: Brill Academic Publishers, Inc., 1970.

Plato. *Republic.* Translated by Paul Shorey. Two vols. Vol. 1. Loeb Classical Library 237. Cambridge, MA: Harvard University Press, and London: William Heinemann, Ltd, 1937.

Plummer, A. *A Critical and Exegetical Commentary on the Gospel according to St Luke.* New York: T&T Clark, 1960.

Popovich, Justin. *Tolkovanie na Evangelie ot Matfeya: Svyatosavvye kak filosofiya zhizni* [Commentary on the Gospel according to Matthew: The holy path of St Sava as a philosophy of life]. In *Sobranie tvorenii prepodobnogo Iustina (Popovicha)* [Collected works of the Venerable Justin Popovich]. Moscow, 2014.

Puig i Tarrech, A. *Jesus: A Biography.* Waco: Baylor University Press, 2011.

Renan, Ernest. *Renan's Life of Jesus.* Translated by William G. Hutchison. London: Walter Scott, Ltd., 1897.

Santos, Narry E. *Slave of All: The Paradox of Authority and Servanthood in the Gospel of Mark.* London: Bloomsbury, 2003.

Schäfer, H. *Jesus in psychiatrischer Beleuchtung.* Berlin, 1910.

Schmemann, Alexander. *Of Water and the Spirit: A Liturgical Study of Baptism.* Crestwood, NY: St Vladimir's Seminary Press, 1974.

Schnackenburg, Rudolf. *The Gospel according to St. John.* Vol. 2. New York: Crossroad Publishing Co., 1990.

Schneider, G. *Das Evangelium nach Lukas.* Würzburg: Güttersloh Verlagshaus, 1977.

Schürmann, H. *Das Lukasevangelium. Ester Teil. Kommentar zu Kap. 1,1–9,40.* Freiburg: Herder, 1969.

Schweitzer, A. *Geschichte der Leben-Jesu Forschung.* 5th edition. Tübingen, 1933.

_____. *The Quest of the Historical Jesus: A Critical Study of its Progress from Reimarus to Wrede*. Translated by W. Montgomery. London: A. & C. Black, Ltd, 1911.

Shargunov, Alexander. *Evangelie dnya* [The Gospel of the day]. 2 vols. 2nd ed. Moscow: Sretensky Monastery, 2010.

Spinoza, B. *Theological and political treatise*. Translated by Martin D. Yaffe. Newburyport, MA: Focus Publishing, 2004.

Strakhov, N. N. *Vospominaniya o Fedore Mikhailoviche Dostoevskom* [Memories of Fyodor Mikhailovich Dostoevsky]. In F. M. Doestoevsky. *Polnoe sobranie sochinenii* [Complete collected works] in fourteen volumes; 1:169–329. St. Petersburg, 1883.

Strauss, David Friedrich. *The Life of Jesus, Critically Examined*. Volumes 1 and 2. Translated by Marian Evans. New York: C. Blanchard, 1860.

Swete, Henry Barclay. *The Gospel according to St. Mark*. London, 1898.

Talmud, Babylonian. Treatise *Shabbat*.

Taylor, V. *The Gospel according to St Mark*. 2nd edition. Grand Rapids: Bake Book House, 1981.

Theissen, Gerd. *The Gospels in Context: Social and Political History in the Synoptic Tradition*. New York: T & T Clark, 1992.

Theissen, Gerd. *The Miracle Stories of the Early Christian Tradition*. Edinburgh: First Fortress Press, 2007.

Tolbert, Mary Anne. *Sowing the Gospel: Mark's World in Literary-Historical Perspective*. Minneapolis: Fortress Press, 1989.

Tolstoy, Leo. *The Four Gospels Harmonized and Translated*. Vol. 1. Translated by Leo Wiener. In *The Complete Works of Count Tolstoy*. Vol. 14. Boston: Dana Estes & Co., 1904.

Twelftree, G. H. *Jesus the Miracle Worker*. Downers Grove, IL: InterVarsity Press, 1999.

_____. *Paul and the Miraculous*. Grand Rapids, MI: Baker Academic, 2013.

Tyson, J. B. *The New Testament and Early Christianity*. New York: Macmillan, 1984.

Velimirovich, Nikolai. *Tvoreniya* [Collected works]. Three volumes. Moscow, 2010.

Von Balthazar, Hans Urs. *A Theological Anthropology*. Eugene, OR: Wipf & Stock, 1967.

Wachsman, S. "The Galilee Boat: 2000-Year Old Hull Recovered." *Biblical Archaeology Review* 14 (1988): 18–33.

Walker, W. O. "Mary and Martha in the Third and Fourth Gospels." In *Resourcing New Testament Studies: Literary, Historical and Theological Essays in Honor of David L. Dungan*, edited by A. J. McNicol, D. B. Peabody, J. S. Subramanian, 123–135. London: T & T Clark, 2009.

Wilkinson Duran, Nicole. *The Power of Disorder: Ritual Elements in Mark's Passion Narrative*. London; New York, 2008.

Wilkinson, J. *The Bible and Healing. A Medical and Theological Commentary*. Edinburgh, 1998.

Williams, Joel F. *Other Followers of Jesus: Minor Characters as Major Figures in Mark's Gospel*. Sheffield: Sheffield Academic Press, 1994.

Wilson, Andrew P. *Transfigured: A Derridean Rereading of the Markan Transfiguration*. New York and London: T & T Clark, 2007.

Wilson, Walter T. *Healing in the Gospel of Matthew*. Minneapolis, 2014.

Winkler, L. L., and R. Frenkel. *The Boat and the Sea of Galilee*. Jerusalem: Gefen Publishing House, 2010.

Wrede, W. *The Messianic Secret*. Translated by J. C. G. Greig. Cambridge and London: James Clarke and Co., 1971.

Wright, George Ernest. *Biblical Archeology*. Philadelphia: Westminster Press, 1960.

Wright, N. T. *The Resurrection of the Son of God*. Minneapolis: Fortress Press, 2003.

Zimmerman R. "Narrative Hermeneutics of John 11: Learning with Lazarus How to Understand Death, Life, and Resurrection." In *The Resurrection of Jesus in the Gospel of John*, edited by C. R. Koester and R. Bieringer, 75–101. Tübingen: Mohn/Siebeck, 2008.